2016

上海浦东新区统计年鉴

SHANGHAI PUDONG NEW AREA STATISTICAL YEARBOOK

上海市浦东新区统计局
SHANGHAI PUDONG NEW AREA STATISTICAL BUREAU
国家统计局浦东调查队
PUDONG SURVEY TEAM OF NATIONAL STATISTICS BUREAU

（总第23期 No.23）

中国统计出版社
China Statistics Press

浦东创新 Innovative pudong

新区生产总值(亿元)
Gross Output Value of Pudong New Area (100 million yuan)

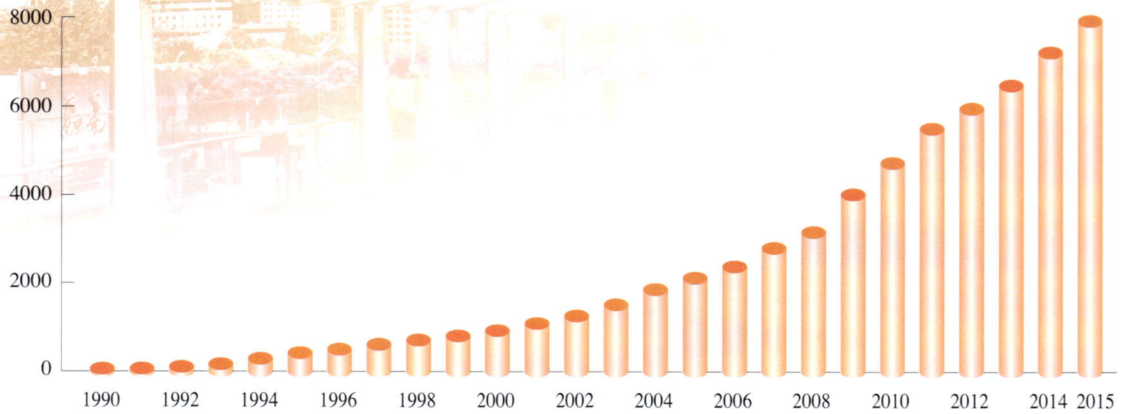

新区生产总值构成(%)
Composition of GDP of PNA (%)

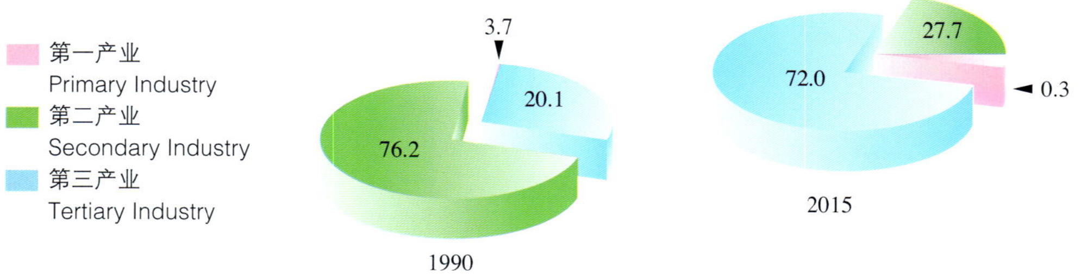

第三产业增加值构成(%)
Composition of Value Added of Tertiary Industry (%)

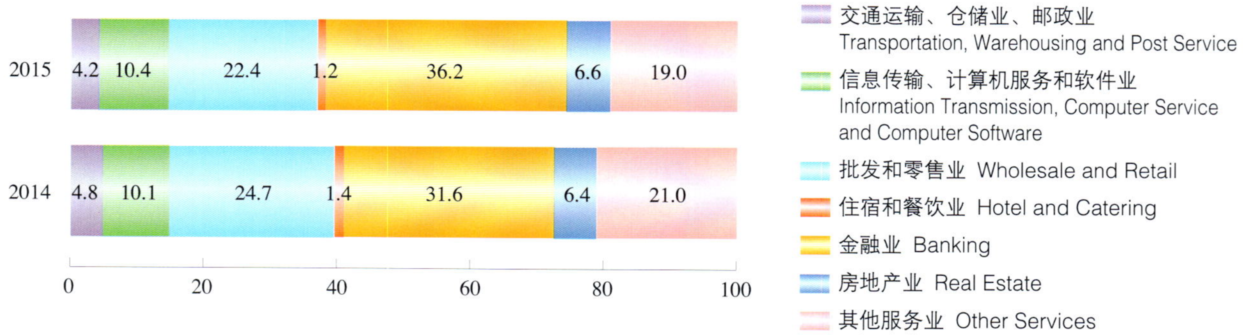

财政收入(亿元)
Fiscal Revenue (100 million yuan)

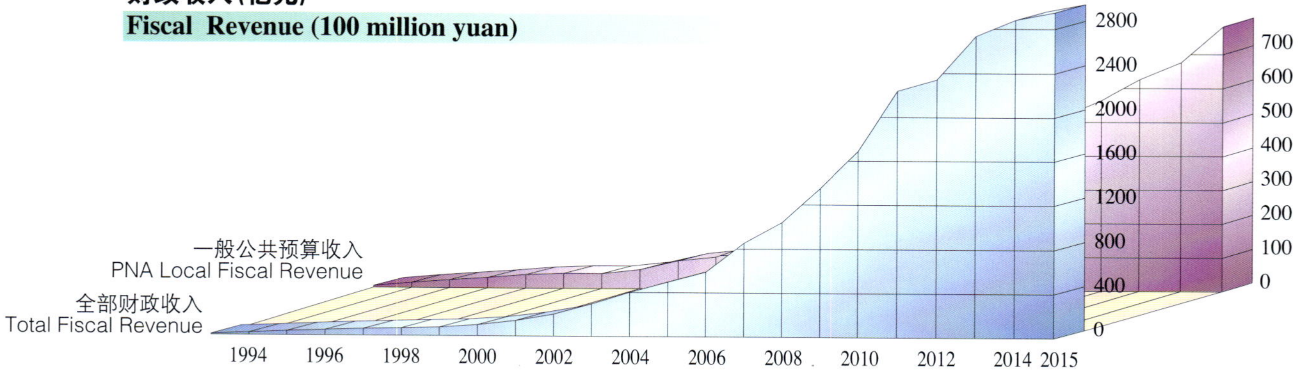

农业总产值(亿元)
Gross Output Value of Agriculture (100 million yuan)

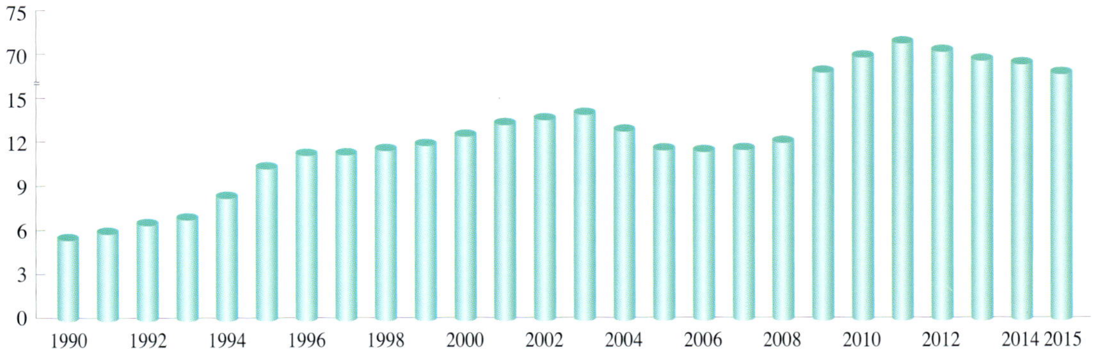

进出口货物总值(亿美元)
Total Value of Imports and Exports (USD 100 million)

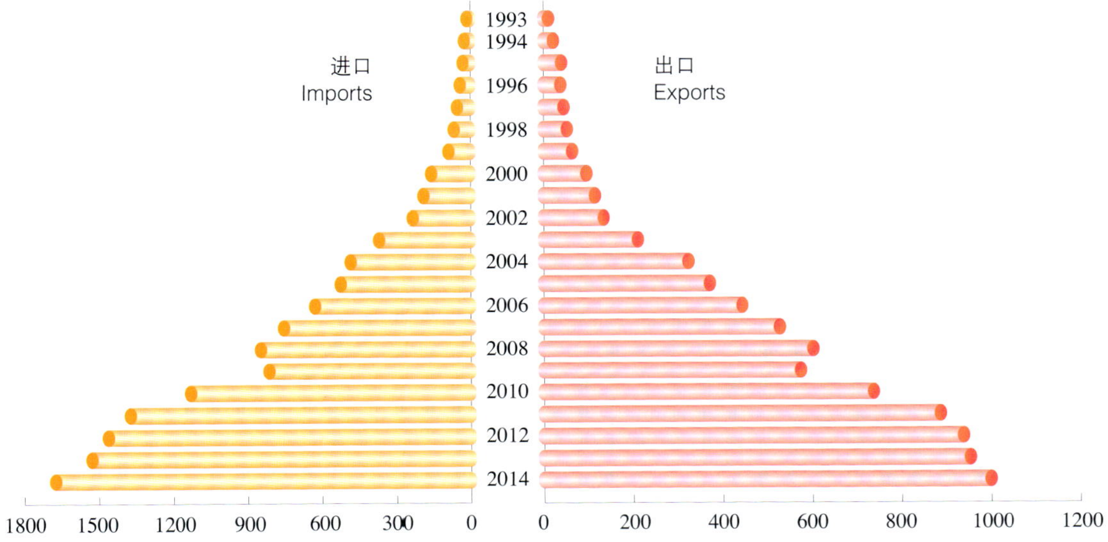

2015年六个工业重点发展行业产值构成(%)
Composition of Gross Output Value of Six Key Industries in 2015 (%)

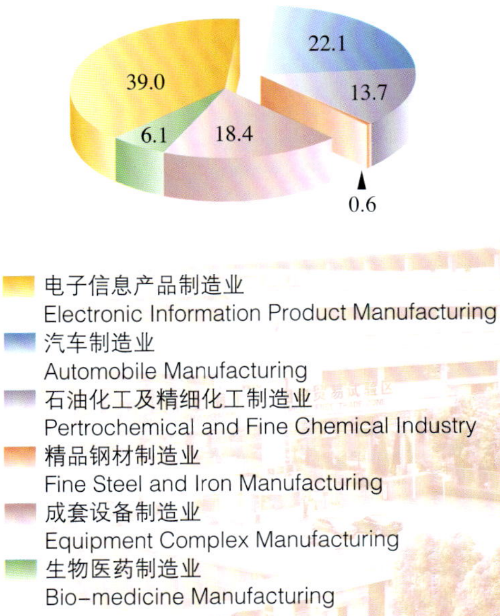

城市基础设施投资额构成(%)
Composition of Urban Infrastructure Investment (%)

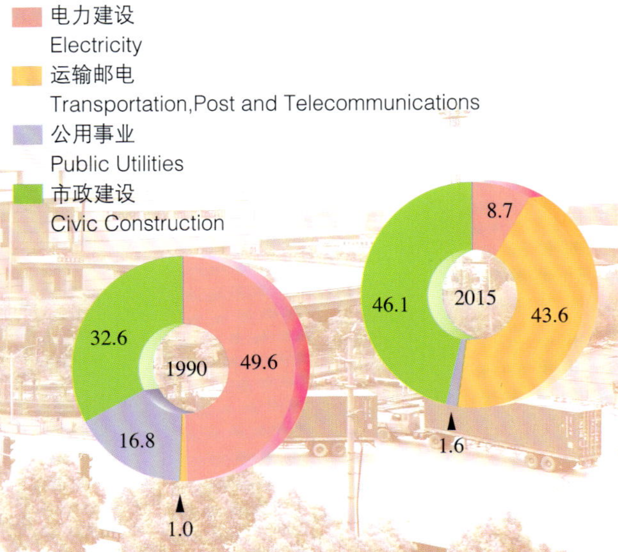

固定资产投资和城市基础设施投资(亿元)
Total Investment in Fixed Assets and Urban Infrastructure (100 million yuan)

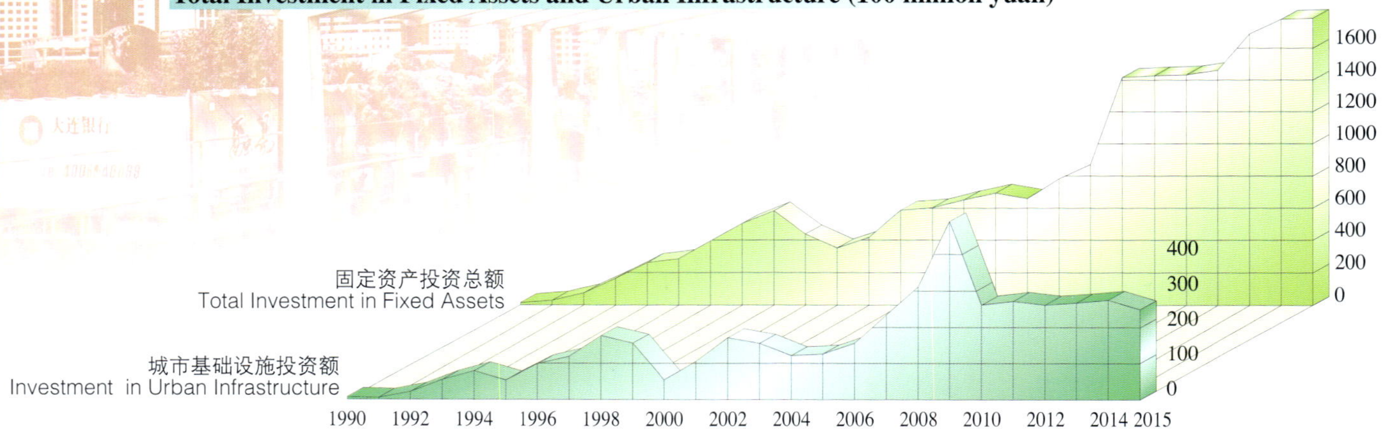

中外资银行本外币存贷款年末余额(亿元)
Balance of RMB and Foreign Currencies Deposits and Loans in Chinese and Foreign Banks (100 million yuan)

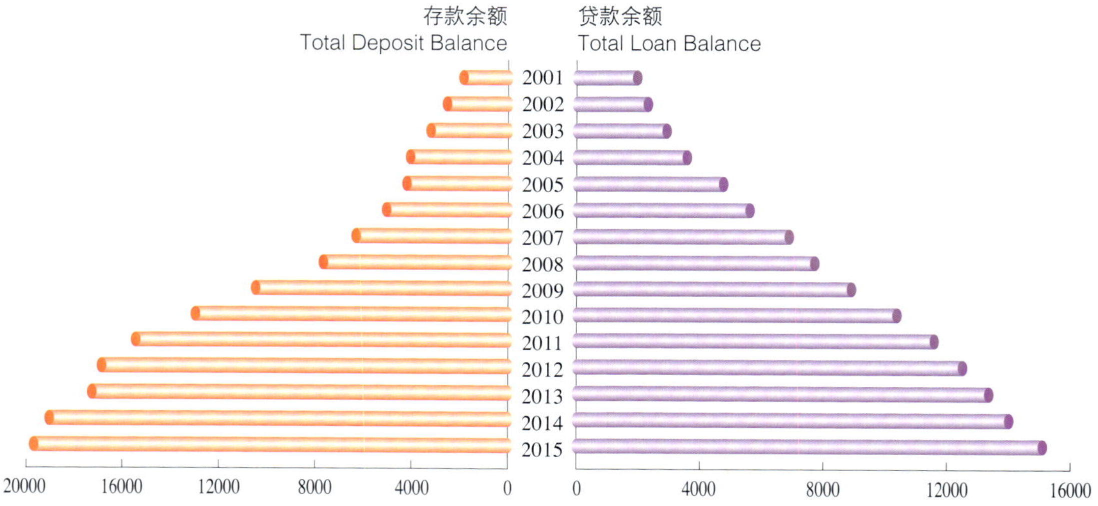

上海证券交易所市价总值(亿元)
Market Value of Shanghai Stock Exchange (100 million yuan)

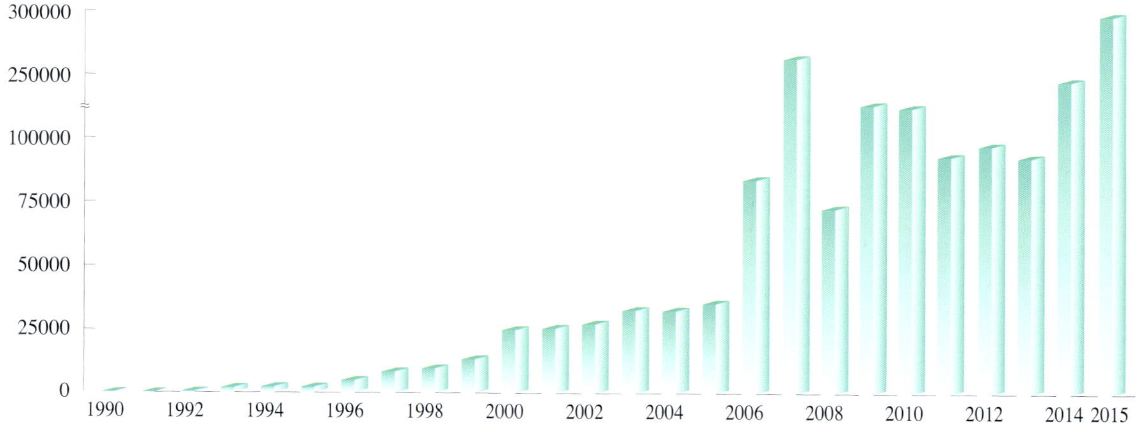

社会消费品零售总额(亿元)
Total Retail Sales of Consumer Goods (100 million yuan)

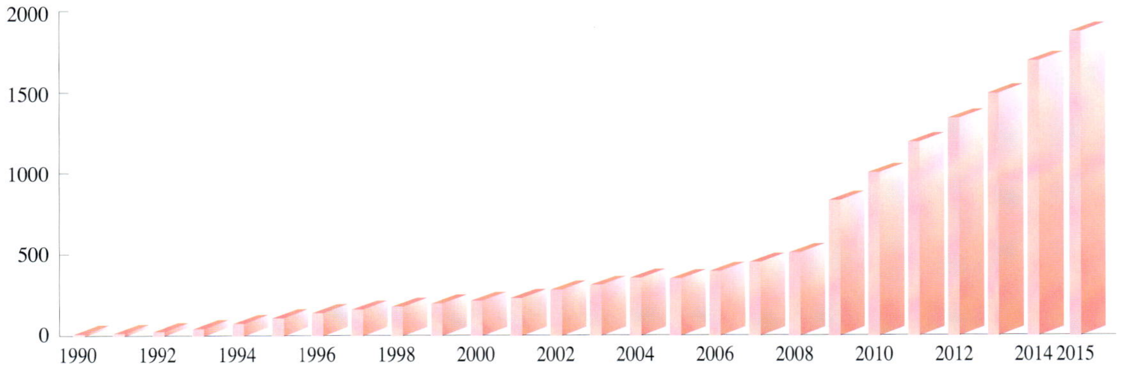

外商合同投资额的投资方式构成(%)
Composition of Contract Value of Foreign Investment by Ways of Investment (%)

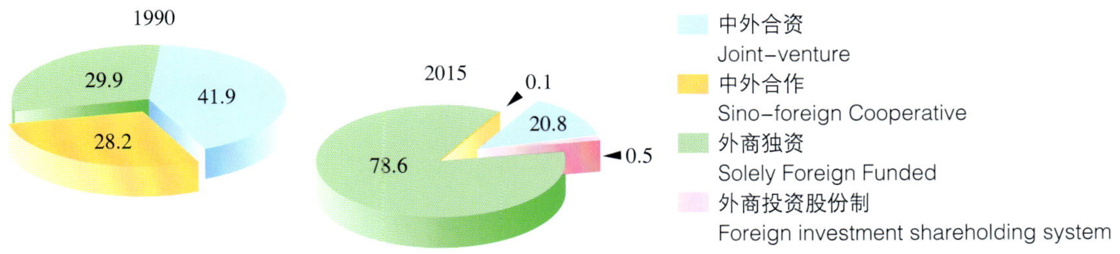

居民储蓄存款年末余额(亿元)
Resident Savings Deposit (100 million yuan)

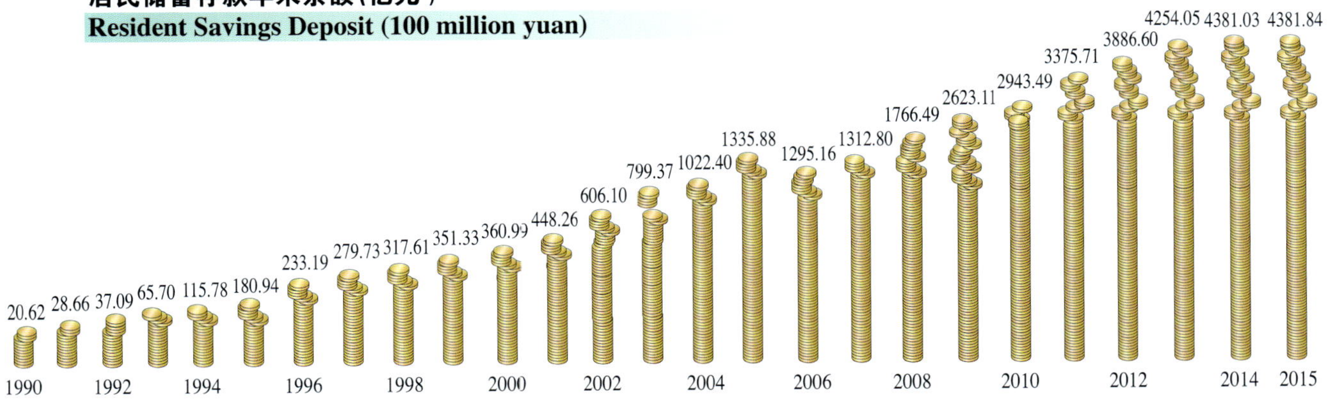

2015年城镇居民家庭消费支出构成(%)
Composition of Consumption Expenditure of Urban Families in 2015 (%)

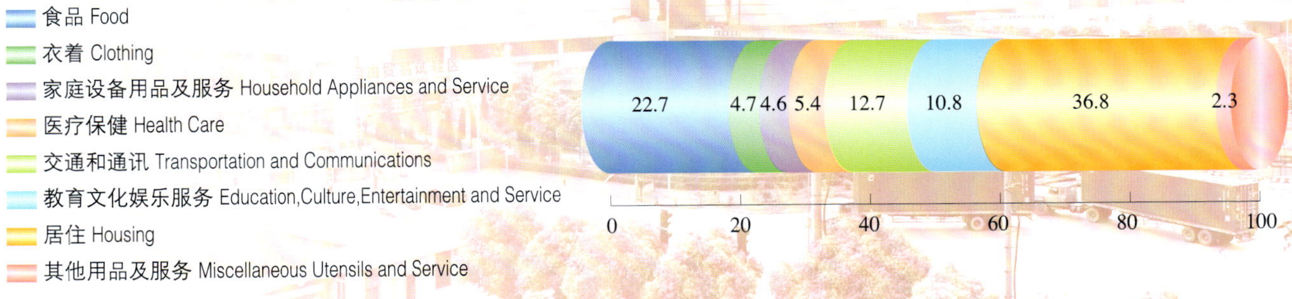

从业人员三次产业构成(%)
Employed Persons by Industry (%)

人口自然增长率和净迁移率(‰)
Natural Growth Rate and Net Migration Rate of Population (‰)

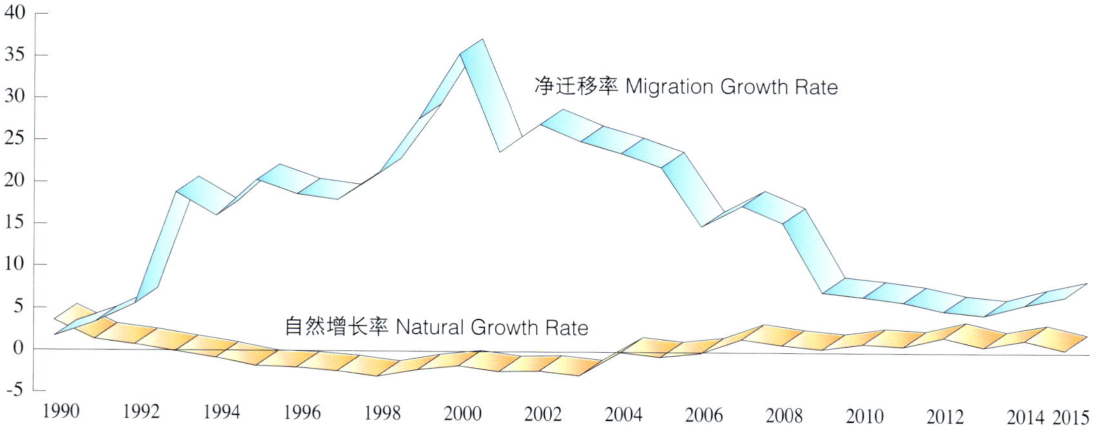

集装箱吞吐量(万标箱)
Container Handling Capacity (10000TEU)

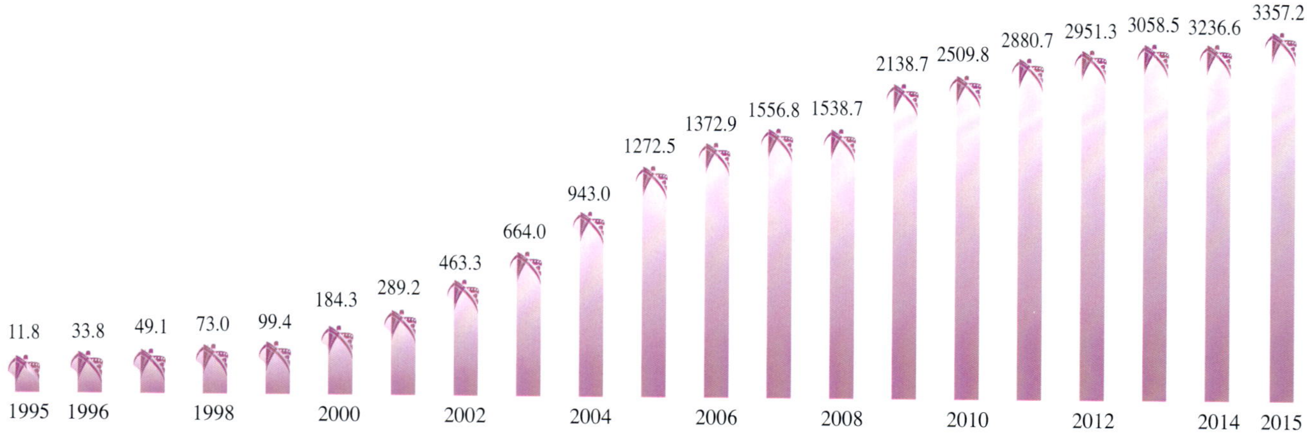

人均公共绿地面积(平方米)
Public Green Space Per Capita (sq.m)

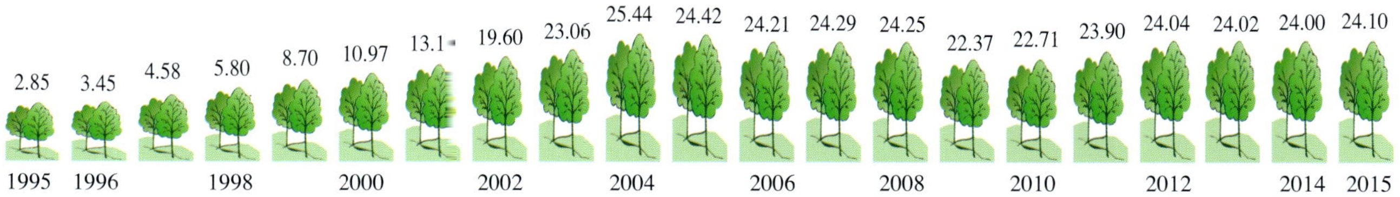

水电消耗情况
Consumption of Tap Water and Electricity

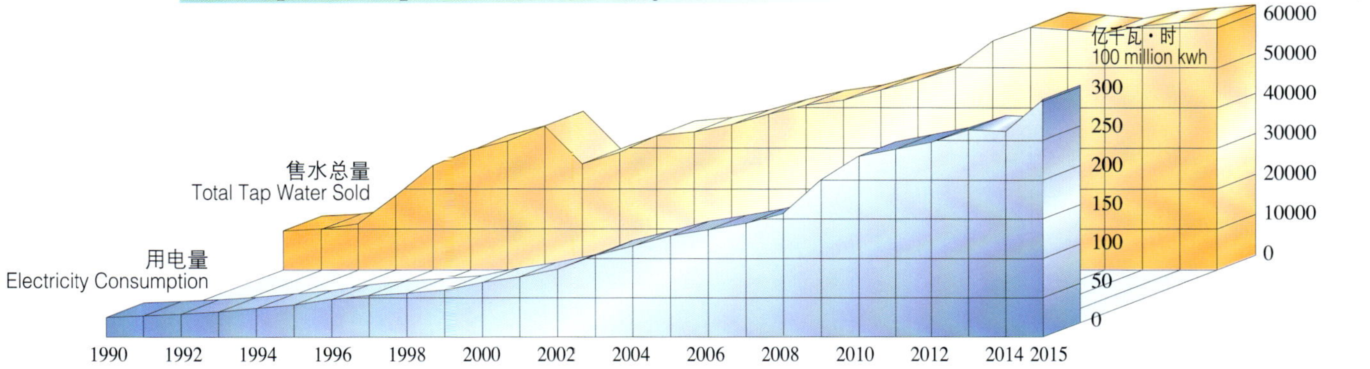

2015年前十位疾病死亡原因构成(%)
Composition of Top 10 Death-Causing Diseases in 2015 (%)

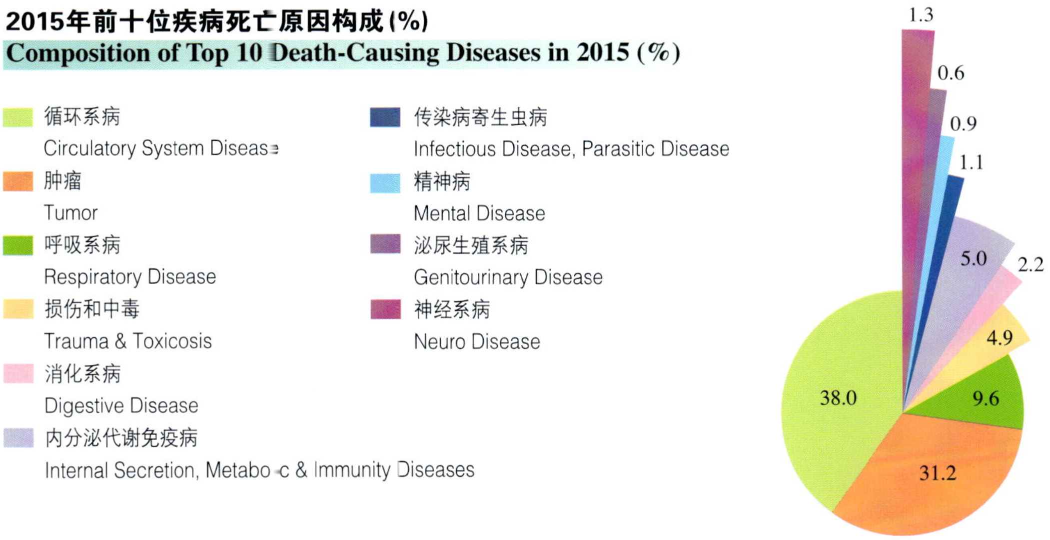

各级学校在校学生数构成(%)
Composition of Students Enrollment by Various Schools (%)

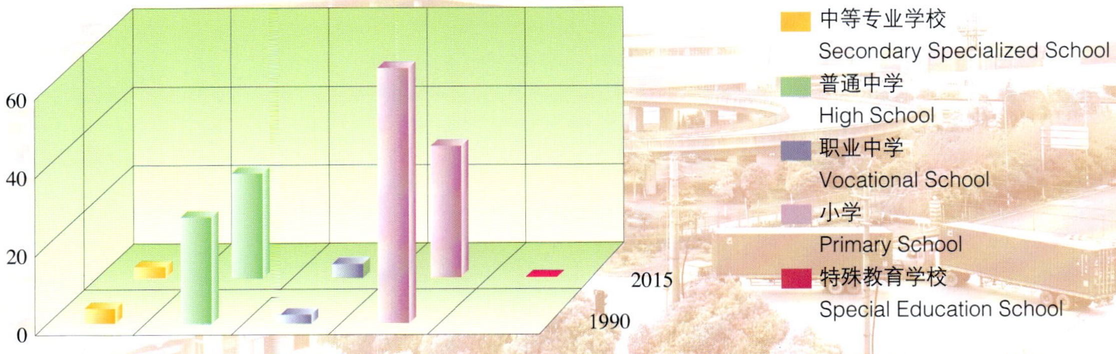

编者说明

一、《上海浦东新区统计年鉴—2016》是一部集浦东新区资料于一体的大型工具书。全书通过大量的统计数据，以中英文对照的形式记录了浦东新区开发开放以来社会经济发展的历程，全面展示了2015年浦东新区在二次创业的新阶段中，经济、社会、科技和重点开发区等各方面的发展变化。年鉴为各级领导、理论研究和实际工作者，以及国内外各界关心浦东开发开放的人士了解浦东、研究浦东、参与浦东开发建设提供了案头工具。

二、2009年，浦东新区行政体制发生重大变化。4月24日，国务院批准南汇区行政区域划入浦东新区。5月6日，上海市人民政府正式宣布两区合并。由于两区以前年度很多数据在统计方法、统计口径、统计范围等方面的不一致，数据无法简单相加，追溯存在一定难度。因此除特别注明外，本年鉴自2009年起，统计数据均为新浦东数据（即含原南汇地区），以前年度仍为原浦东数据。

三、2011年和2012年，浦东新区进行部分街镇行政区划调整。2011年10月28日，上海市人民政府批准撤销川沙新镇、六灶镇建制，设立新的川沙新镇；撤销祝桥镇建制，设立新的祝桥镇，其行政区域范围作相应调整。2012年8月30日，经批准撤销申港街道、芦潮港镇建制，设立南汇新城镇，同时行政区域范围也作相应调整。

四、本年鉴中平均增长速度根据每年的环比增长速度相乘再开方得到。

五、全书内容分为二十一个篇目。内含：1. 综合；2. 人口；3. 固定资产投资；4. 招商引资；5. 农业；6. 工业；7. 建筑业；8. 金融业及要素市场；9. 房地产；10. 国内外贸易；11. 服务、旅游和住宿业；12. 科学技术；13. 人民生活；14. 就业与社会保障；15. 教育；16. 文化和体育；17. 卫生；18. 法律、社会治安及其他；19. 城市建设和环境保护；20. 重点开发区和街镇；21. 上海市统计资料。

六、资料中使用的度量衡单位均采用国际统一标准计量单位。

七、本年鉴部分数据总计数或相对数由于单位取舍不同，产生的计算误差均未作机械调整。

八、浦东新区在行政管理体制上于1995年11月撤乡建镇，实行镇管村体制。因此，本年鉴中有关“镇”和“镇及镇以上工业”等指标含义与全国的“乡”和“乡及乡以上工业”等指标的含义相同。

九、本年鉴中的符号使用说明：“#”表示某一指标的其中主要项；“…”表示数据不足本表最小计量单位数；“空格”表示该项统计指标数据不详或无该项数据或数据为零。

十、根据国务院和国家统计局有关我国GDP核算和数据发布制度的规定，浦东新区国内生产总值自2004年起更名为“浦东新区生产总值”，简称“新区生产总值”。

十一、本年鉴中各项增加值和总产值绝对数均按当年价格计算，增长速度按可比价格计算。

十二、在使用统计资料时，凡与本年鉴有出入的，均以本年鉴为准。

十三、《上海浦东新区统计年鉴》公开出版以来，受到国内外广大读者的爱护和支持，对此我们深表谢意，并竭诚欢迎读者继续对本年鉴的不足之处给予批评和指正。

本年鉴的编制得到了上海市统计局、浦东新区各委、办、局及各开发区管委会等有关单位的大力支持，在此一并表示谢意。

EDITOR'S NOTE

Ⅰ. Statistical Yearbook of Shanghai Pudong New Area (PNA) — 2016 is a large, comprehensive reference book. With great amount of data and in both Chinese and English versions, it records recent years' social and economic development in PNA. It describes the changes in economy, society, science and technology, and key development zones in PNA's new stage of "Second Startup for Business" in 2015. It is a desktop tool - book meant for leaders at all levels, theorists, practitioners, and people at home and abroad who are interested in PNA, want to do research work on Pudong and intend to participate in its development and its construction.

Ⅱ. Great changes happened to the administrative system of Pudong New Area in 2009. On April 24, the State Council approved to add the administrative area of Nanhui District into Pudong New Area. On May 6, the Shanghai Municipal government formally announced the combination of these two districts. Because of data of previous years in these two districts can not be added simply while they had been produced with different statistical methods, approached and areas and it is hard to trace them. Unless specified, the statistical data in this Yearbook are those of new PNA (including former Nanhui District) since 2009, and the data of previous years are those of former PNA.

Ⅲ. In 2011 and 2012, administrative divisions of some towns in PNA were readjusted. On October 28, 2011, Shanghai People's Government approved the establishment of the new Chuansha New Town after rescinding the former Chuansha New Town and Liuzao Town, approved the establishment of the new Zhuqiao Town after rescinding the former Zhuqiao Town, and readjusted the administrative divisions of these two new towns. On August 30, 2012, the municipal government approved the establishment of the new Nanhui New Town after rescinding Shengang Sub - district and Luchaogang Town, and readjusted its administrative division.

Ⅳ. The annual average growth rate in this Yearbook is extracted from the multiplication of the annual chain growth rates.

Ⅴ. This book falls into nineteen chapters: 1. General Survey; 2. Population; 3. Investment in Fixed Assets; 4. Business Promotion and Foreign - fund Attraction; 5. Agriculture; 6. Industry; 7. Construction; 8. Finance and Banking, and Factor Markets; 9. Real Estate; 10. Domestic and Foreign Trades; 11. Services, Tourism and Hotels; 12. Science and Technology; 13. People's Livelihood; 14. Employment and Social Security; 15. Education; 16. Culture and Sports; 17. Public Health; 18. Laws, Public Order and Others; 19. Urban Construction and Environmental Protection; 20. Key Development Zones and Sub - districts and Towns; 21. Statistics of Shanghai Municipality.

Ⅵ. The units of measurement in this book are consistent with international standards.

Ⅶ. No adjustment has been made to correct the deviations of some of the figures in the Yearbook caused by different methods used in rounding.

Ⅷ. In November 1995, PNA rescinded township system and adopted town system. Villages are supervised by towns in the town system. Therefore, in this book, the meanings of "town" and "town and town - above industry" are the same as "township" and "township and township - above industry" in other Chinese statistical books.

Ⅸ. Notations used in this Yearbook:

"#" indicates the major item of a certain indicator,

"…" indicates the figure which is too small to be measured by the smallest unit in the table,

"blank" indicates the data unavailable or none in certain statistical indicator.

Ⅹ. According to relevant stipulations by the State Council and National Bureau of Statistics, GDP of Pudong New Area is to be renamed as Gross Output Value of Pudong New Area, shortened as PNA Gross Output Value starting from 2004.

Ⅺ. All added values and gross output vales in the Yearbook are listed in terms of current prices while growth rates listed in terms of comparable prices.

XII. If any statistical data from other sources conflict with the data in the present Yearbook, data in the present Yearbook shall apply.

XIII. The publication of Pudong New Area Statistical Yearbook has received great attention. Our gratitude and appreciation go to all the readers who have offered their comments. We welcome and are open to more comments and suggestions from our readers when presenting this new edition.

We appreciate the great support and efforts of Shanghai Statistics Bureau, all the commissions, offices and bureaus, and administrations of all the development zones in PNA during compilation of the present Yearbook.

目　　录

CONTENTS

综　述
ABSTRACT

第一篇　综　合
CHAPTER　1　GENERAL SURVEY

第二篇　人　口
CHAPTER 2　POPULATION

第三篇　固定资产投资
CHAPTER 3　INVESTMENT IN FIXED ASSETS

第四篇　招商引资
CHAPTER 4　BUSINESS PROMOTION AND FOREIGN-FUND ATTRACTION

第五篇　农　业
CHAPTER 5　AGRICULTURE

第六篇　工　业
CHAPTER 6 INDUSTRY

第七篇　建筑业
CHAPTER 7　CONSTRUCTION

第八篇　金融业及要素市场
CHAPTER 8　FINANCIAL INDUSTRY AND FACTOR MARKETS

第九篇　房地产
CHAPTER 9　REAL ESTATE

第十篇　国内外贸易

CHAPTER 10 DOMESTIC AND FOREIGN TRADES

第十一篇　服务、旅游和住宿业
CHAPTER　11　SERVICES, TOURISM AND HOTELS

第十二篇　科学技术
CHAPTER　12　SCIENCE AND TECHNOLOGY

第十五篇　教　育
CHAPTER 15 EDUCATION

第十六篇　文化和体育
CHAPTER 16 CULTURE AND SPORTS

第十七篇　卫　生
CHAPTER　17　PUBLIC HEALTH

第十八篇　法律、社会治安及其他
CHAPTER　18　LAWS, PUBLIC ORDER AND OTHERS

第十九篇 城市建设和环境保护

CHAPTER 19 URBAN CONSTRUCTIONS AND ENVIRONMENTAL PROTECTION

第二十篇 重点开发区和街镇

CHAPTER 20 KEY DEVELOPMENT ZONES AND SUB - DISTRICTS AND TOWNS

第二十一篇　上海市统计资料
CHAPTER 21 STATISTICS OF SHANGHAI MUNICIPALITY

2015年浦东新区经济和社会发展情况

2015年是全面完成“十二五”规划的收官之年。面对全球经济复苏缓慢、国内经济下行压力加大的宏观背景，浦东新区在市委、市政府的领导下，认真贯彻党的十八届四中、五中全会精神和“四个全面”要求，牢牢把握稳中求进工作总基调，坚持创新驱动发展、经济转型升级，坚持深化改革、扩大开放、先行先试，坚持推进自贸试验区扩区建设和推进科创中心建设引领发展全局，经济社会发展平稳有序、符合预期，年度计划执行情况总体良好，约束性指标全面完成，多数预期性指标得以实现，“十二五”规划的各项指标也顺利完成。

一、经济转型成效进一步显现

1、经济总量平稳增长。今年以来，为适应“新常态”，新区积极采取各项措施，努力保持经济平稳增长，经济运行总体平稳、符合预期。2015年，地区生产总值达到7898.35亿元，增长9.1%，高于全市平均增幅2.2个百分点。一般公共预算收入完成788.19亿元，增长13.7%。全社会固定资产投资全年完成1772.94亿元。招商引资保持快速增长的势头，实到外资达到64.6亿美元，增长44.3%；新增内资企业注册资本10578亿元，增长1.3倍。镇域经济平稳发展，全年镇级区级地方税收完成121.5亿元，增长3.8%（不含管镇联动和临港招商统筹相关镇）。节能减排工作稳步推进，单位增加值综合能耗下降5.42%，顺利完成全年计划下降目标。

2、质量效益不断提升。第三产业增加值增长12.5%，占生产总值的比重达到72%，对经济增长的拉动作用明显大于二产。第三产业中金融业贡献最大，增长24.9%，占比36%。工业总产值增长2.4%，其中“三大三新”行业在电子信息产品制造业带动下，实现产值5787亿元，占工业总产值比重达到63%。高技术产业发展迅速，产值增速快于工业总产值增速9.8个百分点。

3、产业结构调整有力推进。出台了产业结构调整实施意见和资金管理办法，制定了产业结构调整三年行动计划。全年完成442项产业结构调整项目，完成率达到110%。同时聚焦重点区域，推动合庆、周浦区域产业结构调整工作。2015年全年共完成减量化立项审批552件，减量化总面积429公顷，其中198区域361公顷。

二、自贸试验区带动改革开放深入推进

1、自贸试验区扩区建设成效明显。投资管理改革方面，在新扩展区域全面实施外商投资和境外投资备案管理制度，推动内资注册“单一窗口”从企业设立向变更环节延伸，外资注册从“五证联办”向“七证联办”拓展。大力实施“三证合一、一照一码”改革，全市近半数新增外资项目落户自贸试验区，全年累计办结境外投资项目636个。贸易便利化改革方面，海关、检验检疫分别推出“一区注册、四地经营”、“空检海防”等32项便利化举措；国际贸易“单一窗口”1.0版上线运行，涉及17个口岸和贸易监管部门、1000多家企业上线办理业务；启动实施航运保险产品注册制改革，开展外贸进出口集装箱沿海捎带业务，货物状态分类监管试点扩大到保税区所有物流企业，洋山进境水果指定口岸获批。金融制度创新方面，进一步拓展自由贸易账户功能，启动外币服务功能。截至12月底，共有40家机构接入分账核算单元体系，开设FT账户44186个，账户收支总额22053亿元；累计有246家企业发生跨境双向人民币资金池业务，资金池收支总额4175亿元；上海首家民营银行（华瑞银行）开业，中外合资专业健康医疗保险机构太保安联健康保险股份有限公司设立。加强事中事后监管方面，加快探索以自贸试验区理念推进政府职能转变，系统设计政府职能转变的整体方案。推进“浦东新区公共信用信息服务平台”建设，为推进社会信用体系建设、创新事中事后监管机制提供信息技术和大数据支撑。积极扩大信用信息和信用产品应用，鼓励社会力量参与市场监管，构建政企合作的“互联网+信用”监管模式。

2、各片区功能持续优化。保税区片区继续保持先发优势，充分发挥特殊监管区贸易便利化优势，进一步做强总部经济，拓展国际贸易和航运功能。推进亚太营运商计划，已有两批42家跨国企业获得集团总部授权,启动筹建10家大宗商品现货交易市场。陆家嘴(世博)片区利用金融创新开放优势,加强国际化、高能级要素市场和总部机构集聚,贝莱德、安本、桥水等国际知名资产管理机构落户;支持上交所、上期所、中金所等拓展国际业务;推动央企、国内知名大企业设立地区总部或金融平台。张江片区加快规划建设国际领先的科技城,启动建设张江空服中心,探索复制推广保税研发和通关便利化等创新举措;推动科技与金融结合,促进创业投资机构集聚,支持创新企业在新三板和上海股交中心挂牌。金桥片区着力推进新兴金融、移动视频、电子商务等生产性服务业发展;依托中科院机器人研究总院、新松机器人等机构和企业,大力发展以机器人为重点的智能制造行业。

3、综合配套改革不断深化。围绕简政放权加快政府职能转变,制定发布权力清单、责任清单"1.0版本"。完成行政审批中介服务事项的全面清理,初步形成《浦东新区行政审批中介服务改革实施意见》。"三合一"的知识产权局顺利运作,"多合一"的城市管理行政执法局成立。在张江地区率先开展"管镇联动"试点。临港地区招商统筹改革取得突破。陆家嘴金融城管理体制创新方案基本形成。全面落实浦东国资国企改革的18条意见,按照"一司一策"的工作推进原则,分批实施新区直属国有企业的改革方案。政府信息共享和社会信用体系建设有序推进。完成信用信息服务平台一期建设,录入信用数据500万余条。强化基层基础建设,推进社会治理创新和城乡发展一体化。在全区12个街道全面推行"6+2"模式,统一设置8个党政内设机构。"镇管社区"组织架构和运作机制进一步完善。推进网格化综合管理与大联勤大联动融合对接,构建城市管理网、综合治理网、公共服务网"三网合一"。

三、科技创新推进力度明显加大

1、重点聚焦张江科技城规划建设。积极落实全市科创中心建设22条意见和"双自联动"实施方案,制定出台《上海建设具有全球影响力的科技创新中心浦东新区行动方案(2015-2020年)》。成立依托市区两级推动科技城建设的联合工作组,开展张江科技城功能定位和体制机制研究,启动张江科技城规划设计的国际方案征集。

2、创新环境持续优化。建设开放式孵化器空间或基地。积极引导科研机构、企业、民间资本、海外人才等共建创新型孵化器,本年度分别获得市、区孵化器和众创空间认定12家和21家。完善科技金融支撑体系。强化知识产质押融资的宣传和申报工作,扩大政策受益面。继续推动科技银行试点工作,探索投贷联动机制。深入开展"创业在浦东"系列活动,聚焦科技、媒体和通信、生物医药、绿色节能环保等领域,服务科技创业项目150多个,为17家企业获得约2亿元融资。在全国率先推出"知识产权金融卡",复合提升企业专利、商标、版权等无形资产价值,已有超过200家科技型企业获得银行融资超过3亿。

3、创新创业成效显现。全年获得专利授权13299件,其中发明专利4654件,增长48.3%,每万人口发明专利拥有量约35件左右;完成高新技术成果转化项目139项;技术交易合同金额177.06亿元。自主创新型本土企业发展较好,中信国健、现代制药等企业保持了高速增长。新型企业设立踊跃,"互联网+"、4G等新兴经济成为发展亮点。无店铺零售业快速增长,网上销售零售额106亿元,增长20.4%。

四、核心功能资源配置能力进一步增强

1、金融功能加速提升。2015年新区中外资银行本外币存贷款余额分别增长4.0%和6.6%。证券市场实现成交额266万亿元,增长1.1倍。金融机构继续快速集聚,新增持牌金融机构55家,股权投资、融资租赁、财富管理等新兴金融机构增长3482家。建立面向国际的交易平台,黄金国际板正式运行,获批开展原油期货交易,全国性信托登记平台取得突破性进展。"互联网+金融"加快发展,联想、万达、海尔、小米等企业在浦东设立互联网金融平台。兴业银行组建了兴业云金融,光大集团组建了光大云付互联网金融公司,支付宝总部迁至陆家嘴。

2、航运功能持续发展。全年港口集装箱吞吐量3357.2万标箱,增长3.7%;洋山港集装箱吞吐量1540.7万标箱,其中水水中转量占比49.6%,浦东国际机场货邮吞吐量327万吨,增长2.8%。国际航运要素进一步集聚,全球排名第一的威仕船舶管理公司及哥伦比亚船舶管理公司相继入驻,中外运长航集团航运总部、太平、美亚航运保险运营中心落户。打造陆家嘴洋泾国际航运服务创新区,围绕自贸区航运功能创新,探索搭建航运法律等政府服务平台。积极推进航空城前期规划研究等工作,努力发挥航空枢纽对区域经济发展的带动作用。

3、商业贸易总体平稳。全年商品销售总额29838.4亿元,增长8%,高于全市1.6个百分点;社会消费品零售总额1883.8亿元,增长8.3%。迪士尼旗舰店等新增商业设施保持良好销售势头;通讯器材类电子产品销售旺盛,增长1.5倍;大众餐饮消费直接拉动社会消费品零售总额增长近1个百分点。全年外贸进出口16903亿元,增长2.7%。总部经济持续发展,全年新增跨国公司地区总部16家;新增亚太区总部5家;累计获得认定的跨国公司地区总部245家。

五、社会建设全面深入推进

1、就业和保障工作平稳有序。实施新一轮促进就业政策,积极开展就业援助月、民营企业招聘周、应届生就业服务月等各类就业专项活动。全年新增就业岗位15.1万个,开展职业技能培训9.8万人,共帮助1825人成功创业。抓好各类社会保障政策落实,城乡居保每人每月增加120元,惠及8.3万人。征地养老人员每人每月增加170元,惠及2629人。审核批准各类救助帮困对象140.23万人次,发放各类救助帮困资金64270.88万元。加快推进为老实事项目,新增养老床位1287张。为5.9万多名老人提供居家养老服务,因地制宜推进"长者照护之家"和农村养老睦邻互助点的建设。居民收入平稳增长,全年居民人均可支配收入增长8.6%。市区两级52项实事工程项目全部完成。

2、重点社会事业加快发展。加快建设36所公建配套学校,积极推进川沙中学迁建、杨思职业技术学校新建等项目。深入推进学区化集团化办学试点,开展"新优质学校"创建工作。率先在南汇新城镇推行"教育六条",加强农村教育人才队伍建设。东方医院改扩建项目积极推进,浦南医院综合楼顺利启用,高行、芦潮港等一批社区卫生服务中心开工建设。积极开展以家庭医生为核心的社区卫生服务综合改革,实施"卫生八条",鼓励优秀卫生人才和大学生向农村地区流动。实施川沙体育场征地改扩建、周浦体育中心新建等重大体育项目,新建11条百姓健身路径、4个百姓健身房、5个社区公共运动场、15个农民体育健身工程等健身设施。

3、文化影响力逐步提升。"东方财经·浦东频道"正式开播。建成开放金海文化艺术中心等区域性公共文化设施,外高桥文化艺术中心、谢稚柳陈佩秋艺术馆等设施基本建设完成,抓紧推进新场、横沔等古镇的保护性开发。积极打造浦东文化品牌,成功开展庆祝浦东开发开放25周年系列文化活动,进一步扩大浦东文化艺术节、简单生活节等品牌活动的影响力,参与主办首届上海国际喜剧节。国家公共文化示范区创建工作有力推进,塘桥社区文化活动中心社会化专业化管理经验在全国推广。

4、"三农"工作取得积极成效。全力推进浦东国家现代农业示范区建设,完成181个共5.3万亩粮食高产创建示范方。大力发展家庭农场、农民合作社、农业龙头企业等新型农业经营主体,全区粮田40%由446家家庭农场经营。启动73座农桥改造,申报航头镇牌楼村、新场镇果园村、祝桥镇新如村、大团镇赵桥村等4个村创建市级美丽乡村示范村。继续实施治理不规范畜禽养殖三年计划,完成退养205户,治理面积16.2万平方米。组建经济薄弱村联合发展平台,帮助经济薄弱村及村民获得稳定收益。加强农村集体"三资"监督管理,全区累计已有357个村完成集体经济组织产权制度改革。

六、多方参与的社会治理格局初步形成

1、基层社区治理不断优化。稳步推进社区自治体系、社区共治体系、社区支撑体系、社区服务体系工作,着力推进形成政社互联、多元互动、功能互补的城乡社区治理服务格局。全区36个街镇基本完成"一口受理"达标工作。顺利完成全区1217个居村委换届选举。全面推广实施"1+1+X"基层自治工作法,实现居村全覆盖。成立36家街镇社区发展基金,其中2家为社区基金会。

2、社会组织规范有效运作。全区社会组织总量累计达到1882家。推进公益项目"供需对接一站式服务"平台建设,目前正在为67个公益服务项目提供一站式服务,其中52个公益项目供需对接成功。社工队伍不断发展壮大,具有国家职业资格证书的社会工作者达到近4000人,拥有专业社工机构43家。

3、人口综合管理服务工作有序推进。采取有力措施,加大对"无合法稳定居住,无合法稳定就业"来沪人员的调控力度。截至12月上旬,整治取缔群租7047套,整治取缔无证无序设摊7614个,行政处置无证六小行业3243户、取缔1233户,规范学前儿童看护点154个、关闭179个。截至2015年12月底,新区实有来沪人员237.16万人,下降5.6%。

七、城市建设管理不断优化

1、新兴区域加快建设。世博地区A、B片区加快已出让商办楼宇地块项目建设,部分项目年底全部完工并可交付使用,C片区先行启动区加快土地出让;前滩地块企业天地项目进展顺利,铁狮门、前滩中心、休闲公园等项目加快推进,部分已进入收尾阶段。耀华地块SK大厦和上海合景广场等工程稳步推进。国际旅游度假区核心区"四个一"(中心湖、围场河、西入口大道、公交枢纽)基本建成,外围配套8条9段道路基本全部建成。核心区二级市政项目、过渡性开发项目基本建成,轨交11号线迪士尼段工程建成。临港地区中航商发、中移动等一批重点项目按照节点目标有序推进,12英寸大硅片、极地海洋世界等项目正式开工。上海天文馆等一批项目按照节点目标加快推进。陆家嘴"亚太营运中心"加快推进,国际医疗康检中心开工建设,张江创业工坊开业运营。

2、重大基础设施顺利推进。全年重大工程完成投资141.8亿元,超额完成年度计划目标。旧区改造和保障房建设工作积极推进,截至目前完成旧区改造4068户,已超额完成全年2300户的目标。继续推进"城中村"地块改造,有序推进中心城区二级以下旧里和城镇郊区棚户简屋改造。预计全年区级征收安置房开工225万平方米,解决逾期在外过渡居民3029户。提升信息基础设施建设水平,实现约154个试点公共场所的WiFi覆盖建设。

3、生态环境建设力度加大。启动第六轮环保三年行动计划。继续推进各类林地、滨江森林公园二期、外环开天窗补绿、南汇生态专项等项目建设。继续开展污水支管和截污纳管工程建设,推进垃圾转运等环卫设施建设改造。启动城区收费垃圾清运作业按量付费。加强空气质量监测,在全市率先实施空气质量预报预警试运行。

4、城市管理水平不断提高。初步建成城市网格化综合管理信息平台,实现网格化综合管理与联勤联动有效融合。继续保持"三违"整治的高压态势,全年共整治"三违"总量846.3万平方米,其中,违法建筑442万平方米,违法用地87.1万平方米,违规种养317.2万平方米。集中力量开展合庆G1501以东区域综合整治,共计拆除违法建筑73.9万平方米。制定《浦东新区合庆地区环境综合治理实施方案》,明确涉及环境整治和产业结构调整等40项具体工作任务。合庆地区的消防安全执法、"三违"整治、产业结构调整、河道整治等取得积极成效。

Economic and Social Development of the Pudong New District in 2015

2015 was the complete ending year of the Twelfth Five Year Plan. Under the macro-background of slow global economic recovery and downward pressure on the domestic economy, and with the guidance of municipal committee and municipal government, the Pudong New District conscientiously implemented the spirits of the 4th and 5th Plenary Session of the 18th CPC Central Committee and Four Comprehensives, firmly grasping the general tone of the work while maintaining stability, adhering to the innovation-driven development, economic transformation and upgrading, as well as deepening reform, openness and first pilot, insisting on the construction of Free Trade Zone and the Center of Technological Innovation to lead the overall development. Ensuring the stable and orderly development of social and economic which in line with expectations. Making sure the implementation of annual plan is generally good, bounded targets are completed, and most of the indicators are expected to be achieved, so as the indicators of the Twelfth Five Year Plan .

Ⅰ. The effectiveness of economic transformation has further demonstrated.

1. Total economy grows smoothly. In order to adapt to the New Normal this year, Pudong New District took various measures actively to maintain steady economic growth. The economy which in line with expectations was generally smooth. By 2015, the GDP has reached 789.835 billion yuan, with an increase of 9.1%, higher than the city average growth of 2.2%. General public budget revenue has reached 78.819 billion yuan, with an increase of 13.7%. Total fixed asset investment was 177.294 billion yuan by the year. Investment-invitation has maintained a rapid growth momentum: The actual reached foreign capital was 6.46 billion dollars, with an increase of 44.3%; New domestic enterprises registered capital was 1.0578 trillion yuan, with an increase of 1.3 times. Township economy developed smoothly. Township and district-level local taxes has completed 12.15 billion yuan by year, with an increase of 3.8% (excluding Joint Operation and Lingang investment and co-ordinated related towns). Energy saving and emission reduction has promoted steadily. The unit added value of comprehensive energy consumption has fallen 5.42%, thus the annual target goal has successfully achieved.

2. Quality effectiveness is increasing. Tertiary industry add value has increased by 12.5%, accounting for 72% of GDP, which played a greater role in boosting economic growth than the secondary industry. And among these financial sector contributed the most, with the growth of 24.9%, accounting for 36% of GDP. Industrial output increased by 2.4%, of which Three Big Three New driven by electronic information products manufacturing industry, realizing output value of 578.7 billion yuan, accounting for the proportion of 63% among total industrial output value. High-tech industry was developing rapidly, which the output growth rate is 9.8% faster comparing to total industrial output value.

3. Industrial restructuring is promoting effectively. The industrial restructuring implementation suggestion and fund management approach have been introduced, as well as a three-year plan of industrial restructuring. By the end of this year, 442 industrial restructuring projects has been achieved, the completion rate has reached 110%. At the same time Pudong New District focused on key areas, promoting regional industrial structure adjustment including Heqing and Zhoupu. 552 reduction projects have been approved, with 429 hectares total reduction area, of which 361 hectares belonging to "198. district"

Ⅱ. Free Trade Zone promotes further reform and opening up.

1. Free Trade expansion zones made great success. On the aspect of investment management reform, we fully implemented foreign investment and overseas investment record management system in new development area, promoting the domestic registration single window extends from enterprise establishment to alteration, changing foreign registration from Five License Joint to Seven License Joint. Vigorously implement the reform of "Integrate the Business License, the Organization Code Certificate, and the Certificate of Taxation Registration into One Document, One License, One Code", nearly half of the city's new foreign-funded projects settled in FTZ. The annual total overseas investment projects added up to 636. On the aspect of trade facilitation reforms, customs, inspection and quarantine launched One Area Registration, Four District Management, Space and Coastal Defense such facilitation measures, respectively. International trade single window version 1.0 launched, involving 17 ports trade and regulatory authorities, leading over 1000 companies to conduct business on-line. Start the reform of implementation of shipping insurance product registration system, carrying out foreign trade import and export containers coastal incidentally business. Cargo status classification regulation pilot expanded to all logistics enterprises in the bonded area. The Yangshan port has been approved as imported fruit designated port. On the aspect of Innovation in financial system, to further expand free trade account and start foreign currency services. By the end of December, a total of 40 institutions access sub-accounting system, and offered 44186 FT accounts with a total account balance 2.2053 trillion yuan. There is a total of 246 enterprises happened two-way cross-border RMB cashing pool business, with total capital pool balance 417.5 billion yuan; Shanghai's first private bank (RAE Bank) opened. A joint venture company specializing in health insurance institution Allianz Health Insurance Co., Ltd established. Strengthening supervise in and after the process, and accelerating further transformation of government functions overall plan based on FTZ. Promoting the construction Pudong New District Public Credit Information Service Platform, providing support for the social credit system construction, innovative things in the post-regulatory mechanisms to provide information technology and big data. Actively expand credit information and credit product applications. Encourage social forces to participate in market supervision, and build "Internet + Credit" supervision model between government and enterprises.

2. Keep on optimizing functions of areas. Bonded Area kept to maintain first-mover advantage, giving full play to trade facilitation advantages as special surveillance zone. Further strengthen the headquarters economy, and the expansion of international trade and navigation functions. Promoting Asia-Pacific operators plan. There were already two batches of 42 transnational enterprises gotten authorization from headquarter. 10 commodity spot trading markets were started to build. Lujiazui (Expo) Area took financial innovation advantages to strengthen aggregation of international, high energy level factor market and headquarter. BlackRock, Aberdeen and Bridgewater and other renowned international asset management institutions settled here. Support Shanghai Stock Exchange, SHFE and CFFE international business expansion. promote the central enterprises, domestic well-known large enterprises to set up regional headquarters or financial platform. Zhangjiang Area sped up to plan and construction the world's leading science and technology city, and started construction of Zhangjiang flight center, exploring replicated bonded research and development and facilitation of customs clearance and other innovative initiatives. To promote combining science with finance, strengthen aggregation of venture capital organizations, and supporting innovative enterprises listing at NEEQ and Shanghai Stock and Exchange Center. Jinqiao area focused on promoting the development of emerging financial, mobile video, e-commerce such producer services; relying on the CAS robot research Institute, SIACU robot and other institutions and enterprises to strive to develop intelligent manufacturing industries focusing on robots.

3. Deepen comprehensive supporting reform. Accelerate the transformation of government functions around streamline administration and institute decentralization; formulate releasing power list and the list of responsibilities version 1.0. Accomplished the comprehensive clean-up of administrative examination and approval intermediary service, the Implementation of the Reform of Pudong New District Administrative Examination and Approval on Intermediary Services has taken initial shape. Triple play Intellectual Property Office run smoothly, at the same time, All in

One City Urban Administrative and Law Enforcement Bureau set up. Zhangjiang area took the lead in Joint Operation pilot work. Lingang area made a breakthrough about reform on attracting investment and overall planning. Innovative management system of financial center of Lujiazui was basically formed. We have fully implemented the 18 state owned enterprise reform opinions of Pudong New District, according to the principle One Company, One Policy, promoting the reform to State-owned enterprises directly under New District in batches. Government Information Sharing and social credit system were pushed forward. Complete the first phase construction Credit information service platform and input the credit data of more than 5 million. Strengthen grass-root infrastructure, promote the innovation of society governance and the integration of urban and rural development. We were fully implementing the "6 + 2 model" in the region of 12 streets, unified the set of eight Party and government organs. Further improve Town Managing Community organizational structure and operational mechanism. Promote integration and docking of grid integrated management and joint logistics as well as big linkage, building in triple play including urban management network, comprehensive management network, and public service network.

Ⅲ. Significantly increase on promoting scientific and technological innovation.

1. Focus on Zhangjiang Sci-tech City Planning and Construction. Actively implement 22 comments on the construction of Kechuang Center and Double Self-linkage implementing plan. Formulated the Shang Global Influence on the Action Programme of Pudong New District Scientific and Technological Innovation Center (2015-2020) Establish a joint working group relying on the government at municipal and district levels to promote sci-tech city construction. Carry out functional orientation and institutional research at Zhangjiang Sci-tech City. Start international collection of design plan about Zhangjiang Sci-tech City.

2. Continually optimize innovation environment. Build open Construction of open incubator space or base. Actively guide the scientific research institutions, enterprises, private capital, and other overseas talent to joint build innovative incubator. By the year, 12 of them have accredited by municipal and district level incubator and 21 have accredited by Maker Space. Improve Science and technology support system. Strengthen the propaganda and declaration work of IPRs pledge loan to expand policy benefit area. Continue to promote pilot of technology bank, to explore investment and loans linkage mechanism. Deeply develop Entrepreneurship in Pudong series of activities, focusing on technology, media, communications, bio-medicine, environmental protection and other green areas, serving over 150 STVP, financing about 200 million dollars for 17 companies. we take the lead in putting out Intellectual Property debit card nationwide to enhance the value of intangible assets among enterprises patents, trademarks, copyrights, etc.. More than 200 science and technology enterprises have obtained bank financing over 300 million yuan.

3. Innovation and entrepreneurship have achieved remarkable success. It was estimated to obtain about 13299 patents, including 4654 or so patents for invention, with an increase of 48.3%; about 35 patents per million people; 139 have transformed into tech achievements; technology trading contracts have reached amount 17.70 billion yuan. The in-depended innovation of local enterprises developed well, in which CPGJ and Shyndec Pharm have maintained a rapid growth. The establishment of new enterprises was enthusiastically. Internet +, 4G and other emerging economies became the highlights. Non-store retailing increased rapidly with retail sales of 10.6 billion yuan, growing by 20.4%.

Ⅳ. The enhanced ability of allocating resources in core functional areas.

1. The financial functions of the region have been rapidly improved. In 2015, the Balance of deposits and loans counted in domestic currency, or foreign currency, both in Chinese and foreign banks operating in the New District has increased by 4.0% and 6.6%, respectively. Securities market turnover reached to 266 trillion yuan, an 1.1 times of increase compared to that of last year. There is an momentum of agglomeration among the financial institutions, with 55 new licensed financial institutions set up, and emerging financial institutions working on equity investment, financial leasing, and asset management adding up to 3482. An international trading platform has been established. The international board of Shanghai Gold Exchange officially starts running. The region has been approved to carry out crude oil futures trading. The national trust registration platform has made a breakthrough. A business op-

erating pattern of "Internet + Finance" has been developing rapidly, as enterprises like Lenovo, Wanda, Haier, millet and other companies chose to establish financial platform in Pudong. In the region, Societe Generale Bank established the Societe Generale financial cloud, Everbright Group set up a finance company to facilitate payments through the Internet, and Alipay has moved its headquarter to Lujiazui.

2. The shipping function of the region has developed in a sustainable way. Annual container throughput of the ports in the region has reached to 33.572 million TEUs, an increase of 3.7%; container throughput of Yangshan Port is 15.407 million TEUs, in which water-water transit accounted for more than 49.6%. The cargo throughput of Pudong International Airport is 3.27 million tons, an increase of 2.8%. The region has attracted more international shipping powers. V-ship, the world's largest ship management company, and Columbia Ship management Ltd, have settled in. The headquarters for shipping management of Sinotrans & CSC Holdings Co. Ltd., the shipping insurance operation center of China Taiping Insurance Group Ltd., and that of American International Group, Inc. have also moved in this region. We are developing the international shipping service innovation zone in Yangjing, Lujiazui, and innovate shipping functions serving the FTZ. We try to build governmental services platforms providing legal and other supports concerning shipping activities. We actively accelerate preliminary work of constructing the aviation city, and make the aviation hub a leading role in regional economic development.

3. Commercial trades are generally stable. Annual total sales of goods reaches to 2.98 trillion yuan, an increase of 8%, and 1.6% higher than that of the whole city; total retail sales of social consumer goods reaches to 188.38 billion yuan, an increase of 8.3%. Disney's new flagship store and other commercial facilities maintain good sales momentum; communications equipment and electronic products sell well, and are up 1.5 times; mass catering consumption directly stimulates social retail sales to increase by nearly 1%. Annual imports and exports come up to 1.69 trillion yuan, an increase of 2.7%. The economic influence created by headquarters has increased in an sustainable way. There are 16 new regional headquarters of multinational companies, 5 new Asia-Pacific headquarters. Thus, the total number of certified regional headquarters of multinationals comes up to 245.

Ⅴ. Promoting comprehensive social construction.

1. The employment and social security works have been carried out in a smooth and orderly way. We have implemented the new policy for promoting employment, and have actively held various activities for boosting employment such as employment-assistance month, private- enterprises-recruitment week, graduates-employment-service month. This year 151 000 new jobs have been created, and 98,000 people have received vocational skills training. Those efforts help 1825 people start their own businesses. We have ensured the implementation of various social security policies, and the insurance subsidy for urban and rural residents has increased by 120 yuan per month per person, benefiting 8.3 million people. Such subsidy increases by 170 yuan per month per senior citizen whose farmland is requisitioned, benefiting 2629 people. We have approved of various social aid projects aiming at helping 1.4023 million vulnerable people, and have issued various types of aid poverty-relief funds 642,708,800 yuan. We have accelerated the development of practical projects for the old. 1287 new pension beds have been set. We have provided home care services to more than 59,000 elderly people. And we have promoted the construction of Elderly Care Home and service points for rural endowment through good-neighborliness and mutual assistance, according to local conditions. The residents` income remains a steady growth, with the annual per capital disposable income increasing by 8.6%. 52 practical projects on the urban level have been completed.

2. Key social undertakings develop at a high speed. We have accelerated the construction of 36 public facilitate schools, and have actively promoted the relocation of Chuansha secondary school, and the rebuilding of the Yangsi vocational -technical school. We have further tried to run schools following group-running methods within a district system. And we have carried out the plan to build new superior schools. We have firstly implemented the 6 regulations on education in Nanhui Xincheng, and have focused on the reserve of talents for the education in rural areas. The building expansion project of Oriental Hospital advances well. The comprehensive building of Punan Hospital is successfully commissioned. A number of community health centers in Gaohang, Luchaogang are under construction.

3. Cultural influence gradually improved. Oriental Financial, Pudong Channel has officially launched. Gimhae Arts and Cultural Center and other regional public cultural facilities opened to the public. Waigaoqiao Cultural Arts Center, Xiezhiliu Chenpeiqiu Art Museum have completed basic facilities. we pay close attention to promote the protective development of Xinchang and Hengmian. We build Pudong cultural brand actively, and successfully carried out to celebrate the 25th anniversary of the Pudong development and opening up series of cultural activities, to further expand the influence of Culture and Art Festival and Simple Life Festival in Pudong. Participate in and host the inaugural Shanghai International Comedy Festival. Effectively promote national public cultural demonstration area construction work, and professional management experience of Tangqiao community cultural centers nationwide.

4. Agriculture work has made positive achievements. Pudong made great efforts to promote the construction of national modern agriculture demonstration area, and has completed 5. 3 million mu, a total of 181 high-yield pilot projects. Strive to develop new agricultural business entities including family farms, farmers´cooperatives, agricultural enterprises. 40% of the region's grain fields were operated by 446 family farms. Start 73 farming Bridge Rebuilding. Declare Pailou Village in Hangtou County, Guoyuan Village in Xinchang County, Xinru Village in Zhuqiao County, Zhaoqiao Village in Datuan County such four villages to create municipal beautiful countrysides and model villages. Continue to implement three-year governance program on denormalization of livestock breeding, in which 205 families have finished breeding, 162 thousand square meters have been control. Build joint development platform for weakness villages to help them get stable benefits. Strengthen supervision and management of the rural collective 3-capital Industry. 357 villages have accomplished the reform of collective economy organization institution.

Ⅵ. Formation of participatory social management pattern.

1. The governance of grass-root communities has been continuously optimized. We steadily upgrade our community autonomy system, community cohabitation system, community support system, community service system, and take an effort to forge an governmental service pattern for urban and rural communities, which is politically and socially connected, multiple-interactive, and functionally complemented. A reform, a window handling all necessary formalities, in 36 street communities and towns in the district is basically completed and meets expected standards. The general election of 1217 villages in the region is successfully completed. We have comprehensively promoted the implementation of the 1 + 1 + X grassroots autonomous working method, with an aim to cover both urban and rural residential areas. 36 funds for promoting the development of street communities and towns, which include 2 community founds, have been established.

2. Social organizations operates orderly and effectively. The total number of social organizations in the region has reached 1882. We actively support the building of One-stop Service platforms to match the supply and demand for public projects. And we, currently, have provided these services for 67 public service projects, of which 52 public projects succeed. The number of social workers is increasing, and nearly 4000 members obtained national vocational qualification certificates. There are 43 professional social work organizations in the region.

3. Population management services work in an orderly way. We have taken effective measures to regulate and control the flowing populations who are out of lawful and stable residence or employment in Shanghai. Up to the first half of December, 7047 houses in multiple accommodation, 7614 disordered and desertification booths have been regulated or banned; 3243 food stall, small food shops, food processing workshops, cybercafes, KTVs and game centers are rectified under the order of the administrative authority, with other 1233 banned; 154 preschool childcare points have been regulated, with other 179 closed. As of the end of December 2015, there are 2. 3716 million new comers in Shanghai, and this number has dropped by 5. 6%.

Ⅶ. Optimization of the management of urban construction.

1. The construction of New District has been accelerated. The construction of commercial office buildings on leased land in the Zone A and Zone B of the Expo Area ha sped up. Some building projects can be completed by the end of this year and, then, ready for delivery. We have accelerated the land transfer of the first experimental area of the Zone C ; the project of building a Corporate Avenue in Qiantan area is progressing well. The projects of Tieshi

Men, of Qiantan Center, and leisure parks develop steadily, and some of them have entered the final phase. Yaohua SK Tower, Shanghai Hejing Square and other projects have operates well. The construction of "four major ancillary facilities", namely the Zhongxin lake, the Weichang river, the west entrance avenue, and the transit hub, in the international tourist resort core area is basically completed. 8 auxiliary roads consisting of 9 sections on the periphery of the core area are completed. Two municipal projects, transitional development project in the core area are basically completed, the construction of Disneyland segment of the rail line 11 is completed. According to the schedule, some key projects like that of ACAE(AVIC Commercial Aircraft Engine Co., Ltd.) and China Mobile in the Lingang region are carried out in an orderly manner. The project of 12-inch silicon and of the Polar Sea World, along with other projects, are under construction. A number of projects including the Shanghai planetarium have been accelerated in accordance with schedule. We have accelerated the construction of the Lujiazui Asia-Pacific Regional Operations Center, and have initiated the building of the International Medical Health Inspection Center. Zhangjiang Venture Workshop opens and start to operate.

2. We have smoothly accelerate the construction of key infrastructures. Annual investment into the major instruction building projects reaches 14.18 billion yuan, which is more than target amount set in the annual plan. we have actively carried forward the reconstruction of the old area and the work of building affordable houses. So far, we have completed 4068 cases of house renovation, an amount that has exceeded the full-year target of 2300. We will continue to promote the reconstruction of City Village and orderly renovate the old house in the shanty towns and the outskirts of the city center. The estimated whole-year acreage of resettlement house will be 2.25 million square meters. Those houses will be supplied to 3029 residents living in transitional accommodation for a unexpectedly long time. We have upgraded information service infrastructure and provided WIFI services in 154 pilot public places.

3. We have enhanced the construction of ecological environment. We have started the sixth round of three-year environmental action plan. We continue to accelerate the projects concerning all types of woodland protection, the building of Binjiang Forest Park (the second phase), road greening plan enabling people to see the green when they open the window in the car roof, Nanhui ecological development plan. We continue to expand the scale of the construction of sewage conduit in order to collect waste water. And we have upgraded the environment sanitation facilities like refuse transfer stations. The paid waste collection service in urban area is started and the service is charged according to the amount of the waste. We enhance monitoring of air quality in the city and is the first region where the air quality forecasting and early warning system has been put into experimental use.

4. The urban management has been improved. We have initially built an integrated information platform for city grid management, and integrated the city grid management with combined service forces. We continue to keep the high pressure on the Three Violations, and the renovated area where those Three Violations prevailed, totally reached 8.463 million square meters, in which illegal building counts for 4.42 million square meters, illegal land use counts for 871000 square meters, and illegal planting counts for 3.172 million square meters. We have concentrated our effort on the comprehensive renovation of the area on the east of Heqing region G1501 and teared down illegal buildings covering 739000 square meters. We have formulated a regulation of pudong New District Regional Environment Comprehensive Management Plan in which we set down 40 specific tasks concerning environmental remediation and industrial structure adjustment. Works of the enforcement of firefighting and safety law, the remediation of Three Violations, the industrial restructuring, and the river training in Heqing region have led to positive results.

第一篇

CHAPTER 1

综合

GENERAL SURVEY

表 1-1 行政区划
Administrative Regions
(2015)

单位:个 (unit)

地 区	Subdistrict/Town	居民委员会 Neighborhood Committee	村民委员会 Village Committee
街镇总计(36 个)	**Total (36)**	**876**	**365**
街 道(12 个)	**Subdistricts (12)**	**402**	
潍坊新村街道	Weifangxincun Subdistrict	27	
陆家嘴街道	Lujiazui Subdistrict	31	
周家渡街道	Zhoujiadu Subdistrict	32	
塘桥街道	Tangqiao Subdistrict	23	
上钢新村街道	Shanggang xincun Subdistrict	23	
南码头路街道	Nanmatoulu Subdistrict	27	
沪东新村街道	Hudongxincun Subdistrict	33	
金杨新村街道	Jinyangxincun Subdistrict	48	
洋泾街道	Yangjing Subdistrict	38	
浦兴路街道	Puxinglu Subdistrict	40	
东明路街道	Dongminglu Subdistrict	37	
花木街道	Huamu Subdistrict	43	
镇(24 个)	**Towns (24)**	**474**	**365**
川沙新镇	Chuansha New Town	40	42
高桥镇	Gaoqiao Town	31	14
北蔡镇	Beicai Town	51	9
合庆镇	Heqing Town	6	29
唐 镇	Tangzhen Town	11	17
曹路镇	Caolu Town	23	31
金桥镇	Jinqiao Town	11	3
高行镇	Gaohang Town	30	3
高东镇	Gaodong Town	14	11
张江镇	Zhangjiang Town	26	8
三林镇	Sanlin Town	53	16
惠南镇	Huinan Town	28	29
周浦镇	Zhoupu Town	29	10
新场镇	Xinchang Town	8	13
大团镇	Datuan Town	4	16
康桥镇	Kangqiao Town	34	11
航头镇	Hangtou Town	14	13
祝桥镇	Zhuqiao Town	25	40
泥城镇	Nicheng Town	9	11
宣桥镇	Xuanqiao Town	6	12
书院镇	Shuyuan Town	5	13
万祥镇	Wanxiang Town	3	7
老港镇	Laogang Town	2	7
南汇新城镇	Nanhui New Town	11	1

表 1-2 气象概况
Climate
(2015)

月 份 Month		气 温(℃) Temperature(℃) 平均气温 Average Temperature	平 均 最高气温 Average Highest Temperature	极 端 最高气温 Utmost Highest Temperature in Each Month	平 均 最低气温 Average Lowest Temperature	极 端 最低气温 Utmost Lowest Temperature in Each Month	35℃以上高温日数(天) >35℃(day)	0℃以下低温日数(天) <0℃(day)
年平均	**Annual Average**	**17.0**	**21.0**	**38.7**	**13.7**	**-4.3**	**11**	**12**
1 月	January	6.3	10.8	19.7	2.8	-4.3		5
2 月	February	6.9	10.5	18.5	3.9	-3.2		4
3 月	March	10.7	14.9	29.2	7.1	-1.3		1
4 月	April	15.7	21.1	30.5	11.3	3.6		
5 月	May	20.2	24.4	28.4	16.7	10.1		
6 月	June	24.0	27.7	34.9	21.3	17.7		
7 月	July	26.5	30.3	38.6	23.5	17.2	6	
8 月	August	27.6	31.5	38.7	24.7	22.2	5	
9 月	September	24.2	27.9	31.5	20.8	17.6		
10 月	October	19.3	23.9	27.8	15.4	10.3		
11 月	November	14.1	17.3	27.6	11.5	-1.7		1
12 月	December	8.1	11.8	18.0	4.8	-1.2		1

表 1-2 续表 Continued

月 份 Month		日 照(小时) Sunshine (hour)	降 水 Rainfall 雨量(毫米) Rainfall (mm)	雨日(天) Rainy Day (day)	大雾日(天) Fog Days (day)	霾日(天) Haze Days (day)	平均相对湿度(%) Relative Humidity(%)
全年总计	**Annual Total**	**1 579.0**	**1 730.5**	**156**	**47**	**70**	**76**
1 月	January	118.1	64.1	10	3	19	70
2 月	February	103.9	87.5	11	2	10	72
3 月	March	147.3	98.8	15	5	11	73
4 月	April	171.7	107.6	10	2	9	70
5 月	May	162.1	102.4	13	2		74
6 月	June	89.7	444.0	18	5		83
7 月	July	132.0	172.6	15	4	4	81
8 月	August	167.7	223.5	14	4	2	78
9 月	September	155.8	146.4	10		1	76
10 月	October	164.9	75.3	7	4	3	75
11 月	November	62.5	126.9	20	9	4	82
12 月	December	103.3	81.4	13	7	7	74

注：2015 年极端最高气温 38.7 ℃，出现在 8 月 4 日；极端最低气温 -4.3℃，出现在 1 月 2 日；初霜日 12 月 7 日，终霜日 3 月 12 日，无霜期 269 天。

Note: In 2015, the utmost highest temperature amounted to 38.7 ℃ on July and the utmost lowest temperature came to -4.3 ℃ on January The frost season started on November and ended on March . There were frost-free days in .

表 1-3 主要年份经济发展主要指标
Major Indicators of Economic Development in Main Years

指 标	Indicators	1993	2005	2010	2014	2015
国民经济预算	**Domestic Economic Accounts**					
新区生产总值(亿元)	Gross Domestic Product of PNA (100 million yuan)	164.00	2 108.79	4 707.52	7 109.74	7 898.35
第一产业	Primary Industry	2.12	6.09	31.47	29.73	26.92
第二产业	Secondary Industry	114.45	1 070.96	2 036.58	2 319.38	2 186.52
第三产业	Tertiary Industry	47.43	1 031.74	2 639.47	4 760.63	5 684.91
财 政	**Finance**					
财政收入(亿元)	Financial Revenue (100 million yuan)	11.15	494.94	2 046.17	2 900.77	3 089.88
#一般公共预算收入	Local Financial Revenue	5.53	155.31	428.82	684.51	788.19
一般公共预算支出(亿元)	Local Financial Expenditure (100 million yuan)	9.53	198.79	524.06	820.36	920.22
固定资产投资总额(亿元)	**Total Investment in Fixed Assets(100 million yuan)**	**164.56**	**693.61**	**1 432.30**	**1 765.73**	**1 772.94**
#房地产开发投资	Investment in Real Estate Development		287.92	555.74	897.87	969.22
#城市基础设施投资额	Investment in Urban Infrastructure	54.73	125.95	261.92	303.80	256.40
招商引资	**Business Promotion and Foreign-Fund Attraction**					
外商直接投资合同项目(项)	Projects of Foreign Direct Investment(unit)	924	1734	906	2185	3722
外商直接投资合同金额(亿美元)	Project Amount of Foreign Direct Investment (USD 100 million)	17.57	56.54	56.25	143.07	440.82
期末内资企业注册数(个)	Number of Registered Domestically-Funded Enterprises at End of Term (unit)			10 961	13 271	15 075
科技创新	**Technological Innovations**					
研发机构数(个)	Number of R&D Institutions (unit)		161	393	525	555
专利申请数(项)	Patent Claiming(item)		3 141	17 587	19 002	22 493
专利授权数(项)	Number of Authorized Patents (Piece)		1 204	12 764	10 896	13 299

注：1. 2015 年起，外贸进出口数据计量单位改为人民币结算，后续相关指标口径相同。
2. 2005 年至 2008 年，"港口货物吞吐量"和"集装箱吞吐量"为外高桥港区数据；2009 年起"港口货物吞吐量"和"集装箱吞吐量"为外高桥港区和洋山深水港区数据。

Note: 1. The unit of mensurement for import and export data has been changed to RMB since 2015, hereinafter remains the same.
2. The items of "Volume of Cargo Handled at Port" and "Container Handling Capacity" are the data at Waigaoqiao Port form 2005 to 2008. These two items are the data at Waigaoqiao Port and Yanghan Deepwater Port since 2009.

表1-3 续表 Continued

指 标 Indicators		1993	2005	2010	2014	2015
工业总产值(亿元)	**Gross Output Value of Industry (100 million yuan)**	**604.40**	**4 242.47**	**8 591.50**	**9 495.40**	**9 454.88**
#高技术工业	Industrial Output of High Technologies		1 190.72	2 259.08	2 727.63	2 963.32
国内外贸易	**Domestic and Foreign Trades**					
商品销售总额(亿元)	Aggregate Sales of Commodities (100 million yuan)		2 807.47	8 263.56	27 640.16	29 838.38
社会消费品零售总额(亿元)	Total Retail Sales of Consumer Goods (100 million yuan)	41.92	353.69	1 036.88	1 740.23	1 883.80
外贸进出口总额(亿美元)	Total Imports and Exports (USD 100 million)	25.92	894.75	1 865.62	2 678.71	16 903.70
出口总额	Total Exports	12.02	372.12	738.79	1 006.10	6 019.88
进口总额	Total Imports	13.90	522.63	1 126.83	1 672.61	10 883.82
功能开发	**Functional Development**					
中外资金融机构数(个)	Number of Chinese and Foreign Financial Institutions (unit)		369	649	844	900
中外资银行本外币存款余额(亿元)	Balance of RMB and Foreign Currencies Deposits in Chinese and Foreign Banks (100 million yuan)		4 244	13 079	19 130	19 887
中外资银行本外币贷款余额(亿元)	Balance of RMB and Foreign Currencies Loans in Chinese and Foreign Banks (100 million yuan)		4 668	10 436	14 018	14 942
期末认定跨国公司地区总部入驻数(户)	Settled Headquarters of Transnational Companies at End of Term (in number)		64	150	229	244
举办展览(博览)(次)	Number of Exhibitions Hosted (time)		114	120	220	247
举办国际性会议(次)	Number of International Conferences Hosted (time)		199	26	2 068	2 679
接待国内外游客总数(万人次)	Foreign and Domestic Tourists Received (10 000 person-times)		1 660	3 215	3 639	3 634
浦东国际机场旅客吞吐量(万人次)	Passenger Capacity at Pudong International Airport (10 000 person-times)		2 358	4 041	5 169	6 009
浦东国际机场货邮吞吐量(万吨)	Volume of Cargo Handled at Pudong International Airport (10 000 tons)		185	322	318	327
港口货物吞吐量(万吨)	Volume of Cargo Handled at Port (10 000 tons)	9 017	10 646	22 470	29 918	30 162
集装箱吞吐量(万标箱)	Container Handling Capacity (10 000 TEUs)		1 272.5	2 509.8	3 236.6	3357.2

表 1-4 主要年份社会发展主要指标
Major Indicators of Social Development in Main Years

指 标	Indicators	1993	2005	2010	2014	2015
人 口	**Population**					
年末常住人口(万人)	Permanent Population at Year end (10 000 persons)		279.19	504.44	545.12	547.49
年末户籍总人口(万人)	Registered Population at Year end (10 000 persons)	143.73	184.81	275.80	288.44	291.87
年末总户数(万户)	Total Households at Year end (10 000 households)	48.63	68.95	106.08	111.84	113.55
自然增长率(‰)	Natural Growth Rate(‰)	-0.08	-0.58	1.06	1.87	0.19
少年人口抚养比(%)	Youth Dependency Ratio(%)				14.50	15.10
老年人口抚养比(%)	Elderly Dependency Ratio(%)				24.52	25.88
劳动就业	**Labor and New Jobs**					
从业人员(万人)	Employed Persons (10 000 persons)	104.40	144.08	235.11	302.39	294.70
第一产业	Primary Industry	4.98	1.99	14.78	13.63	1.65
第二产业	Secondary Industry	66.37	57.07	123.90	150.33	106.37
第三产业	Tertiary Industry	33.05	85.02	96.43	138.43	182.03
职工人数(万人)	Staff and Workers (10 000 persons)	78.88	70.16	85.02	197.81	199.19
新增就业岗位(万人)	Number of New Jobs (10 000 persons)		11.50	14.04	15.07	15.10
期末城镇登记失业人数(万人)	Number of Registered Unemployed Persons in Towns at End of Term (10 000 persons)		4.29	4.35	4.18	3.99
人民生活	**People's Livelihood**					
*居民人均年可支配收入(元)	Annual Disposable Income Per Capita of Urban Residents (yuan)		19 089	32 330	46 709	50 726
平均期望寿命(岁)	Life Expectancy (year)	76.10	80.85	82.57	83.32	83.18

注：根据国家住户调查城乡一体化改革，2015 年住户调查数据为城乡一体化新口径数据，同前期老口径数据没有可比性，为方便使用，带"*"指标 2014 年数据为推算数据。

Note: According to the integration reform of National Suvery of Ubarn and Rural Households, the survey data in 2015 use the new statistical approach, which is not comparable to data in previous years. For convience, 2014 data with the sign of "*" are forecasted data in that year.

表 1-4 续表 Continued

指 标 Indicators		1993	2005	2010	2014	2015
教 育	**Education**					
中等学校在校学生数(人)	Student Enrollment at High Schools(person)	79 751	149 407	171 968	166 740	160 235
小学在校学生数(人)	Student Enrollment at Primary Schools (person)	131 204	92 062	165 009	201 261	201 482
市实验性、示范性高中和区重点高中就读学生比例(%)	Rate of Students Enrolled in Municipal Experimental and Demonstration High Schools and District-Key High Schools(%)			73	81	81
学龄儿童入学率(%)	Rate of School-age Child Enrollment (%)	99	100	100	100	100
幼儿园幼儿数(人)	Young Child Enrollment at Kindergartens (person)	42 378	44 554	83 313	109 807	119 113
卫 生	**Health**					
医疗机构数(个)	Healthcare Institutions (unit)	378	630	1 057	1 044	1 057
#医 院	Hospitals	47	57	56	64	65
医院病床(张)	Hospital Bed (bed)	4 840	6 520	15 164	20 043	21 098
卫生技术人员(人)	Healthcare Professionals (person)	7 717	9 794	18 925	28 341	29 237
#执业医生	Medical Practitioners	4 102	4 726	7 644	10 309	10 466
注册护士	Registered Nurses	2 179	3 390	7 448	12 283	12 741
城市建设、环境保护	**Urban Construction and Environmental Protection**					
建成区绿化覆盖率(%)	Coverage of Urban Green Areas in PNA (%)		37.8	36.1	36.2	36.0
城镇污水纳管率(%)	Rate of Sewage Pipe in Towns(%)		70.4	81.9	89.0	87.2
空气质量优良率(%)	Rate of Fine Air Quality (%)		89.3	92.6	76.7	73.6
人均公共绿地(平方米)	Public Green Space Per Capita (sq·m)	3.40	24.42	22.71	24.00	24.10

表1-5 历年社会经济主要指标增长率(以上年为基期)
(1993~2015)

单位:%

指 标 Indicators		1993	1994	1995	1996	1997	1998	1999	2000
年末总户数	Total Households at Year-end		2.6	3.1	3.1	2.8	3.4	3.1	4.1
年末户籍总人口	Registered Population at Year-end	2.2	1.7	1.7	1.7	1.5	1.8	2.5	3.0
男	Male	2.3	1.9	1.8	1.8	1.5	2.0	2.6	3.2
女	Female	2.0	1.6	1.5	1.6	1.5	1.7	2.4	2.8
年末常住人口	Permanent Population at Year-end								
新区生产总值	Gross Output Value of PNA	30.2	28.6	22.0	20.2	18.3	16.8	16.1	16.5
第一产业	Primary Industry	-8.5	5.1	14.2	1.9	5.3	5.9	3.8	4.9
第二产业	Secondary Industry	22.0	21.6	21.9	17.4	16.3	14.0	13.5	15.2
第三产业	Tertiary Industry	46.6	42.8	22.6	30.0	24.3	24.2	22.5	19.6
工业总产值	Gross Domestic Product of Industry	28.7	20.1	19.3	18.2	18.4	15.1	17.3	18.9
财政收入	Financial Revenue		1.2倍 (times)	62.9	30.5	21.4	13.0	13.2	30.1
#一般公共预算收入	Local Financial Revenue		1.8倍 (times)	51.6	32.1	30.0	10.2	-0.5	27.6
一般公共预算支出	Local Financial Expenditure		1.1倍 (times)	93.9	10.1	18.2	10.8	4.8	19.1
固定资产投资总额	Total Investment in Fixed Assets	1.2倍 (times)	58.7	9.2	38.6	27.7	15.6	-24.9	-19.9
#房地产开发投资	Investment in Real Estate Development								6.6
城市基础设施投资额	Investment in Urban Infrastructure	1.5倍 (times)	43.9	-32.2	84.7	20.9	48.5	-11.7	-65.2
商品销售总额	Aggregate Sales of Commodities			16.7	21.2	28.3	-1.6	93.8	26.9
社会消费品零售总额	Total Retail Sales of Consumer Goods	48.5	97.4	32.9	27.5	15.7	10.3	10.8	8.5
外贸进出口总额	Total Imports and Exports		82.7	52.0	12.2	22.6	21.0	28.2	65.9
出口总额	Total Exports		93.1	70.8	-2.2	18.3	15.1	26.3	43.7
进口总额	Total Imports		73.7	33.9	30.0	26.5	26.1	29.8	82.9

注:凡财政指标均为2004年财税体制改革后的同口径对比数,后续相关指标口径相同。
Note: Every financial indicator is the comparative number with the same approach after reforms of finance and taxation system in 2004, hereinafter the same.

Growth Rate of Major Indicators of Social Economy (the Previous Year as Base)

(%)

2001	2002	2003	2004	2005	2006	2007	2008	2009	2010	2011	2012	2013	2014	2015
2.3	2.4	2.6	2.3	3.3	1.7	1.8	1.3	1.3	2.6	1.2	1.0	1.3	1.8	1.5
2.2	2.6	2.2	2.4	2.2	1.5	1.9	1.6	1.4	1.3	1.0	0.9	1.0	1.6	1.2
2.3	2.7	2.4	2.4	2.1	1.4	1.8	1.4	1.3	1.2	0.9	0.9	0.9	1.7	1.2
2.0	2.5	2.1	2.3	2.2	1.5	2.1	1.9	1.4	1.4	1.0	0.9	1.0	1.6	1.2
3.1	3.0	3.0	3.1	3.1	2.2	7.0	0.1	1.7	20.4	2.6	1.7	2.8	0.8	0.4
16.1	16.7	17.5	16.4	12.1	13.4	15.2	11.6	10.5	12.4	11.1	10.1	9.7	9.3	11.1
6.1	4.9	1.6	-7.3	-4.0	-5.1	-5.4	-5.8	-2.7	-2.7	-0.9	-6.8	-8.8	-4.5	-9.5
16.3	16.4	19.3	17.2	10.5	12.1	10.1	9.1	6.3	15.3	9.5	3.7	2.4	3.4	-5.7
16.1	17.1	15.8	15.7	14.0	15.0	20.4	14.0	14.5	10.3	12.4	14.9	14.4	12.7	19.4
20.1	21.0	26.4	22.4	11.8	13.3	14.3	9.4	6.7	21.1	11.2	1.1	1.0	1.1	-0.4
39.1	41.2	46.1	25.7	10.5	18.7	45.4	22.0	5.8	25.4	10.3	4.6	17.0	5.0	6.5
47.2	14.6	41.6	20.9	13.0	14.8	46.3	16.0	9.1	12.0	16.7	10	11.0	12.1	15.1
26.9	36.9	32.6	20.7	2.7	12.0	29.1	28.9	7.1	10.2	17.4	8.4	10.8	11.1	12.2
18.5	41.1	2.5	8.3	6.4	-4.8	18.8	11.3	16.2	0.8	0.2	1.4	15.4	5.2	0.4
6.5	93.6	13.9	13.7	3.0	-10.5	-4.0	13.1	6.2	28.8	6.1	1.8	37.6	8.7	7.9
93.3	62.6	-9.2	-22.1	3.9	23.9	50.3	32.7	33.3	-46.6	3.9	-3.7	2.2	2.8	-6.8
33.5	77.9	35.5	21.0	-4.3	4.9	22.7	28.6	13.7	39.9	27.1	38.5	12.8	15.0	8.0
8.3	22.0	10.2	14.4	13.2	13.1	14.0	15.5	14.4	20.6	16.1	12.1	11.5	8.9	8.3
16.9	21.9	57.5	39.0	10.7	19.9	19.3	13.2	-12.9	34.2	21.1	6.1	4.0	7.3	2.7
15.0	18.2	55.8	52.8	14.9	19.5	18.8	14.4	-16.9	28.2	20.3	5.7	2.0	5.0	-2.6
17.9	24.2	58.6	31.1	7.9	20.2	19.7	12.4	-9.8	38.5	21.7	6.4	5.4	-6.1	5.9

单位:%

表 1-5 续表 Continued

指 标	Indicators	1993	1994	1995	1996	1997	1998	1999	2000
浦东国际机场旅客吞吐量	Passenger Capacity at Pudong International Airport								
浦东国际机场货邮吞吐量	Volume of Cargo Handled at Pudong International Airport								
港口货物吞吐量	Volume of Cargo Handled at Port	21.8	-7.8	-27.6	19.7	2.9	-5.8	-1.3	10.1
集装箱吞吐量	Container Handling Capacity				1.9倍 (times)	45.3	48.7	36.2	85.4
外商直接投资合同项目	Projects of Foreign Direct Investment	63.0	12.0	-19.0	-4.3	-23.2	-9.9	-15.2	47.4
外商直接投资合同金额	Contracted Amount of Foreign Direct Investment	29.9	47.6	25.6	-44.4	-0.5	55.0	-61.5	1.7倍 (times)
中外资银行本外币存款余额	Balance of RMB and Foreign Currencies Deposits in Chinese and Foreign Banks								
中外资银行本外币贷款余额	Balance of RMB and Foreign Currencies Loans in Chinese and Foreign Banks								
城镇居民人均年可支配收入	Annual Disposable Income Per Capita of Urban Residents								
农村居民人均年可支配收入	Annual Disposable Income Per Capita of Rural Residents								
居民储蓄存款年末余额	Residents' Savings Deposit Balance (Year End)	77.1	76.2	56.3	28.9	20.0	13.5	10.6	2.7
高等学校在校学生数	Student Enrollment of Higher Education	26.4	11.3	13.0	6.6	11.9	29.0	21.7	34.4
中等学校在校学生数	Student Enrollment at High Schools	9.6	17.1	15.6	8.2	5.0	5.9	6.2	0.8
小学在校学生数	Student Enrollment at Primary Schools	7.7	0.2	-1.8	-0.1	1.3	-2.7	-6.7	-6.7
幼儿园幼儿数	Young Child Enrollment at Kindergartens		-12.0	-3.5	-9.0	0.5	-0.5	1.0	3.0
医院病床	Hospital Beds	3.1	3.7	4.8	2.8	-1.2	3.4	9.8	2.2
卫生技术人员	Healthcare Professionals	3.4	4.0	2.3	4.4	5.2	3.1	1.2	1.4
#执业医生	Medical Practitioners	6.6	5.1	3.0	6.4	4.5	2.6	1.6	1.5
注册护士	Registered Nurses	3.7	4.9	2.6	3.7	7.6	5.1	2.7	2.6
期末认定跨国公司地区总部入驻数	Settled Headquarters of Transnational Companies at End of Term								

(%)

2001	2002	2003	2004	2005	2006	2007	2008	2009	2010	2011	2012	2013	2014	2015
	64.9	36.3	39.7	12.1	13.1	8.6	-2.8	13.4	26.2	2.5	8.3	5.2	9.5	16.3
	79.5	81.8	38.5	-1.1	16.8	16.2	4.8	-2.4	26.8	-3.4	-5.1	-1.4	9.3	2.8
20.9	36.9	16.5	36.0	33.2	6.6	15.3	0.4	-4.9	14.3	17.2	3.4	5.4	4.3	0.8
56.9	60.2	43.3	42.0	34.9	7.9	13.4	-1.2	-9.7	17.4	14.8	2.5	3.6	5.8	3.7
27.0	9.5	73.4	1.0	2.7	-16.6	-13.3	-36.0	-12.1	16.2	9.8	-1.9	5.7	1.1倍	70.3
-30.6	33.3	7.8	12.1	75.4	-14.4	2.2	0.9	0.3	1.7	17.3	10.4	-1.3	99.0	2.1倍
				25.3	18.8	25.0	22.2	22.9	24.2	18.9	9.6	2.3	9.7	4.0
				21.4	20.2	23.8	12.0	7.6	16.9	11.8	8.1	6.6	4.2	6.6
				12.4	12.4	13.2	14.5	9.3	11.0	13.9	11.1	10.5	9.8	2.2
				11.4	11.6	12.2	12.5	9.2	12.1	14.1	11.2	10.7	11.7	
24.2	35.2	31.9	27.9	30.7	17.1	1.4	34.6	18.2	12.2	14.7	15.1	9.5	3.0	持平
28.0	86.2	21.3	9.6	8.5	5.9	8.2	19.0	4.7	29.5	10.2	-3.7	1.1	-6.3	取消
-1.0	0.2	-1.5	12.3	-2.0	-4.1	-3.8	-3.0	-0.5	-0.7	0.3	-1.2	2.0	-4.0	-3.9
-6.3	-2.3	-0.6	-11.4	3.3	3.5	3.3	3.1	17.3	3.2	6.9	3.8	6.9	2.8	0.1
-1.9	11.0	6.4	7.3	5.4	4.2	9.9	5.5	9.1	10.6	13.7	9.1	5.2	1.0	8.5
5.3	6.0	4.6	-0.6	-5.4	17.4	5.6	2.7	2.5	7.8	16.9	2.4	4.6	5.5	5.3
0.9	-1.3	-0.1	12.3	0.1	6.5	19.6	10.5	3.2	-1.8	22.1	5.9	8.2	7.0	3.2
0.5	-8.4	-0.2	3.7	-0.1	1.4	9.9	9.6	1.8	2.8	16.0	4.1	3.1	8.3	1.5
3.9	9.9	0.6	7.4	1.6	18.0	18.2	8.4	8.9	4.4	29.3	7.9	9.6	7.8	3.7
					29.7	15.7	19.8	17.4	11.1	14.0	12.9	10.9	7.0	6.6

表1-6 社会经济主要指标年均增长速度
Average Annual Growth Rate of Main Social Economic Indicators

单位:% (%)

指 标	Indicators	平均每年增长 Annual Growth Rate 1993~2015	1991~1995	1996~2000	2001~2005	2006~2010	2011~2015
年末户籍总人口	Registered Population at Year-end	1.8	2.1	2.1	2.3	1.5	1.1
新区生产总值	Gross Domestic Product in PNA	15.6	23.0	17.6	15.7	13.1	10.3
第一产业	Primary Industry	-0.1	2.4	4.4	0.1	0.5	-6.2
第二产业	Secondary Industry	12.3	20.0	15.3	15.9	11.6	2.5
第三产业	Tertiary Industry	19.7	29.8	24.1	15.7	14.9	14.7
工业总产值	Gross Output Value of Industry	14.3	20.3	17.6	20.3	14.9	2.2
*财政收入	Financial Revenue	25.9		21.4	36.8	22.8	8.6
* #一般公共预算收入	Local Financial Revenue	25.4		19.2	22.5	18.9	12.9
*一般公共预算支出	Local Financial Expenditure	22.1		12.5	23.4	17.1	11.9
社会消费品零售总额	Total Retail Sales of Consumer Goods	18.6	50.4	14.4	14.0	16.7	11.3
*外贸进出口总额	Total Imports and Exports	22.5		28.8	28.6	15.8	6.1
*出口总额	Total Exports	21.1		19.3	31.2	14.7	5.8
*进口总额	Total Imports	23.5		37.5	26.9	16.6	6.3
中外资银行本外币存款余额	Balance of RMB and Foreign Currencies Deposits in Chinese and Foreign Banks	7.5				20.8	8.7
中外资银行本外币贷款余额	Balance of RMB and Foreign Currencies Loans in Chinese and Foreign Banks	5.8				19.2	7.4
居民储蓄存款年末余额	Balance of Residents´Savings Deposits at Year-end	22.8	54.4	14.8	29.9	21.6	8.3

注：1. 带"*"指标宾栏第一栏年均增长速度的年份为"1994~2015"。
2. 带"*"指标宾栏第二栏因仅有二年增长速度，故不再计算该指标的年均增长速度。

Note：1. The year with the annual growth rate in the first horizontal column that is indicated with the symbol of "*" is from 1994 to 2015.
2. Because the second column in the field of indicators with the sign of "*"only has the growth rate of the recent two years, we will not calculate the annual growth rate of this indicator.

表1-7 社会经济结构主要指标
Main Indicators of Economic and Social Structures

单位:% (%)

指标	Indicators	2005	2010	2014	2015
第三产业增加值占GDP比重	Ratio of Added Value of the Tertiary Industry in GDP	48.9	56.1	67.0	72.0
新区财政收入相当于GDP比例	Ratio of PNA Financial Revenue in GDP	23.5	36.1	40.8	39.1
一般公共预算收入相当于GDP比例	Ratio of Local Financial Revenue in GDP	7.4	9.0	9.6	10.0
固定资产投资相当于GDP比例	Ratio of Fixed Capital Investment in GDP	32.9	30.4	24.8	22.4
外贸进出口总额相当于GDP比例	Ratio of Total Volume of Foreign Trade in GDP	342.4	262.5	230.5	214.0
外贸出口总额相当于GDP比例	Ratio of Total Exports of Foreign Trade in GDP	142.4	103.9	86.6	76.2
社会消费品零售总额相当于GDP比例	Ratio of Total Volume of Retail Sales for Social Consumer Goods in GDP	16.8	22.0	24.5	23.9
六个重点发展行业总产值占工业总产值比重	Ratio of Total Output Value of Six Key Industries in Total Value of Industrial Output	68.1	70.0	69.7	70.8
高技术产业工业总产值占工业总产值比重	Ratio of Total Output Value of High-tech Industries in Total Value of Industrial Output		26.3	28.7	31.3
城市基础设施投资占固定资产投资总额比重	Ratio of Investment for Urban Infrastructure in Gross Investment in Fixed Assets	18.2	18.3	17.2	14.5
房地产开发投资占固定资产投资总额比重	Ratio of Investment for Real Estate Development in Gross Investment in Fixed Assets	41.5	38.8	50.8	54.7
机电产品出口占外贸出口商品总额比重	Ratio of Exports of Machinery and Electrical Equipment in Total Exports of Foreign Trade	61.0	66.4	68.4	70.5
高新技术产品出口占外贸出口商品总额比重	Ratio of Export of High and New Technological Products in Total Export of Foreign Trade	33.4	36.6	43.1	46.8
第三产业实到外资占新区实到外资金额比重	Ratio of Foreign Investment in Place for the Tertiary Industry in Total of Foreign Investment in Place in PNA	71.8	86.8	93.5	85.5
发明专利申请量占专利申请量比重	Ratio of the Number of Applications for Invention Patents in the Volume of Patent Applications	57.1	37.4	54.1	50.5

表1-8 主要年份社会经济部分指标平均每天水平
Daily Average Level of Major Economic and Social Indicators in Main Years

指 标	Indicators	单 位 Unit	2005	2010	2014	2015
新区生产总值	Gross Output Value in PNA	万元 10 000 yuan	57 775	128 973	194 787	216 393
工业总产值	Gross Output Value of Industry	万元 10 000 yuan	116 232	235 384	260 148	259 037
财政收入	Financial Revenue	万元 10 000 yuan	13 560	56 059	79 473	84 654
#一般公共预算收入	Local Financial Revenue	万元 10 000 yuan	4 255	11 748	18 754	21 594
固定资产投资额	Total Investment in Fixed Assets	万元 10 000 yuan	19 003	39 241	48 376	48 573
新增固定资产	Newly Acquired Fixed Assets	万元 10 000 yuan	10 409	17 066	19 422	16 638
商品销售总额	Total Sales of Commodities	万元 10 000 yuan	76 917	226 399	757 265	817 489
社会消费品零售额	Retail Sales of Consumer Goods	万元 10 000 yuan	11 370	28 408	47 678	51 611
外贸出口货物总额	Total Exports Value of Commodities in Foreign Trade	万美元 USD 10 000	10 195	20 241	27 564	164 928
外商直接投资合同项目	Projects of Foreigin Direct Investment	个 unit	4.75	2.48	5.99	10.20
外商直接投资合同金额	Contracted Amount of Foreign Direct Investment	万美元 USD 10 000	1 549	1 541	3 920	12 077
港口货物吞吐量	Volume of Cargo Handled at Port	万吨 10 000 tons	29.17	61.56	81.97	82.63
自来水售水量	Sales of Tap Water	万立方米 10 000 cu.m	114.87	164.62	166.74	166.87
售电量	Electricity Sales	万千瓦·时 10 000 kwh	3 512	6 293	7 151	7 573
管道燃气售气量	Sales of Pipelined Gas	万立方米 10 000 cu·m	121.37	175.89	205.13	218.76
公交车辆乘客人数	Passengers Carried by Public Vehicles	万人次 10 000 person-times	173.12	206.02	163.66	151.11
医院诊疗人数	Outpatients Treated	万人次 10 000 person-times	3.49	8.12	12.76	13.22
出生人数	Birth	人 person	34	61	74	64
死亡人数	Death	人 person	37	53	59	62

表1-9　主要年份社会经济人均指标
Annual Average Level of Major Social and Economi Indicators Per Capita in Main Years

指　标	Indicators	单 位　Unit	2005	2010	2014	2015
工业总产值	Gross Output Value of Industry	元 yuan	154 244	186 066	174 866	173 070
财政收入	Financial Revenue	元 yuan	17 995	44 314	53 420	56 560
#一般公共预算收入	Local Financial Revence	元 yuan	5 647	9 287	12 606	14 428
固定资产投资额	Total Investment in Fixed Assets	元 yuan	25 218	31 019	32 517	32 453
新增固定资产	Newly Acquired Fixed Assets	元 yuan	13 813	13 490	13 055	11 117
社会消费品零售额	Total Retail Sales of Consumer Goods	元 yuan	12 859	22 456	32 048	34 483
外贸出口总额	Total Exports Value of Foreign Trade	美元 USD	13 529	16 000	18 528	110 193
外贸进口总额	Total Imports Value of Foreign Trade	美元 USD	19 001	24 404	30 803	199 226
居民年末储蓄存款余额	Balance of Savings Deposits at Year-end	元 yuan	40 209	63 747	80 680	80 209
职工年平均工资	Annual Average Wage of Staff and Workers	元 yuan	33 186	89 424	113 668	117 626
居民年可支配收入	Annual Disposable Income Per Capita of Urban Residents	元 yuan	19 089	32 330	49 629	50 726
公共绿地占有面积	Public Green Area	平方米 sq・m	24.42	22.71	24.00	24.10
邮政订销报刊数	Total Circulation of Newspapers and Magazines	份 in number	43	16	33	32
每万人拥有病床数	Number of Sick-beds per 10 000 Persons	张 bed	23.35	32.84	36.91	38.62
每万人拥有医生数	Number of Doctors per 10 000 Persons	人 person			18.98	19.15
每万名中小学生拥有教职员工数	Number of Teaching Staff per 10 000 Primary and Middle School Students	人 person	882	821	799	818
实有人口万人发案率	Ratio of Criminal Cases per 10 000 Persons	起/万人 in number/10000persons	61.76	50.93	44.14	54.18
每万人拥有律师数	Number of Lawyers per 10 000 Persons	人 person	5.4	6.4	7.6	8.2

注：1. 上述指标除特别注明外，人均水平均采用常住人口计算。
　　2. 居民年人均可支配收入为住户调查资料。

Note：1. The average level per capita has been calculated in the permanent population except the above-mentioned indicators are otherwise specified.
　　2. The data of annual disposable income per capita are surveyed from household residents.

表1-10　历年新区生产总值

Gross Domestic Product in PNA

(1990~2015)

单位:亿元　　　　(100 million yuan)

年　份 Year	新区生产总　值 Gross Domestic Product of PNA	第一产业 Primary Industry	第二产业 Secondary Industry	#工　业 Industry	第三产业 Tertiary Industry	#金　融 Banking	房地产 Real Estate
1990	60.24	2.22	45.89	43.13	12.13	3.07	
1991	71.54	2.41	53.45	50.46	15.68	4.46	
1992	101.49	1.89	73.72	70.25	25.88	6.96	
1993	164.00	2.12	114.45	108.16	47.43	16.40	
1994	291.20	3.19	197.13	177.45	90.88	23.73	
1995	414.65	4.22	283.92	260.07	126.51	28.59	36.52
1996	496.47	4.57	320.31	286.32	171.59	39.08	40.61
1997	608.22	4.95	376.87	325.38	226.40	69.10	46.20
1998	704.27	5.30	412.82	349.97	286.15	101.31	52.68
1999	801.36	5.47	435.66	388.88	360.23	138.35	47.26
2000	923.51	5.72	488.60	445.43	429.19	159.88	55.36
2001	1 087.53	6.06	560.29	508.62	521.18	170.12	70.39
2002	1 244.00	6.38	635.54	579.86	602.08	166.04	100.51
2003	1 510.32	6.67	767.53	708.98	736.12	183.48	129.12
2004	1 850.13	6.00	952.25	894.13	891.88	218.13	168.25
2005	2 108.79	6.09	1 070.96	1 009.47	1 031.74	249.69	174.48
2006	2 365.33	5.88	1 194.47	1 133.76	1 164.98	313.98	169.24
2007	2 793.39	6.06	1 306.49	1 237.36	1 480.84	474.83	185.38
2008	3 150.99	5.88	1 430.25	1 351.44	1 714.86	553.46	181.49
2009	4 001.39	30.61	1 706.29	1 581.82	2 264.49	708.28	258.94
2010	4 707.52	31.47	2 036.58	1 899.04	2 639.47	825.78	250.08
2011	5 484.35	34.46	2 306.32	2 154.27	3 143.57	991.61	229.71
2012	5 929.91	32.89	2 320.75	2 171.00	3 576.27	1 069.11	269.46
2013	6 448.68	31.28	2 262.39	2 085.15	4 155.01	1 253.67	319.54
2014	7 109.74	29.73	2 319.38	2 135.40	4 760.63	1 503.34	303.56
2015	7 898.35	26.92	2 186.52	2 010.80	5 684.91	2 055.89	374.46

表1-11　历年新区生产总值结构
Structure of Total Gross Domestic Product in PNA
(1990～2015)

单位:%　　　　(%)

年　份 Year	新区生产总值 Gross Domestic Product of PNA	第一产业 Primary Industry	第二产业 Secondary Industry	#工　业 Industry	第三产业 Tertiary Industry	#金　融 Banking	房地产 Real Estate
1990	100.0	3.7	76.2	71.6	20.1	5.1	
1991	100.0	3.4	74.7	70.5	21.9	6.2	
1992	100.0	1.9	72.6	69.2	25.5	6.9	
1993	100.0	1.3	69.8	66.0	28.9	10.0	
1994	100.0	1.1	67.7	60.9	31.2	8.1	
1995	100.0	1.0	68.5	62.7	30.5	6.9	8.8
1996	100.0	0.9	64.5	57.7	34.6	7.9	8.2
1997	100.0	0.8	62.0	53.5	37.2	11.4	7.6
1998	100.0	0.7	58.6	49.7	40.7	14.4	7.5
1999	100.0	0.7	54.4	48.6	44.9	17.3	5.9
2000	100.0	0.6	52.9	48.2	46.5	17.3	6.0
2001	100.0	0.6	51.5	46.8	47.9	15.6	6.5
2002	100.0	0.5	51.1	46.6	48.4	13.4	8.1
2003	100.0	0.5	50.8	46.9	48.7	12.1	8.6
2004	100.0	0.3	51.5	48.3	48.2	11.8	9.1
2005	100.0	0.3	50.8	47.9	48.9	11.8	8.3
2006	100.0	0.2	50.5	47.9	49.3	13.3	7.2
2007	100.0	0.2	46.8	44.3	53.0	17.0	6.6
2008	100.0	0.2	45.4	42.9	54.4	17.6	5.7
2009	100.0	0.8	42.6	39.5	56.6	17.7	6.5
2010	100.0	0.7	43.2	40.3	56.1	17.5	5.3
2011	100.0	0.6	42.1	39.3	57.3	18.1	4.2
2012	100.0	0.6	39.1	36.6	60.3	18.0	4.5
2013	100.0	0.5	35.1	32.3	64.4	19.4	5.0
2014	100.0	0.4	32.6	30.0	67.0	21.1	4.3
2015	100.0	0.3	27.7	25.5	72.0	26.0	4.7

表 1-12 主要年份新区生产总值(新行业分类)
Gross Domestic Product in Main Years(Grouped by New Sectors)

单位:亿元 (100 million yuan)

指 标	Indicators	2005	2010	2014	2015
新区生产总值	**Gross Gross Domestic Production of PNA**	**2 108.79**	**4 707.52**	**7 109.74**	**7 898.35**
第一产业	Primary Industry	6.09	31.47	29.73	26.92
第二产业	Secondary Industry	1 070.96	2 036.58	2 319.38	2 186.52
工 业	Industry	1 009.47	1 899.04	2 135.40	2 010.80
建筑业	Construction	61.49	137.54	183.98	175.72
第三产业	Tertiary Industry	1 031.74	2 639.47	4 760.63	5 684.91
交通运输、仓储业、邮政业	Transportation, Warehousing and Post Service	88.88	170.97	230.75	241.13
信息传输、计算机服务和软件业	Information Transmission, Computer Service and Computer Software	73.34	233.07	481.36	588.84
批发和零售业	Wholesale and Retail	212.05	608.27	1 177.16	1 272.51
住宿和餐饮业	Hotel and Catering	28.13	53.03	66.50	69.83
金融业	Banking	249.69	825.78	1 503.34	2 055.89
房地产业	Real Estate	174.48	250.08	303.56	374.46
其他服务业	Other Services	205.17	498.27	997.96	1 082.25
构 成(%)	**Composition(%)**	**100.0**	**100.0**	**100.0**	**100.0**
第一产业	Primary Industry	0.3	0.7	0.4	0.3
第二产业	Secondary Industry	50.8	43.2	32.6	27.7
工 业	Industry	47.9	40.3	30.0	25.5
建筑业	Construction	2.9	2.9	2.6	2.2
第三产业	Tertiary Industry	48.9	56.1	67.0	72.0
交通运输、仓储业、邮政业	Transportation, Warehousing and Post Service	4.2	3.6	3.2	3.1
信息传输、计算机服务和软件业	Information Transmission, Computer Service and Computer Software	3.5	5.0	6.8	7.5
批发和零售业	Wholesale and Retail	10.1	12.9	16.6	16.1
住宿和餐饮业	Hotel and Catering	1.3	1.2	0.9	0.9
金融业	Banking	11.8	17.5	21.1	26.0
房地产业	Real Estate	8.3	5.3	4.3	4.7
其他服务业	Other Services	9.7	10.6	14.0	13.7

表 1-13 历年新区生产总值指数
Gross Domestic Product Indexes of PNA
(1991 ~2015)

(以 1990 年为 100) (Taking 1990 as 100)

年份 Year	新区生产总值 Gross Domestic Product of PNA	第一产业 Primary Industry	第二产业 Secondary Industry	#工业 Industry	第三产业 Tertiary Industry	#金融 Banking	房地产 Real Estate
1991	113.9	101.2	113.1		119.5	141.0	
1992	138.0	102.3	137.6		143.8	179.1	
1993	179.7	93.6	167.9	121.9	210.7	332.7	
1994	231.1	98.4	204.2	148.0	301.0	408.5	
1995	282.0	112.4	248.9	172.1	369.0	440.0	105.2
1996	339.0	114.5	292.2	199.8	479.7	576.9	111.6
1997	401.0	120.6	339.9	227.4	596.2	856.7	120.8
1998	468.3	127.7	387.4	256.7	740.5	1 210.5	132.1
1999	543.8	132.6	439.7	301.4	907.1	1 571.2	105.4
2000	633.5	139.1	506.5	352.9	1 084.9	1 850.9	127.7
2001	735.5	147.6	589.1	406.2	1 259.6	1 937.9	157.4
2002	858.3	154.8	685.7	473.3	1 475.0	1 941.7	214.3
2003	1 008.5	157.3	818.0	570.3	1 708.1	2 145.6	250.3
2004	1 173.9	145.8	958.7	678.1	1 976.3	2 488.9	276.5
2005	1 315.9	140.0	1 059.4	752.0	2 253.0	2 854.8	273.5
2006	1 492.2	132.9	1 187.6	849.0	2 591.0	3 565.6	261.7
2007	1 719.0	125.7	1 307.5	935.6	3 119.5	4 963.3	267.7
2008	1 918.5	118.3	1 426.7	1 019.8	3 555.9	5 712.8	257.0
2009	2 119.9	115.1	1 516.6	1 080.9	4 071.6	7 369.5	314.1
2010	2 382.8	112.0	1 748.6	1 253.8	4 491.0	7 819.0	282.7
2011	2 647.3	111.0	1 914.7	1 381.8	5 047.8	8 663.5	257.5
2012	2 914.7	103.5	1 985.6	1 435.7	5 799.9	9 694.5	299.3
2013	3 197.4	94.4	2 033.2	1 457.2	6 635.1	11 691.5	311.5
2014	3 494.8	90.2	2 102.3	1 506.7	7 477.8	13 889.5	281.9
2015	3 811.8	76.9	2 159.2	1 543.5	8 410.6	17 346.8	285.2

注：工业增加值以 1992 年为 100，房地产增加值以 1994 年为 100。
Note: The added industrial value takes the data of 1992 as 100, and the added real estate value takes the data of 1994 as 100.

表1-14 历年新区生产总值增长速度
Gross Domestic Product Growth Rate of PNA
（1991～2015）

单位:%　　　　(%)

年 份 Year	新区生产总值 Gross Domestic Product of PNA	第一产业 Primary Industry	第二产业 Secondary Industry	#工 业 Industry	第三产业 Tertiary Industry	#金 融 Banking	房地产 Real Estate
1991	13.9	1.2	13.1	13.8	19.5	41.0	
1992	21.2	1.1	21.7	20.1	20.3	27.0	
1993	30.2	-8.5	22.0	21.9	46.6	85.8	
1994	28.6	5.1	21.6	21.4	42.8	22.8	
1995	22.0	14.2	21.9	16.3	22.6	7.7	5.2
1996	20.2	1.9	17.4	16.1	30.0	31.1	6.1
1997	18.3	5.3	16.3	13.8	24.3	48.5	8.2
1998	16.8	5.9	14.0	12.9	24.2	41.3	9.4
1999	16.1	3.8	13.5	17.4	22.5	29.8	-20.2
2000	16.5	4.9	15.2	17.1	19.6	17.8	21.1
2001	16.1	6.1	16.3	15.1	16.1	4.7	23.3
2002	16.7	4.9	16.4	16.5	17.1	0.2	36.1
2003	17.5	1.6	19.3	20.5	15.8	10.5	16.8
2004	16.4	-7.3	17.2	18.9	15.7	16.0	10.5
2005	12.1	-4.0	10.5	10.9	14.0	14.7	-1.1
2006	13.4	-5.1	12.1	12.9	15.0	24.9	-4.3
2007	15.2	-5.4	10.1	10.2	20.4	39.2	2.3
2008	11.6	-5.8	9.1	9.0	14.0	15.1	-4.0
2009	10.5	-2.7	6.3	6.0	14.5	29.0	22.2
2010	12.4	-2.7	15.3	16.0	10.3	6.1	-10.0
2011	11.1	-0.9	9.5	10.2	12.4	10.8	-8.9
2012	10.1	-6.8	3.7	3.9	14.9	11.9	16.2
2013	9.7	-8.8	2.4	1.5	14.4	20.6	4.1
2014	9.3	-4.5	3.4	3.4	12.7	18.8	-9.5
2015	9.1	-14.8	2.7	2.4	12.5	24.9	1.2

表1-15 历年第三产业增加值增长速度(旧行业分类)
Growth Rate of Value Added in Tertiary Industry(Grouped By Old Sectors)
(1991~2000)

单位:% (%)

年 份 Year	第三产业增加值 Value Added in Tertiary Industry	#交通、运输、仓储、邮电通讯业 Transportation, Warehousing, Post and Telecommunications	批发和零售贸易、餐饮业 Wholesale, Retail and Catering	金融保险 Banking and Insurance	房地产 Real Estate
1991	19.5	8.8	8.1	41.0	
1992	20.3			27.0	
1993	46.6	37.3	24.8	85.8	
1994	42.8	5.4	54.1	22.8	
1995	22.6	15.2	72.8	7.7	5.2
1996	30.0	28.4	58.9	31.1	6.1
1997	24.3	12.2	18.5	48.5	8.2
1998	24.2	17.0	18.3	41.3	9.4
1999	22.5	22.1	29.1	29.8	-20.2
2000	19.6	17.9	19.1	17.8	21.1

表1-16 历年第三产业增加值增长速度(新行业分类)
Growth Rate of Value Added in Tertiary Industry(Grouped by New Sectors)
(2001~2015)

单位:% (%)

年 份 Year	第三产业增加值 Value Added in Tertiary Industry	#交通运输、仓储业、邮政业 Transportation, Warehousing and Post Service	信息传输、计算机服务和软件业 Information Transmission, Computer Service and Computer Software	批发和零售业 Wholesale and Retail	金融业 Banking	房地产业 Real Estate
2001	16.1	27.5	9.4	21.6	4.7	23.3
2002	17.1	27.1	9.7	16.9	0.2	36.1
2003	15.8	15.8	64.3	13.6	10.5	16.8
2004	15.7	22.2	21.4	12.6	16.0	10.5
2005	14.0	18.6	18.3	14.8	14.7	-1.1
2006	15.0	15.2	19.1	12.9	24.9	-4.3
2007	20.4	15.7	16.4	14.7	39.2	2.3
2008	14.0	10.9	20.3	15.4	15.1	-4.0
2009	14.5	-5.3	5.4	14.3	29.0	22.2
2010	10.3	16.5	10.9	20.1	6.1	-10
2011	12.4	12.3	18.4	16.6	10.8	-8.9
2012	14.9	3.4	16.3	18.2	11.9	16.2
2013	14.4	5.5	15.8	12.3	20.6	4.1
2014	12.7	1.0	14.5	14.1	18.8	-9.5
2015	12.5	2.9	7.5	6.9	24.9	1.2

表1－17　中国（上海）自由贸易试验区主要经济指标
Major Economic Indicators in China (Shanghai) Free Trade Zone (2015)

指　标	Indicators	单　位　Unit	2015
税收总额	Total Amount of Tax Revenues	亿元 100 million yuan	1 022.20
一般公共预算收入	General Public Budget Revenue	亿元 100 million yuan	444.74
外商直接投资合同项目	Projects of Foreign Direct Investemnt	个 unit	3 072
外商直接投资合同金额	Contractd Amount of Foreign Direct Investment	亿美元 100 million US dolloars	396.26
外商直接投资实际到位金额	Actual Paid Amount of Foreign Direct Investment	亿美元 100 million US dolloars	48.21
新增内资企业注册户数	Number of Newly-Registered Domestic Enterprises	个 unit	12 891
新增内资企业注册资本	Registered Capital of Newly-Registered domestic Enterprises	亿元 100 million yuan	8 173.38
全社会固定资产投资总额	Total Investment in Fixed Assets	亿元 100 million yuan	563.11
工业总产值	Gross Value of Industrial Output	亿元 100 million yuan	3 901.03
社会消费品零售额	Total Retail Sales of Social Consumer Goods	亿元 100 million yuan	1 051.35
商品销售总额	Gross Sales of Commodities	亿元 100 million yuan	26 866.48
服务业营业收入	Operating Income of Service Industries	亿元 100 million yuan	3 599.06
外贸进出口总额	Total Volume of Foreign Trade	亿元 100 million yuan	7 415.46
#出口额	Amount of Exports	亿元 100 million yuan	2 027.02
经认定的企业研发机构	Number of Approved R&D Institution of Enterprise	个 unit	555
发明专利授权数	Number of Patent Authorizations	个 unit	3 541
期末监管类金融机构	Number of End-term Regulatory Financial Institutions	个 unit	758
新兴金融机构	Emerging Financial Insititutions	个 unit	4 154
跨境人民币结算总额	Total Amount of Cross-border RMB Settlements	亿元 100 million yuan	12 026.40
跨境人民币境外借款金额	Amount of Cross-border RMB Borrowing	亿元 100 million yuan	69.82

注：1、自贸区按照注册地口径统计，统计范围为120.72平方公里。
2、一般公共预算收入按照开发区财力结算口径。
3、外贸进出口总额仅包括自贸区保税区片区。

Note：1. Data above incluede those registered in Free Trade Zone. The statistical range is 120.72 square kilometers。
2. General public budget revenue refers to the budgeted expenditure of financial resources in the Economy and Technology Zone.
3. The total volume of foreign trade only includes Tax-free zone.

表1-18 社会经济主要指标占全市比重
The Proportion of Major Economic and Social Indicators in Shanghai

指标 Indicators		2014 浦东新区 PNA	2014 全市 Shanghai	2014 比重(%) Proportion (%)	2015 浦东新区 PNA	2015 全市 Shanghai	2015 比重(%) Proportion (%)
土地面积(平方公里)	Land Area (sq. km)	1 373.82	6 340.50	21.7	1 373.82	6 340.50	21.7
年末常住人口(万人)	Permanent Population at Year-end (10 000 persons)	545.12	2 425.68	22.5	547.49	2 415.27	22.7
年末户籍总人口(万人)	Registered Population at Year-end (10 000 persons)	288.44	1 438.69	20.0	291.87	1 442.97	20.2
从业人员(万人)	Employment (10 000 persons)	302.39	1 365.63	22.1	294.70	1 361.51	21.6
生产总值(亿元)	Gross Domestic Product (100 million yuan)	7 109.74	23 567.70	30.2	7 879.35	25 123.45	31.4
第一产业	Primary Industry	29.73	124.26	23.9	26.92	109.82	24.5
第二产业	Secondary Industry	2 319.38	8 167.71	28.4	2 186.52	7 991.00	27.3
#工业	Industry	2 135.40	7 362.84	29.0	2 010.80	7 162.33	28.0
第三产业	Tertiary Industry	4 760.63	15 275.73	31.2	5 684.91	17 022.63	33.4
#金融	Banking	1 503.34	3 400.41	44.2	2 055.89	4 162.70	49.4
房地产	Real Estate	303.56	1 530.96	19.8	374.46	1 699.78	22.0
工业总产值(亿元)	Gross Output Value of Industry (100 million yuan)	9 495.40	34 071.19	27.9	9 454.88	33 211.57	28.4
固定资产投资总额(亿元)	Total Investment in Fixed Assets (100 million yuan)	1 765.73	6 016.43	29.3	1 722.94	6 352.70	27.9
城市基础设施投资额(亿元)	Investment in Urban Infrastructure (100 million yuan)	275.25	1 057.25	26.0	256.40	1 425.08	18.0
一般公共预算收入(亿元)	Local Government Revenue (100 million yuan)	684.51	4 585.55	14.9	788.19	5 519.50	14.3
一般公共预算支出(亿元)	Local Government Expenditure (100 million yuan)	820.36	4 923.44	16.7	920.22	6 191.56	14.8

表 1-18 续表 Continued

指 标 Indicators		2014 浦东新区 PNA	2014 全市 Shanghai	2014 比重(%) Proportion (%)	2015 浦东新区 PNA	2015 全市 Shanghai	2015 比重(%) Proportion (%)
商品销售总额(亿元)	Aggregate Sales of Commodities (100 million yuan)	27 640.16	87 829.31	31.5	29 838.38	93 406.57	31.9
社会消费品零售总额(亿元)	Retail Sales of Consumer Goods (100 million yuan)	1 740.23	9 303.49	18.7	1 883.80	10 131.50	18.6
年末居民储蓄存款余额(亿元)	Savings Deposit Balance of Rural and Urban Residents (100 million yuan)	4 381.03	21 995.54	19.9	4 381.84	23 384.73	18.7
外贸进出口商品总额(亿美元)	Total Value of Imports and Exports (USD 100 million)	2 678.71	4 666.22	57.4	16 903.70	28 060.88	60.2
#出口总额	Value of Exports	1 006.10	2 102.77	47.8	6 019.88	12 228.55	49.2
外商直接投资合同项目(个)	Projects of Foreigin Direct Investment (unit)	2 185	4 697	46.5	3 722	6 007	61.9
外商直接投资合同金额(亿美元)	Contracted Amount of Foreign Direct Investment (USD 100 million)	143.07	316.09	45.3	440.82	589.43	74.8
外商直接投资实际到位金额(亿美元)	Foreign Direct Investment Actually Absorbed (USD 100 million)	44.76	181.66	24.6	64.60	184.59	35.0
港口货物吞吐量(万吨)	Volume of Cargo Handled at Port (10 000 tons)	29 918	75 529	39.6	30 162	71 740	42.0
集装箱吞吐量(万标箱)	Container Handling Capacity (10 000 TEUs)	3 236.6	3 528.5	91.7	3 357.2	3 653.70	91.9
各级各类学校在校学生数(万人)	Student Enrollment by Level and Type of Schools (10 000 persons)	53.65	189.38	28.3	36.24	146.93	24.7
医院病床(张)	Number of Hospital Beds (bed)	20 043	98 261	20.4	21 098	103 526	20.3
专业卫生技术人员(万人)	Medical Technical Personnel (10 000 persons)	2.83	16.40	17.3	2.92	17.02	17.2
#执业医生	Medical Practitioners	1.03	6.13	16.8	1.04	6.31	16.5
申请专利(项)	Patent Claiming (item)	19 002	81 664	23.3	22 493	100 006	22.5

表1-19 财政收支
Fiscal Revenue and Expenditure

单位:万元 (10 000 yuan)

指 标	Indicators	2000	2010	2014	2015
全部财政收入	**Total Financial Revenue**	**1 032 077**	**20 461 744**	**29 007 708**	**30 898 752**
一般公共预算收入	**PNA Government Revenue**	**564 020**	**4 288 216**	**6 845 097**	**7 881 870**
区级财政收入	**PNA Financial Revenue**	**355 863**	**6 866 283**	**9 973 518**	**10 564 048**
#增值税	Value Added Tax	44 293	695 060	1 621 000	1 641 693
营业税	Business Income Tax	122 200	1 478 656	1 296 685	1 533 311
企业所得税	Enterprise Tax	72 712	911 281	1 452 600	1 671 034
个人所得税	Individual Income Tax	77 662	447 612	732 877	880 337
城市维护建设税	Tax on Urban Construction and Maintenance	11 603	64 066	163 982	170 421
房产税	Tax on Real Estate	13 418	78 264	149 939	183 455
印花税	Stamp Tax	3 588	124 409	211 325	231 698
契 税	Contract Tax	7 107	315 205	404 045	561 272
一般公共预算支出	**PNA Government Expenditure**	**695 999**	**5 240 626**	**8 203 595**	**9 202 182**
#一般公共服务	Ordinary Community Services		337 484	406 499	432 633
公共安全	Public Security		217 982	301 104	315 038
教 育	Education		493 988	919 851	897 053
科学技术	Technology		239 029	406 902	383 505
文化体育与传媒	Culture, Sports and Media		55 135	87 792	112 665
社会保障和就业	Social Security and Employment		456 319	690 176	851 218
医疗卫生与计划生育	Medical hegienism and Birth Control		260 061	439 777	453 358
节能环保	Lower Power Consumption and Environment Protection		61 191	39 322	52 104
城乡社区事务	Urban and Suburban Community Affairs		1 475 828	1 904 908	2 834 509
农林水事务	Agricultural, Forest and Water Affairs		285 049	388 434	575 389
交通运输	Traffic and Transportation		153 107	429 758	285 133
资源勘探信息等支出	Resource Prospect Information Expend		879 267	1 666 568	1 535 928
商业服务业等支出	Business Services Expend		63 436	120 673	76 582
金融支出	Finanacial Expend		88 000	76 000	76 000

注:1. 2007 年财政部进行财税体制改革,起用新科目,2000 及 2005 年口径数据无法提供。
2. 2010 年起财政收入数按"十二五"市财税体制改革确定的新体制口径填列。

Note: 1. This table is provided by PNA Financial Bureau. The Financial Department has started the reform of the finance and taxation system since 2007, which began to use the new subject. Data approached in 2000 and those in 2005 are not available.
2. The number of financial revenue are filled in according to the new system approach determined by the municipal financeand system reforms during the "Twelfth-Five-Year Planning" since the year of 2010.

主要统计指标解释

气 温

气温是指空气的温度,一般以摄氏度(℃)为单位表示。气象观测的温度表是放在离地面约1.5米处通风良好的百叶箱里测量的,因此,通常说的气温指的是离地面1.5米处百叶箱中的温度。其统计计算方法为:

月平均气温是将全月各日的平均气温相加,除以该月的天数而得。

年平均气温是将12个月的月平均气温累加后除以12而得。

降水量

降水量是指从天空降落到地面的液态或固态(经融化后)水,未经蒸发、渗透、流失而在地面上积聚的深度。其统计计算方法为:

月降水量是将全月各日的降水量累加而得。

年降水量是将12个月的月降水量累加而得。

日照时数

日照时数是指太阳实际照射地面的时间。其统计方法与降水量相同。

生产总值(原国内生产总值)

国内生产总值是指按市场价格计算的一个地区所有常住(驻)单位在一定时期内生产活动的最终成果。生产总值有三种表现形态,即价值形态、收入形态和产品形态。从价值形态看,它是所有常驻单位在一定时期内所生产的全部货物和服务价值超过同期投入的全部非固定资产货物和服务价值的差额,即所有常住(驻)单位的增加值之和;从收入形态看,它是所有常住(驻)单位在一定时期内所创造并分配给常住(驻)单位和非常住(驻)单位的初次(分配)收入之和;从产品形态看,它是所有常住单位在一定时期内最终使用的货物和服务减去进口货物和服务。在实际核算中,生产总值有三种计算方法(其三种表现形态体现为三种计算方法),即生产法、收入法和支出法。三种方法分别从不同的方面反映生产总值及其构成。根据国务院和国家统计局有关我国GDP核算和数据发布制度的规定,浦东新区国内生产总值自2004年起更名为"浦东新区生产总值",简称"浦东新区GDP"。

三次产业

根据社会生产活动历史发展的顺序对产业结构的划分,产品直接取自自然界的部门称为第一产业,对初级产品进行再加工的部门称为第二产业,为生产和消费提供各种服务的部门称为第三产业。

第一产业:农林牧渔业(包括农业、林业、畜牧业、渔业和农林牧渔服务业)。

第二产业:包括采矿业、制造业、电力、燃气及水的生产和供应业与建筑业。

第三产业:除第一、第二产业以外的其他各业。

指 数

指数是一种表明社会经济现象动态的相对数。运用指数可以测定不能直接相加和直接对比的社会经济现象的总动态;可以分析社会经济现象总变动中各因素变动的影响程度;可以研究总平均指标变动中各组标志水平和总体结构变动的作用。它是在把各个年份的产值换算成可比价格的基础上,根据定基数等于相应各个环比指数的连乘积这个换算关系计算出来的。

平均每年增长速度

在我国计算平均增长速度有两种方法,一种是习惯上经常使用的"水平法",又称几何平均法,是各以间隔期最后一年的水平同基期水平对比来计算平均每年增长(或下降)速度。另一种是"累计法",又称代数平均法或方程法,是以间隔期内各年水平的总和同基期水平对比来计算平均每年增长(或下降)速度。

在一般正常情况下,两种方法计算的平均每年增长速度比较接近,但在经济发展不平衡,出现大起大落时,两种方法计算的结果差别较大。

本年鉴内所列的平均每年增长速度,除固定资产投资、直接吸收外资是用"累计法"计算以外,其余均用"水平法"计算。

财政收入

指国家财政参与社会产品分配所取得的收入,是实现国家职能的财力保证。财政收入所包括的内容几经变化,目前主要包括:

(1)各项税收:包括增值税、营业税、消费税、土地增值税、城市维护建设税、资源税、城市土地使用税、企业所得税、个人所得税、关税、证券交易印花税、车辆购置税、农牧业税和耕地占用税等。

(2)专项收入:包括排污费收入、城市水资源费收入、矿产资源补偿费收入、教育费附加收入等。

(3)其他收入:包括利息收入、基本建设贷款归还收入、基本建设收入、捐赠收入等。

(4)国有企业亏损补贴:此项为负收入,冲减财政收入。主要包括对工业企业、商业企业、粮食企业的补贴。

中央财政收入和一般公共预算收入

指按现行分税制财政体制划分的中央本级收入和一般公共预算收入。1994年实行分税制财政体制以后，属于中央财政的收入包括关税、海关代征消费税和增值税，消费税，中央企业所得税，地方银行和外资银行及非银行金融企业所得税，铁道部门、各银行总行、各保险总公司等集中缴纳的营业税、利润和城市维护建设税，车辆购置税，船舶吨税，增值税的75%部分，证券交易税（印花税）94%部分，个人所得税中的利息所得税，利息所得税之外的个人所得税中央分享的部分，海洋石油资源税。属于一般公共预算的收入包括营业税，地方企业所得税，利息所得税之外的个人所得税地方分享的部分，城镇土地使用税，固定资产投资方向调节税，城镇维护建设税，房产税，车船使用税，印花税，屠宰税，农牧业税，农业特产税，耕地占用税，契税，土地增值税、国有土地有偿使用收入，增值税25%部分，证券交易税（印花税）6%部分和除海洋石油资源税以外的其他资源税。

一般公共预算支出

一般公共预算支出指根据政府在经济和社会活动中，按照政府的责权划分确定的支出。地方财政支出主要包括地方行政管理和各项事业费，地方统筹的基本建设、技术改造支出，支援农村生产支出，城市维护和建设经费，价格补贴支出等。

港口货物吞吐量

指经水运进出港区范围，并经过装卸的货物数量，包括邮件及办理托运手续的行李、包裹以及补给运输船舶的燃、物料和淡水。货物吞吐量按货物流向分为进口、出口吞吐量，按货物交流性质分为外贸货物吞吐量和国内贸易货物吞吐量。货物吞吐量的货类构成及其流向，是衡量港口生产能力大小的重要指标。

国际标准集装箱吞吐量

凡经过水运进、出港区范围，并经过装卸的集装箱箱数和重量（含集装箱自重），通常是按进港和出港分别统计。

TEU是“折合20英尺标准箱”的英文缩写。它是指各种尺寸的国际标准集装箱的自然箱数，按各自的换算比例，折算为20英尺标准箱的换算箱数。其换算比例为：40英尺箱1∶2；35英尺箱1∶1.75；20英尺箱1∶1；10英尺箱1∶0.5。

EXPLANATORY NOTES TO MAJOR STATISTICAL INDICATORS

Temperature

Temperature refers to the air temperature. It often uses centigrade as the unit. The thermometry used for weather observation is put in a breezy shutter, which is 1.5 meters high from the ground. Therefore, the commonly used temperature refers to the temperature in the breezy shutter 1.5 meters away from the ground. The calculation method is as follows:

Monthly average temperature is the summation of average daily temperature of one month divided by the actual days of that particular month.

Annual average temperature is the summation of monthly average of a year divided by 12 months.

Volume of Precipitation

Volume of Precipitation refers to the deepness of liquid state or solid state (thawed) water falling from the sky to the ground that has not been evaporated, infiltrated or run off. The calculation method is as follows:

Monthly precipitation is the summation of daily precipitation of a month.

Annual precipitation is the summation of 12 months precipitation of a year.

Sunshine Hours

Sunshine Hours refers to the actual hours of sun irradiating the earth. The calculation method is the same as that of the precipitation.

Gross Domestic Product

Gross Domestic Product refers to the final products at market prices by (of) all resident units of a region during a certain period of time. Gross product is expressed in three different forms, i. e value, income, and products respectively. The form of value added refers to the total value of all products and services produced by all resident units during a certain period of time minus the total value of inputs of non fixed-assets products and services or the summation of the value added of all resident units; the form of income includes all the income items produced by all resident units and distributed primarily to all resident and non-resident units; the form of product refers to all final goods and services minus imports of goods and services. In the practice of national accounting, it is calculated by three approaches, i. e. product approach, income approach, and expenditure approach, respectively, to reflect Gross Product and its composition of different aspects. According to the regulations of GDP national accounting and data release issued by the State Council and National Bureau of Statistics, since 2004 Pudong New Area Gross Domestic Product has been renamed as Pudong New Area Gross Product Value, for short PNA GDP.

Three Industries

Three Industries have been classified according to the historical sequence of development. Primary industry refers to extraction of natural resources; secondary industry involves processing of primary products; and tertiary industry provides services of various kinds for production and consumption.

Primary industry: Agriculture, forestry, animal husbandry and fishery. (including farming, forestry, animal husbandry, fishery industry and service industry for farming, forestry, animal husbandry and fishery).

Secondary industry: Mining, manufacturing, power, steam and water production and supply and construction.

Tertiary industry: All other industries not included in primary or secondary industries.

Index

Index refers to the relative figures indicating social and economic phenomena and developments. Index is used to evaluate the overall development of social and economic phenomena which can not be determined by simple addition or direct comparison. It is also used to analyze the outcome of various changes in the general phenomenon movement of social and economic development, and to study the level of each sub-index in the changes of general average index and the role of the changes of the overall structure. It is calculated at the comparable prices conversed from the output value of each year, using the formula of index number with fixed base period equal to the continuous product of its relative chain index.

Average Annual Growth Rate

Two methods for calculating Average Annual Growth Rate are applied in China, one is often called "level approach" or geometry average, which is derived by comparing the growth rate for the last year of the interval with that of the beginning year; the other is called "accumulating approach" or algebraic average or equation method, which is calculated by comparing the total growth rate of each year for the interval with that of base year.

Usually the results calculated by the two methods are fairly close, but they differ sharply when imbalance occurred in economic development with striking fluctuations in growth.

The Average Annual Growth Rates listed in this statistical yearbook are calculated by "level approach" except for the growth rate of investment in fixed assets and foreign capital absorbed.

Government Revenue

Government Revenue refers to the revenue of the government finance by means of participating in the distribution of the social products, which is the financial resources for ensuring the government to function. The contents of government revenue have been changed several times. Now it includes the following main items:

(1) Various tax revenues, including value added tax, business tax, consumption tax, land value added tax, tax on city maintenance and construction, resources tax, tax on use of urban land, enterprise income tax, personal income tax, tariff, stamp tax on security transactions, tax on purchase of motor vehicles, tax on agriculture and animal husbandry and tax on occupancy of cultivated land, etc.

(2) Special revenues, including revenues from the fee on sewage treatment, fee on urban water resources, fee for the compensation of mineral resources and extra-charges for education, etc.

(3) Other revenues, including revenue from interest, revenue from the repayment of capital construction loan, revenue from capital construction projects, and donations and grants.

(4) Subsidies for the losses of the state-owned enterprises. This is an item of negative revenue, consisting of subsidies to industrial, commercial and grain purchasing and supply enterprises.

Revenue of the Central Government and Revenue of the Local Government

Revenue of the central government and revenue of the local governments: refers to the revenue of the central government and that of the local governments as defined by the decentralized taxation system starting from 1994. In accordance with this system, the revenue of the central government includes tariff, consumption tax and value added tax levied by the customs, consumption tax, income tax of the enterprises subordinate to the central government, income taxes of the local banks, foreign-funded banks and non-bank financial institutions, business tax and profits of railways, head offices of banks, head office of insurance company , which are handed over to the government in a centralized way, tax on city maintenance and construction, tax on purchasing motor vehicles, tonnage tax of ships, 75% of the value added tax, 94% of the tax on stock dealing (stamp tax), interest income tax in the personal income tax, proportion of the personal income tax (other that interest income tax) to be shared by the central government, and tax on ocean petroleum resources. The revenue of the local governments includes business tax, income tax of the enterprises subordinate to the local government, proportion of the personal income tax (other that interest income tax) to be shared by the central government, tax on the use of urban land, tax on the adjustment of the investment in fixed assets, tax on town maintenance and construction, tax on real estates, tax on the use of vehicles and ships, stamp tax, slaughter tax, tax on agriculture and animal husbandry, tax on special agricultural products, tax on the occupancy of cultivated land, contract tax, value-added tax on land, income from charges on use of state-owned land, 25% of the value added tax, 6% of the tax on stock dealing (stamp tax) and tax on resources other than the ocean petroleum resources.

Expenditure of the Local Government

Expenditure of the local government includes mainly the administrative expenses and various operating expenses at the level of local governments, the expenditure for capital construction and technological innovation with the funds raised by the local government, expenditure for supporting rural production, expenditure for city maintenance and construction and expenditure for price subsidies, etc.

Volume of Freight Handled in Ports

Volume of Freight Handled in Ports refers to the volume of cargo passing in and out the harbor area of the ports and having been loaded and unloaded. The volume includes that of the postal matters, registered luggage and fuels, materials and fresh water as supplies of the ships. The volume of freight handled may be classified by direction of flow as freight for import and freight for export, or by nature of cargo as freight for domestic trade and freight for foreign trade. As an important indicator, the volume of freight handled by type of cargo and by main flow direction reflects the production capacity of ports.

International Container Throughput Capacity

International Container Throughput Capacity refers to number and weight of containers which are loaded or unloaded within port area via water carriage. It is often calculated by entering and leaving port, respectively. TEU was the abbreviation of twenty foot equivalent unit, which refers to converted number of all kinds of containers. The conversion method is based on respective conversion ratio and the number of all kinds of container is converted to the standard number of twenty foot equivalent unit. The conversion ratio is: 40 feet container 1 : 2, 35 feet container 1 : 1.75, 20 feet container 1 : 1, 10 feet container 1 : 0.5.

第二篇

CHAPTER 2

人口

POPULATION

表2-1 历年常住人口、户籍人口、流动人口情况
(1990～2015)

单位:万人

年 份 Year	年末常住人口 Permanent Population at Year-end	常住人口密度 (人/平方公里) Density of Permanent Population (Persons/sq·km)	年末户籍人口 Registered Population at Year-end	按户籍 Grouped by Types of 非农业 Non-agriculture
1990			133.94	81.67
1991			137.34	85.45
1992			140.67	89.65
1993			143.73	97.78
1994			146.20	104.63
1995			148.63	109.73
1996			151.11	113.84
1997			153.40	119.20
1998			156.18	123.70
1999			160.08	128.51
2000	240.23	4 503	164.87	134.57
2001	247.56	4 641	168.45	139.85
2002	255.11	4 782	172.82	146.25
2003	262.89	4 616	176.69	153.46
2004	270.91	4 756	180.90	160.13
2005	279.19	4 902	184.81	170.17
2006	285.30	5 009	187.56	175.24
2007	305.35	5 361	191.16	179.90
2008	305.70	5 367	194.29	183.62
2009	419.05	3 462	272.28	240.32
2010	504.44	3 908	275.80	245.06
2011	517.50	4 007	278.53	248.63
2012	526.39	3 832	281.12	252.24
2013	540.90	3 937	283.79	255.37
2014	545.12	3 968	288.44	260.87
2015	547.49	3 985	291.87	265.11

Permanent Population, Household Registered Population and Migrating Population

(10 000 Persons)

性质分 Residence Registration	按性别分 Grouped by Sex		户籍人口密度（人/平方公里）Density of Registered Population (persons/sq. km)	期末登记流动人口数 Number of Registered Migrating Population
农业 Agriculture	男 Male	女 Female		
52.27	66.41	67.53	2 584	
51.89	68.22	69.12	2 650	
51.02	69.96	70.71	2 714	
45.95	71.59	72.14	2 749	
41.57	72.92	73.28	2 797	
38.90	74.23	74.40	2 843	
37.27	75.53	75.58	2 891	
34.20	76.70	76.70	2 934	
32.48	78.21	77.97	2 988	
31.57	80.22	79.86	3 001	
30.30	82.75	82.12	3 091	
28.60	84.66	83.79	3 158	
26.57	86.97	85.85	3 240	67.94
23.23	89.03	87.66	3 102	80.16
20.77	91.20	89.70	3 176	82.58
14.64	93.12	91.69	3 245	93.73
12.32	94.45	93.11	3 293	119.75
11.26	96.13	95.03	3 356	130.97
10.67	97.48	96.81	3 411	127.30
31.96	136.00	136.28	2 249	169.53
30.74	137.60	138.20	2 137	218.33
29.90	138.87	139.65	2 156	206.50
28.88	140.18	140.94	2 046	238.32
28.42	141.49	142.30	2 066	266.81
27.57	143.86	144.59	2 100	252.11
26.76	145.55	146.32	2 125	237.16

表2-2 土地面积、户数、人口、人口密度及人口迁移情况
(2015年底)

单位:人

地 区	Subdistrict/Town	土地面积(平方公里) Land Area (sq. km)	户 数(户) Household (household)	年末人口 Population Year-end	按户籍性质分 Grouped by Types of Residence Registration	
					非农业 Non-agriculture	农 业 Agriculture
总 计	**Total**	**1 373.82**	**1 135 490**	**2 918 699**	**2 651 066**	**267 633**
街道小计	**Subdistrict Tot**	**85.69**	**443 659**	**1 171 281**	**1 171 237**	**44**
潍坊新村街道	Weifangxincun Subdistrict	3.74	31 954	92 228	92 228	
陆家嘴街道	Lujiazui Subdistrict	6.89	38 368	118 085	118 085	
周家渡街道	Zhoujiadu Subdistrict	5.52	42 806	111 316	111 316	
塘桥街道	Tangqiao Subdistrict	3.86	21 890	57 718	57 718	
上钢新村街道	Shanggangxincun Subdistrict	7.54	35 995	98 989	98 989	
南码头路街道	Nanmatoulu Subdistrict	4.25	29 953	79 707	79 707	
沪东新村街道	Hudongxincun Subdistrict	5.39	28 718	72 653	72 653	
金杨新村街道	Jinyangxincun Subdistrict	8.02	52 767	132 419	132 419	
洋泾街道	Yangjing Subdistrict	7.38	41 038	109 938	109 938	
浦兴路街道	Puxinglu Subdistrict	6.25	42 320	104 597	104 597	
东明路街道	Dongminglu Subdistrict	5.95	28 305	68 444	68 409	35
花木街道	Huamu Subdistrict	20.90	49 545	125 187	125 178	9
镇小计	**Town Tot**	**1 288.13**	**691 831**	**1 747 418**	**1 479 829**	**267 589**
川沙新镇	Chuansha New Town	96.70	58 357	155 600	122 786	32 814
高桥镇	Gaoqiao Town	39.00	34 991	90 095	85 774	4 321
北蔡镇	Beicai Town	23.71	52 752	134 918	131 408	3 510
合庆镇	Heqing Town	41.86	23 133	57 938	38 550	19 388
唐 镇	Tangzhen Town	32.30	18 148	46 292	43 777	2 515
曹路镇	Caolu Town	45.40	26 493	75 808	65 152	10 656
金桥镇	Jinqiao Town	25.20	11 248	29 647	29 175	472
高行镇	Gaohang Town	22.80	22 485	57 424	57 387	37
高东镇	Gaodong Town	35.10	14 363	36 929	33 146	3 783
张江镇	Zhangjiang Town	45.00	29 055	81 891	81 877	14
三林镇	Sanlin Town	34.19	55 815	139 617	136 014	3 603
惠南镇	Huinan Town	65.38	47 309	116 853	102 719	14 134
周浦镇	Zhoupu Town	42.68	34 293	83 131	77 500	5 631
新场镇	Xinchang Town	53.44	22 836	54 637	36 537	18 100
大团镇	Datuan Town	50.57	29 157	66 754	35 682	31 072
康桥镇	Kangqiao Town	41.55	28 440	71 991	70 897	1 094
航头镇	Hangtou Town	59.51	27 643	66 829	51 531	15 298
祝桥镇	Zhuqiao Town	160.19	55 002	138 054	105 872	32 182
泥城镇	Nicheng Town	59.27	25 037	57 618	43 174	14 444
宣桥镇	Xuanqiao Town	45.81	19 099	43 222	35 072	8 150
书院镇	Shuyuan Town	54.20	22 801	52 080	28 607	23 473
万祥镇	Wanxiang Town	23.14	10 037	24 710	16 582	8 128
老港镇	Laogang Town	38.90	13 483	33 721	18 957	14 764
南汇新城镇	Nanhui New Town	152.23	9 854	31 659	31 653	6

Land Area, Households, Population, Density of Population and Migration of Population (End of 2015)

(person)

按性别分 Grouped by Sex		平均每户人口 Average Persons Per Household	人口密度（人/平方公里） Population Density (persons/sq·km)	人口迁移情况 Population Mobility		
男 Male	女 Female			迁入 Population Moved-in	迁出 Population Moved-out	净迁入 Net Mobility
1 455 539	**1 463 160**	**2.57**	**2 125**	**26 167**	**9 756**	**16 411**
584 305	**586 976**	**2.64**	**13 669**	**9 525**	**1 557**	**7 968**
45 567	46 661	2.89	24 660	812	77	735
57 843	60 242	3.08	17 139	844	346	498
54 985	56 331	2.60	20 166	580	86	494
28 447	29 271	2.64	14 953	402	34	368
49 208	49 781	2.75	13 129	376	58	318
39 287	40 420	2.66	18 755	424	51	373
37 039	35 614	2.53	13 479	652	89	563
66 265	66 154	2.51	16 511	993	117	876
54 962	54 976	2.68	14 897	916	415	501
53 547	51 050	2.47	16 736	1 241	106	1 135
34 903	33 541	2.42	11 503	569	57	512
62 252	62 935	2.53	5 990	1 716	121	1 595
871 234	**876 184**	**2.53**	**1 357**	**16 642**	**8 199**	**8 443**
77 140	78 460	2.67	1 609	856	90	766
44 953	45 142	2.57	2 310	645	87	558
67 795	67 123	2.56	5 690	1 348	279	1 069
28 480	29 458	2.50	1 384	200	35	165
23 283	23 009	2.55	1 433	857	75	782
37 768	38 040	2.86	1 670	1 729	2 015	-286
14 983	14 664	2.64	1 176	359	34	325
29 077	28 347	2.55	2 519	802	61	741
18 417	18 512	2.57	1 052	218	31	187
41 728	40 163	2.82	1 820	2 432	760	1 672
69 329	70 288	2.50	4 084	997	65	932
57 632	59 221	2.47	1 787	628	374	254
41 579	41 552	2.42	1 948	714	223	491
27 110	27 527	2.39	1 022	275	21	254
33 236	33 518	2.29	1 320	67	13	54
36 436	35 555	2.53	1 733	990	633	357
33 260	33 569	2.42	1 123	337	19	318
68 237	69 817	2.51	862	390	69	321
28 550	29 068	2.30	972	128	24	104
21 377	21 845	2.26	944	209	31	178
25 784	26 296	2.28	961	77	21	56
12 261	12 449	2.46	1 068	27	7	20
16 704	17 017	2.50	867	54	11	43
16 115	15 544	3.21	208	2 303	3 221	-918

表2-3 各街镇户籍人口自然变动

Natural Change of Registered Population in Subdistricts and Towns (2015)

单位：人 (person)

指 标	Indication	出生人口 Birth Population			死亡人口 Death Population			自然增加人口 Natural Growth		
		合 计 Total	男 Man	女 Female	合 计 Total	男 Man	女 Female	合 计 Total	男 Man	女 Female
总 计	**Total**	**23 541**	**12 120**	**11 421**	**22 973**	**12 237**	**10 736**	**568**	**-117**	**685**
街道小计	**Subdistrict Tot**	**9 520**	**4 979**	**4 541**	**9 891**	**5 248**	**4 643**	**-371**	**-269**	**-102**
潍坊新村街道	Weifangxincun Subdistrict	731	380	351	803	390	413	-72	-10	-62
陆家嘴街道	Lujiazui Subdistrict	965	484	481	964	488	476	1	-4	5
周家渡街道	Zhoujiadu Subdistrict	733	390	343	1 146	626	520	-413	-236	-177
塘桥街道	Tangqiao Subdistrict	457	235	222	466	255	211	-9	-20	11
上钢新村街道	Shanggangxincun Subdistrict	564	292	272	1 125	567	558	-561	-275	-286
南码头路街道	Nanmatoulu Subdistrict	539	280	259	763	421	342	-224	-141	-83
沪东新村街道	Hudongxincun Subdistrict	543	274	269	667	371	296	-124	-97	-27
金杨新村街道	Jinyangxincun Subdistrict	959	498	461	1 054	568	486	-95	-70	-25
洋泾街道	Yangjing Subdistrict	917	475	442	767	429	338	150	46	104
浦兴路街道	Puxinglu Subdistrict	987	521	466	789	432	357	198	89	109
东明路街道	Dongminglu Subdistrict	608	317	291	654	333	321	-46	-16	-30
花木街道	Huamu Subdistrict	1 517	833	684	693	368	325	824	465	359
镇小计	**Town Tot**	**14 021**	**7 141**	**6 880**	**13 082**	**6 989**	**6 093**	**939**	**152**	**787**
川沙新镇	Chuansha New Town	1 246	607	639	1 082	572	510	164	35	129
高桥镇	Gaoqiao Town	608	299	309	731	382	349	-123	-83	-40
北蔡镇	Beicai Town	1 202	621	581	1 141	597	544	61	24	37
合庆镇	Heqing Town	354	173	181	467	243	224	-113	-70	-43
唐 镇	Tangzhen Town	558	296	262	324	164	160	234	132	102
曹路镇	Caolu Town	563	294	269	570	311	259	-7	-17	10
金桥镇	Jinqiao Town	249	126	123	186	103	83	63	23	40
高行镇	Gaohang Town	591	320	271	405	244	161	186	76	110
高东镇	Gaodong Town	202	100	102	379	198	181	-177	-98	-79
张江镇	Zhangjiang Town	1 001	516	485	480	238	242	521	278	243
三林镇	Sanlin Town	1 201	626	575	1 101	586	515	100	40	60
惠南镇	Huinan Town	895	460	435	806	450	356	89	10	79
周浦镇	Zhoupu Town	739	368	371	628	348	280	111	20	91
新场镇	Xinchang Town	449	231	218	428	235	193	21	-4	25
大团镇	Datuan Town	360	186	174	559	298	261	-199	-112	-87
康桥镇	Kangqiao Town	810	406	404	484	232	252	326	174	152
航头镇	Hangtou Town	514	245	269	488	259	229	26	-14	40
祝桥镇	Zhuqiao Town	911	457	454	1 097	590	507	-186	-133	-53
泥城镇	Nicheng Town	325	176	149	417	215	202	-92	-39	-53
宣桥镇	Xuanqiao Town	302	157	145	362	223	139	-60	-66	6
书院镇	Shuyuan Town	331	179	152	400	198	202	-69	-19	-50
万祥镇	Wanxiang Town	159	69	90	203	109	94	-44	-40	-4
老港镇	Laogang Town	192	96	96	216	123	93	-24	-27	3
南汇新城镇	Nanhui New Town	259	133	126	128	71	57	131	62	69

表2-4　主要年份户籍人口变动
Change of Registered Population in Main Years

单位:人　(person)

指　标	Indicators	1990	1993	2000	2005	2010	2014	2015
人口自然变动	**Natural Changes in Population**							
出生人口	Births	13 459	9 785	8 229	12 363	22 337	26 980	23 541
出生率(‰)	Birth Rate (‰)	10.20	6.88	5.07	6.76	8.10	9.35	8.07
死亡人口	Deaths	8 711	9 899	11 007	13 423	19 415	21 582	22 973
死亡率(‰)	Death Rate (‰)	6.60	6.96	6.78	7.34	7.04	7.48	7.87
自然增长人口	Natural Growth	4 748	-114	-2 778	-1 060	2 922	5 398	568
自然增长率(‰)	Natural Growth Rate (‰)	3.60	-0.08	-1.71	-0.58	1.06	1.87	0.19
人口迁移变动	**Population Mobility**							
迁入人口	Population Moved-in from Other Provinces and Chongming	18 079	59 214	160 975	128 476	27 440	25 031	26 167
#市外迁入	Non-Shanghai Population Moved-in	8 102	10 469	18 522	18 346	26 845	24 158	25 110
迁出人口	Population Moved-out to Other Provinces and Chongming	15 820	32 457	103 486	88 315	9 119	9 741	9 756
#迁出市外	Population Moved Out of Shanghai	5 843	3 356	5 734	2 612	8 434	9 143	9 068
移入人口	Population Moved-in from other districts in Shanghai			70 435	51 427	38 696	52 290	47 213
移出人口	Population Moved-out to other districts in Shanghai			33 274	27 544	24 737	26 341	29 853

表2-5 年末流动人口登记情况
Registered Migrating Population at Year-end

单位:人 (person)

指 标	Indicators	2005	2010	2014	2015
总 计	**Total**	**937 331**	**2 183 277**	**2 521 103**	**2 380 524**
潍坊新村街道	Weifangxincun Subdistrict	10 975	30 057	30 867	29 277
陆家嘴街道	Lujiazui Subdistrict	17 538	53 091	51 685	48 818
周家渡街道	Zhoujiadu Subdistrict	13 614	28 984	25 847	25 084
塘桥街道	Tangqiao Subdistrict	7 319	19 797	22 917	21 780
上钢新村街道	Shanggangxincun Subdistrict	9 998	17 907	17 995	17 113
南码头路街道	Nanmantoulu Subdistrict	9 295	19 957	27 222	25 746
沪东新村街道	Hudongxincun Subdistrict	11 559	23 289	23 120	21 939
金杨新村街道	Jinyangxincun Subdistrict	27 016	42 152	46 739	44 213
洋泾街道	Yangjing Subdistrict	19 041	50 032	43 153	41 874
浦兴路街道	Puxinglu Subdistrict	15 898	38 169	51 548	49 557
东明路街道	Dongminglu Subdistrict	14 981	26 787	29 439	28 795
花木街道	Huamu Subdistrict	36 626	60 266	71 046	69 773
申港街道	Shengang Subdistrict		11 759		
水上派出所	Boat Police Station	333			
世博园区	Shibo Park		14	14 491	16 231
外高桥保税区	Waigaoqiao Free Trade Zone	3 036	3 443	7 890	8 962
川沙新镇	Chuansha New Town	123 566	173 882	156 903	147 848
高 桥 镇	Gaoqiao Town	51 477	84 918	99 415	93 857
北 蔡 镇	Beicai Town	75 586	140 747	159 041	151 078
合 庆 镇	Heqing Town	40 144	72 050	85 393	81 835
唐 镇	Tangzhen Town	49 296	79 778	94 847	87 736
曹 路 镇	Caolu Town	55 245	96 229	118 033	107 013
金 桥 镇	Jinqiao Town	69 312	65 756	52 747	46 881
高 行 镇	Gaohang Town	45 035	63 057	80 057	71 337
高 东 镇	Gaodong Town	59 380	71 851	74 219	69 491
张 江 镇	Zhangjiang Town	51 157	124 278	129 512	119 490
三 林 镇	Sanlin Town	119 904	196 584	211 042	194 010
惠 南 镇	Huinan Town		92 325	122 836	117 471
周 浦 镇	Zhoupu Town		67 239	100 347	94 780
新 场 镇	Xinchang Town		42 297	48 222	46 524
大 团 镇	Datuan Town		13 800	16 562	15 283
芦潮港镇	Luchaogang Town		12 406		
康 桥 镇	Kangqiao Town		152 304	184 907	177 325
航 头 镇	Hangtou Town		59 749	76 572	73 534
六 灶 镇	Liuzao Town		18 292		
祝 桥 镇	Zhuqiao Town		46 462	114 549	106 308
泥 城 镇	Nicheng Town		21 397	28 045	28 039
宣 桥 镇	Xuanqiao Town		26 775	32 426	29 288
书 院 镇	Shuyuan Town		19 569	23 145	22 880
万 祥 镇	Wanxiang Town		3 440	6 736	6 733
老 港 镇	Laogang Town		12 388	11 041	9 981
南汇新城镇	Nanhui New Town			30 547	32 177
三甲港边防派出所	Sanjiagang Border Police Station				132
滨海边防派出所	Binhai Border Police Station				331

表2-6 户籍人口年龄结构
Age Structure of Registered Population

单位:万人 (10 000 persons)

指 标 Indicators		年末人口数 Population at the End of the Year		比重(%) Percentage	
		2014	2015	2014	2015
户籍人口年龄构成	**Age Structure of Registered Population**				
合 计	**Total**	**288.44**	**291.87**	**100.0**	**100.0**
17 岁及以下	17 and below	34.98	36.14	12.1	12.4
18 ~ 34 岁	18 ~ 34	61.25	59.89	21.2	20.5
35 ~ 59 岁	35 ~ 59	114.31	113.52	39.6	38.9
60 岁及以上	60 and above	77.90	82.31	27.0	28.2
户籍老年人口年龄构成	**Age Structure of Registered Aging Population**				
合 计	**Total**	**77.90**	**82.31**	**100.0**	**100.0**
60 ~ 64 岁	60 ~ 64	27.03	28.73	34.7	34.9
65 ~ 79 岁	65 ~ 79	37.38	39.53	48.0	48.0
80 岁及以上	80 and above	13.49	14.05	17.3	17.1

表2-7　主要年份婚姻登记和计划生育情况
Marriage Registration and Family Planning in Main Years

单位:人　　(person)

指　标	Indicators	1993	2000	2005	2010	2014	2015
婚姻登记	**Marriage　Registration**						
准予登记结婚(对)	Registered Marriage (couple)	7 362	11 083	14 602	23 831	28 853	30 410
离婚登记(对)	Registered Divorce (couple)	489	2 102	4 402	7 511	12 065	13 832
计划生育	**Planned Births**						
出　生	**Births**						
出生人数	Number of Births	9 785	9 958	12 363	22 337	26 980	23 541
第一孩	First Child	9 309	9 669	11 928	20 893	23 120	18 279
第二孩	Second Child	471	285	424	1 423	3 811	5 220
多　孩	≥ Third Child	5	4	11	21	49	42
符合计划生育人数	Planned Parenthood	9 760	9 903	12 323	22 273	26 919	23 480
计划生育率(%)	Rate of Planned Birth (%)	99.74	99.45	99.68	99.71	99.80	99.74
节　育	**Birth　Control**						
已婚育龄妇女人数(万人)	Married Women at Child-bearing Age (10 000 persons)	31.69	32.34	29.33	45.08	45.14	45.18
已领独生子女证人数(万人)	Persons Who Have Applied for One-child Certificate (10 000 persons)	22.66	15.48	10.84	13.80	13.72	11.69
独生子女领证率(%)	Rate of One-child Certificate (%)	71.50	47.86	36.98	30.60	30.40	25.88
晚　婚	**Late Marriage**						
女性初婚人数	Number of First Marriage of Female	5 712	7 564	11 594	12 054	13 784	14 911
#23岁以上	≥ 23 Years Old	2 115	4 217	8 941	10 289	12 811	14 126
晚婚率(%)	Rate of Belated Marriage (%)	37.03	55.75	77.12	85.36	92.94	94.74

主要统计指标解释

人口数

为每年12月31日的年末总人口。根据统计口径的不同,分为户籍人口和常住人口。户籍人口是指在公安部门办理了户籍登记的人口。常住人口是指实际上经常居住在一个地方(住所)的人口,一般都以在其住所居住半年以上者为常住人口。年鉴中除特别注明是常住人口、实有人口等统计口径外,其他均为户籍人口数。

农业人口、非农业人口

是人口按经济特征分组的主要指标。农业人口指依靠从事农业(包括种植业、林业、牧业、渔业)维持生活的全部人口,即包括从事农、林、牧、渔业生产的人口以及由他们抚养的人口。非农业人口指依靠从事农业以外职业的人口以及由他们抚养的人口。但长期来在户籍管理上,往往把在农村中就业并按工资形式获得劳动报酬及由其抚养的人口统计为非农业人口;在农村劳动并参加农村合作经济收益分配的人,及由其抚养的人口作为农业人口统计。

出生率(又称粗出生率)

指在一定时期内(通常为一年)一定地区的出生人数与同期平均人数(或期中人数)之比,一般用千分率表示。计算公式:

$$出生率=\frac{年出生人数}{年平均人数}\times 1000‰$$

出生人数是指活产婴儿,即胎儿脱离母体时(不管怀孕月数),有过呼吸或其他生命现象。年平均人数是年初、年底人口数的平均数,也可用年中人口数代替。

死亡率(又称粗死亡率)

指在一定时期内(通常为一年)一定地区的死亡人数与同期平均人数(或期中人数)之比,一般用千分率表示。计算公式:

$$死亡率=\frac{年死亡人数}{年平均人数}\times 1000‰$$

人口自然增长率

指在一定时期内(通常为一年)人口自然增加数(出生人数减死亡人数)与该时期内平均人数(或期中人数)之比,一般用千分率表示。计算公式:

$$人口自然增长率=\frac{本年出生人数-本年死亡人数}{年平均人数}\times 1000‰$$

人口自然增长率 = 人口出生率 - 人口死亡率

EXPLANATORY NOTES TO MAJOR STATISTICAL INDICATORS

Population

Population refers to the total population by December 31 every year. According to different statistical approaches, there are two definitions of population named as population with registered residence and population with permanent residence. The former refers to the population with registration in the police while the latter refers to the population that actually reside in a place (residence) permanently ,usually longer than half a year. Unless the statistical approaches are specified as permanent population and present population, the others are the number of registered population in this Yearbook.

Agricultural Population, Non-agricultural Population

Agricultural Population, Non-agricultural Population are main indicators of population grouped by economic features. Agricultural Population refers to the total number of people who live on agriculture, including farming, forestry, husbandry and fishery, and their dependents. Non-agricultural Population refers to the number of people who live on non-agricultural jobs and their dependents. According to the resident registering control system, however, the people who are employed in rural area, receive income, and their dependents are actually registered as non-agricultural population. The people who work in rural area and receive their income from agricultural collective units and their dependents are statistically defined as agricultural population.

Birth Rate

Birth Rate (or gross birth rate) means the ratio of the number of births in a certain period (usually a year) to the average population in the same period (or mid-year figure). It is usually calculated in terms of permillage and its calculating formula is:

$$\text{Birth Rate}=\frac{\text{Number of Births}}{\text{Average Number of Popualtion}}\times 1000‰$$

Number of Births refers to live births, when babies have showed any vital phenomena regardless of the length of pregnancy.

Average Number of Population is the average of the number of population at the beginning of the year and that at the end of the year, sometimes substituted for with mid-year population.

Death Rate

Death Rate (or Gross Death Rate) refers to the ratio of number of deaths to the average population (or mid-year population) during a certain period of time (usually a year), which is often presented as permillage. Its calculating formula is :

$$\text{Death Rate} = \frac{\text{Number of Deaths}}{\text{Average Number of Population}} \times 1000‰$$

Natural Growth Rate of Population

Natural Growth Rate of Population refers to the ratio of natural increase in population (number of births minus number of deaths) in a certain period of time (usually a year) to the average population (or mid-year population) of the same period, which is often presented as permillage. The following formula are applied:

$$\text{Natural Growth Rate of Population} = \frac{\text{Number of Births-Number of Deaths}}{\text{Average Number of Population}} \times 1000‰$$

Natural Growth Rate of Population = Birth Rate-Death Rate

第三篇

CHAPTER 3

固定资产投资

INVESTMENT IN FIXED ASSETS

表3-1　固定资产投资主要指标
(2015)

指　标	Indicators	合　计 Total	内　资 Domestic Investment	国　有 State-owned	集　体 Collective-owned
本年完成投资额(亿元)	**Completed Investment in This Year (100 million yuan)**	**1 772.94**	**1 343.92**	**345.37**	**19.01**
按构成分	**By Composition**				
建筑安装工程	Construction and Installation	978.84	789.68	237.94	5.93
设备工具器具购置	Purchase of Equipment and Instrument	206.67	78.74	37.06	0.08
其他费用	Others	587.43	475.50	70.37	13.00
按建设性质分	**By Type of Construction**				
#新　建	New Construction	556.15	419.77	272.48	1.32
改　建	Reconstruction	88.72	41.20	23.23	
扩　建	Expansion	46.46	38.65	32.72	
按三次产业分	**By Industry**				
第一产业	Primary Industry	1.26	1.26		0.07
第二产业	Secondary Industry	280.27	140.85	64.29	
第三产业	Tertiary Industry	1 491.41	1 201.81	281.08	18.94
按主要行业分	**By Main Sector**				
#工　业	Industry	280.12	140.71	64.14	
交通运输、仓储和邮政业	Transportation, Warehousing and Post Service	104.76	101.67	47.12	0.90
信息传输、计算机服务和软件业	Information Transmission, Computer Service and Computer Software	29.50	22.49	18.18	
批发和零售业	Wholesale and Retail	10.94	10.94	5.60	
住宿和餐饮业	Hotel and Catering	14.51	3.37		
金融业	Banking	22.15	22.15	10.76	
新增固定资产	**Newly-increased Fixed Assets**	**607.32**	**426.02**	**68.48**	**1.97**
固定资产交付使用率(%)	Rate of Fixed Assets Put into Use (%)	34.30	31.70	19.80	10.30
房屋建筑面积(万平方米)	**Floor Area of Buildings (10 000 sq. m)**				
施工面积	Floor Area Under Construction	4 366.95	3 865.43	324.69	28.96
#住　宅	Residential Housing	2 121.44	1 946.45	5.36	22.04
竣工面积	Floor Area Completed	541.50	476.26	11.46	0.59
#住　宅	Residential Housing	341.23	299.15	2.47	

注：按建设性质分不含房地产开发投资
Note: The field of "By Type of Construction" does not include the investment in real estate development.

Major Indicators of Investment in Fixed Assets

联 营 Jointly Operated	有限责任公司 Companies with Limited Liability	股份有限公司 Companies Limited by Shares	私营及个 体 Private/ Individual	其 他 Others	港澳台商投资 Hong Kong/ Macao/Taiwan Funded	# 独资企业 Solely Foreigner Funded Enterprises	外商投资 FIE	# 独资企业 Solely Foreigner Funded Enterprises
1.53	**635.57**	**105.57**	**230.15**	**6.72**	**173.07**	**113.62**	**255.95**	**63.26**
0.69	355.97	51.28	131.33	6.54	74.64	42.98	114.52	8.38
0.71	11.27	8.57	20.87	0.18	15.85	13.04	112.08	50.12
0.13	268.33	45.72	77.95		82.58	57.60	29.35	4.76
1.53	71.77	29.79	42.88		11.88	11.10	124.50	9.65
	16.77	0.56	0.46	0.18	2.25	0.66	45.27	0.72
	2.29	1.44	2.20		1.27	0.33	6.54	1.81
			1.19					
0.71	29.30	10.14	36.23	0.18	17.37	14.48	122.05	45.55
0.82	606.27	95.43	192.73	6.54	155.70	99.14	133.90	17.71
0.71	29.30	10.14	36.23	0.18	17.37	14.48	122.03	45.55
	13.10	27.97	12.59		0.04	0.04	3.05	0.75
	3.03		1.29		0.90		6.11	6.11
0.17	5.11		0.06					
	2.00		1.37				11.14	0.11
	11.40							
0.71	216.12	4.37	133.81	0.57	28.76	21.77	152.54	86.20
46.50	34.00	4.10	58.10	8.50	16.60	19.20	60.30	136.30
0.07	2 426.96	212.00	872.75		333.00	179.39	168.52	80.42
	1 501.78	42.24	375.03		97.21	80.37	77.78	23.97
	327.75		136.46		11.00	10.07	54.24	39.31
	248.09		48.60		10.32	9.38	31.75	19.40

表3-2　历年固定资产投资总额
Total Investment in Fixed Assets
(1990~2015)

单位:亿元　　(100 million yuan)

年　份 Year	投资总额 Total Investment	#城市基础设施 Investment in Urban Infrastructure	#房地产开发 Real Estate Development	#工　业 Industry
1990	14.15	7.50		
1991	28.95	5.42		
1992	75.00	21.84		
1993	164.56	54.73		
1994	261.13	78.76		
1995	285.07	53.42	18.26	
1996	395.04	98.68	95.45	112.55
1997	504.36	119.32	125.00	140.95
1998	583.22	177.24	134.87	209.11
1999	438.20	156.54	103.88	135.50
2000	351.06	54.51	110.74	140.65
2001	416.18	105.36	111.66	161.48
2002	587.20	171.36	215.80	192.87
2003	602.16	155.63	245.81	191.00
2004	651.94	121.21	279.49	200.29
2005	693.61	125.95	287.92	144.61
2006	659.97	156.04	257.81	139.56
2007	784.10	234.54	247.46	224.59
2008	872.68	311.30	279.97	158.59
2009	1 420.77	490.77	431.36	298.71
2010	1 432.30	261.92	555.74	336.72
2011	1 435.39	272.02	589.45	361.03
2012	1 454.98	261.86	600.30	356.55
2013	1 679.22	267.63	826.13	329.40
2014	1 765.73	275.25	897.87	303.80
2015	1 772.94	256.40	969.22	280.12
1990~2015年累计 Accumulated from 1990 to 2015	19 329.91	4 295.20	7 384.19	4 418.08

表3-3 各行业固定资产投资情况
Investment in Fixed Assets by Sector
(2015)

指　标	Indicators	施工项目(个) Projects Under Construction (unit)	竣工项目(个) Projects Completed (unit)	本年完成投资额(亿元) Investment (100 million yuan)	新增固定资产(亿元) Newly Increased Fixed Assets (100 million yuan)
总　计	**Total**	**949**	**249**	**1 772.94**	**607.32**
农、林、牧、渔业	Agriculture, Forest, Animal Husbandry and Fishery	9	7	1.26	0.96
工　业	Industry	271	105	280.12	161.93
# 制造业	Manufacturing	202	60	253.26	145.3
电力、热力、燃气及水生产和供应业	Production and Supply of Electricity, Thermal Power, Gas and Water	69	45	26.86	16.63
建筑业	Construction			0.15	
批发和零售业	Wholesale and Retail	6	1	10.94	0.06
交通运输、仓储和邮政业	Transportation, Warehousing and Postal Service	48	11	104.76	17.63
住宿和餐饮业	Hotel and Catering	6	1	14.51	0.34
信息传输、软件和信息技术服务业	Information Transmission, Computer Services and Software	14	2	29.5	9.39
金融业	Banking	5	1	22.15	8.68
房地产业	Real Estate	348	68	973.38	373.74
租赁和商务服务业	Leasing and Commercial Services	23	1	47.51	2.12
科学研究和技术服务业	Scientific Research and Technology Services	22	7	16.35	3.87
水利、环境和公共设施管理业	Water Conservancy, Environment and Public Facilities Management	151	38	121.48	22.94
居民服务、修理和其他服务业	Residents' Services, Repair and Other Services				
教　育	Education	19	4	41.5	2.04
卫生和社会工作	Healthcare and Social Work	8	1	5.98	1.56
文化、体育和娱乐业	Culture, Sports and Entertainment	11	1	98.49	1.71
公共管理、社会保障和社会组织	Public Management, Social Guarantee and Social Organizations	8	1	4.86	0.35

表3-4 固定资产投资房屋建筑面积
Floor Space of Housing and Buildings in Fixed Assets Investment

单位:万平方米 (10 000 sq·m)

指 标	Indicators	2005	2010	2014	2015	1990~2015年累计 Accumulated Investment (1990~2015)
房屋施工面积	**Floor Area Under Construction**					
合 计	**Total**	**2 483.56**	**4 322.59**	**4 470.67**	**4 366.95**	
住 宅	Residential Housing	1 510.04	2 086.26	2 222.93	2 121.44	
厂房仓库	Factory Building and Warehouse	120.52	308.28	450.56	312.69	
商业营业用房	Commerce	276.76	491.29	404.39	399.72	
办公楼	Offices	196.68	601.15	475.54	568.82	
教育用房	Education	20.35	48.36	66.70	102.83	
医疗用房	Healthcare	7.39	9.20	15.23	0.40	
其 他	Others	351.82	778.05	835.32	861.05	
房屋竣工面积	**Floor Area Completed**					
合 计	**Total**	**615.37**	**646.98**	**797.31**	**541.50**	**14 733.16**
住 宅	Residential Housing	408.44	297.89	474.53	341.23	8 830.22
厂房仓库	Factory Building and Warehouse	43.89	55.50	68.76	11.21	1 530.40
商业营业用房	Commerce	85.64	61.83	71.08	57.90	993.73
办公楼	Office	54.08	93.82	41.39	14.95	1 284.12
教育用房	Education	8.37	10.06	19.85	4.07	285.90
医疗用房	Healthcare		4.56	8.73	0.03	93.11
其 他	Others	14.95	123.32	112.97	112.11	1 715.68

表3-5 历年新增固定资产
Newly Increased Fixed Assets
(1994～2015)

指 标 Indicators		1994	1995	1996	1997	1998	1999	2000
新增固定资产(亿元)	Newly Increased Fixed Assets (100 million yuan)	141.03	150.76	260.75	329.84	331.79	396.22	379.60
固定资产交付使用率(%)	Rate of Fixed Assets Transferred in Use (%)	54.0	52.9	66.8	65.4	56.9	90.4	108.1

表3-5 续表1 Continued

指 标 Indicators		2001	2002	2003	2004	2005	2006	2007
新增固定资产(亿元)	Newly Increased Fixed Assets (100 million yuan)	261.82	279.79	407.66	633.37	379.92	522.56	380.96
固定资产交付使用率(%)	Rate of Fixed Assets Transferred in Use (%)	62.9	47.6	67.7	97.2	54.8	79.2	48.6

表3-5 续表2 Continued

指 标 Indicators		2008	2009	2010	2011	2012	2013	2014	2015
新增固定资产(亿元)	Newly Increased Fixed Assets (100 million yuan)	638.70	656.15	622.89	789.74	663.74	711.60	708.92	607.32
固定资产交付使用率(%)	Application Rate of Fixed Assets (%)	73.2	46.2	43.5	55.0	45.6	42.4	40.1	34.3

表3-6 主要年份固定资产投资资金来源
Capital Resources of Investment in Fixed Assets in Main Years

单位:亿元 (100 million yuan)

指 标 Indicators		2010	2014	2015
资金来源合计	**Total Capital Resources**	**2 045.60**	**2 891.75**	**2 910.80**
上年末结余资金	Balance at End of Previous Year	363.69	828.04	886.16
本年资金来源小计	Sub-total of Capital Resources in this Year	1 681.91	2 063.71	2 024.64
国家预算内资金	State Budgetary Funds	23.97	97.52	108.59
国内贷款	Domestic Loans	381.47	571.27	530.15
债 券	Bonds	8.00		
利用外资	Foreign Investment	79.00	90.95	37.23
#外商直接投资	Foreign Direct Investment	42.14	87.30	36.63
自筹资金	Self-Financed Capital	872.50	864.48	830.84
#企事业自有资金	Self-Financed by Enterprises and Institutions	515.87	535.58	514.02
其他资金	Other Capitals	316.97	439.49	517.83
#集 资	Raised Funds	2.86		
本年各项应付投资款	Investment Payable in this Year	196.79	297.96	293.56
#工程款	Project Funds	85.70	172.66	195.98

表3-7　城市基础设施投资额
Investment in Urban Infrastructure

指　标	Indicators	2010	2014	2015	1990~2015年累计 Accumulated Investment (1990~2015)
投资额总计(亿元)	**Total Investment (100 million yuan)**	**261.92**	**275.25**	**256.40**	**4 295.20**
电力建设	Electricity	24.38	28.69	22.32	464.40
运输邮电	Transportation, Post and Telecommunications	116.85	107.21	111.90	1 880.29
#市内公共交通	Urban Public Transportation	31.48	51.42	46.59	593.94
公用设施	Public Facilities	120.69	139.35	122.18	1 950.51
公用事业	Public Utilities	3.85	2.88	4.04	153.99
自来水	Tap Water	2.56	0.99	2.68	77.36
燃　气	Gas	1.29	1.89	1.36	76.63
市政建设	Civic Construction	116.85	136.47	118.14	1 796.52
市政工程	Civic Projects	100.51	119.37	100.70	1 619.39
园林绿化	Garden/Park	14.08	14.26	16.70	136.96
环境卫生	Environmental Sanitation	2.10	2.84	0.74	31.00
其　他	Others	0.17			9.17
构　成(%)	**Composition(%)**				
投资额总计	**Total Investment**	**100.0**	**100.0**	**100.0**	**100.0**
电力建设	Electricity	9.3	10.4	8.7	10.8
运输邮电	Transportation, Post and Telecommunications	44.6	39.0	43.6	43.8
#市内公共交通	Urban Public Transportation	12.0	18.7	18.2	13.8
公用设施	Public Facilities	46.1	50.6	47.7	45.4
公用事业	Public Utilities	1.5	1.0	1.6	3.6
自来水	Tap Water	1.0	0.4	1.0	1.8
燃　气	Gas	0.5	0.7	0.5	1.8
市政建设	Civic Construction	44.6	49.6	46.1	41.8
市政工程	Civic Projects	38.3	43.4	39.3	37.7
园林绿化	Garden/Park	5.4	5.2	6.5	3.2
环境卫生	Environmental Sanitation	0.8	1.0	0.3	0.7
其　他	Others	0.1			0.2

表3-8 工业各行业投资主要指标
Main Indicators of Investment by Industrial Sectors
(2015)

指 标	Indicators	施工项目(个) Projects Under Construction (unit)	全部建成投产项目(个) Projects Completed and Put into Production (unit)	建成投产率(%) Rate of Projects Completed and Put into Use(%)	工业本年完成投资额(亿元) Completed Investment in Industry in This Year (100 million yuan)
总 计	**Total**	**271**	**105**	**38.7**	**280.12**
#制造业	**Manufacturing**	**202**	**60**	**29.7**	**253.26**
农副食品加工业	Farm and Sideline Food Processing	2			1.40
食品制造业	Food Manufacturing	3			1.15
酒、饮料和精制茶制造业	Alcohol, Beverage, and Tea Manufacturing	1			0.38
烟草制品业	Tobacco Manufacturing	1			8.20
纺织业	Textile Industry	2	1	50.0	0.16
纺织服装、服饰业	Textile Clothes and Accessories	2			1.09
造纸和纸制品业	Paper-making and Paper Products	2	1	50.0	0.48
印刷业和记录媒介复制业	Printing and Record Medium Reproduction	1			0.38
石油加工、炼焦和核燃料加工业	Petroleum Processing, Coking and Nuclear Fuel Processing	4	2	50.0	1.80
化学原料和化学制品制造业	Chemical Materials and Chemical Products	12	11	91.7	4.38
医药制造业	Medicine Manufacturing	6	2	33.3	3.32
橡胶和塑料制品业	Manufacturing of Rubber and Plastic Products	25	6	24.0	21.48
非金属矿物制品业	Manufacturing of Non-metal Mineral Products	3	1	33.3	2.34
黑色金属冶炼和压延加工业	Manufacturing of Smelting and Processing of Ferrous Metals	3	1	33.3	1.23
有色金属冶炼和压延加工业	Manufacturing of Smelting and Processing of Non-ferrous Metals	8	4	50.0	3.02
金属制品业	Manufacturing of Metal Products	13			6.96
通用设备制造业	Manufacturing of General-use Equipment	21	2	9.5	18.74
专用设备制造业	Manufacturing of Special Equipment	33	5	15.2	47.38
汽车制造业	Manufacturing of Automobiles	8			15.28
铁路、船舶、航空航天和其他运输设备制造业	Manufacturing of Railway, Ship, Aviation and Aerospace, and Other Transportation Equipment	11	3	27.3	7.92
电气机械和器材制造业	Manufacturing of Electric Machinery and Apparatus	23	17	73.9	95.97
计算机、通信和其他电子设备制造业	Manufacturing of Computer, Telecommunications and Other Electronic Equipment	5	2	40.0	1.59
仪器仪表制造业	Manufacturing of Instrument and Meter	12	2	16.7	8.20
废弃资源综合利用业	Comprehensive Recycling of Discarded Resources	69	45	65.2	26.86
其他制造业	Other Manufacturings	1			0.41
电力、热力、燃气及水生产和供应业	**Production and Supply of Electricity, Thermal Power, Gas and Water**	**63**	**41**	**65.1**	**22.82**
电力、热力生产和供应业	Electricity&Heat Production and Supply	3	3	100.0	1.36
燃气生产和供应业	Gas Production and Supply	3	1	33.3	2.68
水的生产和供应业	Water Production and Supply				

表3-9　主要年份建设改造投资主要指标

Major Indicators of Investment on Constructions and Transformations

指　标	Indicators	2014	2015
投资总额(亿元)	**Total Investment (100 million yuan)**	**867.86**	**803.72**
按建设性质分	**Grouped by Type of Construction**		
#新　建	New Construction	652.53	558.94
改建和技改	Reconstruction and Technologic Reforms	93.91	88.72
扩　建	Expansion	35.59	46.46
按产业分	**Grouped by Type of Industry**		
第一产业	Primary Industry	5.49	1.26
第二产业	Secondary Industry	303.80	280.27
第三产业	Tertiary Industry	558.57	522.19
按行业分	**Grouped by Sectors**		
农、林、牧、渔业	Farming, Forestry, Animal Husbandry and Fishery	5.49	1.26
工　业	Industry	303.80	280.12
建筑业	Construction		0.15
批发和零售业	Wholesale and Retail	122.03	104.76
交通运输、仓储和邮政业	Transportation, Storage and Post Service	15.58	29.50
住宿和餐饮业	Hotel and Catering	7.41	10.94
信息传输、软件和信息技术服务业	Information Transmission, Software and Information Technology Services	16.87	14.51
金融业	Financial Industry	18.38	22.15
房地产业	Real Estate Industry	3.92	4.16
租赁和商务服务业	Leasing and Business Service	58.37	47.51
科学研究和技术服务业	Scientific Research andTechnology Service	25.61	16.35
水利、环境和公共设施管理业	Water Conservancy, Environment and Public Facilities Management	142.11	121.48
居民服务、修理和其他服务业	Residents' Services, Repair and Other Services	0.37	
教　育	Education	54.74	41.50
卫生和社会工作	Healthcare and Social Work	4.32	5.98
文化、体育和娱乐业	Culture, Sports and Entertainment	88.03	98.49
公共管理、社会保障和社会组织	Public Management, Social Insurance and Social Organizations	0.83	4.86
新增固定资产	**Newly Increased Fixed Assets**		
固定资产交付使用率(%)	Application Rate of Fixed Assets(%)	30.5	29.8
房屋建筑面积(万平方米)	**Floor Area of Buildings (10 000 sq. m)**		
施工面积	Floor Space Under Construction	731.45	643.49
#住　宅	Residential Housing		23.62
竣工面积	Floor Space Completed	92.45	32.59
#住　宅	Residential Housing	0.02	13.60

表3-10 主要年份住宅投资(按经济类型分)
Investment in Residential Housing in Main Years (by Ownership)

单位:亿元 (100 million yuan)

指 标	Indicators	2010	2014	2015
住宅投资额总计	**Total Investment in Residential Housing**	**343.57**	**518.60**	**501.09**
占固定资产投资额比重(%)	Percentage of Investment in Fixed Assets (%)	23.8	29.4	28.3
内 资	Domestic Investment	309.32	412.01	426.29
国 有	State-owned	48.69	4.74	1.13
集 体	Collective-owned	30.06	1.52	4.07
联 营	Jointly-operated	26.31		
有限责任公司	Companies with Limited Liability	115.45	286.53	290.31
股份有限公司	Companies Limited by Shares	0.92	4.67	25.16
私 营	Private	87.88	114.55	105.62
港澳台商投资	Hong Kong/Macao/Taiwan Invested	12.16	50.27	60.45
#港澳台商独资	Solely Hong Kong/Macao/Taiwan Funded	6.18	48.42	42.67
外商投资	FIE	22.09	56.32	14.35
#外商独资	Solely Foreigner Funded	21.37	6.57	4.68

表3-11 主要重大项目(浦东部分)投资完成额
Amount of Completed Investment in Key Civic Projects in PNA
(2015)

单位:亿元 (100 million yuan)

序号 No.	指标	Indication	计划总投资 Total Planned Investment	累计完成投资 Accumulated Investment	#2015年完成投资 Investment Completed in 2015
1	上海迪士尼乐园项目	Shanghai Disneyland	293.70	238.86	84.77
2	中环线浦东段(军工路隧道—高科中路)	Pudong Central Link (Jungong Road Tunnel-Middle Gaoke Road)	122.55	97.56	25.91
3	上海轨道交通9号线三期东段工程	Phase III of Shanghai Metro Line 9	102.82	38.90	25.00
4	通用汽车设计与工程技术中心金桥基地暨金桥扩能项目	Jinqiao Auto Expasion Project by Gerneral Motors Design and Engineering Technology Center	78.00	34.85	9.21
5	东西通道	East-West Aisles	71.95	68.51	13.80
6	C919大型客机研制保障条件能力建设项目	Research and Maintainance Capability Project for C919 Large Airplane of Shanghai Airplane Manufacturing Co., Ltd.	69.85	56.90	4.23
7	中航商用航空发动机有限责任公司临港基地项目	ACAE Lingang Project	66.01	137.03	6.39
8	浦东新区环城绿带开天窗补绿工程	Around-city Greenbelt Re-greening Project in Pudong New District	64.50	47.79	2.90
9	上海世博会地区B02、B03地块地下空间工程	Parcel B02 & B03 Underground Space Construction in Shanghai Expo Area	61.13	40.72	4.28
10	上海烟草浦东科技创新园区建设项目	Shanghai Tabacco Corporation Construction Project in Pudong Hi-Tech Park	58.90	21.73	8.20
11	上海浦东国际机场第五跑道工程	Shanghai Pudong International Airport 5th Runway Project	54.06	39.36	4.56
12	上海通用汽车增资生产新一代中级、中高级轿车项目	GM Shanghai Capital Increase for New Intermerdiate Car Production	52.00	42.34	1.71
13	上海迪士尼乐园配套项目	Shanghai Disneyland Supporting Project	45.26	35.98	11.02
14	上海科技大学新校区一期工程	Shanghai Technology University New Campus Project Phase I	35.03	40.88	19.35
15	上海国际金融中心上交所项目	Shanghai Stock Exchange at Shanghai IFC Project	35.00	23.16	3.00
16	中国商飞总部基地	COMAC Headquater Base	34.49	29.73	5.27
17	国家电网世博园区办公楼项目	State Grid Corporation of China-Shanghai Expo Zone Office Building Project	33.28	26.24	4.38
18	滨江大道及绿化工程	Binjiang Avennue Construction and Greening Project	30.23	21.90	1.50
19	远东宏信广场	Far East Hongxin Square	28.00	11.40	11.40
20	滴水湖环湖80米景观带工程	80-metre Landscape Around Dishui Lake Construction Project	25.25	0.18	0.18
21	中国商飞大型客机研保条件建设项目	Research and Maintainance Capability Project for Commercial Aircraft Corporation of China Ltd.	25.05	21.77	1.44
22	华能上海大厦	Huaneng Shanghai Building Construction Project	24.39	18.69	5.58
23	上海建桥学院临港新校区迁建项目一期工程	Shanghai Jianqiao Univerisity Lingang Campus Removal Project Phase I	23.79	24.79	6.54
24	申江路(中环线-S2)高架专用道新建工程	Shenjiang (Cental Link-S2) Elevated Road Construction Project	23.25	22.00	2.04
25	两港公路(拱极路-A15)	Lianggang Road (Gongji Road-A15)	21.04	18.35	0.68

表3-12 当年建成部分大项目一览表
Major Projects Completed in Current Year
(2015)

单位:亿元 (100 million yuan)

序号 No.	指标	Indication	计划总投资 Total Planned Investment	累计完成投资 Accumulated Investment	#2015年完成投资 Investment Completed in 2015
1	中环线浦东段(军工路隧道—高科中路)	Pudong Central Link (Jungong Road Tunnel-Middle Gaoke Road)	122.55	97.56	25.91
2	上海科技大学新校区一期工程	Shanghai Technology University New Campus Construction Project Phase I	35.03	40.88	19.35
3	士韵家园	Shiyunjiayuan Project	27.88	35.40	8.11
4	上海二十一世纪中心大厦	Shanghai Tower Project Phase I	24.66	24.66	0.09
5	上海建桥学院临港新校区迁建项目一期工程	Shanghai Jianqiao Univerisity Lingang Campus Removal Project Phase I	23.79	24.79	6.54
6	鹏利海景公寓	Ocean One Construction Project	21.00	21.19	0.35
7	上海保障性住房三林基地6号地块	Shanghai Idemnificatory housing Sanlin Base Pacel 6	17.75	21.31	2.01
8	轨道交通七号线浦江耀华站所在街坊(18-1)站综合开发项目—环通商业广场	Metro Line 7 Pujiangyaohua Station Area Comprehensive Development Project-Huantong Commerial Plaza	16.35	16.52	0.64
9	绿地景汇佳苑	Lvdi Jinghui Jiayuan	16.00	16.00	0.32
10	临港大道	Lingang Avenue	14.55	14.65	0.93
11	上天马第5.5代Am-OLED显示线(一期)项目	Am-OLED Display Line (G5.5) Project (Phase I) Project of Shanghai Tianma Co. Ltd.	14.30	14.89	8.39
12	周浦镇08单元06—07地块绿地商业	Lane 08 Parcel 06-07 in Zhoupu Town-Lvdi Commercial	13.00	13.00	6.39
13	御珑公馆	Yulonggongting Construction Project	12.79	15.60	2.00
14	上海市保障性住房三林基地5号地	Shanghai Idemnificatory housing Sanlin Base Pacel 5	12.07	8.11	0.24
15	旭辉亚瑟郡	Xuhui Yase Jun Project	9.18	9.41	0.35
16	丽都华庭	Liduhuating Project	8.70	8.96	0.30
17	中国银联研发中心工程	China UnionPay R&D Center Construction Project	8.68	8.68	3.74
18	印象春城六街区	Yin Xiang Chun Cheng Block 6	8.66	8.65	4.90
19	锦绣15#地块二期	Jinxiu Project Parcel 15 Phase II	8.50	6.95	0.94
20	明天华城三期	Ming Tian Hua Cheng Project Phase III	8.40	8.40	0.03
21	中化集团上海世博B03C-02地块商办楼	Sinochem Group-Commerial Office Building in Shanghai Expo Area Parcel B03C-13	8.17	9.73	3.03
22	江畔御庭	Jiang Pan Yu Ting Construction Project	8.12	9.16	1.35
23	浦东新区川沙新镇C08-13地块配套	Chuansha New Town Parcel C08-13 Supporting Project in Pudong New District	7.91	6.97	1.46
24	汤巷五街坊B地块配套商品房	Ancillary Commercial Housing in Tangxiang Fifth Street Parcel B	7.51	7.51	0.01
25	新金桥阳光欧洲城商务中心	New Jinqiao Yangguang European City Commerial Center	6.93	6.08	0.88

主要统计指标解释

全社会固定资产投资

固定资产投资是国民经济再生产活动的一个重要部分。固定资产投资额是以货币形式表现的在一定时期内建造和购置固定资产的工作量以及与此有关的费用总称。它是反映固定资产投资规模、结构和发展速度的综合性指标。按照现行国家统计制度，全社会固定资产投资包括建设改造、房地产开发、城乡集体经济单位、城乡私人建房和其他经济单位投资。

从2011年起，固定资产投资统计起点为500万元(含500万元)以上项目。

房地产开发投资

指各种登记注册类型的房地产开发公司、商品房建设公司及其他房地产开发法人单位和附属于其他法人单位实际从事房地产开发或经营活动的单位统一开发的包括统代建、拆迁还建的住宅、厂房、仓库、饭店、宾馆、度假村、写字楼、办公楼等房屋建筑物和配套的服务设施，土地开发工程(如道路、给水、排水、供电、供热、通讯、平整场地等基础设施工程)的投资；不包括单纯的土地交易活动。

固定资产投资按国民经济行业分

固定资产投资按国民经济行业分是根据建设项目建成投产后的主要产品或主要用途及社会经济活动性质来确定国民经济行业。一般情况下，一个建设项目或一个企业、事业单位只能属于一种国民经济行业。

固定资产投资按构成分

(1)建筑工程(建筑工作量)包括：

①各种房屋如厂房、仓库、办公室、住宅、商店、学校、医院、俱乐部、食堂、招待所等工程，包括列入房屋工程预算内的暖气、卫生、通风、照明、煤气等设备的价值及装饰油饰工程，列入建筑工程预算内的各种管道(如蒸汽、压缩空气、石油、给排水等管道)、电力、电讯电缆导线的敷设工程。

②设备基础、支柱、操作平台、梯子、烟囱、凉水塔、水池、灰塔等建筑工程；炼焦炉、蒸汽炉等各种窑炉的砌筑工程及金属结构工程。

③为施工而进行的建筑场地的布置、工程地质勘探，原有建筑物和障碍物的拆除，平整土地、施工临时用水、电、气、道路工程，以及完工后建筑场地的清理、环境绿化美化工作等。

④矿井的开凿，井巷掘进延伸，露天矿的剥离，石油、天然气钻井工程和铁路、公路、港口、桥梁等工程。

⑤水利工程，如水库、堤坝、灌溉以及河道整治等工程。

⑥防空、地下建筑等特殊工程。

(2)安装工程(安装工作量)包括：

①生产、动力、起重、运输、传动和医疗、实验等各种需要安装设备的装配和安装，与设备相连的工作台、梯子、栏杆等装设工程，附属于被安装设备的管线敷设工程，被安装设备的绝缘、防腐、保温、油漆等工作。

②为测定安装工程质量，对单个设备、系统设备进行单机试运，系统联动无负荷试运工作(投料试运工作不包括在内)。在安装工程中，不得包括被安装设备本身价值。

(3)设备、工具、器具购置：是指把工业生产的产品转为固定资产的购置活动，包括建设单位或在企、事业单位购置或自制达到固定资产标准的设备、工具、器具的价值。固定资产的标准按财务部门规定。新建单位及扩建单位的新建车间，按照设计和计划要求购置或自制的全部设备、工具、器具，不论是否达到固定资产标准均计入“设备、工具、器具购置”中。

①设备：指各种生产设备、传导设备、动力设备、运输设备等。分为需要安装的设备和不需要安装的设备两种。

需要安装的设备(简称“需安设备”)：是指必须将其整体或几个部位装配起来，安装在基础上或建筑物支架上才能使用的设备。如轧钢机、发电机、蒸汽锅炉、变压器、塔、换热器、各种泵、机床等。有的设备虽不要基础，但必须进行组装工作，并在一定范围内使用，如生产用电铲、塔吊、门吊、皮带运输机等也作为需要安装的设备统计。

不需要安装的设备(简称“不需安设备”)：指不必固定在一定位置或支架上就可以使用的各种设备，如电焊机、叉车、汽车、机车、飞机、船舶以及生产上流动使用的空压机、泵等。

②工具、器具：是指具有独立用途的各种生产用具、工作工具和仪器。如生产和维修用的切削工具、压延工具、铆焊工具、模压器、铸型、风镐等，检验、实验测量用的各种计量、分析、化验仪器，以及达到固定资产标准的包装容器等。

购置旧设备：是指从外单位购入的，已经使用过的各种设备。不包括从国外购进的旧设备。旧设备一般是指在国内其他单位作为固定资产使用过的设备(单纯购置旧设备不纳入固定资产投资统计)。

用于更新的设备：是指为更换陈旧设备而购置的投资。用于更新的设备与原有设备在台数和价值上不一定相等。购置的设备如不是用于更换原有设备，而是用于新增或扩大生产能力的，不能作为用于“更新的设备”统计。

(4)其他费用：指不属于上述几项的投资完成额。包括计入固定资产的费用(如农林建设单位牲畜购置费、各种经济林木营造费、办公和生活用家具、器具购置费、建设单位管理费、土地、青苗补偿和安置补偿费、勘察设计费、研究试验费、负荷联合试运费、引进技术和进口设备项目的其他费用)。

固定资产投资按建设性质分

按建设项目情况填写。

（1）新建：指从无到有“平地起家”开始建设的项目。现有企业、事业、行政单位投资的项目一般不属于新建。但如有的单位原有基础很小，经过建设后新增的固定资产价值超过该企业、事业、行政单位原有固定资产价值（原值）三倍以上的，也应作为新建。

（2）扩建：是指企（事）业单位在厂内或其他地点，为扩大原有产品的生产能力（或效益）或增加新的产品生产能力，而增建主要生产车间（或主要工程）独立的生产线、分厂等。行政、事业单位在原单位增建业务用房（如学校增建的教学用房、医院增建门诊部、病房）也作为扩建。

现有企、事业单位为扩大原有主要产品生产能力或增加新的产品生产能力，增建一个或几个主要生产车间（或主要工程）、总厂之下的分厂，如同时进行一些更新改造工程的建设，则也应作为扩建。

（3）改建和技术改造：是指现有企业、事业单位对原有设施进行技术改造或更新（包括相应配套的辅助性生产、生活福利设施）的建设项目。改建项目包括现有企业、事业单位为适应市场变化的需要，而改变企业的主要产品种类（如军工企业转民产品等）的建设项目，原有产品生产作业线由于各工序（车间）之间能力不平衡，为填平补齐充分发挥原有生产能力而增建不增加本企业主要产品设计能力的车间的建设项目。技术改造是指企业、事业单位在现有基础上，用先进的技术代替落后的技术，用先进的工艺和装备代替落后的工艺和装备，以改变企业落后的技术经济面貌，实现以内涵为主的扩大再生产，达到提高产品质量、促进产品更新换代、节约能源、降低消耗、扩大生产规模、全面提高社会经济效益的目的。技术改造具体包括以下内容：机器设备和工具的更新改造；生产工艺改革、节约能源和原材料的改造；厂房建筑和公共设施的改造；保护环境进行的“三废”治理改造；劳动条件和生产环境的改造等。

（4）单纯建造生活设施：是指企（事）业及行政单位在不扩建、改建生产性工程和业务用房的情况下，单纯建造职工住宅、托儿所、子弟学校、医务室、浴室、食堂等生活福利设施。

（5）迁建：指为改变生产能力布局或由于城市环境保护和安全生产的需要等原因搬迁到另地建设的企、事业单位。在搬迁另地建设过程中，不论是维持原来规模还是扩大规模都按迁建统计。

（6）恢复：是指因自然灾害、战争等原因，使原有固定资产全部或部分报废，以后又投资恢复建设的单位。不论是按原规模恢复还是在恢复的同时进行扩建的都按恢复项目统计。尚未建成投产的基本建设项目，因自然灾害而损坏重建的，仍按原有建设性质划分。

（7）单纯购置：是指现有企、事业、行政单位单纯购置不需要安装的设备、工具、器具而不进行工程建设的单位。有些单位当年虽然只从事一些购置活动，但其设计中规定有建筑安装活动，应根据设计文件的内容来确定建设性质，不得作为单纯购置统计。

新增固定资产

新增固定资产又称交付使用的固定资产，是指已经完成建造和购置过程，并已交付生产或使用单位的固定资产价值。新增固定资产是表示固定资产投资成果的价值量指标，也是反映建设进度、计算固定资产投资效果的必要数据。

固定资产交付使用率

固定资产交付使用率又称固定资产运用系数，是指一定时期新增固定资产与同期完成投资额的比率。它反映各个时期固定资产动用速度，衡量建设过程中宏观投资效果的综合性指标。

施工项目

施工项目指报告期内进行过建筑或安装施工活动的项目。凡是报告期内施过工的建设项目，不论施工时间长短，均作为施工项目统计。施工项目个数可以反映一定时期固定资产投资的实际规模，与同期建成投产的建设项目个数相比，可以从建设速度的角度反映固定资产投资的效果。根据建设项目施工活动的不同性质，施工项目又分为：本年正式施工项目、本年收尾项目和以前年度全部停缓建项目。

全部投产项目

工业项目指设计文件规定形成生产能力的主体工程及其相应配套的辅助设施全部建成，经负荷试运转，证明具备生产设计规定合格产品的条件，并经过验收鉴定合格或达到竣工验收标准，与生产性工程配套的生活福利设施可以满足近期正常生产的需要，正式移交生产的建设项目。非工业项目指设计文件规定的主体工程和相应的配套工程全部建成，能够发挥设计规定的全部效益，经验收鉴定合格或达到竣工验收标准，正式移交使用的建设项目。

EXPLANATORY NOTES TO MAJOR STATISTICAL INDICATORS

Total Investment in Fixed Assets

Investment in Fixed Assets constitutes an important portion of the national economic reproduction. Fixed assets investment is a general term for both the work volume of production and purchase of fixed assets and relevant expenditure, in the form of currency, during a certain period. It is a comprehensive indicator of scale, structure and development speed of fixed assets investment. As stipulated in the current national statistics regulations, the social fixed assets investment includes the investment into infrastructure and reformation, real estate development, urban and rural collective economic bodies, private house construction in urban and rural areas and other economic bodies.

Since the year of 2011, the fixed assets items have only include those with an investment of 5 million yuan and above.

Investment in Real Estate Development

Investment in Real Estate Development refers to the investment by the real estate development companies, commercial buildings construction companies and other real estate development units of various types of ownership in the construction of house buildings, such as residential buildings, factory buildings, warehouses, hotels, guesthouses, holiday villages, office buildings, and the complementary service facilities and land development projects, such as roads, water supply, water drainage, power supply, heating, telecommunications, land leveling and other projects of infrastructure. It excludes the activities in pure land transactions.

Investment in Fixed Assets by Sector

Investment in Fixed Assets by Sector refers to determining the classification of construction projects by the major products or the purpose of the projects when they are put into production or use, and by the nature of their social economic activities. In general, one project or one enterprise or institution can only be classified into one sector.

Investment in Fixed Assets by Composition

(1) Construction Projects (work volume of construction) include:

① Various kinds of houses and buildings such as workshops, warehouses, offices, residential buildings, shops, schools, hospitals, clubs, canteens and hostels, including the value of equipment such as heating, sanitation, lighting, and gas that are covered by the budget of housing projects and some decoration and polishing projects, various kinds of pipelines such as steam, compressed air, petroleum, tap water and sewage that are covered by the budget of construction projects and the pavement for cable conductors of electricity and telecommunications.

② Construction projects such as equipment foundations, pillars, operating platforms, ladders, chimneys, cooling towers, pools and gray towers, the masonry of various kinds of kilns and stoves for coke and stream ovens, and the metal structure work.

③ Site layout and geological explorations for the construction, demolition of the old buildings and barriers, site leveling, projects of temporary tap water, electricity , gas and road for the construction, and clearing up and green environment after the construction.

④ The mine excavation, the excavation and extension of roadway, the stripping of open pits, drilling engineering works for petroleum and natural gas, and the projects of railway, highway, ports and bridges.

⑤ Projects of water conservancy, such as reservoirs, dams, irrigation and river regulation.

⑥ Special projects such as air-raid shelters and underground constructions.

(2) Installation Projects (work volume of installation) include:

① Various assembly and installations that need equipment for installation, such as production, power, lifting, transportation, transmission and medical experiments, decoration projects that are connected with the equipment, such as tables, ladders and railings, pipeline laying works that are attached with the installed equipment, and works such as isolation, anti-corrosion and painting for the installed projects.

② In order to determine the quality of the installation project, the system equipment will be operated on trial separately and the system will be connected without any load (excluding the trial with feeding). The installation project will not include the value of the installed equipment itself.

(3) Purchase of equipment, tools and instruments refers to the total value of equipment, tools, and instruments purchased or self-produced which come up to standards for fixed assets by the construction units or the enterprises or institutions. The standards for fixed assets are specified by the financial departments. All of the equipment, tools and instruments purchased or self-produced for new workshops by newly established or expanded units are categorized as "purchase of equipment, tools and instruments" no matter whether they come up to the standards for fixed assets.

① Equipment refers to various kinds of equipment for production, transmission, power and transportation. It is divided into two categories: one that need installation and the other that need not be installed.

Equipment that need installation refers to the equipment that must be assembled in whole or in several parts, and mounted on the base or on the brackets of the building for normal operation, such as rolling machines, generators, steam boilers, transformers, towers, heat exchangers, pumps and machine tools. Although some equipment need not a base, they need the job for assembly and can only be used in a certain scope, such as shovels, cranes, gantry cranes and belt conveyors for production.

Equipment that need not be installed refers to various kinds of equipment that are not necessarily installed at a certain place or bracket and can be put into use, such as welding machines, forklifts, cars, motorcycles, planes, ships, and air compressors and pumps that are used in a non-fixed place during the production.

② Tools and instruments refer to various production supplies, working tools and instruments with their independent uses, such as cutting, rolling and riveting tools, molded devices and picks for production and repair, various measurement, analysis, laboratory equipment for inspection and experiment, and containers that can meet the standards of fixed assets.

Purchase of old equipment refers to various kinds of used equipment that have been bought from other units, which exclude used equipment purchased from foreign countries. Old equipment generally refers to the equipment that other domestic units have used as fixed assets (Simple purchasing of old equipment will not be covered in the statistical investment of fixed assets).

Equipment for updating refers to the investment that is purchased for updating the old equipment. Equipment for updating does not necessarily have the same number and value as those of the original equipment. If the purchased equipment is not used to replace the old equipment but to increase or enlarge its production capability, it can not be identified as "Equipment for updating".

(4) Other Expenses refer to the completed investment that are other than those mentioned above, which include expenses that are covered by fixed assets, such as purchasing livestock, planting economic trees, furniture and appliances for office and living, manage-

ment, land, compensation for young crops, resettlement compensation, survey and design, research and test, joint trial for load and combination, introduction of foreign technology and imported equipment by construction units of agriculture and forest.

Investment in Fixed Assets by Property of Construction

It is filled out according to the specific construction project.

(1) New construction refers to completely new construction from scratch. Projects of the existing enterprises, institutions or administrative units are not considered as new construction. In case the assets of the existing unit are quite small, and the value of newly added fixed assets exceeds the original value of assets by three times, the expansion will also be considered as new construction.

(2) Expansion refers to construction of new major production workshop, branch factory or independent production line within a factory or in other locations, for the purpose of increasing the production capacity (or improving efficiency) of the original products. Newly constructed houses for the operation of institutions and administrative organizations (such as the newly constructed buildings for teaching in schools, buildings for clinics or wards in hospitals, etc.) are also classified as expansion.

Also included in the expansion are investments by existing enterprises or institutions in building major production line(s) or branch factory(ies) along with some work on innovation, for the purpose of expending the production capacity of original products or producing new products.

(3) Reconstruction and technological reforms refers to construction projects by existing enterprises or institutions in innovation or technical transformation of the old facilities (including auxiliary production equipment and welfare facilities). Also considered as reconstruction is the construction of new workshops by the existing enterprises or institutions to change the variety of products to meet the market demand (such as the production of civil products by defense industries), or to bring the designed production capacity into full play through a more balanced production process on production lines. Technological reforms refer to the fact that enterprises and institutions, on an ongoing basis, replace outdated technology with advanced technology and replace backward process and equipment with advance ones, in order to change the outdated technology of the enterprises and improve the economic benefits while lowering the consumption of the energy. Technological reforms include the following contents: renovation of the machinery and tools, reform of production process, saving energy and raw materials, reform of plant buildings and public facilities, protection of the environment, and reform of the working conditions and environment.

(4) Simple construction of living facilities refers to facilities for living and welfare, such as residential buildings, nurseries, schools, medical rooms, bathrooms and canteens for the staff and workers, simply built by enterprises and institutions without expanding or reconstructing production projects or business buildings.

(5) Relocation: Enterprises and institutions relocate their plants to other places because of the change of production layout or for reasons of protecting the urban environment and safe production. During the construction of relocation to other places, the original or expanded scale of construction will be covered in the statistics.

(6) Restoration: Enterprises and institutions restore the construction with investment after all or part of their original fixed assets has been scrapped due to natural disasters and wars. Restoration to their original scale or any expansion will be covered as restored projects.

(7) Simple purchase: Existing enterprises, institutions and administrative units simply purchase equipment, tools and instruments that need not be installed or any construction. Although some units purchased some equipment in the previous year, there are some construction and installation in their design. These constructions should be determined to the contents of the design files, not being covered as simple purchase.

Newly Increased Fixed Assets

Newly Increased Fixed Assets, also called fixed assets put into operation, refers to the value of fixed assets that has been put into production or handed over to the production units after the completion of the process of construction and purchase. The newly increased fixed asset is a value indicator of the result of investment. It is also the necessary data for reflecting the construction process and the result of investment in fixed assets.

Rate of Fixed Assets Completed and Put into Operation

Rate of Fixed Assets Completed and Put into Operation, also called the fixed assets operation ratio, refers to ratio of newly increased fixed assets to total investment completed in the same period, which is a comprehensive indicator, reflecting the development of fixed assets investment and investment efficiency.

Projects under Construction

Projects under Construction refer to projects with construction and installation activities undertaken in the reference period. All projects that have construction activities undertaken during the reference period are reported as projects under construction irrespective of the length of construction work. The number of projects under construction can reflect the actual size of investment in fixed assets during a given period, and when compared with the number of projects completed and put into use during the same period, it demonstrates the results of investment in fixed assets. Depending on the nature of construction activities, projects under construction can also be classified into projects under construction in current year, winding-up projects in current year and stopped or suspended projects in previous years.

Projects Completely Put into Use

Industrial projects refer to the major projects and accessory facilities completed which result in forming production capacity and have been checked and accepted while the living and welfare facilities have been completed and can ensure normal production and formally put into production. Non-industrial projects refer to the major projects and accessory facilities completed which possess the designed capacity and have been checked, accepted and formally put into production.

第四篇

CHAPTER 4

招商引资

BUSINESS PROMOTION AND FOREIGN FUND ATTRACTION

表4-1　历年外商直接投资情况
(1990～2015)

年　份 Year	外商直接投资合同项目(项) Contracted Projects of Foreign Direct Investment(unit)	#中外合资 Joint-venture	中外合作 Sino-foreign Cooperative	外商独资 Solely Foreigner Funded
1990	28	22	2	4
1991	92	79	4	9
1992	567	467	38	56
1993	924	610	38	275
1994	1 035	547	51	432
1995	838	340	41	455
1996	802	285	38	479
1997	615	132	36	447
1998	554	88	30	435
1999	470	71	18	380
2000	693	109	21	563
2001	880	110	10	758
2002	964	119	14	829
2003	1 563	175	15	1 370
2004	1 688	188	9	1 489
2005	1 734	149	8	1 574
2006	1 446	143	7	1 292
2007	1 254	112	3	1 138
2008	803	90	3	710
2009	780	100	4	676
2010	906	140	1	765
2011	995	181	2	809
2012	976	207	2	763
2013	1 032	274	1	757
2014	2 185	262	4	1 551
2015	3 722	1 169	5	2 542

注：从2004年起，外商直接投资实际到位金额中不包含间接吸收外资。
Note: The actual paid amount of foreign direct investment will not include the indirectly-attracted foreign capital after the year of 2004.

Foreign Direct Investment

外商直接投资合同金额(亿美元) Contracted Value of Foreign Direct Investment (USD 100 million)				外商直接投资实际到位金额(亿美元) Capital in Place of Foreign Direct Investment (USD 100 million)
	#中外合资 Joint-venture	中外合作 Sino-foreign Cooperative	外商独资 Solely Foreigner Funded	
0.34	0.29	0.01	0.05	0.13
1.01	0.92	0.03	0.06	0.68
13.53	7.28	0.82	2.77	2.49
17.57	13.08	1.53	2.78	4.29
25.93	14.14	4.10	7.32	6.85
32.56	10.47	2.56	17.43	12.81
18.09	5.04	5.84	7.21	14.25
18.00	13.39	0.82	3.79	10.13
27.90	13.77	0.63	2.90	15.37
10.73	2.95	0.55	6.91	5.92
28.84	2.73	0.47	25.63	8.85
20.02	4.51	1.12	14.16	23.04
26.68	5.72	1.36	17.22	18.47
28.75	6.47	0.12	21.19	18.01
32.24	5.05	0.56	26.08	23.78
56.54	7.84	0.38	42.20	31.11
48.42	7.67	0.32	39.46	32.20
49.49	5.08	0.39	41.30	33.06
49.92	5.87	0.12	43.12	34.35
55.29	4.80	1.22	47.13	39.08
56.25	8.57	0.01	45.35	38.56
65.97	9.31	0.59	55.00	52.97
72.86	4.21	2.17	62.09	48.30
73.89	9.36	0.04	61.62	50.33
143.07	34.09	2.00	103.83	44.76
440.82	91.59	0.39	346.39	64.60

表4-2　外商直接投资合同项目

Number of Contracted Projects of Foreign Direct Investment

单位:个　　(unit)

指　标	Indicators	2005	2010	2014	2015	至2015年末累计 Accumulated by the End of 2015
总　计	**Total**	**1 734**	**906**	**2 185**	**3 722**	**27 563**
按投资方式分	**By Way of Investment**					
中外合资	Joint-venture	149	140	262	1 169	6 220
中外合作	Sino-foreign Cooperative	8	1	4	5	412
外商独资	Solely Foreigner Funded	1 574	765	1 551	2 541	20 466
外商投资股份制	Foreign investment shareholding system	3		4	7	51
按投资行业分	**By Sector**					
#第二产业	Secondary Industry	209	52	13	42	4 103
#工　业	Industry	188	46	11	26	3 468
第三产业	Tertiary Industry	1 524	854	2 170	3 679	23 431
#批发零售业	Wholesale and Retail	672	476	1 151	1 650	12 452
交通运输、仓储和邮政业	Transportation, Warehousing, Post and Telecommunications	18	20	19	36	847
房地产业	Real Estate	25	3	8	31	391
租赁和商务服务业	Leasing and Commercial Services	295	216	630	772	4 899
按投资国别、地区分	**By Country/Region**					
#中国香港	Hong Kong, China	307	301	890	1 827	9 040
中国澳门	Macao, China	2		9	10	84
中国台湾	Taiwan, China	82	62	214	288	1 829
日　本	Japan	270	101	88	117	2 995
新加坡	Singapore	107	52	99	181	1 565
韩　国	Republic of Korea	80	29	75	110	804
英　国	United Kingdom	35	15	45	78	515
德　国	Germany	52	27	56	86	760
法　国	France	26	10	34	47	284
荷　兰	the Netherlands	24	10	17	25	292
瑞　士	Switzerland	14	8	12	22	226
美　国	United States of America	146	87	183	223	2 817
加拿大	Canada	19	10	64	64	455
澳大利亚	Australia	22	8	56	84	453
海外中资集团	Overseas Chinese Group Companies					

注：当年增资部分不计算项目个数。
Note: The increase of investment in the current year is not listed as new project.

表4-3 外商直接投资合同金额
Contract Value of Foreign Direct Investment

单位:万美元 (USD 10 000)

指 标	Indicators	2005	2010	2014	2015	至2015年末累计 Accumulated by the End of 2015
总 计	**Total**	**565 369**	**562 487**	**1 430 736**	**4 408 231**	**13 626 887**
按投资方式分	**By Way of Investment**					
中外合资	Joint-venture	78 437	85 679	340 876	915 887	2 722 689
中外合作	Sino-foreign Cooperative	3 771	122	20 028	3 865	199 631
外商独资	Solely Foreigner Funded	421 985	453 504	1 052 927	3 463 917	10 285 656
外商投资股份制	Foreign investment shareholding system	61 176	23 182	16 905	24 562	418 911
按投资行业分	**By Sector**					
#第二产业	Secondary Industry	172 056	98 697	21 701	138 919	2 249 794
#工 业	Industry	162 312	95 872	21 029	130 929	1 762 973
第三产业	Tertiary Industry	393 242	463 790	1 408 388	4 266 056	11 370 880
#批发零售业	Wholesale and Retail	61 919	90 922	324 744	509 728	1 037 112
交通运输、仓储和邮政业	Transportation, Warehousing, Post and Telecommunications	114 776	18 896	20 477	28 469	607 144
房地产业	Real Estate	49 390	100 310	26 269	201 154	369 699
租赁和商务服务业	Leasing and Business Service	114 149	163 058	352 719	542 770	1 330 536
按投资国别、地区分	**By Country/Region**					
#中国香港	Hong Kong, China	68 253	200 809	880 058	3 415 746	6 498 857
中国澳门	Macao, China	68		18 008	5 888	32 417
中国台湾	Taiwan, China	2 795	2 936	35 160	39 515	158 007
日 本	Japan	69 789	49 831	39 496	35 934	914 556
新加坡	Singapore	18 363	30 632	98 513	187 760	760 977
韩 国	Republic of Korea	5 438	4 463	4 636	28 608	126 195
英 国	United Kingdom	6 245	10 809	3 628	30 319	150 384
德 国	Germany	54 020	9 016	13 031	12 006	236 042
法 国	France	2 531	21 750	34 366	17 045	183 181
荷 兰	the Netherlands	8 424	9 744	13 770	21 175	271 886
瑞 士	Switzerland	1 340	1 037	1 889	12 376	71 397
美 国	United States of America	41 169	21 172	76 684	143 213	961 387
加拿大	Canada	1 101	-92	7 416	13 483	46 443
澳大利亚	Australia	787	1 024	10 796	8 942	42 043
海外中资集团	Overseas Chinese Group Companies					20 657

表4-4 当年签约投资1.5亿美元以上的外商投资企业

FIEs with Current Year Contracted Investment Over USD 150 Million (2015)

单位:万美元 (USD 10 000)

序号 No.	指标 Indicators		国别(地区) Country/Region	总投资 Total Investment	外商合同投资 Contracted Foreign Investment
1	上海旭泾置业有限公司	Shanghai Xu Jing Real Estate Co. Ltd.	香港 HongKong	119 335	68 658
2	上海华新置业有限公司	Shanghai Hua Xin Real Estate Co. Ltd.	新加坡 Singapore	40 634	36 717
3	上海远汇置业有限公司	Shanghai Yuan Hui Real Estate Co. Ltd.	香港 HongKong	71 725	35 863
4	微创(上海)医疗科学投资有限公司	MicroPort (Shanghai) Investment Co. Ltd.	开曼群岛 Cayman Islands	34 480	34 480
5	上海华虹宏力半导体制造有限公司	Shanghai Huahong Grace Semiconductor Manufacturing Co. Ltd.	香港 HongKong	32 081	32 081
6	诺亚(上海)融资租赁有限公司	Noah (Shanghai) Financial Leasing Co. Ltd.	香港 HongKong	30 000	30 000
7	普新投资(上海)有限公司	Pu Xin Investment (Shanghai) Co. Ltd.	新加坡 Singapore	30 000	30 000
8	上海百轶融资租赁有限公司	Shanghai Baiyi Financial Leasing Co. Ltd.	香港 HongKong	30 000	30 000
9	口碑(上海)信息技术有限公司	Koubei (Shanghai) Information Technology Co. Ltd.	香港 HongKong	29 500	29 500
10	伊丰(中国)融资租赁有限公司	Yifeng (China) Financial Leasing Co. Ltd.	香港 HongKong	28 800	28 800
11	芯鑫融资租赁有限责任公司	Xinxin Financial Leasing Co. Ltd.	开曼群岛 Cayman Islands	91 613	27 097
12	佳腾(中国)融资租赁有限公司	Jiateng (China) Financial Leasing Co. Ltd.	香港 HongKong	26 000	26 000
13	携程旅游信息技术(上海)有限公司	Ctrip Information Technology (Shanghai) Co. Ltd.	香港 HongKong	28 660	25 777
14	知典融资租赁(上海)有限公司	Zhidian Financial Leasing (Shanghai) Co. Ltd.	香港 HongKong	25 631	25 631
15	纽海信息技术(上海)有限公司	Niuhai Information Technology (Shanghai) Co. Ltd.	香港 HongKong	75 900	25 300
16	上海惠苑管理咨询有限公司	Shanghai Huiyuan Management Consulting Co. Ltd.	香港 HongKong	34 800	24 900
17	远东国际租赁有限公司	Far East Learsing Co. Ltd.	香港 HongKong	24 900	24 900
18	上海光明荷斯坦牧业有限公司	Shanghai Guangming Holstan Co. Ltd.	英属维尔京群岛 Britishi Virgin Islands	27 386	24 859
19	上海睿戈投资管理有限公司	Shanghai Ruige Investment & Management Co. Ltd.	香港 HongKong	24 421	24 421
20	巨亿融资租赁(上海)有限公司	Ju Yi Financial Leasing (Shanghai) Co. Ltd.	香港 HongKong	24 400	24 400
21	空气化工产品(中国)投资有限公司	Air Products and Chemicals (China) Investment Co. Ltd.	美国 USA	23 932	23 932
22	彩虹桥(中国)融资租赁有限公司	Rainbow Bridge (China) Financial Leasing Co. Ltd.	香港 HongKong	20 000	20 000
23	东方融资租赁(上海)有限公司	Dongfang Financial Leasing (Shanghai) Co. Ltd.	英属维尔京群岛 Britishi Virgin Islands	20 000	20 000
24	广源鑫融资租赁(上海)有限公司	Guan Yuan Xin Financial Leasing (Shanghai) Co. Ltd.	香港 HongKong	20 000	20 000
25	国信锦城融资租赁有限公司	Guoxin Jingcheng Financial Leasing Co. Ltd.	香港 HongKong	20 000	20 000

单位:万美元　　表 4-4　续表　Continued　　(USD 10 000)

序号 No.	指标 Indicators		国别(地区) Country/Region	总投资 Total Investment	外商合同投资 Contracted Foreign Investment
26	万通凯普达(上海)供应链管理有限公司	Wantong Kaipuda (Shanghai) Supply Chain Management Co. Ltd.	美国 USA	20 000	20 000
27	芯飞跃(中国)融资租赁有限公司	Xin Fei Yue (China) Financial Leasing Co. Ltd.	香港 HongKong	20 000	20 000
28	达疆网络科技(上海)有限公司	Dajiang Network Technology (Shanghai) Co. Ltd.	香港 HongKong	40 512	19 900
29	国森融资租赁(上海)有限公司	Guosen Financial Leasing (Shanghai) Co. Ltd.	香港 HongKong	19 520	19 520
30	上海中城聚鋆投资管理有限公司	Shanghai Zhongcheng Juyun Investment & Management Co. Ltd.	香港 HongKong	29 900	18 500
31	联君融资租赁(上海)有限公司	Lianjun Financial Leasing (Shanghai) Co. Ltd.	香港 HongKong	17 796	17 796
32	福特汽车金融(中国)有限公司	Ford Automative Finance (China) Co. Ltd.	美国 USA	17 502	17 502
33	兴邦融资租赁(上海)有限公司	Xinbang Financial Leasing (Shanghai) Co. Ltd.	香港 HongKong	17 420	17 420
34	乾港融资租赁(上海)有限公司	Qiangang Financial Leasing (Shanghai) Co. Ltd.	香港 HongKong	17 405	17 405
35	上海海智融资租赁有限公司	Shanghai Haizhi Financial Leasing Co. Ltd.	香港 HongKong	17 080	17 080
36	港能国际融资租赁有限公司	China LNG Finance Leasing Co. Ltd.	香港 HongKong	16 500	16 500
37	立远融资租赁有限公司	Liyuan Financial Leasing Co. Ltd.	香港 HongKong	16 357	16 357
38	上海彩曼融资租赁有限公司	Shanghai Caiman Financial Leasing Co. Ltd.	香港 HongKong	16 357	16 357
39	上海信迪融资租赁有限公司	Shanghai Xindi Financial Leasing Co. Ltd.	美国 USA	19 119	16 347
40	显鹤融资租赁(上海)有限公司	Xianhe Financial Leasing (Shanghai) Co. Ltd.	香港 HongKong	16 309	16 309
41	保雅(中国)融资租赁有限公司	Baoya (China) Financial Leasing Co. Ltd.	香港 HongKong	16 281	16 281
42	恩福融资租赁有限公司	Enfu Financial Leasing Co. Ltd.	香港 HongKong	16 271	16 271
43	杉圭(上海)融资租赁有限公司	Shangui (Shanghai) Financial Leasing Co. Ltd.	香港 HongKong	16 267	16 267
44	漓江有色金属有限公司	Lijiang Nonferrous Metals Co. Ltd.	香港 HongKong	16 129	16 129
45	美柏(上海)投资有限公司	Meibo (Shanghai) Investment Co. Ltd.	香港 HongKong	16 129	16 129
46	启风融资租赁(上海)有限公司	Qifeng Financial Leasing (Shanghai) Co. Ltd.	香港 HongKong	16 129	16 129
47	珠江石油化工有限公司	Zhujiang Petrochemical Co. Ltd.	香港 HongKong	16 129	16 129
48	纽世投资管理(上海)有限公司	Niushi Investment & Management (Shanghai) Co. Ltd.	韩国 Korea	16 000	16 000
49	沃尔沃建筑设备投资(中国)有限公司	Volvoce Construction Equipment Investemnt (China) Co. Ltd.	瑞典 Sweden	21 821	15 804
50	上海悦耀置业发展有限公司	Shanghai Yueyao Real Estate Development Co. Ltd.	香港 HongKong	53 713	15 221
51	夏普商贸(中国)有限公司	Sharp Commerce & Trade (China) Co. Ltd.	日本 Japan	70 320	15 096
52	莫仕(中国)投资有限公司	Molex (China) Investment Co. Ltd.	新加坡 Singapore	15 064	15 064

表 4-5 外商直接投资实际到位金额
Capital in Place of Foreign Direct Investment

单位:万美元 (USD 10 000)

指 标	Indicators	2010	2014	2015
总 计	**Total**	**385 567**	**447 577**	**646 002**
按投资方式分	**By Way of Investment**			
#中外合资	Joint-venture	59 492	63 768	108 421
中外合作	Sino-foreign Cooperative	836	72 683	32 171
外商独资	Solely Foreigner Funded	325 239	310 144	503 734
按投资行业分	**By Sector**			
#第二产业	Secondary Industry	50 926	29 143	93 470
#工 业	Industry	48 603	28 692	92 862
第三产业	Tertiary Industry	334 516	418 436	552 532
#批发和零售业餐饮业	Wholesale and Retail Catering	64 727	59 825	65 918
房地产业	Real Estate	64 706	57 573	103 396
租赁和商务服务业	Leasing and Business Service	118 916	90 105	146 909
按投资国别、地区分	**By Country/Region**			
#中国香港	Hong Kong, China	116 495	185 321	331 171
日 本	Japan	37 506	27 903	5 062
新加坡	Singapore	61 672	20 133	143 996
英 国	United Kingdom	4 632	1 811	699
德 国	Germany	8 738	12 740	3 365
法 国	France	14 871	5 454	7 472
荷 兰	the Netherlands	27 020	7 829	9 244
开曼群岛	Cayman Islands	12 702	982	5 894
英属维尔京群岛	British Virgin Islands	17 901	39 742	31 410
美 国	United States of America	21 956	94 518	69 804
萨摩亚	Samoa	1 358	2 795	720

表4-6 内资企业工商注册情况
Registered Domestic Enterprises

指 标	Indicators	单 位 Unit	2014	2015
期末实有注册企业	**Actual Registered Enterprises at End of Term**	**个 unit**	**13 271**	**15 075**
第一产业	Primary Industry	个 unit	146	145
第二产业	Secondary Industry	个 unit	2 361	2 326
#制造业	Manufacturing	个 unit	1 861	1 817
建筑业	Construction	个 unit	442	452
第三产业	Tertiary Industry	个 unit	10 764	12 604
#交通运输、仓储和邮政业	Transportation, Warehousing and Post Service	个 unit	580	653
批发和零售业	Wholesale and Retail	个 unit	3 676	4 013
金融业	Banking	个 unit	417	609
房地产业	Real Estate	个 unit	926	939
期末实际注册资金总额	**Total of Actual Registered Capital at End of Term**	**亿元（100 million yuan）**	**12 614.66**	**16 272.22**
第一产业	Primary Industry	亿元（100 million yuan）	27.16	26.91
第二产业	Secondary Industry	亿元（100 million yuan）	2 485.07	2 827.03
#制造业	Manufacturing	亿元（100 million yuan）	1 516.15	1 761.57
建筑业	Construction	亿元（100 million yuan）	716.84	813.13
第三产业	Tertiary Industry	亿元（100 million yuan）	10 102.43	13 418.29
#交通运输、仓储和邮政业	Transportation, Warehousing and Post Service	亿元（100 million yuan）	1 052.98	1 237.94
批发和零售业	Wholesale and Retail	亿元（100 million yuan）	1 147.76	1 577.30
金融业	Banking	亿元（100 million yuan）	1 121.62	1 652.08
房地产业	Real Estate	亿元（100 million yuan）	1 204.57	1 364.69

注：内资注册数和注册资本含市局登记，不含分支机构。
Note: The number of domestic registered enterprises and that of registered capital included those registered in Shanghai municipal bureaus and excluded those registered in branch bureaus.

表4-7　私营企业基本情况
Statistics of Private Enterprises

指　标	Indicators	户　数（户）Number of Enterprises (unit)		注册资金（亿元）Registered Capital (100 million yuan)	
		2014	2015	2014	2015
总　计	**Total**	**142 104**	**187 898**	**12 880.02**	**25 589.68**
农、林、牧、渔业	Farming, Forestry, Animal Husbandry and Fishery	827	856	17.64	20.74
采掘业	Mining and Quarrying	4	5	1.31	1.36
制造业	Manufacturing	17 164	17 070	433.29	482.63
建筑业	Construction	4 820	5 946	297.20	412.52
交通运输业、仓储和邮政业	Transportation, Warehousing and Post Service	5 066	5 738	243.20	330.07
信息传输、计算机服务	Information Transmission and Computer Service	4 908	7 743	282.67	526.34
批发零售贸易业	Wholesale and Retail	52 711	69 328	2224.72	3582.56
住宿和餐饮业	Accommodation and Catering	2 066	2 443	18.02	25.65
居民服务和其他服务业	Resident Service and Other Services	3 101	3 294	47.23	56.42
房地产	Real Estate	2 814	3 073	563.48	638.05
其　他	Others	48 623	72 402	8 751.26	19 513.34

表4-8 个体工商户基本情况
Self-employment Business

指　标	Indicators	户　数（户）Number of Enterprises (unit)		注册资金（万元）Registered Capital (10 000 yuan)	
		2014	2015	2014	2015
总　计	**Total**	**75 727**	**78 760**	**214 253**	**246 731**
农、林、牧、渔	Farming, Forestry, Animal Husbandry and Fishery	517	525	3 170	3 212
制造业	Manufacturing	1 737	1 778	5 365	5 751
建筑业	Construction	91	93	345	372
交通运输业、仓储业	Transportation and Warehousing	569	621	3 928	4 848
批发零售贸易业、住宿和餐饮业	Wholesale, Retail and Catering Businesses	64 374	66 981	175 542	197 514
批发零售贸易业	Wholesale and Retail	60 558	62 648	160 015	177 835
住宿和餐饮业	Accommodation and Catering	3 816	4 333	15 527	19 679
居民服务和其他服务业	Resident Service and Other Services	7 388	7 691	21 859	30 779
其　他	Others	1 051	1 071	4 044	4 255

主要统计指标解释

外商直接投资

外商直接投资是指外国企业和经济组织或个人(包括华侨、港澳台胞以及我国在境外注册的企业)按我国有关政策、法规,用现汇、实物、技术等在我国境内开办外商独资企业、与我国境内的企业或经济组织共同举办中外合资经营企业、合作经营企业或合作开发资源的投资(包括外商投资收益的再投资)以及企业投资总额内直接投资者对企业的贷款,即外方股东贷款(需在报告期内将相应合同及贷款协议报商务部备案核查)。

合同投资额

是指经有关部门批准的我方与外商正式签订的合同规定的可使用的贷款额、外商投资额和中方对外发行债券、股票总值,以及"补偿贸易"外商提供的设备价款,"国际租赁"境外出租人提供的设备等价款总值。

外商实际投资额

是指按合同(章程)规定,外商以现金、实物及专有技术等工业产权计价的全部实缴资本额,包括经有关部门批准,外商用于扩大再生产、发展企业规模或补充基本建设资金不足而投入的追加资金。外商的实缴资本额一律折成美元计算。

EXPLANATORY NOTES TO MAJOR STATISTICAL INDICATORS

Foreign Direct Investment

Foreign Direct Investment refers to the investments made inside China by foreign enterprises and economic organizations or individuals (including overseas Chinese, compatriots in Hong Kong, Macao and Chinese enterprises registered abroad), in line with the relevant policies and laws of China, for the establishment of wholly foreign-owned enterprises, and joint ventures or development projects launched in China (including re-investment of profits from foreign businesses), and the funds that enterprises borrow from abroad in the total investment of projects which are approved by the relevant departments of the governments and the loans from the direct investors within the total investment of the projects, i. e. foreign shareholders' loans. (The related contracts and loans agreements in the report period should be filed with the Ministry of Commerce.)

Agreed (Contracted) Investment

Agreed (Contracted) Investment includes usable loans which are approved by government departments and with contracts signed formally by Chinese units and foreign investors, investment of foreigners, total value of bonds and stocks issued in international market by Chinese units, the value of equipment provided by foreign investors for compensation trade, the value of equipment which are leased from foreign firms, etc.

Actual Investment of Foreign Investors

Actual Investment of Foreign Investors refers to all foreign investors paid-in capital, in cash, in kind or in special technique, based on contracts, which includes the additional funds used for extensional reproduction, expanding enterprise scale or complements to capital construction. All the foreigners paid-in capital is measured by or converted to US dollars.

第五篇

CHAPTER 5

农 业

AGRICULTURE

表5-1 主要年份农村户数、人口和劳动力
Rural Households, Population and Workforce in Main Years

指 标	Indicators	单 位 Unit	1990	2000	2005	2010	2014	2015
户 数	Household	万户 10 000 households	15.74	13.67	12.67	32.90	31.20	29.80
人 口	Population	万人 10 000 persons	47.00	36.82	35.57	82.96	75.61	72.73
劳动力使用	Workforce	万人 10 000 persons	27.70	19.86	19.66	48.70	45.30	43.60
第一产业	Primary Industry	万人 10 000 persons	6.83	4.04	1.67	10.62	8.68	8.21
第二产业	Secondary Industry	万人 10 000 persons	14.91	8.98	11.53	25.95	26.72	26.03
第三产业	Tertiary Industry	万人 10 000 persons	5.96	6.83	6.46	12.13	9.90	9.36
外省市流入劳动力	Migrant Workforce from Other Provinces	万人 10 000 persons	1.53	9.13	26.52	65.32	67.75	64.82
第一产业	Primary Industry	万人 10 000 persons	0.28	1.47	1.65	4.08	3.91	3.32
第二产业	Secondary Industry	万人 10 000 persons	1.18	5.27	18.44	43.32	42.75	41.80
第三产业	Tertiary Industry	万人 10 000 persons	0.06	2.38	6.43	17.92	21.09	19.70

注：表中涉及的户数、人口和劳动力是指居住在农村地区的本市户籍常住户数和人口。
Note: The numbers of households, population and labor force involved in this table are referred to those live in the rural area of Shanghai.

表5-2 各镇耕地面积
Cultivated Area by Town

单位:公顷 (hectare)

镇 Town		2014年末耕地面积 Cultivated Area (End of 2014)	2015年净减少耕地面积 Net Decrease in Cultivated Area in 2015	2015年末耕地面积 Cultivated Area (End of 2015)	水田 Paddy Field	水浇地 Irrigated Land
川沙新镇	Chuansha New Town	1 749.9	1.4	1 748.5	1 654.0	94.5
高桥镇	Gaoqiao Town	430.4	89.9	340.5		340.5
北蔡镇	Beicai Town	146.0		146.0		146.0
合庆镇	Heqing Town	798.9	2.5	796.4	727.2	69.2
唐镇	Tangzhen Town	175.3	0.2	175.1	7.9	167.2
曹路镇	Caolu Town	524.1	14.0	510.1	510.1	
金桥镇	Jinqiao Town	24.8		24.8	24.8	
高行镇	Gaohang Town	2.3		2.3		2.3
高东镇	Gaodong Town	251.4	5.8	245.6		245.6
张江镇	Zhangjiang Town	211.0		211.0	211.0	
三林镇	Sanlin Town	247.0		247.0		247.0
惠南镇	Huinan Town	1 562.2	-53.4	1 615.6	1 615.6	
周浦镇	Zhoupu Town	571.8	74.1	497.7	422.6	75.1
新场镇	Xinchang Town	2 270.0	99.8	2 170.2	1 027.7	1 142.5
大团镇	Datuan Town	1 334.2	-4.1	1 338.3	1 155.0	183.3
康桥镇	Kangqiao Town	229.7	16.2	213.5	55.8	157.7
航头镇	Hangtou Town	1 755.4	-16.7	1 772.1	1 087.9	684.2
祝桥镇	Zhuqiao Town	2 697.0	-30.4	2 727.4	2 071.4	656.0
泥城镇	Nicheng Town	1 861.6		1 861.6	1 401.6	460.0
宣桥镇	Xuanqiao Town	1 898.2	-6.0	1 904.2	1 082.7	821.5
书院镇	Shuyuan Town	2 453.4	66.8	2 386.6	2 226.6	160.0
万祥镇	Wanxiang Town	922.5	-2.3	924.8	848.5	76.3
老港镇	Laogang Town	1 745.2	0.5	1 744.7	599.5	1 145.2
南汇新城镇	Nanhui New Town	2 533.3		2 533.3	1 627.6	905.7
农场	Farm	26.1		26.1	26.1	
棉种场	Cotton Farm	23.5		23.5	23.5	

注：2013年始批准数指标取消，现各镇反映的数据均为实际经营数。后续相关指标口径相同。

Note: Since 2013, the authorized indicators of cultivated area are cancelled, so the numbers of each town all represent the real operating ones. The same principle goes on in this book.

表5-3　主要年份耕地面积增减情况
Increase and Decrease of Cultivated Land in Main Years

单位:公顷　　(hectare)

指　标 Indicators		2005	2010	2014	2015
年初耕地面积	Cultivated Area (Year Beginning)	9 483	44 001	21 415	20 887
年末耕地面积	Cultivated Area (Year Ended)	8 849	43 551	20 887	20 628
当年减少	Decrease in Current Year	634	450	528	259

注：2013 年起批准数指标取消,为实际经营数。
Note: Since 2013, the authorized indicators of cultivated area are cancelled, so the numbers all represent the real operating ones.

表5-4　主要年份农业总产值
Gross Output Value of Agriculture in Main Years

单位:万元　　(10 000 yuan)

指　标 Indicators		1990	2000	2005	2010	2014	2015
按当年价格计算	**Calculated in Current Year**						
总　计	**Total**	**55 318**	**125 732**	**116 248**	**698 552**	**650 962**	**594 356**
种植业	Planting	24 015	59 584	66 809	396 127	372 813	351 081
林　业	Forestry	234	1 279	25 424	10 420	19 609	23 310
牧　业	Animal Husbandry	29 528	60 837	19 488	183 084	139 810	114 453
渔　业	Fishery	1 541	4 032	4 527	70 921	77 650	68 382
农、林、牧、渔服务业	Agriculture, forestry, animal husbandry and fishery			38 000	38 500	41 080	37 130
构　成(%)	**Composition (%)**						
总　计	**Total**	**100.0**	**100.0**	**100.0**	**100.0**	**100.0**	**100.0**
种植业	Planting	43.4	47.4	57.5	56.7	57.3	59.1
林　业	Forestry	0.4	1.0	21.9	1.5	3.0	3.9
牧　业	Animal Husbandry	53.4	48.4	16.8	26.2	21.5	19.3
渔　业	Fishery	2.8	3.2	3.8	10.2	11.9	11.5
农、林、牧、渔服务业	Agriculture, forestry, animal husbandry and fishery				5.4	6.3	6.2

表5-5 各镇农业总产值
Gross Output Value of Agriculture by Town
(2015)

单位:万元 (10 000 yuan)

指 标	Indicators	农业总产值(按现行价格计算) Gross Output Value of Agriculture (at Current Price)	#种植业 Planting	林 业 Forestry	牧 业 Animal Husbandry	渔 业 Fishery
总 计	**Total**	**594 356**	**351 081**	**23 310**	**114 453**	**68 382**
川沙新镇	Chuansha New Town	40 628	21 844	3 559	11 257	1 468
高桥镇	Gaoqiao Town	1 379	1 330			49
北蔡镇	Beicai Town	439	379			60
合庆镇	Heqing Town	9 931	6 457		3 209	265
唐 镇	Tangzhen Town	1 227	1 057	78		92
曹路镇	Caolu Town	32 110	14 432	643	16 816	159
金桥镇	Jinqiao Town	36		36		
高行镇	Gaohang Town					
高东镇	Gaodong Town	1 871	1 816			55
张江镇	Zhangjiang Town	4 566	4 293	111		162
三林镇	Sanlin Town	3 332	1 287	250		138
惠南镇	Huinan Town	18 987	13 541		3 461	1 985
周浦镇	Zhoupu Town	11 604	9 352		1 646	606
新场镇	Xinchang Town	59 144	45 496		9 805	3 843
大团镇	Datuan Town	44 734	31 363		11 015	2 356
康桥镇	Kangqiao Town	3 275	3 126		149	
航头镇	Hangtou Town	40 392	20 961	2 214	16 005	1 212
祝桥镇	Zhuqiao Town	64 175	49 410		10 303	4 462
泥城镇	Nicheng Town	40 804	30 395	718	980	8 188
宣桥镇	Xuanqiao Town	10 170	5 295		4 196	679
书院镇	Shuyuan Town	35 720	24 650	5	6 748	4 317
万祥镇	Wanxiang Town	14 249	9 181		2 644	2 424
老港镇	Laogang Town	40 271	25 635		11 528	3 108
南汇新城镇	Nanhui New Town	26 294	18 836		968	6 490
其 他	Others	89 018	10 945	15 696	3 723	26 264

表5-6 各镇粮食和蔬菜作物播种面积和产量
Sown Area and Output of Grain Crops and Vegetables by Town
(2015)

指 标	Indicators	粮食播种面积（公顷）Sown Area (hectare)	粮食总产量（吨）Total Output of Grain Crops (ton)	夏粮 Summer Harvested	秋粮 Autumn Harvested	粮食单位面积产量（千克/公顷）Yield Per Unit (kg/hectare)	蔬菜播种面积（公顷）Sown Area of Vegetables (hectare)	蔬菜总产量（吨）Total Output of Vegetables (ton)
总 计	**Total**	**20 768.3**	**151 680**	**31 170**	**120 510**	**7 303**	**21 163.0**	**698 700**
川沙新镇	Chuansha New Town	743.0	5 943	764	5 179	7 999	1 559.6	45 553
高桥镇	Gaoqiao Town						198.6	3 735
北蔡镇	Beicai Town						115.4	1 351
合庆镇	Heqing Town	162.9	1 206	326	880	7 403	471.8	17 165
唐镇	Tangzhen Town	18.5	122	54	68	6 595	64.0	1 384
曹路镇	Caolu Town	156.0	1 259	376	883	8 071	989.9	33 602
金桥镇	Jinqiao Town							
高行镇	Gaohang Town							
高东镇	Gaodong Town						214.9	3 302
张江镇	Zhangjiang Town	109.0	775	248	527	7 110	117.7	3 354
三林镇	Sanlin Town						113.6	3 189
惠南镇	Huinan Town	960.0	7 502	1 743	5 759	7 815	840.5	23 123
周浦镇	Zhoupu Town	535.5	3 657	1 000	2 657	6 829	500.9	12 521
新场镇	Xinchang Town	950.1	7 336	1 111	6 225	7 721	2 573.1	71 952
大团镇	Datuan Town	1 192.8	9 084	1 447	7 637	7 616	728.5	34 154
康桥镇	Kangqiao Town	122.7	827	239	588	6 740	355.7	9 425
航头镇	Hangtou Town	792.9	6 137	837	5 300	7 740	1 719.7	60 680
祝桥镇	Zhuqiao Town	1 972.7	13 738	2 971	10 767	6 964	3 585.1	186 840
泥城镇	Nicheng Town	1 611.8	12 552	2 623	9 929	7 788	2 317.3	56 287
宣桥镇	Xuanqiao Town	374.1	3 072	393	2 679	8 212	2 024.1	40 944
书院镇	Shuyuan Town	2 052.5	14 552	3 444	11 108	7 090	814.1	36 602
万祥镇	Wanxiang Town	904.6	6 681	1 310	5 371	7 386	536.4	16 141
老港镇	Laogang Town	3 175.7	22 325	3 651	18 674	7 030	833.7	25 563
南汇新城镇	Nanhui New Town	4 933.5	34 912	8 633	26 279	7 077	488.4	11 833

表5－7 主要农产品产量
Output of Main Agricultural Products

指 标	Indicators	单 位 Unit	2005	2010	2014	2015
粮食作物	Grain Crops	吨 ton	13 671	148 707	132 657	151 680
夏熟作物	Summer Harvested	吨 ton	1 303	27 147	24 321	31 170
#小 麦	Wheat	吨 ton	1 064	20 291	17 059	24 999
秋熟作物	Autumn Harvested	吨 ton	12 368	121 560	108 336	120 510
#单季晚稻	Single-season Late Harvested Rice	吨 ton	10 580	116 437	105 299	118 561
油菜籽	Rapeseed	吨 ton	89	2 315	2 042	1 249
蔬 菜	Vegetables	万吨 10 000 tons	30	81	80	72
西甜瓜	Watermelons	万吨 10 000 tons	2	23	10	9
水果产量	Output of Fruits	吨 ton	4 219	108 714	76 068	59 557
#柑 桔	Mandarin Oranges	吨 ton	607	56 543	19 023	11 870
生 梨	Pears	吨 ton	274	7 829	9 961	6 224
葡 萄	Grapes	吨 ton	727	4 304	9 243	8 862
桃 子	Peaches	吨 ton		39 153	36 578	31 200
生猪饲养数	Stock of Hogs	万头 10 000 in number	16.72	96.61	90.96	70.04
生猪出栏数	Hogs on Market	万头 10 000 in number	8.80	56.36	51.71	40.68
猪肉产量	Pork Output	万吨 10 000 tons	0.77	3.66	4.42	3.09
牛奶产量	Milk Output	万吨 10 000 tons	1.27	4.43	3.70	3.38
家禽出栏数	Poultry on Market	万羽 10 000 in number	24.28	1 913.32	679.09	375.38
鲜蛋产量	Output of Fresh Eggs	万吨 10 000 tons	0.17	2.26	1.82	1.40
水产品产量	Output of Aquatic Products	万吨 10 000 tons	0.23	2.16	2.14	2.02
海水产品	Sea Products	万吨 10 000 tons		0.32	0.10	0.10
淡水产品	Fresh Water Products	万吨 10 000 tons	0.23	1.84	2.04	1.92

表5-8　种源农业生产、销售情况
Seed Agriculture Production and Selling
(2015)

指　标	Indicators	单　位 Unit	生　产 Production	自产自用 For Self-use	销　售 Sales
总　计	**Total**	**万元 10 000 yuan**	**20 347**	**14 578**	**5 769**
农业(种植业)	**Agriculture(Crop Farming)**	**万元 10 000 yuan**	**986**	**117**	**869**
#粮食种籽	Grain Seed	吨 ton	843	582	261
金　额	Amount	万元 10 000 yuan	126	59	67
蔬菜种籽	Vegetable Seed	公斤 kilogram	25 600	7 595	18 005
金　额	Amount	万元 10 000 yuan	617	10	607
食用菌种	Eatable Mushroom Seed	万元 10 000 yuan	29	11	18
花卉种苗	Flower Seed	万枝 10 000 unit	1 350	305	1 045
金　额	Amount	万元 10 000 yuan	213	36	177
林　业	**Forestry**	**万元 10 000 yuan**	**537**	**45**	**492**
#树　苗	Sapling	百棵 100 unit	13 552	1 361	12 191
金　额	Amount	万元 10 000 yuan	537	45	492
畜牧业	**Animal Husbandry**	**万元 10 000 yuan**	**17 529**	**13 795**	**3 734**
#苗　猪	Procreating Boar	只 unit	239 806	206 152	33 654
金　额	Amount	万元 10 000 yuan	16 412	12 799	3 613
苗　禽	Procreating Bird	万只 10 000 unit	220	210	10
金　额	Amount	万元 10 000 yuan	580	550	30
种　蛋	Procreating Egg	万只 10 000 unit	412	400	12
金　额	Amount	万元 10 000 yuan	482	408	74
羊　羔	Procreating Sheep	只 unit	1 961	1 023	938
金　额	Amount	万元 10 000 yuan	55	38	17
渔　业	**Fishing**	**万元 10 000 yuan**	**1 295**	**621**	**674**
#鱼　苗	Procreating Fish	万尾 10 000 unit	144	88	56
金　额	Amount	万元 10 000 yuan	122	71	51
鳗　苗	Procreating Eel	万尾 10 000 unit	37		37
金　额	Amount	万元 10 000 yuan	363		363

表5-9 浦东新区特色农业发展情况
The Development of Characteristic Agriculture in Pudong New Area

指 标 Indicators		单 位 Unit	2014	2015
农业组织化	**Organised Agriculture**			
农业产业化龙头企业	Top Enterprises of Agriculture Industrialization	个 in number	53	60
家庭农场	Home Farming	个 in number	271	446
农业品牌	**Famous Brand in Agriculture**			
中国驰名商标	Famous Brand in China	个 in number	1	1
市名牌产品	Famous Municipal Product	个 in number	16	20
市著名商标	Famous Municipal Brand	个 in number	21	23
农业科技	**Agro-technology**			
国家级项目	National Project	个 in number	17	
市级项目	Municipal Project	个 in number	34	7
农业设施化、标准化	**Agriculture Standardlization**			
设施粮田面积	Facilitated Grain Land Area	公顷 hectare	5 509.8	5 466.7
设施菜地面积	Facilitated Vegetable Land Area	公顷 hectare	4 650	1 440
设施果园面积	Facilitated Fruit Land Area	公顷 hectare	723.7	1 333.3
标准化畜禽养殖场	Standardlized Livestock Farm	个 in number	41	41
标准化水产养殖场	Standardlized Fishing Lake	个 in number	22	19
农产品认证	**Agricultural product certification**			
“三品一标”认证覆盖率	The Coverage of Harmless Agro-product, Green Food, Organic Agro-product, and Agro-product with Geographical Indications	%	73.4	70.0
无公害农产品认证企业数	Enterprises with Identified Harmless Agro-product	个 in number	400	409
绿色食品认证企业数	Enterprises with Identified Green Food	个 in number	19	20
有机农产品认证企业数	Enterprises with Identified Organic Agro – product	个 in number	9	11
农业旅游	**Agro-tourism**			
旅游景点	Travel Spot	个 in number	42	42
接待人次	Number of Tourists	万人 10 thousand	420	425

表5-10 农业机械拥有量
Farm Machinery Holding

指 标	Indicators	单 位 Unit	2010	2014	2015
农业机械总动力	**Total Power of Farm Machinery**	**千瓦 kw**	**112 420**	**144 525**	**153 409**
耕作机械动力合计	Total Power of Farm Machinery	千瓦 kw	46 605	60 822	66 772
大、中型拖拉机	Large/Medium Tractors	台 set	925	1 319	1 429
小型拖拉机	Walking Tractors	台 set	938	583	577
排灌机械动力	Total Power of Drainage and Irrigation Machinery	千瓦 kw	15 603	18 506	18 431
种植机械动力	Total Power of Cultivation	千瓦 kw	2 897	5 200	6 460
植物保护机械动力	Total Power of Crop Protection Machinery	千瓦 kw	6 141	8 410	8 931
#机动喷雾器	Motorized Sprayers	台 set	2 043	2 826	3 129
		千瓦 kw	6 052	8 410	8 931
收获机械动力合计	Total Power of Harvest Machinery	千瓦 kw	14 293	19 671	24 327
#联合收割机	Combines	台 set	383	376	431
		千瓦 kw	10 176	17 008	20 787
农产品加工机械动力	Power of Farm Processing Machinery	千瓦 kw	6 468	3 893	3 973
积肥机械动力	Power of Manure-Collecting Machinery	千瓦 kw	1 629	1 011	1 011
畜牧机械动力	Power of Animal Husbandry Machinery	千瓦 kw	2 831	3 011	4 651
渔业机械动力	Total Power of Fishery Machinery	千瓦 kw	9 673	19 303	13 659
园艺机械动力	Total Power of Horticultural Machinery	千瓦 kw	492	1 363	1 394
其他农业机械动力	Total Power of Other Agricultural Machineries	千瓦 kw	5 788	3 335	3 800
#农用载重汽车	Trucks for Agricultural Use	辆 in number	75	27	37
机动运输船	Transport Ships with Mechanical Power	艘 in number	43	25	25
每公顷耕地拥有动力	Power Per Hectare	千瓦 kw	5	7	7
每万公顷耕地拥有拖拉机	Tractors Per 10 000 Hectare	台 set	842	911	972

表5-11 农田水利建设情况
Construction of Farmland Water Conservancy

指 标 Indicators		单 位 Unit	2010	2014	2015
有效灌溉面积	Effectively Irrigated Area	公顷 hectare	18 510	16 188	16 253
本年实灌面积	Actually Irrigated Area (Current Year)	公顷 hectare	11 939	11 924	13 954
当年新增改善灌溉面积	Increased and Improved Irrigated Area (Current Year)	公顷 hectare	242	1 331	1 266
旱涝保收面积	Ensured Area from Drought and Flood	公顷 hectare	11 939	11 924	13 954
易涝面积	Area Subjected to Flood	公顷 hectare		286	286
水 闸	Dams	座 unit	11	16	16
堤 防	Dikes	公里 km	180.59	183.12	183.12
#郊区海塘	Rural/Suburban Sea Wall	公里 km	115.28	117.81	117.81
江 堤	Embankment	公里 km	65.31	65.31	65.31
围垦面积	Enclosed Tideland for Cultivation	公顷 hectare			
小机口新增	Newly Increased Small Machinery	座/台套/千瓦 unit /set /kw	29/29/316.5	41/84/1 086	33/69/1 628
新增排涝泵站	Newly Built Pump Houses for Draining Water-logging Fields	座/台套/千瓦 unit /set /kw	1/3/10	2/4/30	2/4/30
新建排涝涵洞	Newly Built Culvert for Draining Water-logging Fields	座/米 unit /meter	57/2 681	2/146	2/60
改造地下渠道	Underground Irrigation Ditch Reformed	公里 km	101.74	286.50	259.20
改造渡槽倒虹吸	Siphon Aqueduct Transformed	条/米 unit/meter	192/3 851	162/8 099	257/10 266

表5-12 历年农田水利工程投资
Investment in Farmland Water Conservancy Projects
(1990～2015)

单位:万元 (10 000 yuan)

年 份 Year	合 计 Total			乡村自筹所占比重(%) Percentage of Village-Funded(%)
		国家投资 State-invested	乡村自筹 Village-Funded	
1990	1 363.74	668.75	694.99	51.0
1991	906.70	354.80	551.90	60.9
1992	826.30	311.90	514.40	62.3
1993	1 517.22	357.80	1 159.42	76.4
1994	2 673.15	1 253.61	1 419.54	53.1
1995	2 426.99	1 262.82	1 164.17	48.0
1996	3 357.97	1 766.90	1 591.07	47.4
1997	4 203.64	2 154.13	2 049.51	48.8
1998	4 849.08	2 419.01	2 430.07	50.1
1999	4 907.60	2 152.70	2 754.90	56.1
2000	6 321.21	2 333.20	3 988.01	63.1
2001	5 627.80	2 787.75	2 840.05	50.5
2002	7 975.97	3 423.95	4 552.02	57.1
2003	7 259.27	3 281.75	3 977.52	54.8
2004	7 137.29	3 583.26	3 554.03	49.8
2005	10 131.48	4 403.23	5 728.25	56.5
2006	15 053.70	6 661.95	8 391.75	55.7
2007	14 859.89	7 510.40	7 349.49	49.5
2008	43 846.67	21 908.07	21 938.60	50.0
2009	37 513.48	15 601.77	21 911.71	58.4
2010	68 474.03	52 745.21	15 728.82	23.0
2011	59 262.87	41 412.45	17 850.42	30.1
2012	89 338.99	66 015.05	23 323.94	26.1
2013	79 466.92	67 345.18	12 121.74	15.3
2014	91 098.12	73 759.35	17 338.77	19.0
2015	112 727.89	94 504.61	18 223.28	16.2

表5-13 农村实用人才基本情况(至2015年末)
The Basic Information of the Applied Personnel in Rural Area(at the end of 2015)

单位:人 (persons)

指 标	Indicators	合 计 In total	按人才类型分 By type of personnel				
			生产型 in Production	经营型 in Operation	技能服务型 in Skill Service	技能带动型 in Skill Driven	社会服务型 in Social Service
合 计	**In total**	**12 215**	**3 047**	**2 474**	**952**	**914**	**4 828**
按学历分	**By Educational Background**						
研究生及以上	Master Degree and Above	41	1	9	22		9
大学本科	Bachelor Degree	814	1	80	214	1	518
高等专科	Junior College	1 958	56	228	193	5	1 476
高中(含中专)	High School	2 688	255	714	186	65	1 468
初中及以下	Junior High School and below	6 714	2 734	1 443	337	843	1 357
按专业技术职称分	**By Technical Title**						
高 级	Senior	54	7	14	23		10
中 级	Medium	476	37	90	136	9	204
初 级	Junior	1 031	60	95	135	31	710
按职业资格分	**By Vocational Qualification**						
高级技师	Senior Technicians	98	8	14	18	9	49
技 师	Technicians	39	9	6	11		13
高级工	Senior Workers	105	10	17	43		35
中级工	Medium Workers	226	11	47	69	3	96
初级工	Junior Workers	587	12	111	100	26	338
专业技能提升渠道	**By Technical Skill Training**						
国家级层面培训	National Training	651	254	90	65	13	229
市级培训	Municipal Training	118	5	11	52		50
区县级培训	County Training	1 088	42	74	415	5	552
街镇级培训	Street Training	951	113	71	87	13	667
本单位培训	Training of Own Company	3 241	636	799	120	275	1 411

主要统计指标解释

农村从业人员

指乡村人口中16岁以上实际参加生产经营活动并取得实物或货币收入的人员，既包括劳动年龄内实际参加劳动人员，也包括超过劳动年龄但实际参加劳动的人员，但不包括户口在家的在外学生、现役军人和丧失劳动能力的人，也不包括待业人员和家务劳动者。劳动者年龄为16岁以上。

农业总产值

农业总产值是以货币表现的农、林、牧、渔业全部产品的总量和对农林牧渔生产活动进行的各种支持性服务活动的价值。它反映一定时期内农业生产的总规模和总成果。

农、林、牧、渔业的统计范围是：

（1）农业　包括农作物种植业和其他农业。

农作物种植业包括谷物、豆类、薯类、棉、油料、糖料、麻类、烟叶、蔬菜、药材、瓜类和其他农作物的种植，以及茶园、桑园、果园的生产经营。

其他农业包括采集野生植物的果实、纤维、树胶、树脂、油料以及柴草、野生药材、菌类等及农民家庭兼营的商品性工业。

（2）林业　包括林木的栽培（不包括茶园、桑园和果园的栽培、管理和收获等活动）、林产品的采集和村及村以下合作经济组织和农户的竹木采伐。

（3）牧业　包括除渔业养殖以外的一切动物饲养和放牧，以及野生动物的捕猎和饲养。

（4）渔业　包括水生动物和海藻类植物的养殖和捕捞。

（5）农林牧渔服务业　包括农林牧渔业生产活动进行的各种支持性服务活动。但不包括各种科学技术和专业技术服务活动。

从所有制看，包括国有经济的各种专业农（农、林、牧、渔）场以及国家各级机关团体学校、科研机构、部队经营的农业；集体所有制的乡镇村各级办农场；农村各种经济组织经营的农、林、牧、渔业以及工矿企业家属集体经营的农业；农民家庭自营的农林牧渔业及兼营商品性工业等。

农业总产值的计算方法通常是按农林牧渔业产品及其副产品的产量分别乘以各自单位产品价格求得，少数生产周期较长、当年没有产品或产品产量不易统计的，则采用间接方法匡算其产值，然后将四业产品产值和服务业产值相加即为农业总产值。

1957年以前的农业总产值中包括了厩肥和农民自给性手工业（如农民自制衣服、鞋、袜，自己从事粮食初步加工等）。1958年及以后的农业总产值，林业中增加了村及村以下竹木采伐产值；牧业中取消了厩肥产值；副业中取消了农民自给性手工业产值，增加了村及村以下办的工业产值；渔业中增加了海洋捕捞水产品产值。1980年及以后的农业总产值，在副业中增加了农民家庭兼营工业商品部分的产值。从1984年起村及村以下办工业产值划归工业。从1993年起，取消副业。将野生动物的捕猎划入牧业，野生植物采集和农民家庭兼营商品性工业划归农业。从2003年起，农业总产值中包括了农林牧渔服务业产值。

当年价格

当年价格（或现行价格）是指报告期的实际价格，如工业品的出厂价格、农产品的收购价格、商品零售价格等。用当年价格计算的一些以货币表现的物量指标或劳务总量指标，如国内生产总值、工农业总产值、社会商品零售额等，反映当年的实际情况，使国民经济各项指标互相衔接，便于考察当年社会经济效益，便于对生产和流通、生产和分配、生产和消费之间进行经济核算和综合平衡。

按当年价格计算的以货币表现的指标，在不同年份之间进行对比时，因包含各年间价格变动的因素，不能确切地反映实物量的增减变动，必须消除价格变动的因素后，才能真实反映经济发展动态。因此，在计算增长速度时都使用按可比价格计算的数字。

可比价格

可比价格指在对不同时期的价值指标对比时，扣除了价格变动的因素，以确切反映物量的变化。按可比价格计算有两种方法，一种是直接按产品产量乘其某一年的不变价格计算；另一种是用价格指数换算。

不变价格

指以同类产品某年的平均价格作为固定价格，用于计算各年的产品价值。按不变价格计算的产品价值消除了价格变动因素，不同时期对比可以反映生产的发展速度。新中国成立后，随着工农业产品价格水平的变化，国家统计局先后五次制定了全国统一的工业产品不变价格和农业产品不变价格。从1952年到1957年使用1952年工（农）业产品不变价格，从1957年到1970年使用1957年不变价格，从1971年到1980年使用1970年不变价格，从1981年到1990年使用1980年不变价格，从1991年到2000年使用1990年不变价格，从2001年开始使用2000年不变价格。

年末耕地面积

年末耕地面积指能够种植农作物，经常进行耕锄的田地。包括熟地、当年新开荒地、新开垦围垦地、连续撂荒未满三年的耕地和当年休闲地（轮歇地）。以种植农作物为主并附带种植桑树、茶树、果树和其他林木的土地，以及沿海、沿湖地区已围垦利用的“海涂”、“湖田”等也应包括在内，但不包括专业性桑园、茶园、果园、果木苗圃、林地、芦苇地、天然草原等。小于一米宽的渠、路、田埂,包括在耕地中。

农作物播种面积

农作物播种面积指报告期内收获农产品的作物的实际播种或移植有农作物的面积。凡是实际种植农作物的面积,不论种植在耕地上还是种植在非耕地上,均包括在农作物播种面积中。在播种季节基本结束后,因遭灾而重新改种和补种的农作物面积,也包括在内。

粮食产量

指全社会的产量。包括国有经济经营的、集体统一经营的和农民家庭经营的粮食产量,还包括工矿企业办的农场和其他生产单位的产量。粮食除包括稻谷、小麦、玉米、高粱、谷子及其他杂粮外,还包括薯类和豆类。其产量计算方法,豆类按去豆荚后的干豆计算;薯类(包括甘薯和马铃薯,不包括芋头和木薯)1963 年以前按每 4 公斤鲜薯折 1 公斤粮食计算,从 1964 年开始改为按 5 公斤鲜薯折 1 公斤粮食计算。城市郊区作为蔬菜的薯类(如马铃薯等)按鲜品计算,并且不作粮食统计。其他粮食一律按脱粒后的原粮计算。1989 年以前全国粮食产量数据主要靠全面报表取得,1989 年开始使用抽样调查数据。

水产品产量

指人工养殖的水产品和天然生长的水产品的捕捞量。包括海水的鱼类、虾蟹类、贝类和藻类以及内陆水域的鱼类、虾蟹类和贝类,不包括淡水生植物。水产品产量是通过各级水产和统计部门逐级上报取得数据。1995 年及以前,贝类中牡蛎按鲜肉计算;蚶、蛤、蛙按 5 斤鲜品折 1 斤计算。1996 年以后则统一按鲜品计算。

猪、牛、羊肉产量

指当年出栏并已屠宰、除去头蹄下水后带骨肉(即胴体重)的重量。包括全社会范围内的产量。1996 年前为各级逐级上报数据。1996 年第一次农业普查以后,由于畜牧业产品年报数据与普查数据之间存在一定的差距,国家统计局农调总队对畜牧业年报数据与普查数据进行衔接。1999 年以后,国家统计局开展了猪、牛、羊、禽等主要畜禽品种的抽样调查,并用抽样数据作为国家定案数据使用。未开展抽样调查的品种,仍使用各级统计部门逐级上报数据。

种源农产品

指农业生产中,农作物的种籽、种苗、菌种;林业生产中的种籽、树苗;畜禽生产中的种畜、种畜精液、仔畜、种禽、种蛋、苗禽;渔业生产中的种鱼、鱼苗、虾蟹苗。

种源农产品生产

指报告期内生产的种源农产品的数量和金额。

种源农产品自产自用

指调查单位和农户自己生产(包括报告期外生产的)的农产品在报告期内进行再生产自用。

种源农产品出售

指报告期内出售自己生产(包括指报告期外生产的)的种源农产品数量和金额。金额按实际成交价格计算。

农业机械总动力

农业机械总动力指用于农、林、牧、渔业生产的各种动力机械的动力总和。动力机械包括耕作、排灌、种植、植物保护、收获、农产品加工、运输、畜牧、渔业、农田水利等各种机械。不包括专门用于乡办工业、基本建设、非农业运输、科学试验和教学等非农业生产方面用的动力机械与作业机械的数量。

EXPLANATORY NOTES TO MAJOR STATISTICAL INDICATORS

Personnel Employed in Rural Areas

Personnel Employed in Rural Areas refers to people in rural areas who are older than 16 years and engaged in production and business activities that generate incomes in cash or in practicality. It includes all working laborers, no matter whether they are within the working age or not, whereas students studying outside but with their registered residence at home, active serviceman, people who lost their ability to work, unemployed people, and those engaged in housework are not included. The working age is defined as older than 16 years.

Gross Output Value of Agriculture

Gross Output Value of Agriculture refers to the total volume of products of farming, forestry, animal husbandry and fishery expressed in the monetary terms and output value of all kinds of service activities that support farming, forestry, animal husbandry and fishery production. It reflects the overall scale and achievements of agricultural production during a given period of time.

The scope of statistics on farming, forestry, animal husbandry, and fishery are as follows:

(1) Farming includes cultivation of farm crops and other agricultural activities.

Cultivation of farm crops include cultivation of grain crops, legume crops, tuber-crops, cotton, oil-bearing crops, sugar crops, bastfiber plants, tobacco, vegetables, medicinal herbs, melon crops, and cultivation and management of tea plantations, mulberry fields and orchards.

Other agricultural activities include harvesting wild fruits, fiber, tree gum, resin, oil-bearing plants, firewood, wild medicinal herbs, fungus, and rural-household commodity industries.

(2) Forestry refers to planting trees of various kinds (excluding tea plantations, mulberry fields and orchards), collection of forestry products and cutting and felling of bamboo and trees by villages and other cooperative organizations under village level.

(3) Animal husbandry refers to raising and grazing of all kinds of farm animals except fishing and aquatic cultivating, and hunting and rising of wild animals.

(4) Fishery refers to cultivation and catching of fish and other aquatic products and cultivation and collection of seaweed and other aquatic plants.

(5) Service Industry for Farming, Forestry, Animal Husbandry and Fishery refers to all kinds of service activities that support farming, forestry, animal husbandry and fishery production, whereas activities of science, technology and professional service are not included.

In terms of ownership, China's agriculture includes specialized state farms (for farming, forestry, animal husbandry, fishery), farms managed by various government agencies, organizations, schools, research institutions, and army; farms managed by rural collective organizations at levels of the township, town, and village; farming, forestry, animal husbandry, fishery run by various rural collective organizations and farming run by collective family members' organizations of mining and industrial enterprises; farming, forestry, animal husbandry and fishery and some commodity industries run by individual farmers.

Gross output value of agriculture is obtained by first multiplying the output of products or by-products by their unit price. For a small number of products, annual output of which is not available or difficult to get due to the long production/growing process involved, the output value will be estimated through an indirect approach. The sum of output value of all products of farming, forestry, animal husbandry and fishery and output value of service activities will then and together to form gross output value of agriculture.

Before 1957, China's gross agricultural output value included the value of barnyard manure and handicraft products for self-consumption (clothes, shoes, stockings, and initial grain processing under-taken by peasants). After 1958, the output value of cutting and felling of bamboo and trees by villages and other cooperative organizations under villages have been included in forestry; value of barnyard manure has been excluded from animal husbandry; the value of self-consumed handicrafts has been excluded from sideline occupations, while output value of industries run by villages and cooperative organizations under village level has been included in sideline occupations and output value of fish catches by motor fishing boats has been added to fishery. Since 1980, the output value of handicraft products made for sale by farmer households has been added to sideline occupations, From 1984, industries run by villages and cooperative organizations under village level have been included in the sector of industry. After 1993, the category of sideline occupations has been canceled and hunting of wild animals has been classified into husbandry, and harvesting of wild vegetation and commodity industry run by rural households have been grouped into the category of agriculture. Since 2003, the output value of service industry for farming, forestry, animal husbandry and fishery is included in the gross output value of agriculture.

Current Prices

Current prices refer to the actual prices in the report period, for example, industrial producers prices, procurement prices of agricultural products, retail prices, and so on. Goods and services measured by the current prices, such as gross national product, gross output value of industry and agriculture, total retail sales, reflect the current-year actual activities. The various national economic indicators, such as current-year social economic efficiency, production, exchange, distribution and consumption could be understood and compared directly if they are measured by the current prices.

The indicators measured by the current prices can not exactly reflect the real change over different years, if the price level changes during the period of time. The comparable prices would be used in measuring growth rates, in order to deflate the price change.

Comparable Prices

Comparable Prices are applied when comparing indicators over time to reflect accurately the changes in real term. Two methods are used for calculating comparable prices: 1. output by constant price of certain year; 2. output in current prices divided by relevant price index.

Constant Price

Constant Price refers to the average price of a given product in certain year, which is used for comparison of output value over time. As the output value at constant prices removes the factor of price changes, it reflects the trend of production development over time. Since 1949, with the changes in general price level, National Bureau of Statistics has issued nationally unified constant prices five times: the 1952 constant prices for 1949 – 1957; the 1957 constant prices for 1957 – 1971; the 1970 constant prices for 1971 – 1981; the 1980 constant prices for 1981 – 1990; the 1990 constant prices for 1991 – 2000; and the 2000 constant prices have been used since 2001.

The Actual Area of Plowland at Year End

The Area of Plowland at Year End refers to the area of arable land and frequently-tended farm-fields at the beginning of a year. It includes cultivated land, the newly-reclaimed wasteland and inning land in the year, the farmland which has been laid idle for no more than three consecutive years, and land on fallow that year. It shall also include farmland with mulberry, tea, fruit and other trees but used mainly for growing crops as well as the reclaimed "beach-land" and "lake-land" along the sea coasts and the lake banks. However, it shall not include the land devoted especially for mulberry and the tea gardens, orchards, nurseries, woodlands, reed marches and natural grasslands. Ditches, pathways and ridges of field which are less than one meter wide are included in plowland.

Sown Area of Crops

Sown Area of Crops refers to area of land sown or transplanted with crops that have been harvested during report period, regardless of being in cultivated area or non-cultivated area. Area of land re-sown due to natural disasters is also included.

Grain Output

Grain Output refers to the total output in the whole country including grains produced by state farms, collective units, rural households, as well as by farms affiliated to industrial and mining enterprises and other production units. Grain includes rice, wheat, corn, sorghum, millet and other miscellaneous grains as well as tubers and bean. Output of beans refers to dry beans without pods. The output of tubers (sweet potatoes and potatoes, not including taros and cassava) was converted into that of grain at the ratio 4 : 1, i. e. 4 kilograms of fresh tubers was equivalent to 1 kilogram of grain up to 1963. Since 1964 the ratio for conversion has been 5 : 1. Tubers supplied as vegetables (such as potatoes) in cities and suburbs are calculated as fresh vegetables and their output is not included in the output of grain. Output of all other grains refers to husked grain. Data on grain production before 1989 were obtained through Comprehensive Statistical Reporting System. Since 1989, data from sample surveys are used.

Output of Aquatic Products

Output of Aquatic Products refers to catches of both artificially cultured and naturally grown aquatic products, including fish, shrimps, crabs and shellfish in sea and inland water as well as seaweed. Freshwater plants are not included. Data on output of aquatic products are reported by aquatic product and statistical agencies level by level. Before 1995, among the shellfish, the oyster was counted as fresh meat; 5 kilograms of ark shell, clams and frogs are equivalent to 1 kilogram of fresh aquatic products; they are all counted as fresh aquatic products since 1996.

Output of Pork, Beef, and Mutton

Output of Pork, Beef, and Mutton refers to the meat of slaughtered hogs, cattle, sheep and goats with head, feet, and offal taken away. Data refers to the production of the whole country. The first agriculture census of China in 1996 revealed some discrepancy between the production of animal products from the annual reports and that from the census. Efforts were made by the Rural Socio-economic Survey Organization of NBS to adjust the output value of animal husbandry to make the figures from the annual reports consistent with the census data. Since 1999, NBS conducted sample survey for the major animal husbandry products, such as hogs, cattle, sheep and goats and fowls, and the data from sample surveys are used as national finalized data. Those products, which are not covered by the sample survey, are still reported by statistical agencies level by level.

Seed Agriculture

Seed agriculture includes four aspects, respectively, the seeds, plants, and strains of crops in farm production; the seeds and plants in forestry production; livestocks and poultry breedings, poultries, sperm, eggs, and procreating birds in livestock production; fish, shrimp, and crab seedlings in fishery production.

Seed Agriculture Production

Seed agricluture production refers to the number and amount of seed agriculture products.

Seed Agriculture Products for Self-use

Seed agriculture products for self – use refers to the farming products that are used for self-use or re-production (including those produced not in the reporting period).

Seed Agriculture Products for Selling

Seed agriculture products for selling refers to the number and amount of the seed agriculture products that are used for selling. The amount is calculated by the real settlement price.

Total Power of Farm Machinery

Total Power of Farm Machinery refers to the total mechanical power of machinery used in farming, forestry animal husbandry and fishery, including machines used for ploughing, irrigation and drainage, crop growing, plant protection, harvesting, farm product processing, transport, stock breeding, fishery and water conservancy. Machinery employed for non-agricultural purposes such as township industry, capital construction, non-agricultural transport, scientific experiments and for teaching is excluded.

第六篇

CHAPTER 6

工 业

INDUSTRY

表6-1 主要年份工业总产值及其构成

单位:亿元

指 标	Indicators	1990	1995	2000	2001	2002	2003	2004
总 计	**Total**	**176.85**	**968.03**	**1 625.77**	**1 888.74**	**2 193.82**	**2 856.68**	**3 519.71**
按隶属关系分	**By Subordination**							
中央工业	Central	42.48	225.99	381.41	386.40	431.13	549.05	677.04
市属工业	Municipal	88.44	491.63	599.57	779.48	805.98	1 082.55	1 254.17
非中央、市属工业	Local	45.93	250.41	644.79	722.86	956.71	1 225.08	1 588.50
按登记注册类型分	**By Type of Registration**							
国 有	State-owned	110.18	449.57	275.85	344.02	241.56	290.97	358.04
集 体	Collective-owned	49.09	122.54	70.91	57.02	49.57	46.02	49.09
港澳台及外商投资	Overseas Invested	7.07	231.94	1 012.34	1 242.91	1 522.31	1 985.30	2 461.66
其 他	Others	10.51	163.98	266.67	244.79	380.38	534.39	650.92
按轻、重工业分	**By Light/Heavy Industry**							
轻工业	Light Industry	72.08	424.42	514.58	535.06	541.28	647.92	764.94
重工业	Heavy Industry	104.77	543.61	1 111.19	1 353.68	1 652.54	2 208.76	2 754.77
按企业规模分	**By Scale of Enterprises**							
大型企业	Large	81.32	632.35	1 138.11	1 294.24	1 564.20	1 229.85	1 426.29
中型企业	Medium	21.40	96.37	187.00	239.26	209.92	862.86	1 083.29
小型企业	Small	74.13	239.31	300.66	355.24	419.70	763.97	1 010.13
构 成(%)	**Composition (%)**							
总 计	**Total**	**100.0**	**100.0**	**100.0**	**100.0**	**100.0**	**100.0**	**100.0**
按隶属关系分	**By Subordination**							
中央工业	Central	24.0	23.3	23.5	20.4	19.7	19.2	19.3
市属工业	Municipal	50.0	50.8	36.9	41.3	36.7	37.9	35.6
非中央、市属工业	Local	26.0	25.9	39.6	38.3	43.6	42.9	45.1
按登记注册类型分	**By Type of Registration**							
国 有	State-owned	62.3	46.4	17.0	18.2	11.0	10.2	10.2
集 体	Collective-owned	27.8	12.7	4.3	3.0	2.3	1.6	1.4
港澳台及外商投资	Overseas Invested	4.0	24.0	62.3	65.8	69.4	69.5	69.9
其 他	Others	5.9	16.9	16.4	13.0	17.3	18.7	18.5
按轻、重工业分	**By Light/Heavy Industry**							
轻工业	Light Industry	40.8	43.8	31.7	28.3	24.7	22.7	21.7
重工业	Heavy Industry	59.2	56.2	68.3	71.7	75.3	77.3	78.3
按企业规模分	**By Scale of Enterprises**							
大型企业	Large	46.0	65.3	70.0	68.5	71.3	43.1	40.5
中型企业	Medium	12.1	10.0	11.5	12.7	9.6	30.2	30.8
小型企业	Small	41.9	24.7	18.5	18.8	19.1	26.7	28.7

注：本篇从6-2表开始,数据均为年主营业务收入2000万元及以上企业。
Note: In this chapter, data from sheet 2 to sheet 14 all refered to enterprises with annual main business income of 20 million yuan and above.

Gross Output Value of Industry and its Composition in Main Years

(100 million yuan)

2005	2006	2007	2008	2009	2010	2011	2012	2013	2014	2015
4 242.47	**4 758.76**	**5 188.12**	**5 649.22**	**7 141.55**	**8 591.50**	**9 553.79**	**9 424.67**	**9 375.57**	**9 495.42**	**9 454.88**
1 321.05	1 538.42	1 663.26	1 999.48	1 653.93	2 216.69	2 278.33	2 235.91	2 299.88	2 213.84	2 185.24
1 135.29	1 249.74	1 373.81	1 289.49	2 010.76	2 043.34	2 284.38	1 986.87	1 983.98	2 061.92	1 916.81
1 786.13	1 970.60	2 151.05	2 360.25	3 476.86	4 331.47	4 991.08	5 201.89	5 091.71	5 219.67	5 352.83
550.18	573.84	662.21	679.71	729.56	885.71	927.97	960.60	834.91	838.06	847.99
38.67	36.87	34.89	31.60	47.87	34.70	34.67	33.63	23.72	30.39	26.41
2 632.70	2 980.46	3 001.98	3 088.54	4 008.58	5 047.75	5 899.02	5 846.88	5 834.32	5 981.89	5 900.75
1 020.92	1 167.59	1 489.04	1 849.37	2 355.54	2 623.34	2 692.13	2 583.56	2 682.62	2 645.09	2 679.73
825.40	878.66	952.26	1 070.62	1 402.71	1 535.63	1 677.47	1 638.43	1 687.97	1 752.95	1 690.52
3 417.07	3 880.10	4 235.86	4 578.60	5 738.84	7 055.87	7 876.32	7 786.24	7 687.60	7 742.47	7 764.36
1 989.45	1 976.08	2 309.39	2 731.96	3 318.52	4 097.63	6 154.87	6 105.36	5 854.97	5 895.29	5 928.21
1 173.99	1 725.62	1 841.13	1 822.86	2 022.62	2 593.18	1 477.88	1 580.14	1 688.82	1 637.61	1 634.38
1 079.03	1 057.06	1 037.60	1 094.40	1 800.41	1 900.69	1 921.04	1 739.17	1 831.78	1 962.52	1 892.28
100.0	**100.0**	**100.0**	**100.0**	**100.0**	**100.0**	**100.0**	**100.0**	**100.0**	**100.0**	**100.0**
31.1	32.3	32.0	35.4	23.2	25.8	23.8	23.7	24.5	23.3	23.1
26.8	26.3	26.5	22.8	28.1	23.8	23.9	21.1	21.2	21.7	20.3
42.1	41.4	41.5	41.8	48.7	50.4	52.3	55.2	54.3	55.0	56.6
13.0	12.1	12.8	12.0	10.2	10.3	9.7	10.2	8.9	8.8	9.0
0.9	0.8	0.7	0.6	0.7	0.4	0.4	0.4	0.3	0.3	0.3
62.0	62.6	57.8	54.7	56.1	58.8	61.7	62.0	62.2	63.0	62.4
24.1	24.5	28.7	32.7	33.0	30.5	28.2	27.4	28.6	27.9	28.3
19.5	18.5	18.4	19.0	19.6	17.9	17.6	17.4	18.0	18.5	17.9
80.5	81.5	81.6	81.0	80.4	82.1	82.4	82.6	82.0	81.5	82.1
46.9	41.5	44.5	48.3	46.5	47.7	64.4	64.8	62.4	62.1	62.7
27.7	36.3	35.5	32.3	28.3	30.2	15.5	16.8	18.0	17.2	17.3
25.4	22.2	20.0	19.4	25.2	22.1	20.1	18.5	19.6	20.7	20.0

表6-2　工业总产值、销售产值和出口交货值
（2015）

单位:亿元

指　标　Indicators		工业总产值（按现行价格计算）Gross Output Value of Industry (at Current Price)
总　计	**Total**	**9 177.80**
按隶属关系分	**By Subordination**	
中央工业	Central	2 185.09
市属工业	Municipal	1 916.19
非中央、市属工业	Local	5 076.52
按登记注册类型分	**By Type of Registration**	
内　资	Domestic Funded	3 304.73
国　有	State-owned	847.50
集　体	Collective-owned	21.79
股份合作制	Share-holding	3.54
联　营	Jointly-operated	4.06
有限责任公司	Companies with Limited Liability	1 108.87
股份有限公司	Companies Limited by Shares	655.30
私　营	Private	663.67
其　他	Others	
港澳台商投资	Hong Kong/Macao/Taiwan Invested	722.92
#港澳台商独资	Solely Hong Kong/Macao/Taiwan Funded	396.90
外商投资	Foreign Invested	5 150.15
#外商独资	Wholly foreign-owned	2 949.17
按轻、重工业分	**By Light/Heavy Industry**	
轻工业	Light Industry	1 588.67
重工业	Heavy Industry	7 589.13
按企业规模分	**By Scale of Enterprises**	
大型企业	Large	5 928.22
中型企业	Medium	1 634.38
小型企业	Small	1 615.20

Gross Output Value, Sales Value and Export Delivery Value

(100 million yuan)

#镇及镇以上 Town and Above	工业销售产值 Sales Value of Industry	#镇及镇以上 Town and Above	出口交货值 Export Delivery Value	#镇及镇以上 Town and Above
4 350.69	**9 152.02**	**4 301.36**	**2 963.96**	**618.46**
2 185.09	2 169.67	2 169.67	456.10	456.10
1 916.19	1 880.65	1 880.65	146.62	146.62
249.42	5 101.70	251.04	2 361.24	15.74
2 340.58	3 265.69	2 319.00	425.73	304.97
841.04	847.61	841.13	4.03	2.90
7.71	19.66	7.14	1.34	0.96
	3.49		0.01	
1.38	4.04	1.36		
917.38	1 099.32	910.45	285.87	241.93
573.06	638.96	558.92	64.44	59.18
	652.60		70.03	
132.76	716.51	136.59	323.06	16.00
	391.55		191.22	
1 877.35	5 169.82	1 845.77	2 215.17	297.48
	2 990.18		1 819.50	
554.86	1 564.86	534.86	288.74	85.94
3 795.83	7 587.15	3 766.50	2 675.22	532.52
3 407.52	5 928.68	3 375.36	2 332.37	496.67
595.49	1 626.55	590.85	372.95	91.49
347.68	1 596.79	335.16	258.64	30.30

表6-3 主要工业产品生产和销售量
Output and Sales Volume of Major Industrial Products
(2015)

产品名称	Products	单 位 Unit	生产量 Output	销售量 Sales Volume	生产量占全市比重(%) PNA/Shanghai(%)
汽 油	Gasoline	万吨 10 000 tons	227.56	230.10	42.4
柴 油	Diesel Oil	万吨 10 000 tons	334.47	337.10	114.2
化学纤维	Chemical Fiber	万吨 10 000 tons	11.55	10.99	25.2
合成纤维聚合物	Synthetic Polymer	万吨 10 000 tons	54.97	55.41	50.2
化学药品原药	Original Chemical Drug	吨 ton	3644.37	3388.77	8.4
钢 材	Steel	万吨 10 000 tons	45.58	46.49	2.1
家用洗衣机	Household Washing Machine	万台 10 000 sets	147.57	147.52	92.1
房间空气调节器	Household Air-conditioner	万台 10 000 sets	136.65	140.03	41.7
数字程控交换机	Program-controlled Exchange	万线 10 000 lines	70.60	71.62	114.9
电话单机	Telephone Set	万部 10 000 sets	128.34	139.61	100.0
电子计算机整机	Electronic Computor	万台 10 000 sets	546.90	569.75	14.8
#笔记本计算机	Including Notebooks	万台 10 000 sets	921.30	93.57	40.1
移动通信基站设备	Mobile Communication Base Station Equipment	信 道	262 396	262 396	100.0
移动通信手持机(手机)	Mobile Phone	万台 10 000 sets	5159.38	5073.91	76.5
液晶(LCD)电视机	Color TV Set	万台 10 000 sets	127.96	128.74	94.5
气体压缩机	Gas Compressor	万台 10 000 sets	1019.27	986.05	61.4
轿 车	Car	万辆 10 000 vehicles	55.59	55.46	27.3
#1升<排量≤1.6升	1L<Displacement≤1.6L	万辆 10 000 vehicles	27.54	27.43	17.8
1.6升<排量≤2.0升	1.6L<Displacement≤2.0L	万辆 10 000 vehicles	21.41	21.38	49.9
2.0升<排量≤2.5升	2.0L<Displacement≤2.5L	万辆 10 000 vehicles	6.60	6.60	100.0
#新能源汽车	in which new-energy-fueled car	辆 vehicle	12 330	11 143	31.5

表6－3 续表 Continued

产品名称 Products		单 位 Unit	生产量 Output	销售量 Sales Volume	生产量占全市比重(%) PNA/Shanghai(%)
集成电路	Integrated Circuit	亿块 100 million pieces	105.00	104.32	48.3
集成电路圆片	IC Wafer	万片 10 000 pieces	318.79	316.92	72.0
起重机	Crane	万吨 10000 tons	45.97	45.76	94.1
微波炉	Microwave Oven	万台 10 000 sets	345.82	345.42	100.0
发电量	Electricity	亿千瓦时 100 mil. kwh	242.81	242.81	30.6
电子元件	Electronic Component	亿只 100 million pieces	113.83	114.22	29.1
光电子器件	Optoelectronic Device	亿只 100 million units	10.01	10.04	89.2
印制电路板	Printed Circuit Board	万平方米 10 000 sq. m.	120.31	119.51	27.9
原电池(折R20标准只)	Size D Battery (R20 standard)	亿只 100 million units	13.07	12.87	70.0
塑料制品	Plastic Product	万吨 10 000 tons	25.54	25.31	14.3
合成橡胶	Synthetic Rubber	万吨 10 000 tons	18.23	16.38	89.0
初级形态的塑料	Plastics in Primary Form	万吨 10 000 tons	64.85	65.24	16.8
涂 料	Paint	万吨 10 000 tons	65.44	66.14	34.3
化学农药原药	Original Chemicals of Chemical Pesticide	吨 ton	1 076.45	987.38	10.4
服 装	Garment	亿件 100 million units	0.68	0.56	15.1
布	Cloth	万米 10 000 meters	697.2	682.3	7.4
乳制品	Dairy Products	万吨 10 000 tons	0.37	0.35	0.7
商品混凝土	Commercial Concrete	万立方米 10 000 cu. m	734.99	734.99	20.0

表6-4 按行业分的工业总产值、销售产值和出口交货值

Gross Output Value, Sales Value and Export Delivery Value by Sector (2015)

单位:亿元 (100 million yuan)

指 标 Indicators		工业总产值(按现行价格计算) Gross Output Value of Industry (at Current Price)	工业销售产 值 Sales Value of Industry	出口交货值 Export Delivery Value
总 计	**Total**	**9 177.80**	**9 152.02**	**2 963.96**
#农副食品加工业	Processing of Agricultural Side-line Food	125.19	124.97	0.88
食品制造业	Food Manufacturing	35.04	33.94	2.11
酒、饮料和精制茶制造业	Manufacturing of Liquor, Beverage and Refined Tea	42.15	42.05	5.16
烟草制品业	Tobacco Products	22.16	20.84	0.05
纺织业	Textile Industry	38.85	39.14	8.67
纺织服装、服饰业	Textile Clothes and Accessories	102.67	101.19	16.26
皮革、毛皮、羽毛及其制品和制鞋业	Leather, Fur, Feather and their Products and Shoe-making	6.86	7.31	1.52
木材加工及木、竹、藤、棕、草制品业	Timber-processing, Bamboo, Cane, Palm Fiber and Straw Products	4.30	4.39	0.04
家具制造业	Furniture Manufacturing	102.12	101.80	21.27
造纸及纸制品业	Paper-making and Paper Products	46.18	46.23	7.51
印刷业和记录媒介复制业	Printing and Record Pressing	45.94	45.36	4.27
文教、工美、体育和娱乐用品制造业	Manufacturing of Cultural, Educational, Arts, Sports and Leisure Products	30.26	29.40	5.31
石油加工、炼焦及核燃料加工业	Petroleum Processing, Coke Products and Processing of Nuclear Fuel	474.34	466.50	52.51
化学原料和化学制品制造业	Raw Chemical Materials and Chemical Products	486.58	487.11	74.95
医药制造业	Medicine Manufacturing	320.51	295.65	17.85

单位:亿元　　表6-4 续表 Continued　　(100 million yuan)

指 标 Indicators		工业总产值(按现行价格计算) Gross Output Value of Industry (at Current Price)	工业销售产值 Sales Value of Industry	出口交货值 Export Delivery Value
化学纤维制造业	Chemical Fiber Manufacturing	3.42	3.24	0.28
橡胶和塑料制品业	Rubber and Plastic Products	110.96	112.67	24.27
非金属矿物制品业	Nonmetal Mineral Products	99.27	100.73	12.75
黑色金属冶炼及压延加工业	Smelting and Pressing of Ferrous Metal	43.13	42.82	1.97
有色金属冶炼及压延加工业	Smelting and Pressing of Nonferrous Metal	55.38	54.44	5.82
金属制品业	Metal Products	143.45	145.76	34.35
通用设备制造业	General Purpose Equipment Manufacturing	655.35	656.49	233.70
专用设备制造业	Special Purpose Equipment Manufacturing	330.37	328.60	114.64
汽车制造业	Automobile Manunfacturing	1 481.08	1 458.71	83.16
铁路、船舶、航空航天和其他运输设备制造业	Manufacturing of Railway, Ships, Aeronautics & Astronautics, and Other Transportation Equipment	388.49	383.16	197.14
电气机械及器材制造业	Electric Equipment and Machinery	470.95	468.01	131.47
计算机、通信和其他电子设备制造业	Manufacturing of Computers, Telecommunications and Other Electronic Equipment	2 410.58	2 451.28	1 849.78
仪器仪表制造业	Manufacturing of Instruments and Apparatuses	116.86	116.18	51.27
其他制造业	Other Manufacturing	23.65	24.04	1.91
废弃资源综合利用业	Comprehensive Reutilization of Discarded Resources	1.08	1.42	0.00
金属制品、机械和设备修理业	Repairing of Metal Products, Machineries and Equipment	24.86	24.95	3.09
电力、热力的生产和供应业	Production and Supply of Electricity and Heating Power	895.14	895.05	0.00
燃气生产和供应业	Production and Supply of Gas	21.58	21.58	0.00
水的生产和供应业	Production and Supply of Tap Water	19.06	16.96	0.00

表6－5　工业重点发展行业主要指标
(2015)

单位:万元

指　标	Indicators	企业单位数(个) Enterprises (unit)	从业人数(人) Employed Persons (person)	工业总产值 Gross Output Value of Industry
总　计	**Total**	**836**	**398 101**	**66 925 909**
按登记注册类型分	**By Type of Registration**			
内　资	Domestic Funded	407	123 828	17 849 711
国　有	State-owned	5	2 977	386 621
集　体	Collective-owned	5	519	52 070
股份合作制	Share-holding	2	203	6 598
联　营	Jointly-operated	1	117	12 114
有限责任公司	Companies with Limited Liability	92	55 056	7 911 249
股份有限公司	Companies Limited by Shares	21	18 552	5 826 628
私　营	Private	281	46 404	3 654 431
港澳台商投资	Hong Kong/Macao/Taiwan Invested	93	38 362	5 263 060
#港澳台商独资	Solely Hong Kong/Macao/Taiwan Funded	60	24 029	3 421 892
外商投资	Foreign Invested	336	235 911	43 813 138
#外商独资	Wholly Foreign-owned	244	160 853	24 915 844
按轻、重工业分	**By Light/Heavy Industry**			
轻工业	Light Industry	133	43 717	6 668 160
重工业	Heavy Industry	703	354 384	60 257 749
按企业规模分	**By Scale of Enterprises**			
大型企业	Large	61	242 809	47 992 728
中型企业	Medium	160	83 205	10 552 810
小型企业	Small	615	72 087	8 380 371
按行业分	**By Industry**			
电子信息产品制造业	Manufacturing of Electronic and Information Technology Products	221	178 966	26 120 168
汽车制造业	Auto Manufacturing	125	73 967	14 810 796
石油化工及精细化工制造业	Manufacturing of Petrochemical and Fine Chemicals	97	24 095	9 198 465
精品钢材制造业	Manufacturing of High Quality Steel Products	14	1 714	377 510
成套设备制造业	Manufacturing of Complete Equipment	289	88 208	12 334 192
生物医药制造业	Manufacturing of Biological Medicine	90	31 151	4 084 777

Major Indicators of Pillar Industries

(10 000 yuan)

工业销售产值 Sales Value of Industry	固定资产原价 Original Value of Fixed Assets	资产总计 Total Assets	负债总计 Total Liabilities	实收资本 Paid-in Capital	主营业务收入 Revenue of Primary Operations	税金 Tax	利润总额 Total Profits
66 682 097	**30 501 978**	**84 601 489**	**40 754 043**	**17 092 194**	**82 821 245**	**2 703 915**	**7 479 808**
17 551 391	9 484 356	39 658 646	14 700 579	7 255 844	19 940 599	1 576 978	3 323 900
388 450	443 368	708 373	151 959	582 765	392 472	11 979	17 249
51 354	10 426	40 968	27 848	6 028	50 708	3 115	1 092
6 443	5 008	8 989	6 549	758	6 425	423	280
12 118	1 614	1 716	614	773	12 118	99	43
7 843 636	4 873 527	14 386 303	8 939 330	3 369 244	9 046 939	83 369	297 302
5 662 186	3 035 876	20 163 538	3 443 392	2 473 272	6 756 689	1 368 182	2 663 058
3 587 204	1 114 538	4 348 759	2 130 888	823 005	3 675 249	109 812	344 875
5 167 078	4 207 950	7 592 057	3 894 251	1 994 832	7 352 542	37 271	343 600
3 363 192	3 556 625	5 315 068	3 041 704	1 380 743	5 380 168	9 825	164 457
43 963 629	16 809 672	37 350 787	22 159 213	7 841 518	55 528 103	1 089 666	3 812 308
25 341 395	8 268 050	14 628 448	7 915 207	4 012 654	26 359 413	4 168	1 073 602
6 395 064	2 143 335	7 229 290	3 110 428	1 623 192	6 541 022	307 365	794 406
60 287 033	28 358 644	77 372 199	37 643 615	15 469 002	76 280 223	2 396 551	6 685 402
48 049 689	23 409 986	62 662 847	30 180 050	11 675 124	62 944 179	2 169 633	5 710 975
10 399 643	3 996 768	12 284 397	6 402 310	2 805 463	11 178 006	224 641	923 492
8 232 766	3 095 225	9 654 246	4 171 682	2 611 607	8 699 060	309 641	845 341
26 535 223	12 506 879	21 895 547	12 793 999	6 500 143	30 069 388	-98 412	614 518
14 587 077	5 850 444	31 210 624	10 187 126	2 979 065	26 523 885	1 057 767	5 317 700
9 112 530	3 902 287	5 805 966	2 388 450	2 430 226	9 500 746	1 432 983	551 248
377 239	305 687	325 472	197 197	387 059	389 382	4 614	-4 085
12 240 074	6 487 127	20 189 585	12 876 300	3 638 183	12 370 226	94 898	525 262
3 829 954	1 449 554	5 174 296	2 310 971	1 157 519	3 967 618	212 066	475 166

表6-6 高技术工业主要指标

(2015)

单位:万元

指 标	Indicators	企业单位数(个) Enterprises (unit)	从业人数(人) Employed Persons (person)	工业总产值 Gross Output Value of Industry
总 计	**Total**	**252**	**202 154**	**29 633 183**
按登记注册类型分	**By Type of Registration**			
内 资	Domestic Funded	91	33 462	2 701 404
国 有	State-owned			
集 体	Collective-owned			
股份合作制	Share-holding			
联 营	Jointly-operated	1	117	12 114
有限责任公司	Companies with Limited Liability	33	20 923	1 811 928
股份有限公司	Companies Limited by Shares	7	2 505	185 644
私 营	Private	50	9 917	691 718
港澳台商投资	Hong Kong/Macao/Taiwan Invested	46	25 784	3 716 966
#港澳台商独资	Solely Hong Kong/Macao/Taiwan Funded	31	16 644	2 437 288
外商投资	Foreign Invested	115	142 908	23 214 813
#外商独资	Wholly foreign-owned	91	123 301	18 955 606
按轻、重工业分	**By Light/Heavy Industry**			
轻工业	Light Industry	87	32 652	4 659 130
重工业	Heavy Industry	165	169 502	24 974 053
按企业规模分	**By Scale of Enterprises**			
大型企业	Large	34	149 650	23 723 564
中型企业	Medium	61	32 759	3 528 607
小型企业	Small	157	19 745	2 381 011
按工业行业分	**By Sector**			
信息化学品制造	Manufacturing of Information Chemicals	1	68	5 919
医药制造业	Manufacturing of Medicine	60	23 468	3 205 083
航空航天器制造	Manufacturing of Aviation and Space Vehicles	5	950	103 005
电子及通信设备制造业	Manufacturing of Electronics and Telecommunications Equipment	108	146 116	21 676 246
电子计算机及办公设备制造业	Manufacturing of Electronic Computers and Office Equipment	13	14 594	2 882 169
医疗设备及仪器仪表制造业	Manufacturing of Medical Equipment and Instrument	65	16 958	1 760 760

Major Indicators of PNA High-Tech Enterprises

(10 000 yuan)

工业销售产值 Sales Value of Industry	固定资产原价 Original Value of Fixed Assets	资产总计 Total Assets	负债总计 Total Liabilities	实收资本 Paid-in Capital	主营业务收入 Revenue of of Floating Assets	税金 Tax	利润总额 Total Profits
29 741 997	**13 683 803**	**26 384 558**	**14 755 301**	**7 667 268**	**33 313 656**	**67 060**	**983 835**
2 575 548	2 362 243	5 306 867	2 824 554	1 744 335	2 707 087	96 843	46 331
12 118	1 614	1 716	614	773	12 118	99	43
1 764 568	2 017 967	4 000 427	2 293 186	1 476 440	1 848 176	59 909	-46 581
156 171	97 274	434 249	144 413	93 124	157 218	10 730	33 372
642 690	245 388	870 474	386 342	173 998	689 576	26 105	59 497
3 635 431	3 353 088	5 777 995	2 894 434	1 537 245	5 536 588	16 095	290 647
2 402 292	2 920 239	4 146 411	2 392 810	1 034 457	4 271 954	4 226	168 680
23 531 018	7 968 472	15 299 696	9 036 313	4 385 688	25 069 981	-45 878	646 857
19 389 023	6 601 785	9 633 033	5 366 914	3 005 676	20 260 509	-150 726	479 256
4 390 636	1 537 083	5 383 714	2 429 973	1 245 002	4 513 789	218 529	466 958
25 351 360	12 146 720	21 000 844	12 325 328	6 422 266	28 799 867	-151 469	516 876
23 915 019	11 342 747	19 204 970	11 720 322	5 723 902	27 230 730	-89 879	413 522
3 470 517	1 381 537	4 265 101	1 977 182	1 056 729	3 664 069	64 493	297 859
2 356 460	959 519	2 914 487	1 057 798	886 638	2 418 856	92 446	272 454
7 018	995	3 656	444	800	7 018	146	468
2 956 538	1 156 646	4 189 405	2 022 018	957 258	3 070 298	190 627	357 110
101 519	77 903	129 483	78 622	114 430	101 519	2 745	16 618
22 055 377	11 867 602	16 898 750	9 168 959	6 093 283	22 670 560	-169 640	433 033
2 865 048	111 764	3 291 650	2 909 403	122 498	5 652 410	21 485	-38 238
1 756 498	468 894	1 871 614	575 855	378 999	1 811 850	21 698	214 843

表6-7　独立核算工业企业主要财务指标
（2015）

单位：万元

指　标	Indicators	企业单位数（个）Enterprises (unit)	从业人数（人）Employed Persons (person)	工业总产值 Gross Output Value of Industry
总　计	**Total**	**1 714**	**591 108**	**91 777 985**
按隶属关系分	**By Subordination**			
中央工业	Central	39	71 408	21 850 864
市属工业	Municipal	89	82 255	19 161 875
非中央、市属工业	Local	1 586	437 445	50 765 247
按登记注册类型分	**By Type of Registration**			
内　资	Domestic Funded	959	221 170	33 047 277
国　有	State-owned	13	19 128	8 475 049
集　体	Collective-owned	16	1 590	217 884
股份合作制	Share-holding	7	1 153	35 424
联　营	Jointly-operated	4	212	40 562
有限责任公司	Companies with Limited Liability	196	77 591	11 088 718
股份有限公司	Companies Limited by Shares	33	22 586	6 552 955
私　营	Private	690	98 910	6 636 684
港澳台商投资	Hong Kong/Macao/Taiwan Invested	171	61 995	7 229 172
#港澳台商独资	Solely Hong Kong/Macao/Taiwan Funded	103	31 855	3 968 971
外商投资	Foreign Invested	584	307 943	51 501 536
#外商独资	Wholly Foreign-owned	426	208 936	29 491 708
按轻、重工业分	**By Light/Heavy Industry**			
轻工业	Light Industry	534	142 065	15 886 701
重工业	Heavy Industry	1 180	449 043	75 891 284
按企业规模分	**By Scale of Entrerprises**			
大型企业	Large	82	301 811	59 282 122
中型企业	Medium	260	137 523	16 343 824
小型企业	Small	1 372	151 774	16 152 039

Major Indicators of Industrial Enterprises with Independent Accounting Systems

(10 000 yuan)

工业销售产值 Sales Value of Industry	实收资本 Paid-in Capital	资产总计 Total Assets	流动资产合计 Total Circulating Assets	固定资产合计 Total Fixed Assets	固定资产原价 Original Value of Fixed Assets
91 520 160	**33 991 165**	**123 980 050**	**64 150 403**	**31 871 002**	**67 240 199**
21 696 680	16 516 916	39 551 741	13 957 240	16 940 349	34 928 742
18 806 497	5 860 392	38 426 188	18 753 336	5 684 898	11 592 833
51 016 983	11 613 857	46 002 122	31 439 827	9 245 756	20 718 624
32 656 862	21 328 324	68 614 239	27 473 376	20 726 810	41 099 316
8 476 071	11 696 290	19 391 486	2 178 824	13 190 404	26 680 270
196 617	11 218	141 868	123 273	15 410	43 045
34 883	5 756	45 112	32 186	11 151	23 012
40 438	5 547	13 321	11 828	1 396	5 142
10 993 174	5 385 665	20 393 426	11 949 254	4 848 289	8 962 192
6 389 647	2 821 476	21 293 910	8 209 014	1 289 823	3 180 402
6 526 032	1 402 372	7 335 116	4 968 996	1 370 337	2 205 254
7 165 134	2 850 404	10 445 944	6 846 573	2 117 075	5 739 786
3 915 453	1 658 652	5 971 964	4 356 483	1 321 641	4 023 295
51 698 164	9 812 437	44 919 867	29 830 454	9 027 117	20 401 097
29 901 782	5 003 434	19 000 817	13 274 855	4 136 968	10 167 814
15 648 649	4 138 360	16 696 117	10 957 693	3 389 648	6 438 408
75 871 511	29 852 805	107 283 934	53 192 710	28 481 355	60 801 791
59 286 837	23 531 047	84 974 587	38 209 541	23 709 590	51 309 733
16 265 452	5 172 144	19 975 405	13 232 504	3 778 930	7 636 438
15 967 870	5 287 975	19 030 058	12 708 358	4 382 483	8 294 028

单位:万元　　　　表6－7　续表　Continued

指　标	Indicators	本年折旧 Depreciation of the Current Year	负债合计 Total Liabilities	所有者权益 Owner's Equity
总　计	**Total**	**3 547 959**	**57 110 867**	**66 727 753**
按隶属关系分	**By Subordination**			
中央工业	Central	1 672 593	18 491 369	20 968 663
市属工业	Municipal	684 380	14 302 058	24 123 677
非中央、市属工业	Local	1 190 987	24 317 440	21 635 413
按登记注册类型分	**By Type of Registration**			
内　资	Domestic Funded	2 100 612	25 521 121	43 074 122
国　有	State-owned	1 273 253	5 543 301	13 848 038
集　体	Collective-owned	4 219	104 083	37 784
股份合作制	Share-holding	1 042	19 438	25 674
联　营	Jointly-operated	156	6 036	7 285
有限责任公司	Companies with Limited Liability	543 638	12 072 932	8 312 839
股份有限公司	Companies Limited by Shares	137 510	3 976 163	17 317 370
私　营	Private	140 794	3 799 168	3 525 132
港澳台商投资	Hong Kong/Macao/Taiwan Invested	203 177	5 554 763	4 898 462
#港澳台商独资	Solely Hong Kong/Macao/Taiwan Funded	117 872	3 354 075	2 611 610
外商投资	Foreign Invested	1 244 171	26 034 983	18 755 170
#外商独资	Wholly Foreign-owned	672 905	10 164 430	8 831 763
按轻、重工业分	**By Light/Heavy Industry**			
轻工业	Light Industry	354 105	8 211 191	8 455 749
重工业	Heavy Industry	3 193 855	48 899 676	58 272 004
按企业规模分	**By Scale of Enterprises**			
大型企业	Large	2 671 648	37 564 360	47 318 217
中型企业	Medium	430 412	10 248 477	9 740 103
小型企业	Small	445 899	9 298 029	9 669 434

(10 000 yuan)

主营业务收入 Revenue of Primary Operations	税金 Tax	#本年应交增值税 Current Year Value-added Tax Payable	营业利润 Operation Profits	利润总额 Total Profits	应付职工薪酬 Wage/Fringe Benefits
108 729 408	**3 724 322**	**1 934 565**	**8 434 563**	**8 980 916**	**6 637 645**
22 081 471	1 767 859	564 336	502 573	671 945	1 332 498
31 151 722	1 275 394	818 728	5 382 882	5 605 271	1 441 537
55 496 215	681 069	551 501	2 549 108	2 703 700	3 863 611
35 486 234	2 296 851	998 872	3 843 052	4 177 690	2 427 208
8 593 333	314 877	288 557	323 677	304 789	477 581
204 031	5 283	4 997	29	594	10 193
36 881	1 947	1 808	1 408	2 678	5 163
40 440	712	659	951	952	982
12 413 778	375 211	214 971	432 989	628 208	943 305
7 474 894	1 370 450	292 103	2 579 700	2 681 031	403 192
6 722 877	228 369	195 777	504 298	559 438	586 791
9 446 270	98 669	86 967	480 423	497 387	574 221
5 929 585	26 405	20 338	190 126	185 030	319 621
63 796 904	1 328 803	848 726	4 111 089	4 305 839	3 636 216
31 247 802	167 880	116 982	1 291 916	1 311 348	2 038 652
16 315 438	730 544	534 949	1 434 782	1 484 086	1 365 150
92 413 970	2 993 778	1 399 616	6 999 782	7 496 830	5 272 495
74 275 609	2 558 489	1 020 456	5 893 429	6 317 661	3 794 421
17 454 690	549 494	371 884	1 254 849	1 300 567	1 522 609
16 999 109	616 339	542 225	1 286 286	1 362 688	1 320 616

表6-8　独立核算大中型工业企业主要指标
(2015)

单位:万元

指　标	Indicators	企业单位数(个) Enterprises (unit)	从业人数(人) Employed Persons (person)	工业总产值 Gross Output Value of Industry
总　计	**Total**	**342**	**439 334**	**75 625 946**
按隶属关系分	**By Subordination**			
中央工业	Central	26	69 346	21 428 552
市属工业	Municipal	47	76 287	17 161 370
非中央、市属工业	Local	269	293 701	37 036 024
按登记注册类型分	**Type of Registration**			
内　资	Domstic Funded	124	133 100	25 213 329
国　有	State-owned	7	18 421	8 449 008
集　体	Collective-owned			
股份合作制	Share-holding			
联　营	Jointly-operated			
有限责任公司	Companies with Limited Liability	52	58 925	8 313 008
股份有限公司	Companies Limited by Shares			
私　营	Private	53	36 088	2 491 645
其他内资	Other Domestic Investment			
港澳台商投资	Hong Kong/Macao/Taiwan Invested	53	46 694	5 725 777
#港澳台商独资	Solely Hong Kong/Macao/Taiwan Funded	25	21 516	2 940 806
外商投资	Foreigner Invested	165	259 540	44 686 840
#外商独资	Solely Foreigner Funded	107	171 838	24 534 153
按轻、重工业分	**By Light/Heavy Industry**			
轻工业	Light Industry	105	90 516	10 891 814
重工业	Heavy Industry	237	348 818	64 734 132
按从业人数分	**By Number of Employees**			
5 000 人及以上	≥5 000 persons	11	150 007	37 893 736
3 000 ~4 999 人	3 000 ~4 999 persons	18	67 024	10 366 658
1 000 ~2 999 人	1 000 ~2 999 persons	57	90 860	11 089 913
999 及以下	≤ 999 persons	256	131 443	16 275 639
按工业总产值分	**By Gross Output Value of Industry**			
5 亿元及以上	≥500 million yuan	172	348 434	71 511 382
10 000 ~49 999 万元	100 ~499.99 million yuan	148	82 520	3 954 700
5 000 ~9 999 万元	50 ~99.99 million yuan	20	7 026	155 041
5 000 万元以下	<50 million yuan	2	1 354	4 824
按固定资产原价分	**By Original Value of Fixed Assets**			
5 亿元及以上	≥500 million yuan	87	261 240	57 500 832
10 000 ~49999 万元	100 ~499.99 million yuan	137	111 217	13 012 464
1 000 ~9 999 万元	10 ~99.99 million yuan	62	34 267	3 398 576
1 000 万元以下	<10 million yuan	56	32 610	1 714 074
按利税总额分	**By Profits and Taxes**			
1 亿元及以上	≥100 million yuan	92	191 567	47 359 403
5 000 ~9 999 万元	50 ~99.99 milion yuan	59	49 466	4 750 895
1 000 ~4 999 万元	10 ~49.99 milion yuan	106	67 659	5 309 419
1 000 万元以下	<10 million yuan	85	130 642	18 206 230

Major Indicators of Large and Medium Industrial Enterprises with Independent Accounting Systems

(10 000 yuan)

工业销售产值 Sales Value of Industry	实收资本 Paid-in Capital	资产总计 Total Assets	流动资产合计 Total Circulating Assets	固定资产合计 Total Fixed Assets	固定资产原价 Original Value of Fixed Assets	本年折旧 Depreciation of the Current Year
75 552 289	**28 703 191**	**104 949 993**	**51 442 045**	**27 488 520**	**58 946 171**	**3 102 060**
21 374 020	16 440 863	39 292 275	13 745 874	16 901 810	34 812 527	1 668 648
16 812 098	4 904 439	35 598 907	17 469 009	4 251 486	9 000 638	553 822
37 366 171	7 357 889	30 058 811	20 227 162	6 335 224	15 133 006	879 591
25 019 298	18 661 733	58 630 857	21 502 019	17 975 017	36 238 024	1 835 178
8 447 863	11 669 629	19 337 937	2 143 331	13 173 044	26 642 745	1 272 582
8 236 600	4 120 118	16 408 129	9 971 065	3 201 290	5 946 505	390 469
2 431 043	283 021	2 406 244	1 618 270	428 454	660 639	44 228
5 651 676	2 129 991	8 325 856	5 539 304	1 585 484	4 742 464	157 911
2 870 856	1 177 597	4 606 360	3 431 652	973 872	3 385 007	83 892
44 881 315	7 911 467	37 993 279	24 400 722	7 928 019	17 965 682	1 108 972
24 959 446	3 707 278	14 085 420	9 392 212	3 358 026	8 471 302	572 271
10 678 225	2 600 552	11 140 263	7 274 496	2 294 647	4 411 441	246 204
64 874 065	26 102 638	93 809 729	44 167 550	25 193 873	54 534 730	2 855 856
38 153 310	16 742 868	62 758 428	25 158 454	18 088 413	38 166 576	1 892 936
10 150 834	3 065 043	8 124 372	4 331 473	2 634 334	7 166 330	362 429
11 050 243	3 782 499	14 622 506	8 945 878	3 257 248	6 075 729	421 327
16 197 903	5 112 781	19 444 687	13 006 241	3 508 524	7 537 535	425 368
71 438 613	26 280 612	96 711 937	46 763 875	25 747 008	55 991 571	2 926 150
3 950 759	2 322 192	7 700 964	4 442 475	1 639 298	2 762 021	161 143
157 980	63 183	278 554	151 145	56 545	127 403	10 092
4 937	37 204	258 537	84 550	45 668	65 176	4 675
57 471 324	25 883 718	86 609 042	37 590 856	25 186 672	54 914 036	2 797 193
12 933 801	2 307 433	12 454 802	8 662 690	1 980 580	3 427 996	253 859
3 392 134	318 665	3 939 293	3 516 613	246 090	449 511	39 423
1 755 030	193 374	1 946 855	1 671 886	75 177	154 627	11 585
46 864 160	22 622 080	81 417 679	35 639 005	22 572 575	49 729 261	2 400 034
4 829 238	1 148 088	5 578 778	3 934 674	1 075 160	2 198 933	125 593
5 274 926	1 338 818	6 145 411	3 960 877	1 311 226	2 185 489	136 923
18 583 965	3 594 204	11 808 125	7 907 489	2 529 559	4 832 487	439 510

单位:万元

表6－8 续表 Continued

指 标	Indicators	负债合计 Total Liabilities	所有者权益 Owner's Equity
总 计	**Total**	**47 812 837**	**57 058 320**
按隶属关系分	**By Subordination**		
中央工业	Central	18 343 964	20 856 601
市属工业	Municipal	12 857 239	22 741 286
非中央、市属工业	Local	16 611 634	13 460 433
按登记注册类型分	**Type of Registration**		
内 资	Domstic Funded	20 306 768	38 322 005
国 有	State-owned	5 516 322	13 821 615
集 体	Collective-owned		
股份合作制	Share-holding		
联 营	Jointly-operated		
有限责任公司	Companies with Limited Liability	9 913 560	6 494 566
股份有限公司	Companies Limited by Shares		
私 营	Private	1 245 824	1 158 338
其他内资	Other Domestic Investment		
港澳台商投资	Hong Kong/Macao/Taiwan Invested	4 587 577	3 751 840
#港澳台商独资	Solely Hong Kong/Macao/Taiwan Funded	2 786 678	1 819 682
外商投资	Foreign Invested	22 918 492	14 984 475
#外商独资	Wholly Foreign-owned	7 904 751.9	6 182 446.6
按轻、重工业分	**By Light/Heavy Industry**		
轻工业	Light Industry	5 598 438	5 553 305
重工业	Heavy Industry	42 214 399	51 505 015
按从业人数分	**By Number of Employees**		
5 000 人及以上	≥5 000 persons	25 306 036	37 362 483
3 000～4 999 人	3 000～4 999 persons	4 623 289	3 499 003
1 000～2 999 人	1 000～2 999 persons	8 031 939	6 590 546
999 及以下	≤ 999 persons	9 851 573	9 606 288
按工业总产值分	**By Gross Output Value of Industry**		
5 亿元及以上	≥500 million yuan	43 906 435	52 713 490
10000～49999 万元	100～499.99 million yuan	3 640 544	4 073 596
5 000～9 999 万元	50 ～99.99 million yuan	142 234	136 320
5 000 万元以下	<50 million yuan	123 623	134 914
按固定资产原价分	**By Original Value of Fixed Assets**		
5 亿元及以上	≥500 million yuan	36 686 471	49 830 581
10000～49999 万元	100～499.99 million yuan	6 993 983	5 460 416
1 000～9 999 万元	10～99.99 million yuan	2 721 813	1 217 478
1 000 万元以下	<10 million yuan	1 410 570	549 845
按利税总额分	**By Profits and Taxes**		
1 亿元及以上	≥100 million yuan	32 866 164	48 459 785
5 000～9 999 万元	50～99.99 milion yuan	2 826 444	2 750 253
1 000～4 999 万元	10～49.99 milion yuan	3 647 454	2 497 573
1 000 万元以下	<10 million yuan	8 472 776	3 350 709

(10 000 yuan)

主营业务收入 Revenue of Primary Operations	税金 Tax	本年应交增值税 Current Year Value-Added Tax Payable	营业利润 Operation Profits	利润总额 Total Profits	应付职工薪酬 Wage/Fringe Benefits
91 730 299	**3 107 983**	**1 392 341**	**7 148 278**	**7 618 228**	**5 317 029**
21 609 346	1 747 962	548 854	475 567	644 028	1 306 923
29 107 717	1 179 331	731 437	5 084 843	5 293 795	1 341 343
41 013 236	180 691	112 049	1 587 868	1 680 406	2 668 763
27 455 731	1 970 610	720 854	3 247 977	3 504 105	1 827 892
8 566 063	313 235	287 254	328 147	306 660	471 707
9 610 236	240 488	97 208	200 997	366 163	744 362
2 439 090	67 509	60 058	191 804	207 962	238 874
7 840 071	64 115	56 838	417 652	451 654	420 630
4 850 963	8 612	5 145	122 907	138 767	208 853
56 434 497	1 073 258	614 649	3 482 649	3 662 469	3 068 507
25 953 633.3	-34 989.6	-70 366	881 926.8	890 687.5	1 587 191.3
11 064 398	512 984	347 292	969 920	985 981	954 452
80 665 901	2 594 999	1 045 048	6 178 358	6 632 247	4 362 577
49 779 653	872 215	409 858	4 793 399	5 094 899	2 159 540
10 967 099	1 452 141	407 909	415 544	471 500	692 247
13 622 948	238 133	206 231	703 869	773 472	993 425
17 360 598	545 494	368 342	1 235 466	1 278 357	1 471 817
87 125 891	2 993 472	1 296 846	6 937 339	7 355 681	4 536 024
4 379 917	106 708	90 190	202 712	237 260	707 971
176 068	7 333	5 222	3 377	3 771	45 242
48 422	471	83	4 850	21 517	27 793
70 005 806	2 733 629	1 071 727	5 949 407	6 368 609	3 559 803
14 182 735	240 587	201 387	943 341	981 139	1 254 890
5 264 157	62 769	55 484	170 210	178 013	267 464
2 277 601	70 999	63 743	85 320	90 467	234 872
59 233 470	3 078 837	1 407 598	7 032 379	7 422 758	3 203 161
5 504 537	123 631	107 531	257 497	291 719	462 616
5 663 173	83 160	67 463	193 042	211 349	607 960
21 329 119	-177 645	-190 252	-334 640	-307 598	1 043 292

表6-9　港澳台及外商投资工业企业主要指标
（2015）

单位：万元

指　标	Indicators	企业单位数（个）Enterprises (unit)	从业人数（人）Employed Persons (person)	工业总产值 Gross Output Value of Industry
总　计	**Total**	**755**	**369 938**	**58 730 709**
按登记注册类型分	**By Type of Registration**			
与港澳台商合资经营企业	China-Hong Kong/Macao/Taiwan Joint Venture	61	24 052	2 189 535
与港澳台商合作经营企业	China-Hong Kong/Macao/Taiwan Cooperative	4	879	43 007
港澳台商独资企业	Solely Hong Kong/Macao/Taiwan Funded	103	31 855	3 968 971
港澳台商投资股份有限公司	Hong Kong/Macao/Taiwan Investment Companies Limited by Shares	3	5 209	1 027 660
其他港澳台商投资	Other HongKong/Macao/Taiwan Investment			
中外合资经营企业	Sino-Foreign Jointly-operated	139	68 404	17 235 004
中外合作经营企业	Sino-Foreign Cooperative	9	5 425	513 659
外商独资企业	Solely Foreigner Funded	426	208 936	29 491 708
外商投资股份有限公司	Foreign Investment Company Limited by Shares	8	24 246	4 144 445
其他外商投资	Other Foreign Investment	2	932	116 721
按行业分	**By Sector**			
农副食品加工业	Processing of Agricultural Side-line Food	10	1 532	789 034
食品制造业	Food Manufacturing	7	3 429	277 487
酒、饮料和精制茶制造业	Manufacturing of Liquor, Beverage and Refined Tea	3	3 858	297 761
烟草制品业	Tobacco Products			
纺织业	Textile Industry	11	1 338	153 825
纺织服装、服饰业	Textile Clothes and Accessories	17	9 191	274 751
皮革、毛皮、羽毛及其制品和制鞋业	Leather, Fur, Feather and their Products and Shoe-making	5	562	15 520
木材加工及木、竹、藤、棕、草制品业	Timber-Processing, Bamboo, Cane, Palm Fiber and Straw Products	2	220	11 604
家具制造业	Furniture Manufacturing	9	5 805	981 408
造纸及纸制品业	Paper-making and Paper Products	14	3 018	325 783

Major Indicators of HK/Macao/Taiwan & Overseas Invested Industrial Enterprises

(10 000 yuan)

工业销售产值 Sales Value of Industry	固定资产原价 Original Value of Fixed Assets	资产总计 Total Assets	负债总计 Total Liabilities	实收资本 Paid-in Capital	主营业务收入 Revenue of of Floating Assets	税金 Tax	利润总额 Total Profits
58 863 298	**26 140 883**	**55 365 811**	**31 589 746**	**12 662 841**	**73 243 174**	**1 427 471**	**4 803 226**
2 216 469	1 453 535	3 451 258	1 834 371	917 757	2 445 519	63 114	266 623
40 789	76 091	62 998	94 445	36 772	39 984	1 309	-39 201
3 915 453	4 023 295	5 971 964	3 354 075	1 658 652	5 929 585	26 405	185 030
992 423	186 864	959 723	271 872	237 222	1 031 182	7 840	84 935
16 979 024	6 292 540	16 171 229	9 353 366	3 118 207	27 634 137	1 139 044	2 856 440
533 413	331 254	500 016	255 798	198 221	614 895	25 988	18 456
29 901 782	10 167 814	19 000 817	10 164 430	5 003 434	31 247 802	167 880	1 311 348
4 143 663	3 537 726	9 102 235	6 226 175	1 414 286	4 175 092	-5 744	115 536
140 282	71 763	145 571	35 214	78 290	124 979	1 635	4 059
789 087	116 612	665 440	339 812	79 197	992 830	24 822	34 285
266 681	160 218	181 962	311 120	108 900	261 419	17 609	-68 324
304 200	270 682	237 008	163 454	208 930	356 932	18 731	13 371
155 173	56 624	158 102	84 995	45 051	154 914	1 605	5 306
267 449	54 823	216 921	174 548	34 484	268 755	9 645	-9 619
15 457	3 596	9 455	5 515	3 677	15 460	230	-533
12 374	628	5 199	3 437	1 094	11 435	894	651
978 536	179 574	1 023 118	703 758	106 010	976 895	26 954	184 261
324 600	311 172	418 870	202 086	197 512	331 010	9 259	7 476

单位:万元　　　　表6-9　续表　Continued

指　标	Indicators	企业单位数（个）Enterprises (unit)	从业人数（人）Employed Persons (person)	工业总产值 Gross Output Value of Industry
印刷业、记录媒介的复制	Printing and Record Medium Reproduction	8	1 817	106 268
文教、工美、体育和娱乐用品制造业	Manufacturing of Cultural, Educational, Arts, Sports and Leisure Products	10	1 477	58 278
石油加工、炼焦及核燃料加工业	Petroleum Processing, Coke Products and Processing of Nuclear Fuel	4	691	140 105
化学原料及化学制品制造业	Raw Chemical Materials and Chemical Products	61	14 781	3 994 219
医药制造业	Medicine Manufacturing	29	12 418	2 014 150
化学纤维制造业	Chemical Fiber	1	87	4 131
橡胶和塑料制品业	Rubber and Plastic Products	42	10 688	544 949
非金属矿物制品业	Nonmetal Mineral Products	25	5 474	439 584
黑色金属冶炼及压延加工业	Smelting and Pressing of Ferrous Metal	5	1 278	316 194
有色金属冶炼及压延加工业	Smelting and Pressing of Nonferrous Metal	6	990	257 984
金属制品业	Metal Products	35	8 291	682 005
通用设备制造业	General Purpose Equipment Manufacturing	125	40 034	5 575 117
专用设备制造业	Specialized Equipment Manufacturing	69	18 507	2 361 306
汽车制造业	Automobile Manufacturing	57	41 360	11 413 237
铁路、船舶、航空航天和其他运输设备制造业	Manufacturing of Railway, Ships, Aeronautics & Astronautics, and Other Transportation Equipment	16	2 884	230 182
电气机械及器材制造业	Electric Equipment and Machinery	62	23 597	2 785 002
计算机、通信和其他电子设备制造业	Manufacturing of Computers, Telecommunication and other Electronic Equipment	77	140 431	23 157 370
仪器仪表制造业	Manufacturing of Instrument and Apparatus	33	10 344	1 083 216
其他制造业	Other Manufacturing	5	3 814	224 788
金属制品、机械和设备修理业	Repairing of Metal Products, Machine and Equipment	3	734	89 944
电力、热力生产和供应业	Production and Supply of Electricity and Heating Power	3	236	23 449
水的生产和供应业	Production and Supply of Tap Water	1	1 052	102 058

(10 000 yuan)

工业销售产值 Sales Value of Industry	固定资产原价 Original Value of Fixed Assets	资产总计 Total Assets	负债总计 Total Liabilities	实收资本 Paid-in Capital	主营业务收入 Revenue of of Floating Assets	税金 Tax	利润总额 Total Profits
105 760	103 568	130 421	60 476	34 447	105 656	6 104	6 291
57 695	18 161	57 612	28 764	15 580	63 293	878	2 939
137 526	35 183	67 853	22 601	18 815	155 764	5 789	12 612
4 001 192	1 660 634	3 569 506	1 442 667	910 483	4 130 992	100 100	420 851
1 856 492	742 635	2 407 502	1 299 080	539 793	1 918 095	119 060	210 443
4 131	1 433	5 643	798	2 700	4 131	124	909
566 546	269 868	508 157	193 205	156 459	578 196	17 038	37 668
473 934	595 669	931 431	284 432	380 464	588 935	27 445	53 615
315 790	281 952	253 789	148 717	368 324	328 328	4 503	-11 229
258 265	146 148	328 516	226 173	87 752	286 192	4 372	4 419
707 857	362 197	764 836	373 802	226 969	731 101	22 353	30 906
5 596 505	3 839 785	9 431 905	6 318 334	1 272 615	5 664 046	89 028	232 532
2 376 027	716 533	2 543 889	1 363 426	485 064	2 565 443	54 693	173 110
11 238 106	3 960 476	10 203 337	5 946 411	1 346 803	21 237 080	954 732	2 473 775
227 233	86 874	240 802	103 864	57 844	238 353	4 900	18 894
2 763 537	812 656	2 124 955	1 018 255	472 176	2 843 706	36 295	253 121
23 556 239	10 057 652	16 887 854	10 043 936	4 928 712	26 879 173	-163 435	507 760
1 076 853	233 470	1 033 131	329 104	204 714	1 115 302	7 797	128 938
228 709	282 020	271 786	53 692	70 241	229 376	17 745	25 256
89 944	74 941	110 439	67 135	109 033	89 944	1 688	15 931
23 449	110 798	114 110	11 607	37 000	32 311	1 609	13 099
87 953	594 300	462 265	264 543	152 000	88 107	4 906	24 514

表6-10　私营工业企业主要指标
（2015）

单位：万元

指　标	Indicators	企业单位数（个）Enterprises (unit)	从业人数（人）Average Number of Employed Persons (person)	工业总产值 Gross Output Value of Industry
总　计	**Total**	**690**	**98 910**	**6 636 684**
按轻、重工业分	**By Light/Heavy Industry**			
轻工业	Light Industry	236	33 232	1 973 355
重工业	Heavy Industry	454	65 678	4 663 330
按主要工业行业分	**By Main Sector**			
#农副食品加工业	Processing of Agricultural Side-line Food	7	3 728	201 081
食品制造业	Food Producing	7	721	41 184
酒、饮料和精制茶制造业	Manufacturing of Liquor, Beverage and Refined Tea	2	279	103 024
纺织业	Textile Industry	12	1 460	115 445
纺织服装、服饰业	Manufacturing of Textile Clothes, Shoes and Hats	47	5 625	254 918
皮革、毛皮、羽毛及其制品和制鞋业	Leather, Fur, Feather and their Products and Shoe-making	11	1 500	42 994
木材加工及木、竹、藤、棕、草制品业	Timber-processing, Bamboo, Cane, Palm Fiber and Straw Products	3	222	28 254
家具制造业	Furniture Making	9	895	36 234
造纸及纸制品业	Paper-making and Paper Products	19	2 051	102 687
印刷业和记录媒介的复制	Printing and Record Medium Reproduction	21	3 127	136 999
文教、工美、体育和娱乐用品制造业	Manufacturing of Cultural, Educational, Arts, Sports and Leisure Products	11	1 492	200 095
石油加工、炼焦及核燃料加工业	Petroleum Processing, Coke Products and Processing of Nuclear Fuel	4	254	31 145
化学原料及化学制品制造业	Raw Chemical Material and Chemical Products	35	3 085	295 407
医药制造业	Medicine Manufacturing	15	3 158	280 657
化学纤维制造业	Chemical Fiber Manufacturing	3	264	30 020
橡胶和塑料制品业	Rubber and Plastic Products	70	7 960	420 044
非金属矿物制品业	Nonmetal Mineral Products	30	2 344	182 881
黑色金属冶炼及压延加工业	Smelting and Pressing of Ferrous Metal	12	1 161	88 818
有色金属冶炼及压延加工业	Smelting and Pressing of Nonferrous Metal	12	399	112 481
金属制品业	Metal Products	69	9 045	497 512
通用设备制造业	Manufacturing of General Purpose Equipment	78	10 698	662 144
专用设备制造业	Manufacturing of Specialized Equipment	40	5 139	316 690
汽车制造业	Automobile Manufacturing	39	11 803	704 815
铁路、船舶、航空航天和其他运输设备制造业	Manufacturing of Railway, Ship, Aviation and Aerospace, and other Transportation Equipment	16	1 913	121 182
电气机械及器材制造业	Manufacturing of Electrical Machinery and Equipment	86	12 353	1 244 517
计算机、通信和其他电子设备制造业	Manufacturing of Computers, Telecommunications and Other Electronic Equipment	18	4 740	290 749
仪器仪表制造业	Manufacturing of Instrument and Meters	8	809	49 140
其他制造业	Other Manufacturings	2	139	8 738
废弃资源综合利用业	Comprehensive Utilization of Waste Resource	1	102	10 775
金属制品、机械和设备修理业	Repairing of Metal Products, Machineries and Equipment	3	2 444	26 054

Major Indicators of PNA Private Industrial Enterprises

(10 000 yuan)

工业销售产值 Sales Value of Industry	固定资产原价 Original Value of Fixed Assets	资产总计 Total Assets	负债总计 Total Liabilities	实收资本 Paid-in Capital	主营业务收入 Revenue of of Floating Assets	税金 Tax	利润总额 Total Profits
6 526 032	**2 205 254**	**7 335 117**	**3 799 168**	**1 402 373**	**6 722 877**	**228 369**	**559 438**
1 910 226	755 658	2 169 299	1 049 188	505 942	1 937 551	85 822	246 102
4 615 806	1 449 596	5 165 818	2 749 980	896 431	4 785 326	142 547	313 336
200 607	68 831	143 404	79 320	16 023	188 760	4 530	12 842
41 384	8 939	46 695	21 077	9 574	39 809	1 801	2 277
97 383	31 178	98 518	63 792	24 912	97 507	16 010	65 697
115 623	25 704	121 704	73 633	15 108	116 383	9 268	9 762
248 199	68 818	191 996	137 240	25 527	250 121	6 583	2 336
47 599	7 088	33 004	25 632	5 438	47 838	1 707	119
28 351	1 002	12 317	7 688	2 000	27 269	432	64
36 021	11 712	40 838	27 032	4 653	35 704	1 274	1 614
101 013	66 035	93 433	49 552	11 891	100 379	3 331	2 292
135 054	94 742	148 278	68 573	24 704	135 794	6 101	12 105
192 298	21 626	175 641	82 005	27 010	193 749	2 581	16 105
16 974	28 446	53 550	19 650	14 614	26 153	814	2 907
302 131	107 281	417 020	140 120	134 283	302 635	10 077	69 318
245 772	97 361	399 993	166 367	54 107	286 187	13 127	30 064
28 224	5 066	21 793	7 528	4 212	28 224	1 131	3 519
415 352	166 916	462 145	200 471	180 853	415 539	15 158	43 499
180 716	65 692	227 579	164 028	36 870	182 882	6 012	5 193
85 663	40 667	98 831	62 696	22 363	85 286	2 035	1 602
110 433	10 847	67 917	54 848	11 926	225 967	437	-336
486 160	187 356	500 473	292 929	61 170	489 709	20 915	20 031
654 130	279 240	785 654	395 270	132 904	669 112	28 883	51 694
319 904	84 125	536 238	297 700	94 885	328 658	12 498	26 020
706 014	191 396	699 500	338 984	78 473	711 305	18 579	87 735
119 115	60 470	145 579	94 542	19 284	116 488	4 678	2 482
1 235 363	363 932	1 439 212	750 619	310 823	1 242 096	27 220	71 668
278 628	81 690	238 880	112 981	49 180	278 921	6 585	15 387
49 244	16 165	97 160	42 375	19 888	53 778	2 649	2 999
8 720	4 116	8 913	8 337	1 600	10 042	207	-718
13 904	5 974	12 994	3 343	7 600	10 705	72	748
26 054	2 838	15 859	10 838	500	25 878	3 675	416

表6-11　工业企业单位数和从业人员平均人数的各种分组
Classification of Industrial Enterprises and Average Number of Persons Employed

指　标　Indicators		企业单位数(个) Enterprises (unit)		从业人员平均人数(人) Average Number of Persons Employed (person)	
		2014	2015	2014	2015
总　计	**Total**	**1 788**	**1 714**	**644 497**	**608 915**
按隶属关系分	**By Subordination**				
中央工业	Central	43	39	71 990	72 893
市属工业	Municipal	92	89	91 577	84 803
非中央、市属工业	Local	1 653	1 586	480 930	451 219
按登记注册类型分	**By Type of Registration**				
内　资	Domestic Funded	986	959	226 806	226 028
国　有	State-owned	13	13	20 203	19 549
集　体	Collective-owned	17	16	2 288	1 581
股份合作	Share-holding	9	7	1 141	1 164
联　营	Jointly-operated	4	4	239	219
有限责任公司	Companies with Limited Liabilities	199	196	76 028	80 296
股份有限公司	Companies Limited by Shares	29	33	22 051	23 444
私　营	Private	715	690	104 856	99 775
港澳台商投资	HK/Macao/Taiwan Invested	186	171	68 147	64 591
#港澳台商独资	Solely HK/Macao/Taiwan Funded	111	103	34 670	33 152
外商投资	Foreign Invested	616	584	349 544	318 296
#外商独资	Wholly Foreign-owned	431	426	234 008	216 968
按轻、重工业分	**By Light/Heavy Industry**				
轻工业	Light Industry	559	534	166 121	146 990
重工业	Heavy Industry	1 229	1 180	478 376	461 925
按企业规模分	**By Scale of Enterprises**				
大型企业	Large	90	82	329 636	310 151
中型企业	Medium	273	260	149 576	142 054
小型企业	Small	1 425	1 372	165 285	156 710

表6-12 工业企业分行业能源消费情况
Energy Consumption of Industrial Enterprises by Sector (2015)

指 标 Indicators		企业单位数（个）Enterprises (in Number)	综合能源消费量（吨标准煤）Comprehensive Energy Consumption (tons of standard coal)	产值能耗（吨标准煤/万元）Energy Consumption of Production Value (tons of standard coal/10 000 yuan
总　计	**Total**	**1 754**	**8 498 493**	**0.096**
农副食品加工业	Processing of Agricultural Side-line Food	21	112 225	0.090
食品制造业	Food Manufacturing	17	26 439	0.075
酒、饮料和精制茶制造业	Manufacturing of Liquor, Beverage and Refined Tea	7	29 977	0.071
烟草制品业	Tobacco Products	1	2 836	0.013
纺织业	Textile Industry	32	47 114	0.125
纺织服装、服饰业	Textile Clothes and Accessories	82	13 068	0.013
皮革、毛皮、羽毛及其制品和制鞋业	Leather, Fur, Feather and their Products and Shoe-making	18	3 085	0.043
木材加工及木、竹、藤、棕、草制品业	Timber-processing, Bamboo, Cane, Palm Fiber and Straw Products	5	805	0.022
家具制造业	Furniture Manufacturing	19	23 762	0.023
造纸及纸制品业	Paper-making and Paper Products	38	187 853	0.402
印刷业和记录媒介复制业	Printing and Record Pressing	40	36 705	0.081
文教、工美、体育和娱乐用品制造业	Manufacturing of Cultural, Educational, Arts, Sports and Leisure Products	26	7 719	0.026
石油加工、炼焦及核燃料加工业	Petroleum Processing, Coke Products and Processing of Nuclear Fuel	14	2 207 887	0.465
化学原料和化学制品制造业	Raw Chemical Materials and Chemical Products	111	634 870	0.131
医药制造业	Medicine Manufacturing	58	135 375	0.042
化学纤维制造业	Chemical Fiber Manufacturing	4	5 535	0.161
橡胶和塑料制品业	Rubber and Plastic Products	130	136 315	0.119
非金属矿物制品业	Nonmetal Mineral Products	73	178 933	0.182
黑色金属冶炼及压延加工业	Smelting and Pressing of Ferrous Metal	22	77 164	0.179
有色金属冶炼及压延加工业	Smelting and Pressing of Nonferrous Metal	24	45 459	0.081
金属制品业	Metal Products	125	99 447	0.069
通用设备制造业	Manufacturing of General Purpose Equipment	225	228 871	0.035
专用设备制造业	Manufacturing of Special Purpose Equipment	123	88 735	0.027
汽车制造业	Automobile Manunfacturing	128	455 729	0.031
铁路、船舶、航空航天和其他运输设备制造业	Manufacturing of Railway, Ships, Aviation and Aerospace, and Other Transportation Equipment	45	62 095	0.080
电气机械及器材制造业	Manufacturing of Electric Machinery and Equipment	170	145 950	0.032
计算机、通信和其他电子设备制造业	Manufacturing of Computers, Telecommunications and Other Electronic Equipment	114	819 567	0.035
仪器仪表制造业	Manufacturing of Instruments and Apparatuses	41	20 705	0.018
其他制造业	Other Manufacturings	9	26 342	0.110
废弃资源综合利用业	Comprehensive Reutilization of Discarded Resources	2	189	0.017
金属制品、机械和设备修理业	Repairing of Metal Products, Machineries and Equipment	12	11 809	0.047
电力、热力的生产和供应业	Production and Supply of Electricity and Thermal Power	11	2 551 855	0.285
燃气生产和供应业	Production and Supply of Gas	2	14 399	0.064
水的生产和供应业	Production and Supply of Tap Water	5	59 675	0.309

表6-13 工业企业分行业主要能源品种消费情况
(2015)

指标 Indicators		原 煤(吨) Raw Coal (tons)	洗精煤(吨) Cleaned Coal (tons)	其他洗煤(吨) Other Washed Coals(tons)
总 计	**Total**	**9 795 035**	**7 918**	**10 124**
#农副食品加工业	Processing of Agricultural Side-line Food	27 737		
食品制造业	Food Manufacturing	5 415		
酒、饮料和精制茶制造业	Manufacturing of Liquor, Beverage and Refined Tea			
烟草制品业	Tobacco Products			
纺织业	Textile Industry	11 343		
纺织服装、服饰业	Textile Clothes and Accessories	14		
皮革、毛皮、羽毛及其制品和制鞋业	Leather, Fur, Feather and their Products and Shoe-making	641		
木材加工及木、竹、藤、棕、草制品业	Timber-processing, Bamboo, Cane, Palm Fiber and Straw Products	30		
家具制造业	Furniture Manufacturing	508		
造纸及纸制品业	Paper-making and Paper Products	144 997	1 600	2 023
印刷业和记录媒介复制业	Printing and Record Pressing	653		
文教、工美、体育和娱乐用品制造业	Manufacturing of Cultural, Educational, Arts, Sports and Leisure Products			
石油加工、炼焦及核燃料加工业	Petroleum Processing, Coke Products and Processing of Nuclear Fuel			
化学原料和化学制品制造业	Raw Chemical Materials and Chemical Products	938 967		
医药制造业	Medicine Manufacturing	20 916		
化学纤维制造业	Chemical Fiber Manufacturing			
橡胶和塑料制品业	Rubber and Plastic Products	9 463	3 735	8 101
非金属矿物制品业	Nonmetal Mineral Products	3 905		
黑色金属冶炼及压延加工业	Smelting and Pressing of Ferrous Metal	1 511		
有色金属冶炼及压延加工业	Smelting and Pressing of Nonferrous Metal			
金属制品业	Metal Products	1 343	2 516	
通用设备制造业	Manufacturing of General Purpose Equipment		52	
专用设备制造业	Manufacturing of Special Purpose Equipment	1 524		
汽车制造业	Automobile Manunfacturing	259	15	
铁路、船舶、航空航天和其他运输设备制造业	Manufacturing of Railway, Ships, Aviation and Aerospace, and Other Transportation Equipment			
电气机械及器材制造业	Electric Equipment and Machinery	3 867		
计算机、通信和其他电子设备制造业	Manufacturing of Computers, Telecommunications and Other Electronic Equipment			
仪器仪表制造业	Manufacturing of Instruments and Apparatuses	12		
其他制造业	Other Manufacturings	2 292		
废弃资源综合利用业	Comprehensive Reutilization of Discarded Resources			
金属制品、机械和设备修理业	Repairing of Metal Products, Machineries and Equipment	23		
电力、热力的生产和供应业	Production and Supply of Electricity and Thermal Power	8 619 615		
燃气生产和供应业	Production and Supply of Gas			
水的生产和供应业	Production and Supply of Tap Water			

Consumption of Main Kinds of Engery in Industrial Enterprises by Sector

煤制品(吨) Coal Products (tons)	焦 炭(吨) Coke (tons)	发生炉煤气(万立方米) Generator Gas (10 000 cu·m)	天然气(气态)(万立方米) Natural Gas (gas state) (10 000 cu·m)	液化天然气(液态)(吨) LNG(liquid state) (tons)	天然原油(吨) Natural Crude Oil (tons)	汽油(吨) Gasoline (tons)
81 212	**2 050**	**2**	**80 318**	**2 508**	**10 437 845**	**36 398**
			650			352
			307			429
			109			48
			3			14
			394			640.53
			19			1 214
				2		199
				9		93
			255			194
			2 472			535
			79			884
						313
			11 136		10 437 845	692
80 712			1 634			2 336
			956			825
						66
			179	4		1 807
104			3 599			879
395	876		2 074			505
	1 119		189			347
	55		1 147	1		1 691
			527	2 035		3 187
			297			1 236
			2 993	434		7 990
			542	23		739
			817			2 453
		2	2 045			1 785
			14			297
			333			87
						8
			18			257
			46 012			3 646
			1 517			450
						198

表 6－13　续表 1　Continued

指标	Indicators	煤油(吨) Kerosene (tons)	柴油(吨) Diesel Oil (tons)
总　计	**Total**	**3 444**	**47 295**
#农副食品加工业	Processing of Agricultural Side-line Food		3 424
食品制造业	Food Manufacturing		1 332
酒、饮料和精制茶制造业	Manufacturing of Liquor, Beverage and Refined Tea		1 063
烟草制品业	Tobacco Products		1
纺织业	Textile Industry		275
纺织服装、服饰业	Textile Clothes and Accessories		547
皮革、毛皮、羽毛及其制品和制鞋业	Leather, Fur, Feather and their Products and Shoe-making		10
木材加工及木、竹、藤、棕、草制品业	Timber-processing, Bamboo, Cane, Palm Fiber and Straw Products		44
家具制造业	Furniture Manufacturing	1	161
造纸及纸制品业	Paper-making and Paper Products	2	952
印刷业和记录媒介复制业	Printing and Record Pressing		1 331
文教、工美、体育和娱乐用品制造业	Manufacturing of Cultural, Educational, Arts, Sports and Leisure Products		69
石油加工、炼焦及核燃料加工业	Petroleum Processing, Coke Products and Processing of Nuclear Fuel		76
化学原料和化学制品制造业	Raw Chemical Materials and Chemical Products	2 341	3 733
医药制造业	Medicine Manufacturing		1249
化学纤维制造业	Chemical Fiber Manufacturing	294	1
橡胶和塑料制品业	Rubber and Plastic Products		1 585
非金属矿物制品业	Nonmetal Mineral Products		4 839
黑色金属冶炼及压延加工业	Smelting and Pressing of Ferrous Metal	1	286
有色金属冶炼及压延加工业	Smelting and Pressing of Nonferrous Metal	500	1 365
金属制品业	Metal Products	87	2 785
通用设备制造业	Manufacturing of General Purpose Equipment	153	11 629
专用设备制造业	Manufacturing of Special Purpose Equipment		496
汽车制造业	Automobile Manunfacturing	47	1 454
铁路、船舶、航空航天和其他运输设备制造业	Manufacturing of Railway, Ships, Aviation and Aerospace, and Other Transportation Equipment	3	1 357
电气机械及器材制造业	Electric Equipment and Machinery	15	1 525
计算机、通信和其他电子设备制造业	Manufacturing of Computers, Telecommunications and Other Electronic Equipment		300
仪器仪表制造业	Manufacturing of Instruments and Apparatuses		45
其他制造业	Other Manufacturings		200
废弃资源综合利用业	Comprehensive Reutilization of Discarded Resources		
金属制品、机械和设备修理业	Repairing of Metal Products, Machineries and Equipment		309
电力、热力的生产和供应业	Production and Supply of Electricity and Thermal Power		4 832
燃气生产和供应业	Production and Supply of Gas		
水的生产和供应业	Production and Supply of Tap Water		19

燃料油 (吨) Fuel Oil (tons)	液化石油气 (吨) LPG (tons)	炼厂干气 (吨) Dry Gas from Refineries (tons)	润滑油 (吨) Lude (tons)	石 蜡 (吨) Ceresin Wax (tons)
3 844	**62 685**	**329 564**	**10 971**	**801**
286				
	19			
	177			
	1			
9	22			
	5			
	10			
95	48			
398				
	5			759
124	41 929	318 474		
422	18 725	11 090	306	30
5	713		1	
1 779	47		8	12
176	5			
5				
362	410		11	
129	62		901	
	11		123	
50	160		9 517	
	38		11	
	155		44	
	141			
	2			
4			49	
	2			

表 6－13　续表 2　Continued

指标	Indicators	溶剂油（吨）Solvent Naphtha (tons)	其他石油制品（吨）Other Petrolium Products (tons)
总 计	**Total**	**10 438**	**890 912**
#农副食品加工业	Processing of Agricultural Side-line Food		770
食品制造业	Food Manufacturing		
酒、饮料和精制茶制造业	Manufacturing of Liquor, Beverage and Refined Tea		
烟草制品业	Tobacco Products		
纺织业	Textile Industry		
纺织服装、服饰业	Textile Clothes and Accessories		
皮革、毛皮、羽毛及其制品和制鞋业	Leather, Fur, Feather and their Products and Shoe-making	5	
木材加工及木、竹、藤、棕、草制品业	Timber-processing, Bamboo, Cane, Palm Fiber and Straw Products		
家具制造业	Furniture Manufacturing		
造纸及纸制品业	Paper-making and Paper Products		
印刷业和记录媒介复制业	Printing and Record Pressing		
文教、工美、体育和娱乐用品制造业	Manufacturing of Cultural, Educational, Arts, Sports and Leisure Products		
石油加工、炼焦及核燃料加工业	Petroleum Processing, Coke Products and Processing of Nuclear Fuel	5 964	870 062
化学原料和化学制品制造业	Raw Chemical Materials and Chemical Products	4 333	19 436
医药制造业	Medicine Manufacturing		
化学纤维制造业	Chemical Fiber Manufacturing	63	
橡胶和塑料制品业	Rubber and Plastic Products	42	31
非金属矿物制品业	Nonmetal Mineral Products		
黑色金属冶炼及压延加工业	Smelting and Pressing of Ferrous Metal		
有色金属冶炼及压延加工业	Smelting and Pressing of Nonferrous Metal		
金属制品业	Metal Products		119
通用设备制造业	Manufacturing of General Purpose Equipment	24	62
专用设备制造业	Manufacturing of Special Purpose Equipment	7	
汽车制造业	Automobile Manunfacturing		332
铁路、船舶、航空航天和其他运输设备制造业	Manufacturing of Railway, Ships, Aviation and Aerospace, and Other Transportation Equipment		
电气机械及器材制造业	Electric Equipment and Machinery		49
计算机、通信和其他电子设备制造业	Manufacturing of Computers, Telecommunications and Other Electronic Equipment	1	15
仪器仪表制造业	Manufacturing of Instruments and Apparatuses		30
其他制造业	Other Manufacturings		6
废弃资源综合利用业	Comprehensive Reutilization of Discarded Resources		
金属制品、机械和设备修理业	Repairing of Metal Products, Machineries and Equipment		
电力、热力的生产和供应业	Production and Supply of Electricity and Thermal Power		
燃气生产和供应业	Production and Supply of Gas		
水的生产和供应业	Production and Supply of Tap Water		

热　力 (百万千焦) Heating Power (1 million KJ)	电　力 (万千瓦时) Electric Power (10 000 KWH)	城市生活 垃圾用于燃料 (吨) City Life Garbage for Fuel(tons)	生物质废料 用于燃料 (吨) Biology Waste for Fuel(tons)	其他燃料 (吨标准煤) Other Fuels (tons/standard coal)
14 720 904	**1 896 481**	**383 451**	**5 714**	**42 698**
1 111 813	12 964			
46 311	4 769			
79 846	7 962			
20 155	695			
2 930	10 765		240	
1 036	3 338	48	230	
	767			
	189			
	5 801		4 204	
79 453	12 578			
81 343	9 537			
	2 038			
8 097 408	110 670			
2 633 463	127 311			
668 323	27 315			
	1 637			
24 920	37 645			
4 964	39 279			
	15 338			
	12 821		314	
18 702	23 948		726	
54 189	64 307			38
16 721	26 811			
474 990	123 723			
7 336	17 175			
21 994	41 788			
614 059	256 216			
	6 653			
	6 644			
	59			
	3 575			
353 635	861 326	383 403		42 660
307 313	1 054			
	19 785			

表6-14　工业企业能源消费分组情况

Energy Consumption of Industrial Enterprises by Group (2015)

指标　Indicators		综合能源消费量（吨标准煤）Comprehensive Energy Consumption (tons of standard coal)	单位产值能耗（吨标准煤/万元）Energy Consumption of Production Value (tons of standard coal/10 000 yuan)
按轻、重工业分	**By Light/Heavy Industry**		
轻工业	Light Industry	919 031	0.058
重工业	Heavy Industry	7 579 463	0.105
按企业规模分	**By Scale of Enterprises**		
大型企业	Large	6 227 746	0.110
中型企业	Medium	956 698	0.062
小型企业	Small	1 314 049	0.083
按高载能行业分	**By High Engery Bearing**		
石油加工、炼焦及核燃料加工业	Petroleum Processing, Coke Products and Processing of Nuclear Fuel	2 207 887	0.465
非金属矿物制品业	Nonmetal Mineral Products	178 933	0.182
化学原料及化学制品制造业	Raw Chemical Materials and Chemical Products	634 870	0.131
黑色金属冶炼及压延加工业	Smelting and Pressing of Ferrous Metal	77 164	0.179
电力、热力的生产和供应业	Production and Supply of Electricity and Thermal Power	2 551 855	0.285
按重点行业分	**By Key Industry**		
电子信息产品制造业	Manufacturing of Electronic and Information Products	938 352	0.036
汽车制造业	Automobile Industry	454 229	0.031
石油化工及精细化工制造业	Petrochemical and Refining Industry	2 769 196	0.301
精品钢材制造业	Manufacturing of Refined Steel Products	61 976	0.163
成套设备制造业	Manufacturing of Complete Equipment	284 523	0.032
生物医药制造业	Manufacturing of Biological Medicine	160 686	0.040
按高技术行业分	**By High-tech Industry**		
信息化学品制造	Manufacturing of Information Chemicals	132	0.022
医药制造业	Manufacturing of Medicines	135 375	0.042
航空航天器制造	Manufacturing of Aviation and Space Vehicles	1 600	0.017
电子及通信设备制造业	Manufacuring of Electronic and Communication Equipment	733 350	0.082
电子计算机及办公设备制造业	Manufacturing of Electronic Computer and Office Equipment	100 358	0.007
医疗设备及仪器仪表制造业	Manufacturing of Medical Equipment, Instrument and Meters	37 202	0.021

主要统计指标解释

工 业

指从事自然资源的开采，对采掘品和农产品进行加工和再加工的物质生产部门。具体包括：(1)对自然资源的开采，如采矿、晒盐等(但不包括禽兽捕猎和水产捕捞)；(2)对农副产品的加工、再加工，如粮油加工、食品加工、缫丝、纺织、制革等；(3)对采掘品的加工、再加工，如炼铁、炼钢、化工生产、石油加工、机器制造、木材加工等，以及电力、自来水、煤气的生产和供应等；(4)对工业品的修理、翻新，如机器设备的修理、交通运输工具(包括小卧车)的修理等。

1984年以前农村的村及村以下办工业归属农业，1984年以后划归工业。

工业统计调查单位为独立核算法人工业企业。

独立核算法人工业企业指从事工业生产经营活动的单位。独立核算法人工业企业应同时具备以下条件：①依法成立，有自己的名称、组织机构和场所，能够承担民事责任；②独立拥有和使用资产，承担负债，有权与其他单位签订合同；③独立核算盈亏，并能够编制资产负债表。

轻工业

指主要提供生活消费品和制作手工工具的工业。按其所使用的原料不同，可分为两大类：(1)以农产品为原料的轻工业，是指直接或间接以农产品为基本原料的轻工业。主要包括食品制造、饮料制造、烟草加工、纺织、缝纫、皮革和毛皮制作、造纸以及印刷等工业；(2)以非农产品为原料的轻工业，是指以工业品为原料的轻工业。主要包括文教体育用品、化学药品制造、合成纤维制造、日用化学制品、日用玻璃制品、日用金属制品、手工工具制造、医疗器械制造、文化和办公用机械制造等工业。

重工业

指为国民经济各部门提供物质技术基础的主要生产资料的工业。按其生产性质和产品用途，可以分为下列三类：(1)采掘(伐)工业，是指对自然资源的开采，包括石油开采、煤炭开采、金属矿开采、非金属矿开采等工业；(2)原材料工业，指向国民经济各部门提供基本材料、动力和燃料的工业。包括金属冶炼及加工、炼焦及焦炭、化学、化工原料、水泥、人造板以及电力、石油和煤炭加工等工业；(3)加工工业，是指对工业原材料进行再加工制造的工业。包括装备国民经济各部门的机械设备制造工业、金属结构、水泥制品等工业，以及为农业提供的生产资料如化肥、农药等工业。

根据上述划分原则，修理业中以重工业产品为修理作业对象的划为重工业，反之划为轻工业。

工业总产值

(1) 定义：工业总产值是以货币形式表现的，工业企业在一定时期内生产的工业最终产品或提供工业性劳务活动的总价值量。它反映一定时间内工业生产的总规模和总水平。

(2) 计算原则：工业生产的原则，即凡是企业在报告期生产的经检验合格的产品，不管是否在报告期销售，均包括在内。

最终产品的原则，即凡是计入工业总产值的产品，必须是本企业生产的经检验合格的，不需要再进行任何加工的最终产品。如果企业有中间产品(半成品)对外销售，则对外销售的中间产品应视为企业的最终产品。

工厂法原则，即工业总产值是以工业企业作为基本计算(核算)单位，即按企业的最终产品计算工业总产值。按这种方法计算的工业总产值，不允许同一产品价值在企业内部重复计算，不能把企业内部各个车间(分厂)生产的成果相加，但允许企业间的重复计算。

(3) 内容及计算方法：1995年全国工业普查对工业总产值(原规定)的内容及计算原则和方法做了某些修订，修订后的工业总产值(新规定)包括三项内容：即本期生产成品价值、对外加工费收入、在制品半成品期末期初差额价值三部分。

本期生产成品价值：指企业本期生产，并在报告期内不再进行加工，经检验、包装入库的全部工业成品(半产品)价值合计，包括企业生产的自制设备及提供给本企业在建工程、其他非工业部门和福利部门等单位使用的成品价值。本期生产成品价值为按自备原材料生产的产品的数量乘以本期不含增值税(销项税额)的产品实际销售平均单价计算；会计核算中按成本价格转帐的自制设备和自产自用的成品，按成本价格计算生产成品价值。生产成品价值中不包括用定货者来料加工的成品(半产品)价值。

对外加工费收入：指企业在报告期内完成的对外承接的工业品加工(包括用定货者来料加工产品)的加工费收入和对外工业修理作业所取得的加工费收入。对外加工费收入按不含增值税(销项税额)的价格计算，可根据会计"产品销售收入"科目的有关资料取得。

对于本企业对内非工业部门提供的加工修理、设备安装的劳务收入，如果企业会计核算基础较好，能取得这部分资料，而且这部分价值所占比重较大，应包括在对外加工费收入中。

自制半成品在制品期末期初差额价值：指企业报告期在制品期末减期初的差额价值，本指标一般可以从会计核算资料中取得。如果会计产品成本核算中不计算半成品、在制品的成本，则总产值中也不包括这部分价值，反之则包括。

(4) 工业总产值统计范围变化和计算方法修订情况：1984年以前工业总产值不包括村办工业，村办工业总产值划归农业。1984年以后工业总产值包括村办工业。

1995年工业普查对工业总产值计算方法做了修订，即从1995年始按新修订(新规定)方法计算工业总产值。新规定与原规定的区别如下：

全价与加工费的计算原则不同:新规定为凡自备原材料,不论其生产繁简程度如何,一律按全价计算工业总产值;凡来料加工,允许按加工费计算工业总产值。原规定则视生产加工的繁简程度不同,规定哪些行业按全价,哪些行业按加工费计算工业总产值。

自制半成品、在产品期末期初差额价值的计算原则不同:新规定要求,凡会计产品成本核算时计算了成本的差额价值,总产值中就应包括,否则可不包括;原规定则按生产周期六个月的界限区分,凡生产周期六个月以上的企业,总产值计算中应包括这部分差额价值,否则可不包括。

计算价格不同:新规定按不含增值税(销项税额)的价格计算;原规定则按含增值税(销项税额)的价格计算。

工业销售产值

是以货币表现的工业企业在一定时期内销售的、本企业生产的工业产品总量。包括已销售的成品、半成品价值,对外提供的工业性作业价值和对本单位基本建设部门、生活福利部门等提供的产品和工业性作业及自制设备的价值。工业销售产值依循的是以产品所有权转移为计算原则,因此,已销售的成品、半成品不论是本期生产的、还是上期生产的,只要是本期销售出去的均包括在内。对外提供的工业性作业是指企业按合同对外提供的工业性劳务。

工业销售产值的计算范围、计算价格和计算方法与工业总产值一致,但两者计算的基础不同,工业销售产值计算的基础是产品销售总量,工业总产值计算的基础是工业产品生产总量。

出口交货值

是指工业企业交给外贸部门或自营(委托)出口(包括销往香港、澳门地区、台湾省)的产品价值;批量销于国内或在过境批量出口等但用外汇价格结算的产品价值;外商来样、来料加工,来件装配和补偿贸易等生产,分别参照计算总产值的规定要求按全价或加工费计算的价值。

大、中、小型企业

根据工业和信息化部、国家统计局、国家发展改革委、财政部《关于印发中小企业划型标准规定的通知》(工信部联企业【2011】300号),依据从业人员、营业收入、资产总额等指标或替代指标,将我国的企业划分为大型、中型、小型、微型等四种类型,原划分办法废止。工业企业划型标准见下表:

指标名称	计量单位	大 型	中 型	小 型	微 型
从业人员(X)	人	X≥1000	300≤X<1000	20≤X<300	X<20
主营业务收入(Y)	万元	Y≥40000	2000≤Y<40000	300≤Y<2000	Y<300

说明:大型、中型和小型企业必须同时满足所列指标下限,否则下划一档;微型企业只须满足所列指标中的一项即可。

独立核算工业企业、非独立核算工业生产单位

工业企业按其行政和财务是否独立,分为独立核算工业企业和非独立核算工业生产单位。

独立核算工业企业应同时具备下列三个条件:(1)行政上有独立的组织形式;(2)经济上独立核算,自负盈亏,编制独立的资金平衡表(或资产负债表);(3)有权与其他单位签订合同,并在银行设有独立帐户。独立核算工业企业不论是单一性生产或联合性生产的企业,均以整个企业作为一个基层单位进行统计,而不按分厂、车间统计。

非独立核算工业生产单位是指不同时具备独立核算工业企业三个条件,附设于其他企业、事业、机关、团体、学校、科研机构、部队等单位的工业生产单位。非独立核算工业生产单位必须同时具备下列三个条件,才可列入工业统计范围,即:(1)有固定的生产场所和生产设备;(2)有固定的生产工人和学徒在10人以上;(3)一般单位常年生产,季节性生产的单位全年开工时间在三个月以上。

资产总计

资产是指企业拥有或者控制的能以货币计量的经济资源,包括各种财产、债权和其他权利。资产按其流动性(即资产的变现能力和支付能力)划分为:流动资产、长期投资、固定资产、无形资产、递延资产和其他资产。该指标根据企业会计"资产负债表"中"资产总计"项目的期末数增列。

流动资产合计

指可以在一年或者超过一年的一个营业周期内变现或者耗用的资产,包括现金及各种存款、短期投资、应收及预付货款、存款等。

流动资产平均余额

指企业在报告期内全部流动资产的平均余额。

固定资产净值年平均余额

指固定资产净值在报告期内余额的平均数。计算公式为:

固定资产净值年平均余额 = 1至12月各月月初、月末固定资产净值之和/24

该指标根据"资产负债表"中"固定资产原价"、"累计折旧"指标的期初、期末数计算填列。

固定资产净值指固定资产原价减去历年已提折旧额后的净额。计算公式为:

固定资产净值 = 固定资产原价 - 累计折旧

负债合计

负债合计是指企业所承担的能以货币计量,将以资产或劳务偿付的债务总计。负债一般按偿还期长短分为流动负债和长期负债。流动负债合计是指企业在一年内或超过一年的一个营业周期内偿还的债务;长期负债合计是指偿还期在一年以上或者超过一年的一个营业周期内偿还债

务。

所有者权益

指企业投资人对企业净资产的所有权。企业净资产等于企业全部资产减去全部负债后的余额，包括企业投资人对企业的最初投入的实际到位的资产及资本公积金、盈余公积金和未分配利润。所有者权益合计数小于零，表示企业资不抵债。

利润总额

指企业生产经营活动的最终成果，是企业在一定时期内实现的盈亏相抵后的利润总额（亏损以"－"号表示），它等于营业利润加上补贴收入加上投资收益加上营业外净收入再加上以前年度损益调整。

EXPLANATORY NOTES TO MAJOR STATISTICAL INDICATORS

Industry

Industry refers to the material production sector which is engaged in extraction of natural resources and processing and reprocessing of minerals and agricultural products, including (1) extraction of natural resources, such as mining, salt production (but not including hunting and fishing); (2) processing and reprocessing of farm and sideline produces, such as rice husking, flour milling, wine making, oil pressing, silk reeling, spinning and weaving, and leather making; (3) manufacture of industrial products, such as steel making, iron smelting, chemicals manufacturing, petroleum processing, machine building, timber processing; water and gas production and electricity generation and supply; (4) repairing of industrial products such as the repairing of machinery and means of transport (including cars).

Prior to 1984, the rural industry run by villages and cooperative organizations under village was classified into agriculture. Since 1984, it has been grouped into industry.

Units of industrial statistics survey corporate industrial enterprises with independent accounting system.

Corporate industrial enterprises with independent accounting system refer to enterprises engaging in industrial production activities, which meet the following requirements: ①They are established legally, having their own names, organizations, location, able to take civil liability; ②They possess and use their assets independently, assume liabilities, and are entitled to sign contracts with other units; ③They are financially independent and compile their own balance sheets.

Light Industry

refers to the industry that produces consumer goods and hand tools. It consists of two categories, depending on the materials used:

(1) Industries using farm products as raw materials. These are branches of light industry which directly or indirectly use farm products as basic raw materials, including the manufacture of food and beverages, tobacco processing, textile, clothing, fur and leather manufacturing, paper making, printing, etc.

(2) Industries using non farm products as raw materials. These are branches of light industry which use manufactured goods as raw materials, including the manufacture of cultural, educational articles and sports goods, chemicals, synthetic fiber, chemical products for daily use, glass products for daily use, metal products for daily use, hand tools, medical apparatus and instruments, and the manufacture of cultural and clerical machinery.

Heavy Industry

refers to the industry which produces capital goods, and provides various sectors of the national economy with necessary material and technical basis. It consists of the following three branches according to the purpose of production or the use of products:

(1) Mining, quarrying and logging industry refers to the industry that extracts natural resources, including extraction of petroleum, coal, metal and non-metal ores.

(2) Raw materials industry refers to the industry that provides various sectors of the national economy with raw materials, fuels and power. It includes smelting and processing of metals, coking and coke chemistry, chemical materials and building materials such as cement, plywood, and power, petroleum refining and coal dressing.

(3) Manufacturing industry refers to the industry that processes raw materials. It includes machine building industry which equips sectors of the national economy, industries of metal structure and cement products, industries producing means of agricultural production, such as chemical fertilizers and pesticides. According to the above principle of classification, the repairing trades which are engaged primarily in repairing products of heavy industry are classified into heavy industry while these engaged in repairing products of light industry are classified into light industry.

Gross Output Value of Industry

(1) Definition: Gross industrial output value is the total volume of final industrial products produced and industrial services provided during a given period. It reflects the total achievements and overall scale of industrial production during a given period.

(2) Principles for calculation: Statistics on industrial production follow the principle that all products produced by the enterprises and accepted during the reference period are to be included no matter whether they are sold or not during the reference period.

Determination of final products follow the principle that all products that are included in the calculation of grow industrial output value are the final products of the enterprise which have been accepted through quality check and require no further processing. If an enterprise has intermediate (semi-finished) products to sell, these intermediate products are considered as the final products of the enterprise.

Gross industrial output value is calculated following the principle of factory approach, i. e. industrial enterprise is used as the basic accounting unit in calculating the gross industrial output value. By this approach, value of the same product is not to be double counted, and the output value of different workshops (branch factories) should not be added. However, this approach does not exclude the possibility of double counting between enterprises.

(3) Content and calculation method: The old definition of gross industrial output value was modified duringthe national industrial census in 1995. The revised (new) definition of gross industrial output value consists of 3 components: value of the finished products during the reference period, income from external processing, and value of change in semi-finished products at the end and at the beginning of the reference period.

Value of the finished products during the reference period: refers to the value of all finished (semi-finished) industrial products that are produced during the reference period without the need for further processing, checked for acceptance, packed and put into the warehouse of the enterprise, including the value of own-produced equipment and the value of products provided to the projects under construction of the enterprise, and to other non-industrial or welfare units. Value of finished products during the reference period is calculated by the quantity of products produced using own materials multiplied by the average unit prices at which products are sold (excluding value-added tax). Own-produced equipment and products produced for own use are value at cost prices as in the case of enterprise accounting. Value of finished products does not include the value of finished products (semi-finished products) that are produced using the materials from the clients who make the orders.

Income from external processing: refers to income from contracted external processing of industrial products (including processing of industrial products using materials from the clients), and the income from industrial repairing work provided to other units. Income from external processing is calculated using information from the item "products sales income" in the enterprise accounting at the prices excluding value-added tax.

For income from services such as processing, repairing and installation of equipment provided to non-industrial units within the enterprise, if the accounting work of the enterprise is good enough to separate it from other records, and the share of such services is significant, it should also be included in the income from external processing.

Value of change in semi-finished products at the end and at the beginning of the reference period: refers to the value of change in semi-finished products at the end and at the beginning of the reference period, which generally can be obtained from accounting records of enterprises. If the enterprise accounting excludes the cost of semi-finished products, then it should not be included in the gross industrial output value, and vice versa.

(4) Changes in the coverage and method of calculation of gross industrial output value: Prior to 1984, the value of rural industry run by villages was classified into agriculture instead of industry. Since 1984, it has been included in the gross industrial output value.

Method of calculation for the gross industrial output value was modified in the industrial census in 1995. The difference in the new method as compared with the old one is outlined below:

Principle in using full value vs. processing fee: The new method stipulates that all products produced using own materials are to be calculated with full value in reporting the gross industrial output value irrespective of sophistication of production, and for external processing, it allows calculation using processing fee. In the old method, however, the use of full value or processing fee was determined by the degree of sophistication of production in different branches of industries.

Principle in determining the value of change in semi-finished products: The new method requires that value of the change in semi-finished products should be included in the gross industrial output value if it is included in the accounting record of the enterprise, otherwise it should not be included. By the old method, it is determined by the type of enterprises in terms of production cycle. If the production cycle is over 6 months, the value of change in semi-finished products is included in the gross industrial output value, otherwise it is excluded.

Difference in prices: The new method uses prices excluding value-added tax in the calculation of gross industrial output value, while the old method used prices including value-added tax.

Sales Output Value of Industry

refers to total sales value of products produced by industrial enterprises during a given period, including sales of finished goods, value of semi-products, value of industrial services provided to other units, value of products provided for capital construction sector, welfare sector and value of industrial services provided and self produced equipment within enterprises. Sales of finished goods andsemi-products in current period are taken into account regardless of their production period.

The coverage, pricing, and calculation method for sales output value of industry are the same as for gross output value of industry except that the former is based on sales of products and the latter is based on the output of products.

Export Delivery Value of Industry

refers to the product value which industrial enterprises deliver to Foreign Trade Department, or value of products which are exported directly from producers (including the sales to Hong Kong, Macao and Taiwan); the product value, (at foreign exchange rate,) of domestic batch sale or transit batch export; full price or processing fee of the production with design, materials, assembling parts supplied by foreign businessmen and compensation trade.

Large, Medium and Small Enterprises

According to the Notice of the Ministry of Industry and Information Technology, National Bureau of Statistics, National Development and Reform Commission and the Ministry of Finance on printing and distributing the classification standard for middle and small enterprises (<2011> No. 300), we will divide our national enterprises into four kinds that are large, middle, small and mini in accordance with the indicators or substitute indicators such as employed persons, operation income and total assets. The former method for classification will be discarded. The classification standard for industrial enterprises are shown as followed.

Indicators	Unit	Large	Middle	Small	Mini
Employed Persons (X)	Persons	X≥1000	300≤X<1000	20≤X<300	X<20
Main Operation Income (Y)	10 000 yuan	Y≥40000	2000≤Y<40000	300≤Y<2000	Y<300

Note: Large, middle and small enterprises must meet all of the lowest limit of the listed indicators, or they will be classified into the lower kind, respectively. Mini enterprises can meet only one of the listed indicators.

Industrial Enterprises with Independent Accounting

Systems and Industrial Production Units with Non-Independent Accounting Systems.

Depending on whether they have independent administration and accounting, industrial enterprises can be divided into industrial enterprises with independent accounting system and industrial production units with non-independent accounting system. An industrial enterprise with independent accounting system shall operate simultaneously under the following three conditions: (1) having an independent organization in terms of administration; (2) economically having independent accounting, taking care of its own profits and losses, and filing independent balance sheets; and (3) enjoying the right to sign contracts with other units and to open independent bank accounts. An industrial enterprise with independent accounting system, no matter under a unitary management or cooperative operation, shall be counted as single grassroots unit in statistics and its branch factories and workshops shall not be calculated separately.

An industrial production unit with non-independent accounting system is an industrial production unit which does not operate simultaneously under the above mentioned three conditions of industrial enterprises with independent accounting systems and is attached to an enterprise, institution, government department, organization, school, scientific research institution, or army unit. An industrial production with non-independent accounting system unit can be included into the industrial statistics only when it operates simultaneously under the following three conditions: (1) having fixed production sites and production equipment; (2) having more than 10 permanent workers and apprentices; and (3) operating all year round if it's a normal production unit or operating more than three months a year if it's a seasonal production unit.

Aggregate Assets

Total Assets refer to all economic resources, in monetary terms, that is owned or controlled by enterprises, including properties, creditors equity and other economic rights of all forms. Classified by the degree of equitability, total assets include circulating assets, long-term investment, fixed assets, intangible assets and deferred assets, and other assets. Data on this indicator can be obtained by the year-end figures of total assets in the Assets and Liability Table of accounting records of enterprises.

Total of Working Capitals

Total of Working Capitals refer to capitals which can be cashed in or spent or consumed in an operating cycle of one year or over one year, including cash, all kinds of deposits, short term investment, receivable and payable payment for goods or deposits.

Average Value of Working Capitals

Average Value of Working Capitals refers to the average value of all working capitals of the enterprise during the reference period.

Annual Average of Net Value of Fixed Assets

refer to average of the net value of fixed assets during the reference period, calculated with the following formula:

Annual Average of Net Value of Fixed Assets = sum of net value of fixed assets at the beginning and at the end of each month from January to December / 24.

Information on this indicator can be obtained from the beginning and ending figures of the original value of fixed assets and cumulative depreciation from the Assets and Liability Table of enterprises.

Net value of fixed assets refers to the original value of fixed assets minus depreciation over the years, i. e. :

Net value of fixed assets = original value of fixed assets-cumulative depreciation

Aggregate Liabilities

Aggregate liabilities refer to the total debts of an enterprise which can be calculated in monetary term and will be repaid in the forms of assets or service. Usually, the debts are divided into liquid liability and long-term debt according to the length of the payback period. The liquid liability is the debt that an enterprise will pay back during an operation cycle which is either shorter or longer than a year. The long-term debt refers to a debt whose payback period is longer than a year or which will be repaid during an operation cycle that is longer than a year.

Creditors' Equity

Creditors' Equity refers to investors ownership of net assets of the enterprise, which is equal to the total assets of the enterprise minus its total liabilities, including the primary input actually received at the enterprise from investors, capital accumulation fund, surplus accumulation fund and undistributed profit. When the total of creditors' equity is less than zero, that indicates the liability of the enterprise is larger that its assets.

Total Profits

Total Profits refer to the final achievements of production and operation of the enterprises, represented by the total profits after deducting losses (loss is expressed by the negative figure). It is the sum of profits from operation, income from subsidies, investment earnings, net income from activities other than operation, and adjustment of profits and losses of previous years.

Ratio of Profits, Taxes and Interests to Average Assets

Ratio of Profits, Taxes and Interests to Average Assets reflects the profit-making capability of all assets of the enterprise and is a key indicator manifesting the performance and management and evaluating the profit-making potential of the enterprise. It is calculated as follows:

Ratio of Profits, Taxes and Interests to Average Assets (%) = [(total profits + total taxes + interest payment) / average assets] ×100%

In the above formula, total taxes is the sum of tax and extra charges on the sales of products and value-added tax payable; and average assets is the arithmetic mean of the sum of beginning assets and ending assets.

第七篇

2016上海浦东新区统计年鉴 SHANGHAI PUDONG NEW AREA STATISTICAL YEARBOOK

CHAPTER 7

建筑业

CONSTRUCTION

表7－1 主要年份建筑业企业主要指标

指 标 Indicators		单 位 Unit	1995
施工企业单位数	Number of Construction Enterprises	个 unit	243
年末从业人员数	Employed Persons（Year End）	人 person	125 627
全年从业人员平均数	Annual Average Employed Persons	人 person	140 994
建筑业总产值	Gross Output Value of Construction	万元 10 000 yuan	1 045 601
#建筑工程	Construction Projects	万元 10 000 yuan	905 848
安装工程	Installation Projects	万元 10 000 yuan	110 763
竣工产值	Output Value of Construction Projects Completed	万元 10 000 yuan	446 202
房屋建筑面积	Floor Space of Buildings		
施工面积	Floor Space Under Construction	万平方米 10 000 sq·m	1 042.05
#本年新开工	New Start in Current Year	万平方米 10 000 sq·m	285.02
竣工面积	Floor Space Completed	万平方米 10 000 sq·m	290.25
#住 宅	Housing	万平方米 10 000 sq·m	150.63
全员劳动生产率	Overall Labor Productivity	元/人 yuan/person	74 159
房屋建筑面积竣工率	Ratio of Floor Space Completed over That under Construction	%	27.9
平均每个职工竣工房屋面积	Floor Space Completed Per Staff Member	平方米/人 sq·m/person	20.59

注：建筑业总产值为建筑业企业自行完成的施工产值。
Note：Gross output value of construction refers to the output value of construction completed by construction enterprises themselves.

Major Indicators of Construction Industry in Main Years

2000	2005	2010	2011	2012	2013	2014	2015
367	398	699	720	651	593	586	565
93 753	159 099	253 822	259 056	268 981	181 421	172 806	277 545
116 722	208 807	361 140	424 530	358 747	277 915	315 666	345 036
935 731	3 353 790	9 801 257	11 353 474	12 231 885	12 936 456	12 923 297	13 470 418
886 356	2 599 981	8 001 415	9 746 424	10 415 352	11 366 000	11 526 916	11 625 282
115 164	643 346	1 526 037	1 440 514	1 602 576	1 383 923	1 213 571	1 582 714
786 808	2 322 347	6 858 981	5 650 019	6 128 065	7 805 169	7 012 587	8 601 977
1 149.25	3 009.91	6 886.55	8 451.28	9 976.65	11 285.84	12 627.52	12 600.12
426.18	1 291.18	2 501.17	2 675.90	3 040.28	3 578.08	3 322.24	2 388.39
520.61	903.45	1 641.86	1 520.70	1 619.20	1 824.35	1 947.10	2 153.51
350.65	523.94	695.52	677.63	843.41	878.72	999.28	988.47
80 167	160 617	271 398	267 436	340 961	465 482	409 398	390 406
45.3	30.0	23.8	18.0	16.2	16.2	15.4	17.1
44.60	43.27	45.46	35.82	45.13	65.64	61.68	62.41

表7-2 建筑业企业主要指标
(2015)

指 标	Indicators	企业单位数(个) Number of Enterprises (unit)	年末从业人员数(人) Employed Persons at Year-end (person)	年从业人员平均数(人) Annual Average Employed Persons (person)	建筑业总产值(万元) Gross Output Value of Construction (10 000 yuan)	竣工产值(万元) Output Value of Completed Construction Projects (10 000 yuan)
合 计	**Total**	**565**	**277 545**	**345 036**	**13 470 418**	**8 601 977**
按注册登记类型分	**By Type of Registration**					
内 资	Domestic Investment	539	268 397	331 861	12 829 249	8 035 407
国 有	State-owned	2	35	544	16 414	3 402
集 体	Collective-owned	5	1 046	1 030	34 119	38 874
股份合作	Share-holding	1	43	43	1 015	1 015
联 营	Jointly-operated	2	381	376	18 489	3 546
国有独资公司	Wholly state-owned Companies	15	17 959	27 798	1 373 989	656 578
有限责任公司	Companies with Limited Liabilities	80	126 751	143 689	6 748 113	4 160 984
股份有限公司	Companies Limited by Shares	11	7 412	31 713	1 035 510	1 137 825
私 营	Private	423	114 770	126 668	3 601 600	2 033 183
港澳台商投资	HK/Macao/Taiwan Invested	11	2 923	3 635	221 266	141 702
外商投资	Foreign Invested	15	6 225	9 540	419 903	424 868
按行业分	**By Sector**					
房屋建筑业	Housing Construction	162	186 522	191 017	7 712 585	5 124 865
土木工程建筑业	Civil Engineering Construction	153	53 356	104 162	3 691 915	2 231 662
建筑安装业	Installation	117	15 052	21 318	914 793	661 208
建筑装饰和其他建筑业	Other Constructions	133	22 615	28 539	1 151 125	584 242
按建筑业资质等级分	**By Qualification of Construction Industry**					
#特 级	Special Grade	2	101 234	97 709	4 844 590	3 276 346
一 级	Grade I	74	57 130	79 590	3 690 472	1 683 652
二 级	Grade II	179	72 824	113 649	3 459 172	2 679 523
三 级	Grade III	303	44 349	49 097	1 305 690	834 006

注：1. 建筑业总产值为建筑业企业自行完成的施工产值；建筑业资质等级为新标准资质。
2. 本表数据不包括外省市在沪建筑业企业。

Note：1. Gross Output Value of Construction refers to the output value of construction completed by construction enterprises themselves. Qualification of construction industry refers to the qualification under new standards.
2. The numbers in this form does not include the construction enterprises that operate in Shanghai, but are registered in other provinces.

Major Indicators of Construction Enterprises

房屋建筑施工面积（万平方米）Floor Space Under Construction (10 000 sq・m)	#本年新开工 New Start in Current Year	房屋竣工面积（万平方米）Floor Space Completed (10 000 sq・m)	#住宅 Residential Housing	全员劳动生产率（元/人）Overall Labor Productivity (yuan/person)	房屋建筑面积竣工率（%）Ratio of Floor Space Completed (%)	平均每个职工竣工房屋面积（平方米/人）Floor Space Completed Per Staff Member (sq・m/person)
12 600.12	**2 388.39**	**2 153.51**	**988.47**	**390 406**	**17.1**	**62.41**
12 476.05	2 349.15	2 080.27	988.47	386 585	16.7	62.68
				301 728		
18.15	10.81	7.34	4.66	331 252	40.4	71.26
		0.49		236 047		113.95
14.70	14.70			491 729		
229.77	68.72	83.35	49.85	494 276	36.3	29.98
9 558.26	1 467.78	1 302.21	716.34	469 633	13.6	90.63
1 295.87	357.58	345.30	72.56	326 525	26.6	108.88
1 359.30	429.56	341.58	145.06	284 334	25.1	26.97
		1.00		608 710		2.75
124.07	39.24	72.24		440 150	58.2	75.72
11 145.41	1 903.41	1 731.08	884.46	403 764	15.5	90.62
1 401.47	478.98	407.35	104.01	354 440	29.1	39.11
48.66	4.42	12.51		429 118	25.9	5.86
4.58	1.58	2.57		403 352	56.1	0.90
9 307.61	1 371.12	1 205.75	660.64	495 818	12.9	123.40
743.38	201.82	189.02	86.43	463 685	25.4	23.75
2 303.53	717.18	665.37	226.20	304 373	28.9	58.55
245.60	98.27	93.37	15.20	265 941	3.8	19.02

表7-3 建筑业财务报表
(2015)

单位:万元

指 标	Indicators	合 计 Total	内 资 Domestic Investment
企业单位数(个)	**Number of Enterprises (unit)**	**565**	**539**
年末资产负债	**Balance Sheet at Year-end**		
资产总计	Total Assets	18 898 188	16 905 488
#流动资产	Floating Assets	14 495 217	12 661 618
固定资产	Fixed Assets	1 216 194	1 076 992
固定资产原价	Initial Value of Fixed Assets	2 017 229	1 840 091
累计折旧	Accumulated Depreciation	889 692	851 631
#本年折旧	Depreciation This Year	102 449	96 221
负债总计	Total Liabilities	13 556 235	11 918 912
流动负债	Current Liabilities	12 808 404	11 172 306
非流动负债	Non-current Liabilities	747 831	746 606
所有者权益总计	Total Rights and Interests of Owners	5 341 953	4 986 576
损益及分配	**Profit and Loss and Their Distribution**		
主营业务收入	Income of Main Operations	16 707 778	15 422 189
主营业务成本	Cost of Main Operations	15 229 364	14 124 020
主营业务税金及附加	Taxes and Additional Taxes of Main Operations	456 938	435 217
管理费用	Administrative Expenses	537 546	457 134
#税 金	Taxes	9 265	8 962
财务费用	Financial Expenses	61 316	66 888
营业利润	Operation Profits	541 578	461 964
利润总额	Total Profits	578 662	495 010

注：以上财务数据不包括外省市在沪建筑业企业。
Note: The above-mentioned financial data exclude construction enterprises from other provinces and cities that enter the construction market in Shanghai.

Financial Statements of Construction Industry

(10 000yuan)

国 有 State-owned	集 体 Collective-owned	股份合作 Share-holding	联 营 Jointly-operated	国有独资公司 Wholly state-owned company	责任有限公司 Companies with Limited Liability	股份有限公司 Companies Limited by Shares	私 营 Private	港澳台商投资 Hong kong/ Macao/ Taiwan Investment	外商投资 FIE
2	**5**	**1**	**2**	**15**	**80**	**11**	**423**	**11**	**15**
19 907	35 841	977	11 216	2 404 402	8 227 326	2 154 881	4 050 938	1 001 458	991 242
19 163	33 718	963	10 052	1 627 554	6 103 443	1 327 573	3 539 152	856 306	977 293
515	1 207	14	1 165	496 245	288 143	64 459	225 244	133 873	5 329
1 078	4 625	103	1 439	818 025	461 580	117 538	435 703	161 084	16 054
563	3 465	89	276	339 339	214 358	67 175	226 366	27 336	10 725
101	239	1	19	22 581	30 433	16 521	26 326	5 348	880
16 345	23 268	247	5 020	1 609 452	6 305 222	1 413 713	2 545 645	836 832	800 491
16 345	23 112	247	5 020	1 499 819	5 810 123	1 379 069	2 438 571	836 772	799 326
	156			109 633	495 099	34 644	107 074	60	1 165
3 562	12 573	730	6 196	794 950	1 922 104	741 168	1 505 293	164 626	190 751
24 236	33 512	981	19 063	1 630 308	8 144 342	1 904 125	3 665 622	710 800	574 789
20 941	30 137	891	17 193	1 409 351	7 543 266	1 771 161	3 331 080	599 239	506 105
713	785	27	626	44 726	237 532	41 718	109 090	11 005	10 716
588	3 412	87	405	62 369	171 130	52 552	166 591	43 054	37 358
8	70	4	283	951	1653	2025	3 968	203	100
-202	-21	-45	-6	12 279	19 623	17 953	17 307	-3 388	-2 184
2 213	-247	21	881	131 787	222 923	62 068	42 318	61 000	18 614
2 358	-125	28	890	134 278	237 012	65 969	54 600	61 659	21 993

主要统计指标解释

建筑业总产值

建筑业总产值是以货币形式表现的建筑业企业在一定时期内生产的建筑业产品和提供的服务的总和。建筑业总产值包括：

（1）建筑工程产值：指列入建筑工程预算内的各种工程价值。

（2）安装工程产值：指设备安装工程价值，不包括被安装设备本身价值。

（3）其他产值：建筑业总产值中除建筑工程、安装工程以外的产值。包括房屋构筑物修理产值、非标准设备制造产值、总包企业向分包企业收取的管理费以及不能明确划分的施工活动所完成的产值。

a. 房屋构筑物修理产值：指房屋和构筑物修理所完成的产值，但不包括被修理房屋、构筑物本身价值和生产设备的修理产值。

b. 非标准设备制造产值：指加工制造没有定型的非标准生产设备的加工费和原材料价值（如化工厂、炼油厂用的各种罐、槽，矿井生产统一使用的各种漏斗、三角槽、阀门等）以及附属加工厂为本企业承建工程制作的非标准设备的价值。

房屋建筑施工面积

房屋建筑施工面积指在报告期内施过工的全部房屋建筑面积，包括本期新开工的房屋面积、上期施工跨入本期继续施工的房屋面积、上期停缓建在本期恢复施工的房屋面积、本期竣工的房屋面积及本期施工后又停缓建的房屋面积。

房屋建筑竣工面积

房屋建筑竣工面积 指在报告期内房屋建筑按照设计要求全部完工，达到了使用条件，经验收鉴定合格的房屋建筑面积。

房屋建筑面积竣工率

指一定时期内房屋竣工面积占同期房屋施工面积的比率。该指标从房屋建筑施工速度的角度反映投资效果的指标。

EXPLANATORY NOTES TO MAJOR STATISTICAL INDICATORS

Gross Output Value of Construction

Gross Output Value of Construction refers to total of construction products and services, expressed in money terms, produced or rendered by (completed by) construction enterprises during a given period of time. It includes:

(1) Output value of construction projects, that is the value of projects covered by the project budgets;

(2) Output value of installation projects, that is the value of the installation of equipment, (excluding the value of the equipment to be installed);

(3) Output value of other projects refers to other output value of gross output value of construction industry besides construction and installation projects. It includes the output value of building repairing, nonstandard equipment manufacturing, the management fees going from subcontractor to original contractor and other construction output value which can not be measure off definitely.

a. Output value of repair of buildings and structures, that is the value created through the repairs of buildings or structures, but does not include the value of buildings or structures being repaired and the value of the repair of production equipment;

b. Output value of manufactured non – standard equipment that is the value of non – standard production equipment (including raw materials and manufacturing cost) made for the construction project, irrespective of whether the equipment is manufactured on the construction site or by subsidiary workshops.

Floor Space of Buildings under Construction

Floor Space of Buildings under Construction refers to floor space of buildings under construction during the reference period, including newly started buildings, buildings started earlier and continued during the reference period, and buildings suspended earlier but restarted during the reference period, buildings completed during the reference period, and buildings under construction and then suspended during the reference period.

Floor Space of Buildings Completed

Floor Space of Buildings Completed refers to the floor space of buildings that are completed in the reference period in accordance with the requirements of the design, up to the standard for putting them into use, and have been checked and accepted by concerned departments as qualified ones.

Completion Rate of Floor Space of Buildings

Completion Rate of Floor Space of Buildings refers to the ratio of the floor space of buildings completed in certain period of time to the floor space of buildings under construction in the same period. This indicator reflects the investment result from the perspective of the speed of construction.

第八篇

CHAPTER 8

金融业及要素市场

FINANCIAL INDUSTRY AND FACTOR MARKETS

表8-1 各类金融机构数
Statistics of all Kinds of Financial Institutions

单位:个 (unit)

指 标	Indicators	2010	2014	2015
总 计	**Total**	**649**	**844**	**900**
银行类机构合计	**Subtotal of Banks**	**211**	**240**	**258**
中资银行	Chinese Banks	29	48	53
外资银行法人行	Foreign Banks and Corporate Banks	18	18	18
外资银行分行	Branches of Foreign Banks	57	55	55
外资银行代表处	Representative Offices of Foreign Banks	60	67	65
银行营运中心及业务分部	Bank Operation Centers and Sectors	23	24	28
非银行金融机构	Non-banking Financial Institutions	24	28	38
开发性金融机构	Developmental Financial Institutions			1
证券类机构合计	**Subtotal of Securities Institutions**	**261**	**358**	**385**
中资证券(包括中介机构)	Chinese Securities Institutions (including intermediary organs)	68	94	96
外资证券(包括代表处)	Foreign Securities Institutions (including representative offices)	53	55	56
基金公司(包括第三方销售)	Fund Companies (including third-party sales agency)	46	87	96
期货公司	Futures Companies	81	103	113
非证券金融机构	Non-securities Financial Institutions	13	19	24
保险机构合计	**Subtotal of Insurance Companies**	**177**	**246**	**257**
人寿保险(包括分公司)	Life Insurance (Including Branch)			47
财产保险(包括分公司)	Property Insurance (Including Branch)			37
资产管理	Asset Mangement			5
保险中介	Agencies of Insurance Companies			107
其 他	Others			61

表8-2 主要年份中资银行人民币存贷款年末余额
Chinese Banks' Year-end RMB Balance of Deposits and Loans in Main Years

单位:亿元 (100 million yuan)

指 标	Indicators	1990	2000	2005	2010	2014	2015
存款余额合计	**Total Deposit Balance**	**36.48**	**1 046.81**	**2 915.41**	**8 848.87**	**12 781.72**	**13 435.91**
#企业存款	Enterprise Deposits	9.67	644.79	1 530.99	5 239.12	7 304.44	7 998.98
居民储蓄存款	Resident Savings Deposits	20.62	360.99	1 105.96	2 943.49	4 381.03	4 381.84
其他存款	Others	1.66	10.61	166.38	427.38	661.24	553.30
贷款余额合计	**Total Loan Balance**	**28.19**	**891.59**	**2 674.76**	**6 434.95**	**8 857.93**	**9 546.47**
#企业贷款	Enterprise Loans			2 014.23	5 343.68	6 955.50	7 216.06
短期贷款	Short Term Loans			716.01	1 504.28	2 012.17	2 384.01
中长期贷款	Medium and Long Term Loans			1 298.22	3 839.40	4 943.33	4 832.05
票据融资	Securities Financing			193.73	82.59	373.61	465.95
个人贷款	Individual Loans			464.40	1 007.62	1 519.35	1 838.84
#住房按揭贷款	Housing Mortgage Loans			431.28	888.58	1 198.72	1 517.15
汽车消费贷款	Car Loans			4.08	14.76	33.60	31.11

表8-3　外资银行主要指标
(2015)

指　标	Indicators	单位数(个) Enterprises (unit)	从业人数(人) Employed Persons (person)	普通贷款(亿美元) Ordinary Loans (USD 100 million)
总　计	**Total**	**66**	**19 269**	**200.67**
按各大洲分	**By Continent**			
亚洲地区	Asia	32	9 502	119.17
欧洲地区	Europe	21	6 493	51.31
美洲地区	America	8	2 890	18.02
其他地区	Others	5	384	12.16
按进驻各大厦分	**By Mansion Where Enterprises Handle Their Businesses**			
环球金融中心大厦	Shanghai World Financial Center	8	2 216	28.60
汇亚大厦	Azia Center	8	2 173	24.60
金茂大厦	Jinmao Building	5	314	9.35
恒生银行大厦	Hangseng Bank Tower	4	417	16.76
国金中心	Shanghai International Financial Center	8	3 384	30.78
其他大厦	Others	33	10 765	90.58
按普通贷款分	**By Regular Loans**			
7亿美元以上	> USD 700 million	12	7 584	136.54
5~7亿美元	USD 500~700 million	2	432	11.71
3~5亿美元	USD 300~500 million	5	693	18.53
1~3亿美元	USD 100~300 million	13	2 039	23.00
1亿美元以下	< USD 100 million	34	8 521	10.89
按普通存款分	**By Regular Deposit**			
10亿美元以上	> USD 1,000 million	7	5 517	89.77
3~10亿美元	USD 300~1,000 million	6	2 907	42.70
1~3亿美元	USD 100~300 million	10	1 838	28.45
1千万~1亿美元	USD 10~100 million	16	910	19.14
1千万美元以下	< USD 10 million	27	8 097	20.62
按资产总额分	**By Total Assets**			
10亿美元以上	> USD 1,000 million	26	15 439	144.08
5~10亿美元	USD 500~1,000 million	13	2 518	34.50
3~5亿美元	USD 300~500 million	9	420	11.51
1~3亿美元	USD 100~300 million	15	708	9.70
1亿美元以下	< USD 100 million	3	184	0.87
按税金分	**By Tax**			
2000万元以上	≥20 million yuan	23	13 845	139.95
500~2000万元	5~20 million yuan	26	3 615	54.23
100~500万元	1~5 million yuan	13	384	6.48
100万元以下	< 1 million yuan	4	1 425	

Major Indicators of Foreign Banks (2015)

普通存款（亿美元）Ordinary Deposits (USD 100 million)	人民币贷款（亿元）RMB Loans (100 million yuan)	人民币存款（亿元）RMB Deposits (100 million yuan)	资产总额（亿美元）Total Assets (USD 100 million)	利润总额（亿元）Operation Profit (100 million yuan)	拆放同业（亿元）Banker Call Loans (100 million yuan)
174.94	**2 498.11**	**4 227.77**	**8 842.84**	**66.09**	**883.67**
87.72	1 340.86	2 009.58	6 499.06	10.29	523.34
54.19	756.94	1 424.01	1 734.17	38.85	226.72
26.70	329.99	713.06	469.92	10.20	111.82
6.33	70.33	81.12	139.68	6.75	21.79
29.86	337.44	508.45	7 483.45	15.41	172.70
29.24	215.88	435.98	133.06	2.85	141.60
2.73	73.68	48.03	61.51	-0.35	63.93
4.14	114.60	156.52	35.90	3.36	58.42
34.29	406.87	936.33	348.00	36.93	76.78
74.68	1 349.65	2 142.46	780.92	7.89	370.24
139.12	1 549.26	3 043.43	6 664.68	68.19	416.87
4.52	133.17	151.59	34.32	10.29	21.44
5.23	93.05	181.92	132.79	0.81	25.73
14.92	479.34	691.18	1 448.54	17.96	204.00
11.15	243.30	159.65	562.50	-31.16	215.64
123.18	1 084.24	2 406.11	6 544.89	55.31	253.03
25.95	633.28	1 015.97	151.22	28.30	283.67
17.28	353.40	535.97	1 493.19	16.44	68.55
8.27	206.81	199.29	81.26	3.17	80.16
0.26	220.38	70.43	572.28	-37.14	198.26
144.60	2 053.09	3 633.04	8 690.46	73.71	760.30
19.53	260.64	316.62	90.38	-13.22	54.65
8.48	84.74	170.20	34.05	3.56	22.22
1.30	75.75	80.32	25.48	1.16	42.01
1.03	23.89	27.60	2.47	0.88	4.50
145.63	2 126.36	3 717.98	8 471.61	96.50	722.00
23.86	330.79	474.93	296.42	-20.53	110.66
5.45	40.97	34.42	41.07	2.53	49.64
		0.44	33.73	-12.41	1.38

表8-4　外资银行存贷款年末余额
Foreign Banks' Year-end Balance of Deposits and Loans

指　标　Indicators		单　位　Unit	2014	2015
外汇存贷款	**Deposits and Loans of Foreign Exchange**			
客户存款	Deposits of Customers	亿美元 USD 100 million	169.93	174.94
#单　位	Corporations	亿美元 USD 100 million	144.68	148.32
同业存款	Inter-bank Deposits	亿美元 USD 100 million	42.16	42.80
存放同业	Due from Banks	亿美元 USD 100 million	137.06	127.83
有价证券及投资	Securities Assets and Investments	亿美元 USD 100 million	1.37	0.16
贷　款	Total Loans	亿美元 USD 100 million	247.55	200.67
#短　期	Short-term Loans	亿美元 USD 100 million	100.31	79.18
#贸易融资	Trade Financing	亿美元 USD 100 million	18.10	14.13
拆放同业	Deposits to Other Banks	亿美元 USD 100 million	201.09	202.82
人民币存贷款	**RMB Deposits and Loans**			
客户存款	Deposits of Customers	亿元 100 million yuan	4 502.57	4 227.77
同业存款	Inter-bank Deposits	亿元 100 million yuan	2 401.98	1 696.01
同业拆借	Inter-bank Lending	亿元 100 million yuan	322.51	314.28
贷　款	Total Loans	亿元 100 million yuan	2 311.73	2 498.11
证券资产	Securities Assets	亿元 100 million yuan	965.09	337.38
拆放同业	Deposits to Other Banks	亿元 100 million yuan	963.76	883.67

表8-5 历年中资保险机构原保险保费收入和赔款支出
Original Premium Income and Indemnity Expenditure of Chinese Insurance Business (1992 ~2015)

单位:亿元 (100 million yuan)

年 份 Year	原保险保费收入 Original Premium Income	财产险 Property Insurance	人身险 Life Insurance	原保险赔款支出 Former Indemnity Expenditure	财产险 Property Insurance	人身险 Life Insurance	赔款率(%) Rate of Indemnity(%)	财产险 Property Insurance	人身险 Life Insurance
1992	1.13	0.75	0.38	0.69	0.20	0.49	61.1	26.7	128.9
1993	2.51	1.42	1.09	0.30	0.06	0.24	12.0	4.2	25.9
1994	5.37	3.30	2.07	1.77	1.63	0.14	33.0	49.4	6.8
1995	13.63	10.42	3.21	3.12	2.97	0.15	22.9	28.5	4.7
1996	22.02	7.70	14.32	3.83	3.41	0.42	17.4	44.3	2.9
1997	38.34	9.19	29.15	4.91	4.71	0.20	12.8	51.3	0.7
1998	44.09	9.93	34.16	6.28	4.48	1.80	14.2	45.1	5.3
1999	51.42	10.84	40.58	7.76	5.71	2.05	15.1	52.7	5.1
2000	63.31	13.40	49.91	7.06	3.87	3.19	11.2	28.9	6.4
2001	99.36	13.73	85.63	9.08	4.92	4.16	9.1	35.8	4.9
2002	118.31	16.55	101.76	10.12	7.17	2.95	8.6	43.3	2.9
2003	129.83	21.88	107.95	20.73	9.04	11.69	16.0	41.3	10.8
2004	118.09	29.52	88.57	19.59	11.62	7.97	16.6	39.4	9.0
2005	140.63	40.03	100.60	23.16	20.09	3.07	16.5	50.2	3.1
2006	171.47	45.51	125.96	26.17	22.16	4.01	15.3	48.7	3.2
2007	182.33	52.47	129.86	29.29	24.54	4.75	16.1	46.8	3.7
2008	230.84	55.25	175.59	37.01	30.99	6.02	16.0	56.1	3.4
2009	221.20	68.75	152.45	43.54	36.26	7.28	19.7	52.7	4.8
2010	329.82	100.41	229.41	45.65	39.93	5.72	13.8	39.8	2.5
2011	295.18	120.53	174.65	61.74	56.19	5.52	20.9	46.6	3.2
2012	319.56	130.38	189.18	80.74	72.11	8.63	25.3	55.3	4.6
2013	371.92	204.10	167.82	126.71	117.86	8.85	34.1	57.7	5.3
2014	426.93	233.59	193.34	139.10	125.90	13.20	32.6	53.9	6.8
2015	474.47	265.38	209.09	156.13	140.94	15.19	32.9	53.1	7.3

表8-6　中资保险机构主要险种的原保险保费收入和赔款支出
Original Premium Income and Indemnity Expenditure of Major Types of Chinese Funded Insurance Business
(2015)

单位:亿元　(100 million yuan)

指　标	Indicators	原保险保费收入 Original Premium Income	原保险赔款支出 Original Indemnity Expenditure	赔款率(%) Rate of Indemnity(%)
总　计	**Total**	**474.47**	**156.13**	**32.9**
财产险小计	Subtotal of Property Insurance	265.38	140.94	53.1
#企业财产险	Enterprise Property Insurance	14.78	4.68	31.7
机动车辆险	Motor Vehicle Insurance	210.74	115.58	54.8
货运险	Cargo Transportation Insurance	7.25	3.92	54.1
责任保险	Liability Insurance	11.58	4.70	40.6
人身险小计	Subtotal of Life Insurance	209.09	15.19	7.3

表8-7　外资保险机构主要险种的原保险保费收入和赔款支出
Original Premium Income and Indemnity Expenditure of Major Types of Foreign Funded Insurance Business
(2015)

单位:亿元　(100 million yuan)

指　标	Indicators	原保险保费收入 Original Premium Income	原保险赔款支出 Original Indemnity Expenditure	赔款率(%) Rate of Indemnity(%)
总　计	**Total**	**238.19**	**11.48**	**4.8**
财产保险小计	Subtotal of Property Insurance	17.83	7.57	42.5
#企业财产险	Enterprise Property Insurance	4.79	0.70	14.6
货运险	Cargo Transportation Insurance	3.36	2.79	83
家财险	Household Property Insurance	0.48	0.06	12.5
责任保险	Liability Insurance	5.93	1.35	22.8
人身险小计	Subtotal of Life Insurance	220.36	3.91	1.8

表8-8 上海证券交易所市场交易主要指标
Statistics of Shanghai Stock Exchange

指 标	Indicators	单 位 Unit	2014	2015
交易天数	**Trading Days**	**天 day**	**245**	**244**
上市证券数	**Number of Securities Traded**	**个 unit**	**3 758**	**5 914**
股 票	Stocks	个 unit	1 039	1 125
A 股	A Share	个 unit	986	1 073
B 股	B Share	个 unit	53	52
优先股	Preferred Stocks	个 unit	5	16
债 券	Bonds	个 unit	2 646	4 538
政府债	Government Bonds	个 unit	267	893
公司债	Corporate Bonds	个 unit	2 336	3 596
债券回购	Repurchase	个 unit	43	49
基 金	Funds	个 unit	68	135
期 权	Option	个 unit		100
认 购	Call Option	个 unit		50
认 沽	Put Option	个 unit		50
股票市价总值	**Total Value of Stock Price**	**亿元 100 million yuan**	**243 974.02**	**295 194.20**
成交金额	**Turnover Value**	**亿元 100 million yuan**	**1 281 497.98**	**2 663 690.84**
股 票	Stocks	亿元 100 million yuan	377 162.12	1 330 992.10
A 股	A Share	亿元 100 million yuan	375 149.95	1 323 231.16
B 股	B Share	亿元 100 million yuan	484.45	2 357.12
股票回购	Repurchase	亿元 100 million yuan	1 527.72	5 403.82
优先股	Preferred Stocks	亿元 100 million yuan	4.27	48.24
债 券	Bonds	亿元 100 million yuan	866 848.59	1 228 533.71
政府债	Government Bonds	亿元 100 million yuan	1 247.47	4 330.72
公司债	Corporate Bonds	亿元 100 million yuan	24 198.95	26 350.38
债券回购	Repurchase	亿元 100 million yuan	841 402.17	1 197 852.61
基 金	Funds	亿元 100 million yuan	37 479.25	103 814.16
期 权	Option	亿元 100 million yuan		236.66
认 购	Call Option	亿元 100 million yuan		126.55
认 沽	Put Option	亿元 100 million yuan		110.11
其 他	Others	亿元 100 million yuan	3.75	65.97
成交数量	**Volume Turnover**	**亿手 100 million contracts**	**48 354.15**	**115 825.36**
股 票	Stocks	亿手 100 million contracts	42 938.82	102 485.63
A 股	A Share	亿手 100 million contracts	42 471.35	101 396.17
B 股	B Share	亿手 100 million contracts	96.01	305.51
股票回购	Repurchase	亿手 100 million contracts	371.46	783.95
优先股	Preferred Stocks	亿手 100 million contracts	0.04	0.47
债 券	Bonds	亿手 100million contracts	865.65	1 225.77
政府债	Government Bonds	亿手 100 million contracts	1.25	4.30
公司债	Corporate Bonds	亿手 100 million contracts	22.99	23.62
债券回购	Repurchase	亿手 100 million contracts	841.41	1 197.85
基 金	Funds	亿手 100 million contracts	4 549.64	12 113.19
期 权	Option	亿手 100 million contracts		0.23
认 购	Call Option	亿手 100 million contracts		0.13
认 沽	Put Option	亿手 100 million contracts		0.10
其 他	Others	亿手 100 million contracts	…	0.07

注：2010 年起，上交所统计口径有调整，原表中"国债现货"和"地方政府债"数据，现合并为"政府债"；原表中"公司债"和"可转债"数据，现合并统称为"公司债"。

Note: Shanghai Stock Exchange has changed its statistical approach for its data since 2010. The data in the fields of "National Debts on Spots" and "Local Government Bonds" in the former table have been merged as those of "Government Bonds" and the fields of "Corporate Debts" and "Convertible Bonds" have been merged as "Corporate Bonds".

表8-9 上海证券交易所市盈率和换手率
P/E Ratio & Turnover Rate of Shanghai Stock Exchange

指 标	Indicators	2005	2010	2014	2015
市盈率(%)	**P/E Rate**	**16.3**	**21.6**	**16.0**	**17.6**
A 股	A Share	16.4	21.6	16.0	17.6
B 股	B Share	12.4	23.9	15.8	26.2
换手率(%)	**Turnover Rate**	**274.4**	**198.5**	**173.8**	**388.5**
A 股	A Share	290.7	199.3	174.4	389.6
B 股	B Share	58.5	119.0	64.6	202.6

表8-10 上海证券交易所市场筹集资金
Capital Raising of Shanghai Stock Exchang

单位:亿元 (100 million yuan)

指 标	Indicators	2005	2010	2014	2015
A股小计	**Subtotal of A Shares**	**308.75**	**5 532.14**	**3 962.59**	**8 712.96**
A股首次发行	IPO of A Shares	28.55	1 891.51	311.77	1 086.90
A股再次发行	Second Issuing of A Shares	280.20	3 640.62	3 650.82	7 626.06
#A股增发	Additional Issuing of A Shares	278.78	2 102.90	2 819.40	6 575.05
A股配股	Rights Issuing of A Shares	1.42	1 415.73	107.61	
A股行权	Rights Claiming of A Shares		84.28		
优先股	**Preferred Stocks**			**1 030.00**	**1 959.00**

表8-11 浦东新区上市公司分行业汇总情况
Listed Companies in PNA by Sector
(2015)

指 标	Indicators	单 位 Unit	地产类 Real Estate	工业类 Industry	公用事业类 Public Utilities	商业类 Commerce	综合类 Comprehens-ive
发行股数	Number of Stocks Issued	亿股 100 million in number	200.50	234.71	416.62	37.79	897.19
流通股数	Number of Stocks Circulated	亿股 100 million in number	82.07	214.58	396.79	35.51	835.14
成交额	Volume	亿元 100 million yuan	7 934.01	22 608.23	17 607.48	5 067.56	41 286.41
成交股数	Number of Stock Transacted	亿股 100 million in number	419.52	1 306.05	1 561.80	255.85	3 189.37
市盈率	P/E Ratio	%	39.1	69.1	27.2	94.2	12.1
换手率	Turnover Rate	%	513.4	632.0	400.4	738.5	442.1
市价总值	Total Market Value	亿元 100 million yuan	3 718.79	3 732.00	3 637.08	962.25	10 813.10
流通市值	Circulating Market Value	亿元 100 million yuan	1 773.02	3 306.51	3 306.35	855.64	9 420.24

注:1. 浦东新区上市公司指公司注册地含"浦东"的公司。
2. 数据包含A股和B股。
3. "成交额"、"成交股数"、"换手率"为2015年整年数据。
4. "发行股数"、"流通股数"、"市盈率"、"市值总值"、"流通市值"为2015年12月31日数据。

Note: 1. Public listed companies in PNA refer to those companies that have been registered in Pudong.
2. The data include both A shares and B shares.
3. The items of Business Volume, Number of Stocks Transacted and Turnover Rate are data in the whole year of 2015.
4. The items of Number of Stocks Issued, Number of Stocks Circulated, P/E Ratio, Total Market Value and Circulating Market Value are data of December 31, 2015.

表8-12 上海期货交易所市场交易主要指标
Major Indicators of Shanghai Futures Exchange

指 标	Indicators	单 位 Unit	2005	2010	2014	2015
会员单位	**Membership**	**户 unit**	**215**	**209**	**203**	**201**
经纪单位	Broking	户 unit	175	164	151	150
非经纪单位	Non-Broking	户 unit	40	45	52	51
交易天数	Business Days in the Year	天 day	242	242	245	244
上市交易品种	Business Lines	个 unit	4	8	12	14
成交量	**Total Volume of Business**	**万手 10 000 contracts**	**6 757.95**	**124 379.64**	**168 458.84**	**210 098.83**
铜	Copper	万手 10 000 contracts	2 470.41	10 157.71	14 102.06	17 663.71
铝	Aluminum	万手 10 000 contracts	425.00	3 452.40	2 785.26	4 580.14
锌	Zinc	万手 10 000 contracts		29 317.87	8 085.87	9 047.49
铅	Lead	万手 10 000 contracts			291.56	262.02
锡	Nickel	万手 10 000 contracts				103.16
镍	Tin	万手 10 000 contracts				12 718.02
黄 金	Gold	万手 10 000 contracts		679.41	4 773.08	5 063.44
白 银	Silver	万手 10 000 contracts			17 726.32	28 957.29
天然橡胶	Natural Rubber	万手 10 000 contracts	1 900.63	33 482.98	38 697.53	16 613.51
燃料油	Fuel Oil	万手 10 000 contracts	1 961.91	2 136.44	0.29	0.78
石油沥青	Bitumen	万手 10 000 contracts			130.03	6 479.56
螺纹钢	Rebar	万手 10 000 contracts		45 122.48	81 615.62	108 207.17
线 材	Wire Rod	万手 10 000 contracts		30.35	0.13	0.07
热轧卷板	Hot Rolled Coils	万手 10 000 contracts			251.08	402.47
成交金额	**Total Value of Business**	**亿元 100 million yuan**	**65 402.03**	**1 234 794.76**	**1 264 706.51**	**1 271 105.26**
铜	Copper	亿元 100 million yuan	40 463.23	296 437.54	337 457.53	351 827.60
铝	Aluminum	亿元 100 million yuan	3 714.46	28 342.48	19 256.91	25 482.69
锌	Zinc	亿元 100 million yuan		255 725.62	66 571.36	64 357.71
铅	Lead	亿元 100 million yuan			2 072.87	1 690.80
锡	Nickel	亿元 100 million yuan				1 124.74
镍	Tin	亿元 100 million yuan				104 094.25
黄 金	Gold	亿元 100 million yuan		18 291.92	119 826.28	119 839.07
白 银	Silver	亿元 100 million yuan			255 570.06	152 302.94
天然橡胶	Natural Rubber	亿元 100 million yuan	15 601.79	426 464.81	230 182.98	204 896.35
燃料油	Fuel Oil	亿元 100 million yuan	5 622.55	9 886.37	4.96	11.50
石油沥青	Bitumen	亿元 100 million yuan			553.71	14 717.63
螺纹钢	Rebar	亿元 100 million yuan		199 517.15	232 408.06	229 898.79
线 材	Wire Rod	亿元 100 million yuan		128.87	0.44	0.17
热轧卷板	Hot Rolled Coils	亿元 100 million yuan			801.36	861.03
年末持仓量	**Year End Contracts**	**万手 10 000 contracts**	**30.95**	**206.46**	**478.68**	**770.03**
铜	Copper	万手 10 000 contracts	10.58	37.31	67.93	77.33
铝	Aluminum	万手 10 000 contracts	7.89	23.73	34.27	69.73
锌	Zinc	万手 10 000 contracts		40.24	25.74	41.11
铅	Lead	万手 10 000 contracts			4.42	3.45
锡	Nickel	万手 10 000 contracts				0.67
镍	Tin	万手 10 000 contracts				53.83
黄 金	Gold	万手 10 000 contracts		7.88	19.48	25.91
白 银	Silver	万手 10 000 contracts			40.69	52.00
天然橡胶	Natural Rubber	万手 10 000 contracts	5.70	21.46	31.13	35.78
燃料油	Fuel Oil	万手 10 000 contracts	6.78	10.44	0.01	
石油沥青	Bitumen	万手 10 000 contracts			0.02	21.09

表 8－12 续表 Continued

指 标	Indicators	单 位 Unit	2005	2010	2014	2015
螺纹钢	Rebar	万手 10 000 contracts		65.40	252.50	379.12
线 材	Wire Rod	万手 10 000 contracts		0.01		
热轧卷板	Hot Rolled Coils	万手 10 000 contracts			2.49	10.01
交割量	**Volume of Transaction**	**万手 10 000 contracts**	**8.73**	**37.69**	**33.07**	**40.23**
铜	Copper	万手 10 000 contracts	3.07	3.84	4.66	6.91
铝	Aluminum	万手 10 000 contracts	2.18	11.52	14.51	13.89
锌	Zinc	万手 10 000 contracts		6.15	3.89	3.84
铅	Lead	万手 10 000 contracts			2.92	1.01
锡	Nickel	万手 10 000 contracts				0.20
镍	Tin	万手 10 000 contracts				1.78
黄 金	Gold	万手 10 000 contracts		0.05	0.37	0.71
白 银	Silver	万手 10 000 contracts			1.77	3.68
天然橡胶	Natural Rubber	万手 10 000 contracts	1.52	2.57	2.51	2.11
燃料油	Fuel Oil	万手 10 000 contracts	1.96	6.90		0.01
石油沥青	Bitumen	万手 10 000 contracts			1.35	2.26
螺纹钢	Rebar	万手 10 000 contracts		6.00	1.07	2.85
线 材	Wire Rod	万手 10 000 contracts		0.66		
热轧卷板	Hot Rolled Coils	万手 10 000 contracts			0.02	0.99
交割金额	**Value of Transaction**	**亿元 100 million yuan**	**88.29**	**349.06**	**320.64**	**350.96**
铜	Copper	亿元 100 million yuan	54.54	113.40	114.43	140.83
铝	Aluminum	亿元 100 million yuan	18.07	90.41	96.96	84.22
锌	Zinc	亿元 100 million yuan		53.77	31.28	29.11
铅	Lead	亿元 100 million yuan			20.03	6.56
锡	Tin	亿元 100 million yuan				2.15
镍	Nickel	亿元 100 million yuan				13.78
黄 金	Gold	亿元 100 million yuan		1.46	9.00	16.16
白 银	Silver	亿元 100 million yuan			24.62	18.31
天然橡胶	Natural Rubber	亿元 100 million yuan	10.79	32.21	15.40	25.68
燃料油	Fuel Oil	亿元 100 million yuan	4.89	30.28	0.03	0.11
石油沥青	Bitumen	亿元 100 million yuan			5.74	5.66
螺纹钢	Rebar	亿元 100 million yuan		24.89	3.09	5.98
线 材	Wire Rod	亿元 100 million yuan		2.64		
热轧卷板	Hot Rolled Coils	亿元 100 million yuan			0.06	2.41
交割率	**Rate of Transaction**					
铜	Copper	%	0.2	0.1	0.1	0.1
铝	Aluminum	%	1.0	0.7	1.2	1.3
锌	Zinc	%		0.1	0.1	0.1
铅	Lead	%			2.3	0.8
锡	Tin	%				0.6
镍	Nickel	%				0.1
黄 金	Gold	%		…	…	…
白 银	Silver	%			…	…
天然橡胶	Natural Rubber	%	0.3	…	…	…
燃料油	Fuel Oil	%	0.2	0.5	2.1	1.7
石油沥青	Bitumen	%			0.4	0.1
螺纹钢	Rebar	%		…	…	…
线 材	Wire Rod	%		2.0		
热轧卷板	Hot Rolled Coils	%			…	0.7

表8-13 上海钻石交易所市场交易主要指标
Major Indicators of Shanghai Diamond Exchange

指 标 Indicators		单 位 Unit	2010	2014	2015
会员单位	**Membership**	**户 Unit**	**283**	**369**	**382**
外资会员	Foreign Member	户 Unit	193	233	234
中资会员	Chinese Member	户 Unit	90	136	148
成交量	**Total Volume of Business**	**万克拉 10 000 carat**	**19 762.53**	**11 094.94**	**32 662.03**
钻石进境量	Volume of Diamond Coming in Border	万克拉 10 000 carat	92.60	172.25	120.07
钻石出境量	Volume of Diamond Leaving our Country	万克拉 10 000 carat	24.03	47.40	44.17
钻石进口量	Volume of Imports	万克拉 10 000 carat	118.53	178.60	494.61
钻石出口量	Volume of Exports	万克拉 10 000 carat	19 518.03	10 345.32	31 987.48
钻石保税交易量	Volume of Bonded Transactions	万克拉 10 000 carat	7.54	350.46	15.03
钻石加工贸易量	Volume of Processing Trade	万克拉 10 000 carat	1.80	0.91	0.67
成交金额	**Total Value of Transactions**	**亿美元 100 million USD**	**28.86**	**51.31**	**41.43**
钻石进境额	Amount of Diamond Coming in Border	亿美元 100 million USD	10.46	18.55	112.98
钻石出境额	Amount of Diamond Leaving our Country	亿美元 100 million USD	3.80	6.45	6.28
钻石进口额	Amount of Imports	亿美元 100 million USD	13.11	22.55	19.85
钻石出口额	Amount of Exports	亿美元 100 million USD	0.13	0.62	0.36
钻石保税交易额	Amount of Bonded Transactions	亿美元 100 million USD	1.30	3.09	1.94
钻石加工贸易额	Amount of Processing Trade	亿美元 100 million USD	0.05	0.05	0.02

表8-14　区属人才交流市场基本情况
Basic Statistics of PNA Professional Resources Market(PPRM)

指　标　Indicators		单　位　Unit	2005	2010	2014	2015
全年举办交流活动	Number of Exchange Activites in the Year	场 in number	133	193	208	202
参与人才招聘单位	Number of Participating Organizations	个 unit	3 859	7 462	6 678	5 836
接待咨询服务人次	Job-seeking Visitors Received	万人次 10 000 person-times	19.67	37.00	30.10	31.00
办理择业登记人数	Job-seeking Visitors Registered	人次 person-time	90 452	211 000	143 000	149 000
达成意向人数	Number of Job-seekers Who Have Signed Letters of Intent	人 person	37 302	39 949	26 828	20 916
获得上海市居住证人数	Number of Persons Who Have Obtained Shanghai Residence Permits	人 person	7 158	30 985	71 134	87 039
后续服务	**Follow-up Services**					
档案保管	File-keeping	件 file	5 691	13 489	16 680	13 054
户籍挂靠(迁入)	Domiciling(immigration)	户 unit	1 605	1 175	4 334	

主要统计指标解释

存　款

是企业、机关、团体或居民等根据资金必须收回的原则,把货币资金存入银行或其他信用机构保管并取得一定利息的一种信用活动形式。根据存款对象的不同可划分为企业存款、财政存款、机关团体存款、储蓄存款等科目。它是银行信贷资金的主要来源。

贷　款

是银行或其他信用机构根据资金必须归还的原则,按一定利率,为企业、个人等提供资金的一种信用活动形式。我国银行贷款分为短期贷款、中期流动资金贷款、中长期贷款、信托贷款以及工业贷款、商业贷款等科目。

居民储蓄存款年末余额

居民和农民个人在银行、信用社等金融机构储蓄存款年末余额。不包括居民的手存现金和企事业单位、部队、机关团体等的集体存款。

保险金额

指保险人承担赔偿或者给付保险金责任的最高限额。

保险费

保险费是指投保人根据保险合同的有关规定,为保险受益人取得因保险事故发生所造成的经济损失予以补偿(或给付)权利,付给保险人的代价。包括财产险和人身险储金类支出。

保险赔款及给付

保险赔款及给付指保险事故发生后,经查证确属保险责任范围以内的保险标的损失,保险人根据保险合同的规定履行赔偿义务,给予被保险人(或投保人指定的受益人)的款项。

市价总值

市价总值即全部股份乘上市场价格。

流通市值

流通市值指在某特定时间内当时可交易的流通股股数乘以当时股价得出的流通股票总价值。

市盈率

市盈率是某种股票每股市价与每股盈利的比率。

市盈率 = 普通股每股市场价格 ÷ 普通股每年每股盈利

换手率

换手率是指在一定时间内市场中股票转手买卖的频率。

金融债券

金融债券,是指银行和非银行金融机构为筹集资金而发行的债券。其债务人为发行债券的金融机构。

企业债券

企业债券通常又称为公司债券,是企业依照法定程序发行,约定在一定期限内还本付息的债券。企业债券代表着发债企业和投资者之间的一种债权债务关系。债券持有人是企业的债权人,不是所有者,无权参与或干涉企业经营管理,但债券持有人有权按期收回本息。企业债券与股票一样,同属有价证券,可以自由转让。

可转换债券

可转换债券,又译可换股债券,是债券的一种,它可以转换为债券发行公司的股票,其转换比率一般会在发行时确定。可转换债券通常具有较低的票面利率,因为可以转换成股票的权利是对债券持有人的一种补偿。另外,将可转换债券转换为普通股时,所换得的股票价值一般远大于原债券价值。可转换债券是在发行公司债券的基础上,附加了一份期权,并允许购买人在规定的时间范围内将其购买的债券转换成指定公司的股票。

持仓量

持仓量指的是在交易所市场上未平仓的期权合约的数量,也指某一种类或系列中未平仓的期权合约的数量。

成交量

成交量指当天成交的股票数量。

交　割

交割概念来源于期货,分为:实物交割和现金交割。

实物交割,是指期货合约的买卖双方于合约到期时,根据交易所制订的规则和程序,通过期货合约标的物的所有权转移,将到期未平仓合约进行了结的行为。商品期货交易一般采用实物交割的方式。

现金交割,是指到期未平仓期货合约进行交割时,用结算价格来计算未平仓合约的盈亏,以现金支付的方式最终了结期货合约的交割方式。这种交割方式主要用于金融期货等期货标的物无法进行实物交割的期货合约。

EXPLANATORY NOTES TO MAJOR STATISTICAL INDICATORS

Deposits

Deposits are a form of credit by which enterprises, institutions, organizations or residents put money into banks and other credit institutions for safekeeping and earn interests under the principle of free withdrawal. According to different depositors, deposits are divided into enterprise deposits, treasury deposits, deposits of institutions and organizations, urban savings deposits and other deposits. Deposits constitute a major source of bank credit funds.

Loans

Loans are a form of credit by which banks and other credit institutions provide funds with a specified interest to enterprises and individuals under the principle of free repayment. Loans from Chinese banks include short term loans, medium term circulating capital loans, long term loans, trust loans, industrial loans and commercial loans.

Savings Deposit Balance of Urban and Rural Residents

Refers to year-end savings deposit balance of urban residents and farmers at banks, credit unions and other financial institutions, excluding cash held by residents and collective savings of enterprises, institutions, military units and government agencies.

Amount Insured

Amount Insured refers to the maximum that the insurant will get for the claim of the case insured .

Premium

Premium is the fee paid by the insurant to the insurer to obtain the obligation of compensation from the insurance within the agreed terms. It includes saving payment for property and life insurance.

Insurance Indemnity

Insurance Indemnity is the compensation paid by the insurer to the insurant or the beneficiary, when an accident has happened to the insured property or life and the loss has been investigated and verified to be within the insurance obligation.

Total Market Value

Total Market Value means all of the stock shares multiplied by their relevant market price.

Circulation Value on the Market

Circulation Value on the Market means the tradable circulation shares multiplied by their relevant share prices during a certain period of time.

P/E Ratio

P/E Ratio refers to the ratio between the price of a certain share and its earnings per year. The P/E ratio is the price of a traded common share divided by its annual earnings.

Exchange Rate

Exchange Rate means the trading frequency of certain stock shares on the market during a certain period of time.

Financial Bonds

Financial Bonds refer to those that banks and non-banking financial institutions issue to raise funds. Their debtors are the financial institutions that issue the bonds.

Corporate Bonds

Corporate Bonds usually refer to business bonds, which will be issued in accordance with the statutory procedures of the business and repay the original investment plus agreed interest within a certain period of time. Corporate bonds represent a kind of debtor-creditor relationship between the issuing enterprises and the investors. Bondholders are creditors of the certain enterprise, not the owners, and they do not have the right to participate or interfere with the business management. However, the bondholders have the right to claim the principal and interest on time. Like the stock shares, corporate bonds belong to marketable securities and can be freely transferable.

Convertible Bonds

Convertible Bonds, also translated into convertible exchangeable bonds, can be converted into the stock shares of the enterprise that issue the bonds. The conversion rate will usually be determined at the time of distribution. Convertible bonds generally have lower nominal interest rates, because the right of being converted into stock shares is a kind of compensation to the bondholders. In addition, when the bonds are converted into ordinary shares, the prices of these shares usually are far higher than the original value of the bonds. In essence, the convertible bonds have an additional option on the basis of the business bonds, and these bondholders are allowed to convert the convertible bonds they have purchased into the stock shares of specific companies during the specific period.

Open Interest

Open Interest refers to the number of open option contracts in the exchange market, also refers to the number of one or series of open option contracts.

Turnover

Turnover refers to the transaction volume of stock shares traded on that certain day.

Delivery

Delivery, its concept comes from futures, can be divided into physical delivery and cash delivery.

Physical delivery refers to the behavior that the vendor and the purchaser finish the open contracts at the end of the term by means of the ownership transfer of the object of futures contracts in accordance with rules and procedures of the stock exchange when the contract expires. The transaction of commodity futures usually adopts the physical delivery.

Cash delivery refers to the way that the two sides finally close their futures contracts by means of cash, with the settlement price used to calculate earnings or loss of the open contracts when the open futures contracts are delivered at the end of term. This kind of delivery is mainly used for futures contracts that their objects can not be dealt with physical delivery such as the financial futures.

第九篇

CHAPTER 9

房地产

REAL ESTATE

表9-1　房地产开发投资

(2015)

单位:亿元

指　标	Indicators	企业个数(个) Enterprises (unit)	本年完成投资 Current Year Investment Completed	建筑工程 Construction Project
总　计	**Total**	**676**	**969.22**	**476.05**
按登记注册类型分	**By Type of Registration**			
内　资	Domestic Invested	569	807.18	402.66
国　有	State-owned	13	11.29	3.17
集　体	Collective-owned	5	23.63	7.90
股份合作	Share-holding			
联　营	Jointly-operated			
有限责任公司	Companies with Limited Liabilities	299	541.88	276.40
股份有限公司	Companies Limited by Shares	14	54.08	27.05
私　营	Private	237	176.31	88.14
其　他	Others	1		
港澳台商投资	Hong Kong/Macao/Taiwan Invested	68	144.27	65.61
#港澳台商独资	Solely Hong Kong/Macao/Taiwan Funded	40	89.39	37.87
外商投资	Foreign Invested	39	17.77	7.78
#外商独资	Wholly Foreign-owned	24	5.23	0.88
按隶属关系分	**By Subordination**			
中央属	Central	173	409.70	205.25
市(局)属	Municipal	45	55.47	32.75
区　属	PNA	101	153.68	68.88
其他属	Others	357	350.37	169.17
按企业资质等级分	**By Qualifications of Enterprises**			
一　级	Grade 1	16	37.33	28.04
二　级	Grade 2	73	137.00	62.51
三　级	Grade 3	92	55.98	38.78
无　级	No Grade	495	738.91	346.72

Investment in Real Estate Development

(100 million yuan)

按构成分 By Composition of Completed Investment			按工程用途分 By Project Use of Completed Investment			
安装工程 Installation	设备工器具购置 Equipment Purchasing	其他费用 Other Cost	住　宅 Residential Housing	办公楼 Office Buildings	商业营业用房 Commerce/ Operation	其　他 Others
49.63	**2.31**	**441.23**	**497.77**	**207.60**	**109.67**	**154.18**
43.46	2.31	358.75	422.96	154.25	89.59	140.38
0.05		8.07	0.15	10.04	0.05	1.06
1.73		14.00	8.89	0.19	0.50	14.06
21.56	1.71	242.20	294.16	96.58	58.33	92.81
0.03	0.03	26.97	14.15	32.15	4.72	3.06
20.08	0.57	67.51	105.62	15.29	26.00	29.40
3.64		75.02	60.45	53.16	17.28	13.38
1.02		50.50	42.67	27.63	12.16	6.93
2.53		7.46	14.36	0.19	2.80	0.42
0.84		3.51	4.68	0.19	0.16	0.19
9.87	0.27	194.30	175.29	120.66	39.73	74.01
2.24	0.01	20.47	29.56	0.37	4.55	20.98
6.17		78.63	68.04	52.16	20.06	13.42
31.35	2.03	147.83	224.88	34.41	45.33	45.77
3.26	0.15	5.88	9.01	21.49	0.92	5.90
3.62	0.11	70.77	89.07	6.20	4.93	36.81
6.19		11.02	25.74	15.19	7.28	7.77
36.56	2.05	353.56	373.95	164.72	96.54	103.70

表9-2　房地产开发企业投资资金来源
（2015）

单位:亿元

指　标	Indicators	本年资金来源合计 Total Sources of Funds	上年末结余资本 Remnant Capital of Previous Year	本年资金来源小计 Subtotal of Current Year
总　计	**Total**	**1 913.30**	**628.95**	**1 284.35**
按登记注册类型分	**By Type of Registration**			
内　资	Domestic Investment	1 435.56	400.85	1 034.70
国　有	State-owned	19.98	15.12	4.87
集　体	Collective-owned	33.74	1.11	32.63
股份合作	Share-holding			
联　营	Jointly-operated			
有限责任公司	Companies with Limited Liabilities	929.40	271.13	658.27
股份有限公司	Companies Limited by Shares	59.34	24.65	34.69
私　营	Private	393.10	88.85	304.25
其　他	Others			
港澳台商投资	Hong Kong/Macao/Taiwan Investment	368.95	167.52	201.43
#港澳台商独资	Solely Hong Kong/Macao/Taiwan Funded	247.36	114.92	132.44
外商投资	Foreign Invested	108.79	60.57	48.22
#外商独资	Wholly foreign-owned	11.56	9.51	2.05
按隶属关系分	**By Subordination**			
中央属	Central	617.63	195.20	422.43
市(局)属	Municipal	84.78	12.88	71.90
区　属	PNA	460.58	227.25	233.34
其他属	Others	750.31	193.62	556.68
按企业资质等级分	**By Qualifications of Enterprises**			
一　级	Grade 1	49.83	2.45	47.38
二　级	Grade 2	273.85	36.21	237.65
三　级	Grade 3	102.49	21.02	81.46
无　级	No Grade	1 487.13	569.27	917.86

Sources of Funds of Investment in Real Estate Development

(100 million yuan)

国内贷款 Domestic Loans	利用外资 Foreign Funds	自筹资金 Self-raised Funds	#自有资金 Self-owned	其他资金来源 Other Funds	本年各项应付款合计 Current Year Total Amount Payable	#工程款 Project Funds
394.80	**0.10**	**387.04**	**179.18**	**502.41**	**167.72**	**98.23**
339.36		303.71	159.24	391.63	142.25	86.82
1.71		0.73	0.73	2.43	0.12	0.08
		26.89	6.00	5.74		
254.98		175.04	97.81	228.25	71.57	50.15
12.60		22.09	22.09		13.39	2.59
70.07		78.97	32.61	155.22	57.16	34.00
48.81	0.10	77.09	14.36	75.43	15.22	7.11
30.81		43.47	0.24	58.16	13.42	5.69
6.63		6.24	5.57	35.35	10.25	4.30
0.05				2.00	0.04	
220.17		119.78	79.35	82.48	54.87	36.95
15.31		37.93	6.72	18.66	10.80	6.30
49.44		73.11	19.62	110.78	25.41	11.35
109.88	0.10	156.22	73.49	290.49	76.64	43.63
8.57		38.81	35.92		24.69	21.06
97.31		42.29	16.64	98.04	18.05	9.25
10.77		43.22	26.96	27.47	22.96	20.01
278.15	0.10	262.72	99.66	376.90	102.02	47.91

表9-3　房地产开发企业房屋施工面积、竣工面积和销售面积（2015）

单位：万平方米

指　标	Indicators	施工面积 Floor Area Under Construction	#新开工面积 Floor Area of New Starts	竣工面积 Floor Area Completed
总　计	**Total**	**3 723.47**	**749.19**	**508.91**
按登记注册类型分	**By Type of Registration**			
内　资	Domestic Investment	3 298.65	649.98	443.87
国　有	State-owned	26.39	7.30	
集　体	Collective-owned	71.61	12.27	
股份合作	Share-holding			
联　营	Jointly-operated			
有限责任公司	Companies with Limited Liabilities	2 250.21	410.84	313.39
股份有限公司	Companies Limited by Shares	171.76	63.13	
私　营	Private	778.68	156.43	130.47
其　他	Others			
港澳台商投资	Hong Kong/Macao/Taiwan Invested	307.70	99.21	11.00
#港澳台商独资	Solely Hong Kong/Macao/Taiwan Funded	162.43	59.32	10.07
外商投资	Foreign Invested	117.12		54.04
#外商独资	Wholly Foreign-owned	59.12		39.31
按隶属关系分	**By Subordination**			
中央属	Central	1 513.14	335.59	141.10
市(局)属	Municipal	316.89	36.89	87.45
区　属	PNA	416.18	90.57	65.05
其他属	Others	1 477.26	286.14	215.31
按企业资质等级分	**By Qualifications of Enterprises**			
一　级	Grade 1	306.26	33.90	22.37
二　级	Grade 2	510.07	153.97	90.25
三　级	Grade 3	303.18	47.46	45.36
无　级	No Grade	2 603.96	513.86	350.93

Floor Space Under Construction, Completed and Sold Floor Space in Real Estate Development

(10 000 sq · m)

			竣工价值(亿元) Completion Value (100 million yuan)	现房销售面积 Sold Floor Space for Completed Housing	期房销售面积 Area of Forward Sale of Future Marketable Housing
#住 宅 Housing	办公楼 Office Building	商业营业用房 Commerce/ Operation			
327.62	**14.95**	**57.90**	**311.22**	**167.27**	**324.26**
285.55	7.78	52.80	244.80	154.98	276.26
				1.38	1.14
					11.28
236.95	5.81	24.72	166.77	117.72	186.07
				0.30	0.06
48.60	1.97	28.08	78.03	35.58	77.71
10.32		0.58	10.52	3.98	27.58
9.38		0.58	8.89	2.53	24.77
31.75	7.17	4.52	55.90	8.31	20.42
19.40	7.17	3.91	49.02	3.53	6.90
107.58		9.81	75.50	82.14	97.31
71.78	1.06	3.16	33.59	5.26	15.85
42.08	7.17	5.10	66.42	12.21	48.00
106.18	6.72	39.83	135.71	67.66	163.10
19.42		1.07	15.75	13.60	17.16
67.24	0.11	3.01	39.53	24.80	46.05
31.03		6.62	12.45	20.92	25.37
209.93	14.84	47.20	243.49	107.95	235.68

表9-4 历年全社会房屋施工面积、竣工面积

Total Floor Space Under Construction and Completed in Main Years (1992～2015)

年 份 Year	施工面积（万平方米） Floor Space Under Construction (10 000 sq · m)	#住 宅 Residential Housing	竣工面积（万平方米） Floor Space Completed (10 000 sq · m)	#住 宅 Residential Housing	房屋建筑面积竣工率（%） Construction Completion Rate(%)	#住 宅 Residential Housing
1992	312.15	123.00	104.70	69.27	33.5	56.3
1993	764.36	285.34	169.44	76.68	22.2	26.9
1994	1 158.24	450.03	458.33	113.92	39.6	25.3
1995	1 577.21	583.96	404.58	199.84	25.7	34.2
1996	2 226.58	904.18	674.49	355.31	30.3	39.3
1997	1 954.70	768.15	581.03	271.64	29.7	35.4
1998	2 014.17	911.68	578.31	301.41	28.7	33.1
1999	1 766.88	856.25	573.20	268.27	32.4	31.3
2000	1 549.57	711.80	544.22	255.21	35.1	35.9
2001	1 526.45	879.01	469.53	249.96	30.8	28.4
2002	2 328.47	1 737.98	611.48	512.11	26.3	29.5
2003	2 242.65	1 607.68	671.70	498.85	29.9	31.0
2004	2 250.62	1 569.76	632.76	453.83	28.1	28.9
2005	2 390.79	1 695.24	684.96	512.42	28.6	30.2
2006	2 204.65	1 589.11	779.65	597.52	35.4	37.6
2007	1 983.86	1 255.32	516.59	419.29	26.0	33.4
2008	1 964.30	1 058.98	477.85	255.77	24.3	24.2
2009	2 977.23	1 792.12	742.28	505.70	24.9	28.2
2010	3 211.12	2 085.07	424.90	296.70	13.2	14.2
2011	3 511.82	2 296.52	487.81	286.14	13.9	12.5
2012	3 527.25	2 280.68	626.96	433.38	17.8	19.0
2013	3 560.04	2 185.40	569.03	350.35	16.0	16.0
2014	3 739.22	2 222.93	704.86	474.53	18.9	21.3
2015	3 723.47	2 097.82	508.91	327.62	13.7	15.6

表9-5 主要年份房地产开发企业房屋建筑面积和造价

Floor Space and Cost of Constructions Developed by Real Estate Companies in Main years

指 标	Indicators	1998	2000	2005	2010	2014	2015
房屋施工面积（万平方米）	**Floor Space Under Construction (10 000 sq·m)**	**1 458.94**	**1 119.67**	**2 390.79**	**3 211.12**	**3 739.22**	**3 723.47**
住 宅	Residential Housing	789.35	712.17	1 695.24	2 085.07	2 222.93	2 097.82
#别墅、高档公寓	Villas and Flats	77.46	72.64	490.51	394.58	412.72	380.34
办公楼	Office Buildings	404.07	199.39	196.68	300.14	475.54	568.82
商业营业用房	Commercial Buildings	155.58	106.63	222.13	389.62	404.39	399.72
其 他	Others	109.94	101.48	276.74	436.30	636.37	657.11
房屋竣工面积（万平方米）	**Floor Space Completed (10 000 sq·m)**	**360.36**	**384.03**	**684.96**	**424.90**	**704.86**	**508.91**
住 宅	Residential Housing	231.94	264.91	512.42	296.70	474.53	327.62
#别墅、高档公寓	Villas and Flats	26.10	23.59	168.59	85.58	38.27	78.38
办公楼	Office Buildings	71.15	54.62	54.08	31.61	41.39	14.95
商业营业用房	Commercial Buildings	41.16	28.10	32.85	35.85	71.08	57.90
其 他	Others	16.11	36.40	85.61	60.74	117.86	108.44
房屋竣工价值（亿元）	**Value of Buildings Completed (100 million yuan)**	**141.19**	**110.16**	**204.11**	**173.20**	**287.70**	**311.22**
住 宅	Residential Housing	61.74	55.36	147.55	127.76	172.47	205.41
#别墅、高档公寓	Villas and Flats	16.91	9.86	61.51	71.53	24.97	72.64
办公楼	Office Buildings	53.89	35.25	26.18	13.98	29.28	15.40
商业营业用房	Commercial Buildings	20.61	11.02	10.09	12.98	42.00	33.79
其 他	Others	4.95	8.53	20.29	18.47	43.94	56.62
竣工房屋平均造价（元/平方米）	**Average Construction Cost (yuan/sq. m)**	**3 918**	**2 869**	**2 980**	**4 076**	**4 082**	**6 115**
住 宅	Residential Housing	2 662	2 090	2 879	4 306	3 635	6 270
#别墅、高档公寓	Villas and Flats	6 481	4 179	3 648	8 358	6 524	9 268
办公楼	Office Buildings	7 575	6 454	4 841	4 423	7 076	10 301
商业营业用房	Commercial Buildings	5 007	3 921	3 075	3 622	5 909	5 836
其 他	Others	3 078	2 345	2 371	3 042	3 728	5 221

表9-6 浦东房地产交易中心交易情况
Transactions in Pudong Real Estate Trading Center

指 标	Indicators	单 位 Unit	2010	2014	2015
商品房交易登记	**Registered Transactions of Commodity Housing**				
#出售套数	Number of Commodity Housing Sold	套 set	73 892	53 791	60 052
出售面积	Floor Space of Commodity Housing Sold	平方米 sq·m	7 197 092	5 015 353	5 421 164
出售金额	Value of Commodity Housing Sold	万元 10 000 yuan	6 799 748	6 419 335	6 756 806
预售套数	Number of Forward Sale of Commodity Housing	套 set	14 905	18 336	20 551
预售面积	Floor Space of Forward Sale of Commodity Housing	平方米 sq·m	1 629 081	1 854 481	2 714 517
预售金额	Value of Forward Sale of Commodity Housing	万元 10 000 yuan	3 283 668	4 390 684	9 812 409
存量房交易登记	**Registered Transactions of Housing at Stock**				
交易过户套数	Trading Number of Housing at Stock	套 set	43 162	38 445	71 544
交易过户面积	Trading Floor Space of Housing at Stock	平方米 sq·m	4 537 343	3 828 179	6 668 774
交易过户金额	Trading Value of Housing at Stock	万元 10 000 yuan	6 277 733	6 997 443	15 162 560

主要统计指标解释

房地产开发投资

指各种登记注册类型的房地产开发公司、商品房建设公司及其他房地产开发法人单位和附属于其他法人单位实际从事房地产开发或经营活动的单位统一开发的包括统代建、拆迁还建的住宅、厂房、仓库、饭店、宾馆、度假村、写字楼、办公楼等房屋建筑物和配套的服务设施，土地开发工程（如道路、给水、排水、供电、供热、通讯、平整场地等基础设施工程）的投资；不包括单纯的土地交易活动。

施工面积

指报告期内施工的全部房屋建筑面积。包括本期新开工的面积和上期开工跨入本期继续施工的房屋面积，以及上期已停建在本期恢复施工的房屋面积。本期竣工和本期施工后又停缓建的房屋，其建筑面积仍计入本期房屋施工面积中。

竣工面积

指在报告期内房屋建筑按照设计要求已经全部完工，达到住人和使用条件，经验收鉴定合格（或达到竣工验收标准），正式移交使用单位的各栋房屋建筑面积的总和。

房屋建筑面积竣工率

指一定时期内房屋竣工面积占同期房屋施工面积的比率。该指标从房屋建筑施工速度的角度反映投资效果的指标。

别墅、高档公寓

指建筑造价和销售价格明显高于一般商品住宅的商品住宅。别墅一般指地处郊区，独立成栋的商品住宅；高档公寓一般指地处市内高尚社区，高层或多层的商品住宅。别墅、高档公寓的确定标准：一是经有房地产投资计划审批权的主管部门审批建设的别墅、高档公寓开发项目；二是销售价格高于当地同等地段商品住宅平均销售价格一倍以上的别墅、公寓开发项目。该指标可以分析房地产投资结构，反映高收入家庭商品住宅的供求平衡情况。

EXPLANATORY NOTES TO MAJOR STATISTICAL INDICATORS

Investment in Real Estate Development

It includes the investment by the real estate development companies, commercial buildings construction companies and other real estate development units of various types of ownership in the construction of house buildings, such as residential buildings, factory buildings, warehouses, hotels, guesthouses, holiday villages, office buildings, and the complementary service facilities and land development projects, such as roads, water supply, water drainage, power supply, heating, telecommunications, land leveling and other projects of infrastructure. It excludes the activities in simple land transactions.

Floor Space under Construction

Floor Space under Construction refers to total floor space of all buildings under construction during the reference period, including floor space of newly started buildings during the reference period, floor space of construction extended from the previous period to the current period, and floor space of construction suspended during the previous period and resumed in the current period. Floor space of construction completed in the current period, and floor space of construction started and then suspended in the current period are also included in the floor space under construction of the current year.

Floor Space of Buildings Completed

Floor Space of Buildings Completed refers to the floor space of all buildings completed in the reference period, which have been appraised and accepted (or come up to the designed standards) and have been transferred to the owners for use.

Completion Rate of Floor Space of Buildings

Completion Rate of Floor Space of Buildings refers to the ratio of the floor space of buildings completed in certain period of time to the floor space of buildings under construction in the same period. This indicator reflects the investment result from the perspective of the speed of construction.

Villas, High-Grade Apartments

Villas, High-Grade Apartments refers to commercial houses whose construction costs and marketing prices are significantly higher than ordinary housing. Villas are independent structures generally located in the suburbs; high-grade apartments are multi-story buildings located in elegant urban neighborhoods. Criteria for villas and high-grade apartments include: 1) projects for the construction of villas or high-grade apartments have to be approved by competent departments in charge of real estate development and investment plans, and 2) prices for projects on villas or high-grade apartments are higher by over 100% compared with the average prices of ordinary commercial housing projects in similar location. This indicator helps to analyze the investment structure of the real estate industry and the demand and supply of housing for high-income households.

第十篇

CHAPTER 10

国内外贸易

DOMESTIC AND FOREIGN TRADES

表 10-1　历年商品销售总额

Total Sales of Commercial Goods
(1994～2015)

单位:亿元　　　　(100 million yuan)

年　份 Year	商品购进总额 Total Value of Goods Purchased	商品销售总额 Total Value of Goods Sold	期末库存 Inventory at Year-end
1994	150.11	171.46	10.40
1995	186.38	200.05	17.03
1996	202.48	242.39	15.90
1997	278.41	274.26	37.23
1998	260.70	306.12	26.75
1999	517.13	593.37	57.62
2000	686.44	752.94	62.63
2001	891.30	1 004.89	64.55
2002	1 152.32	1 787.51	51.08
2003	2 366.49	2 422.87	187.75
2004	2 788.95	2 932.10	258.35
2005	2 499.25	2 807.47	224.16
2006	2 638.45	2 944.96	220.71
2007	3 337.31	3 613.46	245.43
2008	4 174.85	4 646.70	376.29
2009	4 913.26	5 905.20	495.57
2010	8 386.78	8 263.56	1 509.06
2011	12 866.04	10 502.98	2 303.33
2012	12 463.17	14 546.69	1 169.08
2013	24 258.51	24 034.93	1 310.34
2014	27 867.04	27 640.16	1 309.03
2015	30 015.89	29 838.38	1 241.08

注：本篇数据从 2013 年开始根据第三次全国经济普查数据进行了调整。
Note: The numbers in this chapter are adjusted according to the Third National Economic Census from year 2013.

表10-2 历年社会消费品零售总额
Total Retail Sales of Social Consumer Goods
(1993～2015)

单位:亿元 (100 million yuan)

年 份 Year	消费品零售总额 Total Retail Sales of Consumer Goods		按商品用途分 By Usage				商品销售总额 Total Sales of Retail Goods
		#餐 饮 Catering	食 品 Food	衣 着 Clothing	用 品 Articles	燃 料 Fuel	
1993	41.92		14.04	4.74	22.80	0.34	
1994	82.74	3.18	39.58	6.47	36.08	0.61	171.46
1995	110.00	4.07	49.50	8.36	51.59	0.55	200.05
1996	140.21	4.03	53.13	12.17	74.01	0.90	242.39
1997	162.23	5.41	62.89	12.54	84.72	2.08	274.26
1998	178.97	4.78	65.06	16.61	96.27	1.03	306.12
1999	198.31	19.02	74.17	15.26	104.17	4.71	593.37
2000	215.17	25.80	81.55	13.65	117.94	2.03	752.94
2001	233.02	28.50	81.27	13.99	135.28	2.48	1 004.89
2002	284.24	25.19	75.12	14.08	190.61	4.43	1 787.51
2003	313.24	24.50	72.53	14.49	220.21	6.01	2 422.87
2004	358.21	31.49	83.73	17.84	251.42	5.22	2 932.10
2005	353.69	43.80	111.00	27.53	213.52	1.64	2 807.47
2006	400.02	51.55	125.88	32.24	240.83	1.07	2 944.96
2007	456.04	60.52	128.66	35.63	283.45	8.30	3 613.46
2008	526.89	68.16	167.23	45.39	306.53	7.74	4 646.70
2009	859.63	102.74	256.11	77.78	498.41	27.33	5 905.20
2010	1 036.88	138.03	268.69	92.32	604.08	71.79	8 263.56
2011	1 204.04	152.43	309.09	114.46	650.35	130.14	10 502.98
2012	1 349.73	166.78	341.95	124.25	728.03	155.50	14 546.69
2013	1 598.01	187.48	435.95	166.09	769.63	226.34	24 034.93
2014	1 740.23	199.48	490.44	192.01	829.55	228.23	27 640.16
2015	1 883.80	219.03	531.44	205.26	946.97	200.13	29 838.38

表 10-3 连锁商业零售额
Retail Sales of Commercial Chains

单位:亿元 (100 million yuan)

指 标	Indicators	2010	2014	2015
连锁商业零售总额	**Total Retail Sales of Commercial Chains**	**225.96**	**284.08**	**284.93**
超市及大型超市	Supermarkets and Shopping Malls	93.45	101.23	98.45
便利店	Convenience Stores	13.63	28.64	29.69
家居建材商店	Stores of Building Materials for House Decorations	3.60	4.32	4.62
家电连锁店	House Appliance Chain Stores	43.89	37.38	44.38
连锁餐饮	Catering Chains	12.78	16.63	19.09
医药连锁	Pharmcy Chains	1.34	1.97	2.27
成品油连锁	Refined Oil Chains	51.82	86.81	78.13
其他连锁	Other Chains	5.46	7.10	8.30

表 10-4 社会商业商品购、销、存总额
Total Values of Social Products on Purchase, Sales and Inventory

单位:亿元 (100 million yuan)

指 标	Indicators	2010	2014	2015
商品购进总额	**Total Goods Purchased**	**8 386.78**	**27 867.04**	**30 015.89**
#进 口	Imports	1 632.04	3 396.71	3 165.81
商品销售总额	**Total Goods Sold**	**8 263.56**	**27 640.16**	**29 838.38**
商品零售总额	Total Sales of Retail Goods	1 036.88	1 740.23	1 883.80
商品批发销售总额	Total Sales of Wholesale Goods	7 226.68	25 899.93	27 954.58
#出 口	Exports	663.82	1 074.24	1 023.98
年末库存总额	**Total Inventory at Year-end**	**1 509.06**	**1 309.03**	**1 241.08**

表10-5 社会消费品零售总额
Total Retail Sales of Consumer Goods

单位:亿元 (100 million yuan)

指 标	Indicators	2010	2014	2015
社会消费品零售总额	**Total Retail Sales of Consumer Goods**	**1 036.88**	**1 740.23**	**1 883.80**
按登记注册类型分	**By Type of Registration**			
内 资	Domestic Invested	694.79	976.52	1 006.83
国 有	State-owned	69.77	109.34	83.71
集 体	Collective-owned	55.25	33.26	23.11
股份有限公司	Companies with Limited Liability	115.15	172.86	178.71
私 营	Private	215.79	425.97	468.57
其 他	Others	238.83	235.09	252.73
港澳台商投资	Hong Kong/Macao/Taiwan Invested	124.38	356.61	393.34
外商投资	Foreign Invested	217.70	407.10	483.63
按行业分	**By Sector**			
商业零售额	Commerce	898.85	1 540.75	1 664.77
餐饮业零售额	Catering	138.03	199.48	219.03
按商品用途分	**By Use**			
食品类	Food	268.69	490.44	531.44
衣着类	Clothing	92.32	192.01	205.26
用品类	Articles	604.08	829.55	946.97
燃料类	Fuel	71.78	228.23	200.13
构 成(%)	**Composition (%)**			
总 计	**Total**	**100.0**	**100.0**	**100.0**
按登记注册类型分	**By Type of Registration**			
内 资	Domestic Invested	67.0	56.1	53.4
国 有	State-owned	6.7	6.3	4.4
集 体	Collective-owned	5.3	1.9	1.2
股份有限公司	Company with Limited Liability	11.1	9.9	9.5
私 营	Private	20.8	24.5	24.9
其 他	Others	23.1	13.5	13.4
港澳台商投资	Hong Kong/Macao/Taiwan Invested	12.0	20.5	20.9
外商投资	Foreign Invested	21.0	23.4	25.7
按行业分	**By Sector**			
商业零售额	Commerce	86.7	88.5	88.4
餐饮业零售额	Catering	13.3	11.5	11.6
按商品用途分	**By Use**			
食品类	Food	25.9	28.2	28.2
衣着类	Clothing	8.9	11.0	10.9
用品类	Articles	58.3	47.7	50.3
燃料类	Fuel	6.9	13.1	10.6

表10-6 限额以上商业企业主要财务指标
Major Financial Indicators of Above-quota Commercial Enterprises

单位:亿元 (100 million yuan)

指 标	Indicators	2010	2014	2015
企业单位数(个)	**Number of Enterprises (unit)**	**1 524**	**1 783**	**1 713**
年末资产负债	**Assets and Liabilities at Year-end**			
资产总计	Total Assets	3 513.25	8 410.41	8 442.21
#流动资产合计	Total Circulating Assets	2 843.68	6 518.78	6 593.67
#存 货	Goods in Stock	663.75	1 225.93	1 136.64
固定资产合计	Total Fixed Assets	193.64	325.14	313.27
固定资产原价	Original Value of Fixed Assets	271.39	568.98	584.40
累计折旧	Accumulated Depreciation	96.24	244.49	271.45
#本年提取折旧	Depreciation in Current Year	17.76	38.55	39.45
负债总计	Total Liabilities	2 441.40	6 087.29	6 044.89
所有者权益总计	Owner's Equity	1 071.85	2 323.12	2 397.32
#实收资本	Paid-up Capital	411.67	1 167.94	1 091.85
#国家资本	State-owned Capital Assets	147.05	198.99	147.96
港澳台商资本	Hong Kong/Macao/Taiwan Capital Assets	41.41	167.51	208.17
外商资本	Foreign Capital Assets	81.17	225.83	275.04
法人资本	Legal Person Capital Assets	72.67	397.21	350.17
损益及分配(限批发零售贸易业填)	**Profit, Loss and Distribution (Only for Wholesale and Retails)**			
营业收入	Operating Revenue	83 314.34	24 117.56	21 843.51
#主营业务收入	Main Operation Revenue	82 887.94	23 997.11	21 714.87
主营业务成本	Main Operation Cost	77 084.46	22 336.35	20 189.07
营业费用	Operating Expenses	2 360.98	903.19	978.18
业务税金及附加	Operation Tax & Surtax	111.52	22.17	22.33
主营业务利润	Profit From Main Business	5 691.96	1 638.59	1 503.47
其他业务利润	Other Earnings	331.97	65.21	53.49

表 10-7 商品交易市场基本情况
Commodity Market Transactions
(2015)

指 标 Indicators		市场数(个) Number of Markets(unit)	营业面积(平方米) Business Space(sq·m)	成交额(亿元) Transaction Value (100 million yuan)
合 计	**Total**	**156**	**1 043 640**	**3 617.69**
综合市场	**Integrated Markets**	**63**	**265 531**	**153.26**
工业消费品综合市场	Integrated Market for Industrial Consumer Goods	2	11 332	0.35
农产品综合市场	Integrated Market for Agricultural Products	55	189 874	135.78
其他综合市场	Other Integrated Markets	6	64 325	17.13
专业市场	**Professional Markets**	**93**	**778 109**	**3464.43**
生产资料市场	Market for Productive Materials	8	24 908	3155.56
农产品市场	Market for Agricultural Products	42	153 253	44.63
食品饮料烟酒市场	Market of Food, Beverage, Tobacco and Liquor	5	18 080	1.97
纺织品服装鞋帽市场	Market of Textiles, Clothes, Shoes and Hats	10	61 326	3.03
日用品及文化用品市场	Market of Commodities and Stationers´Goods	1	5 000	179.52
家俱、五金装饰材料市场	Market of Furniture, Hardware and Decoration Materials	16	444 000	56.70
汽车及零配件市场	Market of Automobiles and Spare and Accessory Parts	2	35 360	20.24
电器、通讯器材市场	Market of Electric Appliances and Communication Equipment	2	11 005	1.36
花、鸟、鱼、虫市场	Market of Flowers, Birds, Fishes and Insects	2	17 740	1.24
其他专业市场	Other Professional Markets	5	7 437	0.18

表10-8 商品交易市场摊位数量及成交额
Number of Stalls and Transaction Value in Commodity Market
(2015)

指 标	Indicators	数 量（个）Stalls (unit)	成交额（亿元）Transaction Value (100 million yuan)
已出租摊位总计	**Total Stalls Leased**	**19 253**	**3 617.69**
食品、饮料、烟酒类	Food, Beverage, Tobacco and Liquor	9 645	181.87
服装、鞋帽、针、纺织品类	Garments, Shoes, Hats and Knitwear	2 469	4.61
化妆品类	Cosmetics	26	0.02
金银珠宝类	Gold, Silver and Jewelry	7	0.02
日用品类	Articles for Daily Use	481	181.14
五金电料类	Hardware Materials	93	0.37
体育、娱乐用品类	Sports and Recreation Articles	17	0.03
书报杂志类	Books and Newspapers	2	…
电子出版物及音像制品	Electronic Publications and Audio-Video Products	4	…
家用电器和音像器材类	Household Appliances and Audio-Video Equipment	16	0.02
中西药品	Western and Traditional Chinese Medicine	1	…
文化办公用品类	Culture and Office Articles	176	1.83
通讯器材类	Telecommunications Equipment	70	0.13
家具类	Furniture	819	4.30
木材及制品类	Timber and Its Products	19	0.29
石油及制品类	Petroleum and its products	754	1 690.10
金属材料及制品类	Metal Materials and Products	600	1 437.11
建筑及装潢材料类	Building and Decoration Materials	2 160	52.84
汽车类	Automobiles	37	20.24
种子饲料类	Seeds and Feeding Stuff	3	…
其他类	Others	1 854	42.76

表10-9 限额以上主要商品销售量
Sales Amount of Main Above-quota Goods

指 标	Indicators	单 位 Unit	2013	2014	2015
电脑(微型计算机)	Computer (PC)	台 set	2 468 844	2 326 092	2 498 968
煤 炭	Coal	吨 ton	75 372 013	67 034 856	63 395 491
汽 油	Gasoline	吨 ton	2 538 859	7 649 028	7 089 766
柴 油	Diesel Oil	吨 ton	2 932 936	3 351 737	2 419 517
钢 材	Steel Products	吨 ton	23 017 620	24 430 128	19 856 004
铜	Copper	吨 ton	10 830 827	26 400 910	23 176 500
铝	Aluminium	吨 ton	7 227 416	8 412 367	9 636 417
水 泥	Cement	吨 ton	3 076 823	3 992 725	4 899 597
汽 车	Motor Vehicles	辆 unit	1 886 490	2 182 625	2 178 211
#轿 车	Cars	辆 unit	1 543 503	1 822 003	1 682 174

表10-10 电子商务交易情况
Transactions of E-business

单位:亿元 (100 million yuan)

指 标	Indicators	2013	2014	2015
电子商务交易总额	**E-business Trading Total Volume**	**3 144.10**	**3 544.15**	**3 143.00**
B2B	B2B	2 941.20	3 263.15	2 850.00
网络购物(B2C和C2C)	Online Shopping(B2C and C2C)	202.90	281.00	293.00
商品类	Commodity	135.30	205.00	216.00
服务类	Service	67.60	76.00	77.00
第三方支付交易额	**Third-party Payment Trading Volume**	**55 195.00**	**73 850.70**	**72 357.00**

注：2013年起,浦东新区电子商务数据由上海市商务委统一测算。
Note: Since 2013, E-business Data have been collected and calculated by Shanghai Commission of Commerce, thus the statistical calibre and calculation method are both changed.

表10-11　历年进出口货物总值
Total Value of Imports and Exports
(1993～2015)

单位:亿美元　　(USD 100 million)

年　份 Year	进出口总值 Total Value of Imports and Exports	出口总值 Total Export Value	#一般贸易 Ordinary Trade	加工贸易 Processing Trade	海关特殊监管区域物流货物 Goods for Logistics within Special Supervision of the Customs	进口总值 Total Import Value	#一般贸易 Ordinary Trade	加工贸易 Processing Trade	海关特殊监管区域物流货物 Goods for Logistics within Special Supervision of the Customs
1993	25.92	12.02	6.67			13.90	5.26		
1994	47.35	23.21	13.73			24.14	5.60		
1995	71.96	39.63	24.40			32.34	11.72		
1996	80.78	38.75	21.31			42.03	14.12		
1997	99.01	45.86	23.06			53.15	17.00		
1998	119.82	52.80	25.14			67.02	21.74		
1999	153.65	66.67	28.58			86.98	35.90		
2000	254.86	95.80	44.21			159.06	71.91		
2001	297.83	110.22	49.56			187.61	87.74		
2002	368.98	136.02	62.96			232.96	98.94		
2003	581.33	211.92	102.80			369.41	156.60		
2004	808.07	323.78	145.55			484.29	185.68		
2005	894.75	372.12	175.38			522.63	186.52		
2006	1 073.10	444.71	212.50			628.39	198.72		
2007	1 280.52	528.10	257.50			752.42	248.66		
2008	1 449.59	604.23	300.42			845.36	286.70		
2009	1 389.89	576.50	241.40			813.39	332.19		
2010	1 865.62	738.79	306.50	286.05	127.51	1 126.83	430.70	123.24	506.01
2011	2 260.00	888.98	356.82	339.00	167.03	1 371.02	537.42	152.78	600.65
2012	2 398.93	939.83	361.39	359.28	189.68	1 459.1	542.57	145.04	696.28
2013	2 496.08	958.25	368.20	349.06	212.37	1 537.83	648.54	160.29	630.39
2014	2 678.71	1 006.10	384.88	352.41	241.51	1 672.61	733.49	173.04	644.46
2015	16 903.70	6 019.88	2 272.08	2 150.30	1 458.67	10 883.82	4 804.37	1 075.41	4 033.23

注：2015年始数据计量单位改为"人民币亿元"。
Note: The unit of measurement was changed to "CNY 100 million" in 2015.

表10-12 重要商品的出口货物总值
Total Value of Important Exported Goods

单位:万元 (10 000 yuan)

指 标	Indicators	2014	2015
总 计	**Total**	**61 801 452**	**60 198 776**
#机电产品	Mechanic and Electric Products	42 264 862	42 456 706
#高新技术产品	Hi-tech Products	26 601 427	28 171 854
电话机	Telephone Sets	7 369 454	9 413 303
集成电路	Integrated Circuits	5 932 266	7 597 203
服装及衣着附件	Clothing and Accessories	4 520 624	4 037 132
自动数据处理设备及其部件	Automatic Data Processing Equipment and Componets	4 857 681	3 047 281
船 舶	Ships	2 371 804	2 473 849
纺织纱线、织物及制品	Txtile Yarns, Fabrics and their Products	1 949 732	1 931 225
医药品	Medicines	1 192 376	1 246 734
汽车零配件	Automobile Components	1 176 522	1 190 601
自动数据处理设备的零件	Parts of Automatic Dta Processing Equipment	1 004 949	1 125 987
通断保护电路装置及零件	Protection Circuit Devices and their Parts	927 532	890 472
二极管及类似半导体器件	Diodes and Similar Semiconductor Devices	866 525	811 679
液晶显示板	LCDs	1 241 693	805 654
成品油	Refined Oils	1 084 940	717 282
家具及其零件	Furniture and its Parts	638 810	603 720
箱包及类似容器	Boxes and Similar Containers	621 659	586 037
塑料制品	Plastic Products	516 912	492 227
钢 材	Steel	533 108	482 518
农产品	Agricultural Products	499 828	464 912
医疗仪器及器械	Medical Appartus and Instruments	399 892	422 334
珍珠、钻石、宝石及半宝石	Pearls, Diamons, Precious Stones and Half-precious Stones	407 102	402 270
手用或机用工具	Manual or Machine Tools	337 676	327 368
未锻轧铝及铝材	Unwrought Aluminum and Aluminum Products	328 498	313 179

表10-13　重要商品的进口货物总值
Total Value of Important Imported Goods

单位:万元　　(10 000 yuan)

指　标	Indicators	2014	2015
总　计	**Total**	**102 756 370**	**108 838 183**
#机电产品	Mechanic and Electric Products	58 113 447	57 041 673
#高新技术产品	Hi-tech Products	35 933 227	38 690 838
集成电路	Integrated Circuits	14 136 207	16 465 927
汽　车	Automobiles	8 712 294	6 339 231
农产品	Agricultural Products	4 667 945	6 253 730
未锻轧铜及铜材	Unwrought Copper and Copper Products	5 651 045	4 630 123
医药品	Medicines	4 007 324	4 446 420
飞机及其他航空器	Aeroplanes and other Aircraft	3 350 850	3 617 460
初级形状的塑料	Primarily-formed Plastics	3 504 474	3 063 040
计量检测分析自控仪器及器具	Automatically-controlled Equipment and Devices for Measuring and Checking Analysis	2 904 267	2 693 170
自动数据处理设备及其部件	Automatic Dta Processing Equipment and its Components	2 772 714	2 683 140
通断保护电路装置及零件	Protection Circuit Device and its Componets	2 003 419	1 857 218
医疗仪器及器械	Medical Apparatus and Instruments	1 699 993	1 852 468
粮　食	Grain	965 430	1 700 669
钻　石	Diamonds	1 524 092	1 205 324
汽车零配件	Automobile Componets	1 063 657	1 042 133
铁矿砂及其精矿	Iron Ore and Concentrates	640 031	1 002 578
乳　品	Dairy Products	682 578	910 513
成品油	Refined Oil	1 469 021	884 824
电视摄像机、数字照相机及视频摄录一体机	Television Cameras, Digital Cameras and Vedio Recording Machines	673 565	846 460
纺织纱线、织物及制品	Textile Yarns, Fabrics and their Products	811 319	769 467
手　表	Watches	858 282	763 341
电话机	Telephone Sets	781 050	733 562
自动数据处理设备的零件	Parts of Automatic Dta Processing Equipment	757 672	712 006

表10-14 主要年份按国别(地区)分的出口货物总值
Total Value of Exports by Country/Region in Main Years

单位:万美元 (USD 10 000)

国别(地区)	Country/Region	2005	2010	2014	2015
总　计	**Total**	**3 721 174**	**7 387 919**	**10 060 970**	**6 019.88**
#亚　洲	**Asia**	**1 697 530**	**3 340 974**	**4 866 893**	**3 052.14**
#中国香港	Hong Kong, China	468 087	717 639	1 181 388	785.54
中国澳门	Macao, China	1 789	5 557	3 337	5.16
中国台湾	Taiwan, China	130 197	271 421	308 564	170.52
印　度	India	35 233	133 175	236 002	166.26
孟加拉国	Bangladesh	13 023	24 808	33 249	26.90
印度尼西亚	Indonesia	26 669	71 303	136 616	85.69
日　本	Japan	451 176	774 154	989 941	616.17
马来西亚	Malaysia	66 363	244 468	278 828	110.90
巴基斯坦	Pakistan	10 116	15 838	26 424	19.66
菲律宾	Philippines	64 628	71 219	81 494	50.54
沙特阿拉伯	Saudi Arabia	14 897	31 085	55 529	27.55
新加坡	Singapore	109 379	305 192	512 581	260.91
韩　国	Republic of Korea	136 003	260 049	374 890	326.45
斯里兰卡	Sri Lanka	4 348	5 962	20 488	8.09
泰　国	Thailand	33 224	96 554	128 425	101.66
阿拉伯联合酋长国	United Arab Emirates	46 529	100 559	129 415	61.69
欧　洲	**Europe**	**843 460**	**1 893 937**	**2 009 069**	**1 175.07**
#欧　盟	European Union	785 409	1 701 505	1 795 745	1 097.53
#比利时	Belgium	61 105	101 144	72 086	43.02
英　国	United Kingdom	114 380	178 263	246 532	182.71
德　国	Germany	187 924	380 488	344 793	212.84
法　国	France	63 802	166 625	148 752	79.29
爱尔兰	Ireland	15 151	16 467	20 425	7.97
意大利	Italy	51 163	184 868	100 067	55.34
荷　兰	Netherlands	108 070	225 709	417 981	309.57
西班牙	Spain	42 824	78 986	80 555	38.88
波　兰	Poland	12 284	44 788	45 793	26.92
瑞　典	Sweden	22 954	39 060	28 369	15.76
瑞　士	Switzerland	11 441	26 010	22 046	12.42
俄罗斯	Russia	25 442	126 041	153 127	51.01
拉丁美洲	**Latin America**	**144 120**	**384 886**	**471 410**	**246.95**
#阿根廷	Argentina	5 739	24 892	19 241	9.95
巴　西	Brazil	34 310	120 169	113 679	58.08
智　利	Chile	11 408	23 641	34 621	21.22
墨西哥	Mexico	28 773	99 863	134 464	75.40
巴拿马	Panama	19 659	17 688	28 560	20.86
北美洲	**North America**	**863 433**	**1 279 355**	**2 171 301**	**1 202.24**
#加拿大	Canada	92 621	97 013	124 304	52.23
美　国	United States of America	770 807	1 182 329	2 046 981	1 150.01

注：2015年数据计量单位改为“人民币亿元”。
Note: The unit of measurement was changed to "CNY 100 millions".

表10-15　主要年份按国别(地区)分的进口货物总值

Total Value of Imports by Country/Region in Main Years

单位:万美元　　(USD 10 000)

国别(地区)	Country/Region	2005	2010	2014	2015
总　计	**Total**	**5 226 325**	**11 268 269**	**16 726 133**	**10 883.82**
#亚　洲	**Asia**	**3 046 147**	**6 234 946**	**7 341 207**	**4 677.91**
#中国香港	Hong Kong, China	46 910	38 575	59 785	119.22
中国台湾	Taiwan, China	379 850	762 696	878 400	534.81
印　度	India	58 457	184 487	237 949	126.64
印度尼西亚	Indonesia	76 588	84 572	118 387	81.54
日　本	Japan	919 062	1 738 090	1 700 201	993.60
马来西亚	Malaysia	220 785	736 065	835 649	514.07
新加坡	Singapore	199 594	251 998	355 844	283.51
韩　国	Repubic of Korea	511 641	949 805	1 259 741	895.70
泰　国	Thailand	148 120	330 108	241 220	138.37
非　洲	**Africa**	**39 824**	**214 711**	**308 214**	**166.40**
欧　洲	**Europe**	**1 122 993**	**2 515 255**	**5 286 138**	**3 451.41**
#欧　盟	European Union	998 473	2 092 754	4 287 824	2 377.77
#比利时	Belgium	52 002	200 446	205 189	90.47
英　国	United Kingdom	72 078	113 428	829 827	330.72
德　国	Germany	385 695	797 961	1 593 954	947.68
法　国	France	159 106	293 253	535 807	308.89
意大利	Italy	102 266	192 625	318 324	179.02
荷　兰	Netherlands	44 876	77 545	126 482	101.14
西班牙	Spain	19 596	50 883	84 860	44.92
波　兰	Poland	4 920	18 727	46 396	27.44
瑞　典	Sweden	34 688	114 719	103 835	61.93
瑞　士	Switzerland	68 211	214 630	713 686	844.94
俄罗斯	Russia	31 450	144 899	165 335	150.39
拉丁美洲	**Latin America**	**127 155**	**645 571**	**962 790**	**576.17**
#巴　西	Brazil	26 441	107 078	129 454	143.19
智　利	Chile	35 236	299 182	362 612	200.48
墨西哥	Mexico	26 439	103 963	226 750	144.48
北美洲	**North America**	**820 607**	**1 420 899**	**2 129 525**	**1 468.26**
#加拿大	Canada	61 936	129 762	157 912	125.33
美　国	United States of America	758 389	1 291 123	1 971 613	1 342.89
大洋洲	**Oceania**	**69 599**	**235 546**	**695 211**	**542.15**
#澳大利亚	Australia	56 073	173 509	626 410	509.21
新西兰	New Zealand	9 197	52 040	67 041	31.56

注：2015 年数据计量单位改为“人民币亿元”。
Note:The unit of measurement was changed to“CNY 100 millions”.

主要统计指标解释

社会消费品零售总额

指批发和零售业、餐饮业、新闻出版业、邮政业和其他服务业等，售予城乡居民用于生活消费的商品和社会集团用于公共消费的商品之总量。社会消费品零售总额包括：

（1）批发和零售业企业（单位）：

①售予城乡居民的各种生活消费品；

②售予入境旅游的外国人、华侨、港澳台同胞的各类商品；

③售予行政事业单位、社会团体、军队和武警等机构的商品，以及以零售方式售予各类企业的商品。具体包括：用于非生产和社会交往的办公用品，如通讯设备、计算器具和设备、电讯网络设备、文印设备、音像视听器材和设备、纸张、本册、文具及装订文印材料、家具、日用电器、针纺织品、清洁卫生用品、文体用品、奖品、纪念品、礼品等；供内部人员乘坐的交通工具和燃料；用于办公设施修缮的各类配件、材料、工具等；用于取暖和防暑降温的设备、燃料、材料及食品等；专用于教学的用品和设备；非营利医疗机构的中、西药品、中药材和医疗设备器材；非专用的劳动保护用品；不对外营业的内部食堂用的餐具、炊具、设备、清洁卫生工具和食品、燃料等；军队、武警用于其人员生活的衣着品和个人用品；其他各类非生产性设备和用品。

（2）餐饮业出售的主食、菜肴、烟酒饮料和其他商品。

（3）新闻出版业、邮政业售予城乡居民、企事业单位、军队和武警等机构的书报杂志、音像制品、邮品等。

（4）其他服务业出售的食品、烟酒饮料、服装鞋帽、日常生活用品、医药保健用品、艺术品、工艺美术品、玩具、殡葬用品以及其他消费品。

批发零售贸易业商品购、销、存总额

指各种登记注册类型的批发、零售贸易企业（单位）以本企业（单位）为总体的，从上海、上海以外市场购进的商品总量、销售和出口的商品总量、库存商品总量等情况。该指标对促进工农业生产发展、活跃市场、平抑物价、保障供给、满足需求具有举足轻重的作用。该指标可以反映商品流转过程中商品的购进、销售、库存之间的比例关系和存在的问题。

商品购进总额

指从本企业（单位）以外的单位和个人购进（包括从境外直接进口）作为转卖或加工后转卖的商品总额。它反映批发零售贸易业从国内、国外市场上购进商品的总量。商品购进总额包括：①从工农业生产者购进的商品；②从出版社、报社的出版发行部门购进的图书、杂志和报纸；③从各种登记注册类型的批发零售贸易企业（单位）购进的商品；④从其他单位购进的商品，如从机关、团体、企业等单位购进的剩余物资，从餐饮业、服务业购进的商品，从海关、市场管理部门购进的缉私和没收的商品，从居民手中收购的废旧商品等；⑤从国（境）外直接进口的商品。不包括企业（单位）为自身经营用和未通过买卖行为而收入的商品以及销售退回、商品升溢等。

商品销售总额

商品销售总额指对本企业以外的单位和个人出售（包括对国（境）外直接出口）的商品。这个指标反映批发零售贸易业在上海市场以及上海以外市场上销售商品的总量。商品销售总额包括：①售给城乡居民和社会集团消费用的商品；②售给工业、农业、建筑业、运输邮电业、批发零售贸易业、餐饮业、服务业等作为生产、经营使用的商品；③售给批发零售贸易业作为转卖或加工后转卖的商品；④对国（境）外直接出口的商品。不包括：出售本企业自用的废旧包装用品，未通过买卖行为付出的商品，经本单位介绍，由买卖双方直接结算，本单位只收取手续费的业务，购货退出的商品以及商品损耗和损失等。

批发零售贸易业年末库存

是指年末各种经济类型的批发零售贸易企业（单位）已取得所有权的商品，它反映各地区、各批发零售贸易企业的商品库存情况和对市场商品供应的保证程度。期末库存包括；①存放在批发零售贸易业经营单位（如门市部、批发站、经营处）仓库、货场、货柜和货架中的商品；②挑选、整理、包装中的商品；③已记入购进而尚未运到本单位的商品，即发货单或银行承兑凭证已到而货未到部份；④寄放他处的商品，如因购货方拒绝承付而暂存放在购货方的商品和已办完加工成品收回手续而未提回的商品；⑤委托其他单位代销（未作销售或调出）尚未售出的商品；⑥代其他单位购进尚未交付的商品。不包括所有权不属于本单位的商品、拨付除批发零售贸易业以外的其他行业所属独立核算加工厂等加工生产尚未收回成品的商品，代国家物资储备部门保管的商品等。期末库存总额计算方法是：农副产品采购单位按购进价计算；批发单位按进货价计算；零售单位按什么价格核算就按什么价格计算。

主营业务收入

指企业在销售商品、提供劳务等日常活动中所产生的收入总额。

主营业务成本

指企业已销商品应负担的进货原价和商品进价成本。

营业费用

指批发零售贸易企业在购、销、存过程中发生的各项经营费用。包括运输费、装卸费、包装费、保险费、展览费、差旅费、广告费、商品损耗、进出口商品累计佣金、经营人员的工资及福利费等。

外贸进出口总额

外贸进出口总额是指海关统计中按经营单位即进出口企业在海关注册地的行政区域口径统计的数据,它反映的是上海浦东新区行政辖区内各类具有进出口经营权企业(外贸企业)的进出口。它不包含外省市外贸企业途经上海浦东新区口岸由上海海关结关放行及统计的进出口商品,但包含上海浦东新区外贸企业经由非上海口岸进出口结关放行及统计的商品。

电子商务交易总额

指借助网络订单且实际交割的的商品和服务的总金额,包括商品交易以及住宿旅游、订餐、通信等服务交易,但不包含第三方支付交易。借助网络订单指通过网络发送订单。付款可以是网上,也可以是网下进行。

B2B:指企业对企业的电子商务交易。

B2C:指企业对个人的电子商务交易。

C2C:指个人对个人的电子商务交易。

第三方支付:是指非金融机构作为第三方在收付款人之间作为中介机构通过网络提供货币资金转移服务。

EXPLANATORY NOTES TO MAJOR STATISTICAL INDICATORS

Total Retail Sales of Consumer Goods

Total Retail Sales of Consumer Goods refers to the sum of retail sales of commodities sold by wholesale, retail, catering, publishing, post and telecommunications and other service industries to urban and rural households for private consumption and to social institutions for public consumption. Retail sales of consumer goods include:

(1) Sales by wholesale and retail units:

①of consumer goods sold to urban and rural households;

②of commodities sold to foreigners, overseas Chinese and Chinese compatriots from Hong Kong, Macau and Taiwan visiting in China;

③of commodities sold to government agencies, institutions, social organizations, military and armed police units, and commodities sold to enterprises in the form of retail sales. More specifically, they include: office facilities and articles for non-production purposes such as communications equipment, computing equipment and instruments, TV and network equipment, printing and copying equipment, audio-visual equipment and instruments, paper, notebooks, stationeries, furniture, electric appliances, knitwear, sanitation and cleaning articles, cultural and sport articles, articles for prizes, souvenirs, etc.; transport vehicles and fuels for employees; materials, spare parts and tools for the maintenance of office facilities; equipment, fuels, materials and food for winter heating or summer cooling purposes; articles and equipment for teaching purpose; Chinese and western medicines and medical equipment and facilities purchased by non profit-making medical institutes; non-specialized work safety articles; cooking utensils, tableware, equipment, cleaning articles, food and fuels purchased by internal cafeterias; clothes and personal articles purchased by military or armed police units for their officials and soldiers; and other equipment and articles for non-production purposes.

(2) Sales of stable food, cooked dishes, beverages, tobaccos and other articles by catering units.

(3) Sales of books, newspapers, magazines, audio-visual products and post products by publishing, post and telecommunications departments to urban and rural households and to enterprises, institutions, military and armed police units.

(4) Sales of food, beverages, tobaccos, clothing, hats, footwear, articles for daily use, medicines, medical and health articles, work of art, handicrafts, toys, funeral articles and other articles by other service industries.

Purchase, Sales and Stock of Commodities by Wholesale and Retail Trades

Purchase, Sales and Stock of Commodities by Wholesale and Retail Trades refer to the total volume of commodities purchased, total volume of sales and exports, and the stock of commodities by wholesale and retail enterprises (establishments) of different status of registration from Shanghai and out-of-Shanghai markets. This indicator plays an important role in promoting industrial and agricultural production, thriving market, stabilizing prices, ensuring market supply and meeting the needs of consumers. It also reflects the relationship among purchase, sales and stock of commodities in the circulation of goods and reveals the existing problems.

Total Purchase of Commodities

Total Purchase of Commodities refers to purchase of commodities from other establishments or individuals (including direct import abroad) for the purpose of reselling, either with or without further processing of the commodities purchased. This indicator shows the total value of purchases of commodities by wholesale and retail establishments from domestic and overseas markets, they include: ①agricultural and industrial products purchased from producers; ②books, magazines and newspapers purchased from distribution departments of the publishers; ③commodities purchased from wholesale and retail establishments; ④commodities purchased from other units, such as surplus materials purchased from government agencies, enterprises or institutions, commodities purchased from catering and service establishments, confiscated goods purchased from customs authorities or market management agencies, second hand goods and reusable stuff purchased from residents; ⑤commodities directly imported abroad. Excluded are commodities purchased by establishments for their own business operation, commodities obtained without buying or selling procedures, rejected commodities, etc.

Total Sales of Commodities

Total Sales of Commodities refer to the selling of commodities to other establishments and individuals (including direct export). Reflecting the total value of sales of commodities at Shanghai markets and out-of-Shanghai markets, this indicator includes: ① commodities sold to urban and rural households and institutions for their consumption; ② commodities sold to establishments in industry, agriculture, construction, transportation, post and telecommunications, wholesale and retail trade, catering and service trade and public utility for their production and operation; ③ commodities sold to wholesale and retail establishments for re-selling, with or without further processing; and ④ commodities for direct export to other countries. Excluded are selling of waste packaging materials used by enterprises themselves commodities transferred without buying or selling procedures, commission income from brokerage in transactions whose settlement is directly handled by buyers and sellers, rejected commodities in the purchase, loss in commodities, etc.

Commodities Stock of Wholesale and Retail Enterprises at Year-end

refers to total commodities possessed by wholesale and retail enterprises (units of various ownership, which reflects the commodity stock level of various wholesale and retail enterprises and the potential for market supply. This indicator includes; ① commodities located in storage, rooms, garages, counters, and shelves of operating units (such as sales stores, wholesale stations, and operating offices) of wholesale and retail enterprises; ② commodities in the process of selecting, sorting, and packing; ③ commodities not arrived but recorded as purchase in the account, i. e. commodities have not arrived but payment receipts for the commodities from the sellers or the banks have arrived; ④ commodities deposited in other places rather than places mentioned above, for instance; commodities in the hold of purchasers temporarily due to the refusal of payment and commodities not taken back after going through processing procedures; ⑤ commodities entrusted to other units to sell but not sold out yet; ⑥ commodities purchased for other units but not delivered yet. Commodities not included as stock are those not owned by enterprises, those allocated to financially independent factories rather than wholesale and retail enterprises for processing but not taken back yet, and finally those put in stock by wholesale and retail enterprises on behalf of the state material reserves units. The value of commodities stock at the end of period, the value is calculated at purchasing price of agricultural goods purchasing units and wholesale units and retail units at accounting prices.

Prime Operating Revenue

Prime Operating Revenue refers to the earnings a corporation receives in daily activity such as selling goods and offering labor service.

Operating Cost

Operating Cost refers to the cost a corporation paid to buy and deliver the commodities.

Operating Expenses

Operating Expenses refer to the spending that a wholesaler or retailer pays in buying, selling or stocking goods. It includes fees incurred in transport, loading and unloading, packaging, insurance, exhibition, business trip, advertisement, commodity wastage, commissions in import and export, salaries and bonus paid to workers involved.

The Volume of Foreign Trade

The Volume of Foreign Trade is offered by Customs authorities, covering the operation units, or the enterprises involved in import and export, that have registered in the administrative regions where the Customs operate. It reflects the import and export of all the enterprises with import and export rights (foreign trade enterprises) under the administration of Shanghai Pudong New Area Municipality. It excludes those commodities of foreign trade enterprises from out of town that underwent customs clearance at Shanghai Pudong New Area ports but includes commodities of foreign trade enterprises of Shanghai Pudong New Area that underwent customs clearance in non-Shanghai ports.

E-business Trading Total Volume

E-business Trading Total Volume refers to the total volume of commodities and services that have been ordered and actually transacted through the network, including commodity transaction and service transactions, such as hotel booking, meal order, tourism service and so on, not including the third-party transaction. The term of "through the network" means sending orders via internet, but the payment can be made both online and offline.

B2B

B2B refers to E-business transactions from business to business.

B2C

B2C refers to E-business transactions from business to consumer.

C2C

C2C refers to E-business transactions from consumer to consumer.

The Third-party Transaction

The Third-party Transaction refers to the online monetary capital transferance in which the non-financial corporations act as the third party between the payee and the payer.

第十一篇

CHAPTER 11

服务、旅游和住宿业

SERVICES, TOURISM AND HOTELS

表 11－1 主要年份社会服务业经济总量（营业收入）

Total Economics of Social Services in Main Years (Operating Revenue)

单位：亿元 (100 million yuan)

指标	Indicators	2014	2015
总 计	**Total**	**4 427.51**	**4 887.23**
信息传输、软件和信息技术服务业	Information Transmission, Software and Information Technology Service	1 424.43	1 467.29
# 软件开发	Software Development	523.76	1 161.78
租赁和商务服务业	Leasing and Business Services	1 830.31	2 154.50
# 商务服务业	Commercial Services	1 686.51	2 005.19
# 企业管理服务	Business Management Services	966.85	1 227.37
咨询与调查	Consulting and Surveys	354.41	379.16
广告业	Advertising	107.56	104.65
科学研究和技术服务业	Scientific Researches and Technology Service	552.76	577.47
水利、环境和公共设施管理业	Water Conservancy, Environment and Public Facilities Management	110.12	147.02
居民服务、修理和其他服务业	Resident Services, Repair and Other Services	66.36	77.01
教 育	Education	194.06	194.31
卫生和社会工作	Health and Social Work	205.47	219.85
文化、体育和娱乐业	Culture, Sports and Entertainment	44.00	49.79

注：本篇社会服务业相关表式自 2012 年起，采用国民经济行业分类（GB/T 4754－2011）。
Note: The relevant forms in this chapter of social services have been classified by the national economical trades (GB/T 4754－2011) since 2012.

表 11-2 社会服务业经济总量

Total Economics of Social Services

(2015)

单位:亿元 (100 million yuan)

指标	Indicators	营业收入 Operating Revenue	增幅(%) Increased by	比重(%) Percentage
总计	**Total**	**4 887.23**	**10.3**	**100.0**
信息传输、软件和信息技术服务业	Information Transmission, Software and Information Technology Service	1 467.29	5.4	30.0
#软件开发	Software Development	1 161.78	6.7	23.8
租赁和商务服务业	Leasing and Business Services	2 154.50	13.9	44.1
#商务服务业	Commercial Services	2 005.19	15.1	41.0
#企业管理服务	Business Management Services	1227.37	19.0	25.1
咨询与调查	Consulting and Surveys	379.16	11.7	7.8
广告业	Advertising	104.65	7.2	2.1
科学研究和技术服务业	Scientific Researches and Technology Service	577.47	9.5	11.8
水利、环境和公共设施管理业	Water Conservancy, Environment and Public Facilities Management	147.02	11.3	3.0
居民服务、修理和其他服务业	Resident Services, Repair and Other Services	77.01	6.4	1.6
教育	Education	194.31	11.2	4.0
卫生和社会工作	Health and Social Work	219.85	13.7	4.5
文化、体育和娱乐业	Culture, Sports and Entertainment	49.79	3.7	1.0

表 11-3 主要年份社会服务业从业人员数
Number of Employees of Social Services in Main Years

单位:万人 (10 000 persons)

指 标	Indicators	2014	2015
总 计	**Total**	**68.79**	**71.30**
信息传输、软件和信息技术服务业	Information Transmission, Software and Information Technology Service	16.15	16.56
#软件开发	Software Development	8.87	14.84
租赁和商务服务业	Leasing and Business Services	25.93	27.41
#商务服务业	Commercial Services	24.00	26.36
#企业管理服务	Business Management Services	9.10	9.26
咨询与调查	Consulting and Surveys	4.81	5.37
广告业	Advertising	0.54	0.57
科学研究和技术服务业	Scientific Researches and Technology Service	8.46	8.38
水利、环境和公共设施管理业	Water Conservancy, Environment and Public Facilities Management	2.24	2.63
居民服务、修理和其他服务业	Resident Services, Repair and Other Services	3.56	4.18
教 育	Education	6.52	5.86
卫生和社会工作	Health and Social Work	4.37	4.62
文化、体育和娱乐业	Culture, Sports and Entertainment	1.56	1.66

表 11－4　社会服务业从业人员数
Number of Employees of Social Services
(2015)

单位:万人　　(10 000 persons)

指　标	Indicators	从业人员数 Number of Employees	增　幅(%) Increased by	比　重(%) Percentage
总　计	**Total**	**71.30**	**1.1**	**100.0**
信息传输、软件和信息技术服务业	Information Transmission, Software and Information Technology Service	16.56	0.8	23.2
#软件开发	Software Development	14.84	0.9	20.8
租赁和商务服务业	Leasing and Business Services	27.41	2.5	38.4
#商务服务业	Commercial Services	26.36	2.3	37.0
#企业管理服务	Business Management Services	9.26	1.6	13.0
咨询与调查	Consulting and Surveys	5.37	5.5	7.5
广告业	Advertising	0.57	0.3	0.8
科学研究和技术服务业	Scientific Researches and Technology Service	8.38	1.4	11.8
水利、环境和公共设施管理业	Water Conservancy, Environment and Public Facilities Management	2.63	-0.1	3.7
居民服务、修理和其他服务业	Resident Services, Repair and Other Services	4.18	6.2	5.9
教　育	Education	5.86	-9.6	8.2
卫生和社会工作	Health and Social Work	4.62	4.5	6.5
文化、体育和娱乐业	Culture, Sports and Entertainment	1.66	4.3	2.3

表11-5　主要年份接待国内外游客情况
Foreign and Domestic Tourists Received in Main Years

单位:万人次　　(10 000 persons-times)

指　标	Indicators	2005	2010	2014	2015
接待游客总数	**Total Tourists Received**	**1 660**	**3 215**	**3 639**	**3 634**
按接待单位分	By Receiving Agency				
#宾馆接待游客	Hotels	164	278	325	336
旅行社接待游客	Tourist Agencies	111	185	157	215
景点接待游客	Tourist Attractions	1 385	2 752	3 157	3 083
平均每天接待旅游人数(人次/天)	Average Number of Tourists Received Everyday (person-time/day)	45 474	88 094	99 699	99 562

表11-6　旅游景点经营情况
Operation of Tourist Attractions

指　标	Indicators	单　位 Unit	2005	2010	2014	2015
主要景点营业情况	**Business in Major Tourist Attractions**					
主要景点个数	Main Tourist Attractions	个 in number	23	25	34	34
接待参观人次	Visitors Received	万人次 10 000 person-times	1 908	2 752	3 157	3 083
营业收入	Operating Income	万元 10 000 yuan	87 500	144 781	167 941	179 615

表 11-7 主要景点经营情况
The General Development of Main Tourism Spot

指 标 Indicators		营业收入(万元) Operating Income (10 thousand yuan)		接待人数(万人次) Number of Tourists (10 thousand person-time)	
		2014 年	2015 年	2014 年	2015 年
东方明珠	The Oriental Pearl TV Towel	38 432.07	44 442.44	425.87	398.37
上海海洋水族馆	Shanghai Ocean Aquarium	29 122.04	30 833.29	199.27	208.94
上海野生动物园发展有限公司	Shanghai Wild Life Zoo	25 394.20	28 229.31	230.29	254.03
磁悬浮列车	Magnetically Levitated Train	13 285.31	15 204.00	323.99	364.48
上海环球金融中心观光厅	Shanghai World Financial Center Sightseeing Hall	11 401.00	13 230.70	189.36	228.65
上海科技馆	Shanghai Techonology Museum	9 684.05	9 812.18	297.52	292.95
观光隧道	Sightseeing Tunnel	7 847.88	8 214.22	159.33	177.99
上海金茂大厦	Shanghai Jin Mao Tower	6 992.00	7 477.80	123.36	132.98
上海世纪公园管理有限公司	Shanghai Century Park	5 574.33	4 474.80	309.31	193.72
巧克力开心乐园	Chocolate Happy Paradise	5 076.53	3 438.51	38.33	24.51
月亮船(原沙特馆)	Moon Boat	2 016.16	1 539.50	46.77	38.21
鲜花港	Flower Port	1 727.84	1 662.02	50.72	51.12
南汇桃花村	Nanhui Peach Blossom Villiage	1 684.00	1 155.00	11.02	11.11
东方葵园生态农庄	Oriental Sunflower Ecological Farm	1 409.00	1 312.85	11.22	14.77
喜来春国际农庄	Spring Ecological Farm	1 401.51	1 770.00	29.49	39.66
渔乐湾生态园	Fishing Ecological Farm	1 229.25	572.23	29.60	13.05
书院人家	Shuyuan Farm	916.51	1 477.45	12.84	17.12
中国航海博物馆	China Maritime Museum	791.15	869.76	28.31	30.16
凌空农艺大观园	Lingkong Agro Museum	780.15	788.21	7.43	9.19

表11-8　旅馆、旅行社经营情况
Operation of Hotels and Travel Agencies

指　标	Indicators	单　位 Unit	2005	2010	2014	2015
旅馆业	**Hotel Industry**					
接待能力状况	**Receiving Capacity**					
客房数	Rooms	间 room	12 692	15 780	18 100	17 962
客房床位数	Beds	张 bed	20 245	22 652	26 272	25 962
实际住宿人次数	Actual Staying Days	万人次 10 000 person-times	163.84	278.33	324.96	335.77
#境外来沪住宿人次数	Overseas Guests	万人次 10 000 person-times	73.03	99.21	111.57	109.16
实际住宿人天数	Actual Staying Days	万人天 10 000 person · days	371.18	491.33	509.39	563.49
#境外来沪住宿人天数	Staying Days of Overseas Guests	万人天 10 000 person · days	195.58	187.84	182.05	193.45
财务经营状况	**Financial Operation**					
固定资产原值	Original Value of Fixed Assets	亿元 100 million yuan	82.35	119.19	110.17	108.87
营业收入	Operation Earning	亿元 100 million yuan	37.09	55.85	60.39	64.88
#客房收入	Hotel Room Earning	亿元 100 million yuan	21.77	31.87	31.00	33.58
餐饮收入	Catering Earning	亿元 100 million yuan	15.32	19.22	29.39	25.67
旅行社	**Travel Agency**					
旅行社接待人次数	Persons Received by PNA Travel Agencies	万人次 10 000 person-times	110.69	185.25	157.68	214.68
国内旅行社	Domestic Travel Agencies	万人次 10 000 person-times	89.86	154.52	117.19	87.67
国际旅行社	International Travel Agencies	万人次 10 000 person-times	20.83	30.73	40.49	127.01
旅行社营业收入	Operation Earnings of PNA Travel Agencies	亿元 100 million yuan	14.68	30.00	53.21	62.63
国内旅行社	Domestic Travel Agencies	亿元 100 million yuan	8.44	16.08	19.34	20.21
国际旅行社	International Travel Agencies	亿元 100 million yuan	6.24	13.92	33.87	42.42

表11-9 会议、展览情况
Conferences and Fairs

指 标	Indicators	单 位 Unit	2005	2010	2014	2015
举办展览(博览)	**Number of Exhibitions Hosted**	**次 time**	**114**	**120**	**220**	**247**
#国际性	International	次 time	91	100	185	224
#三万平方米及以上	≥30 000 sq. m	次 time	29	38	85	74
#五万平方米及以上	≥50 000 sq. m	次 time	15	28	45	40
展览面积	Display Area	万平方米 10 000 sq · m	238	400	812	706
参展客商	Exhibition-Attending Investors	个 unit	48 412	69 713	122 915	99 794
接待(参观)人数	Visitors Received	万人次 10 000 person-times	266.90	309.70	649.99	542.36
召开会议	Conferences Hosted	次 time	1 583	1 504	14 677	13 539
#跨省市	Trans-provincial	次 time	61	112		
国际性	International	次 time	199	26	2 068	2 679
参加会议人员	Number of Participants	万人次 10 000 person-times	16.69	17.03	185.77	160.48
#海外与会人员	Overseas Participants	万人次 10 000 person-times	3.00	1.34	18.35	28.95

注：2011 年始会议统计的范围为浦东四星级以上宾馆。
Note: The statistical scope for the conferences has referred to the hotels with four stars or more in Pudong since 2011

表11-10　四星级以上酒店宾馆基本情况
Basic Information about Hotels above Four-star Level

指　标　Indicators		标　准 Standard	客房数(间) Number of Rooms
浦东新区香格里拉酒店有限公司	Shangri-la Hotel Pudong New Area	五星级 Five-star	952
金茂君悦大酒店	Grand Hyatt Residence	五星级 Five-star	555
上海国际会议中心有限公司大酒店	Shanghai International Conference Center Hotel	五星级 Five-star	273
上海锦江汤臣大酒店有限公司	Shanghai Jinjiang Tangcheng Intercontinental Hotel	五星级 Five-star	398
上海东锦江大酒店有限公司	Shanghai East Jinjiang Hotel (Doubletree by Hilton Shanghai Pudong)	五星级 Five-star	850
喜来登由由酒店	Sheraton Youyou Hotel	五星级 Five-star	525
上海淳大万丽大酒店	Renaissance Shanghai Pudong Hotel	五星级 Five-star	370
上海东郊宾馆有限公司	Shanghai Dongjiao Hotel	五星级 Five-star	334
上海紫金山大酒店	Shanghai Purple Mountain Hotel	五星级 Five-star	368
上海外高桥皇冠假日酒店	Shanghai Waigaoqiao Crowne Plaza	五星级 Five-star	388
上海红塔豪华精选酒店	Shanghai Hongta Luxury Collection	五星级 Five-star	328
裕景大饭店	Yujing Grand Hotel	四星级 Four-star	460
上海浦东华油实业有限责任公司中油大酒店	Zhongyou Hotel of Huayou Real Estate Shanghai Pudong	四星级 Four-star	318
上海通茂大酒店	Shanghai Tongmao Hotel	四星级 Four-star	298
浦东华美达大酒店	Pudong Ramada Hotel	四星级 Four-star	269
证大丽笙大酒店	Radisson Hotel Pudong Century Park	四星级 Four-star	354
福朋喜来登由由酒店	Fupeng Sheraton Youyou Hotel	四星级 Four-star	316
机场华美达大酒店	Ramada Airport Hotel	四星级 Four-star	374
齐鲁万怡大酒店	Courtyard by Marriott Shanghai Pudong	四星级 Four-star	323
上海海神诺富特大酒店	Novotel Atlantis Shanghai	四星级 Four-star	293
浦东假日酒店	Pudong Holiday Inn	四星级 Four-star	352
明城大酒店	Mingcheng Hotel	四星级 Four-star	222
东怡大酒店	Dongyi Hotel	四星级 Four-star	209
上海宝安大酒店有限公司	Shanghai Baoan Hotel	四星级 Four-star	228
上海嘉瑞酒店有限公司	Shanghai Green Garden Hotel	四星级 Four-star	151

主要统计指标解释

接待国外游客人数

指来上海浦东新区参观、访问、旅行、探亲、访友、休养、考察、参加会议和从事经济、科技、文化、教育、体育、宗教等活动的外国人、华侨、港澳和台湾同胞的人数。不包括来上海浦东新区常住 1 年以上的外国专家、留学生等。上海浦东新区入境的境外旅游人数包括从上海浦东新区口岸入境的境外旅游人数和从我国其他口岸入境的境外旅游人数。

EXPLANATORY NOTES TO MAJOR STATISTICAL INDICATORS

Number of Overseas Tourists

Number of Overseas Tourists refers to the number cf foreigners, overseas Chinese, and compatriots from Hong Kong, Macao and Taiwan coming to Shanghai Pudong New Area for sightseeing, visits, tours, family reunions, meeting friends, vacations, study tours, attending meetings and other activities of an economic, scientific and technological, cultural, physical culture and religious nature. This does not include foreign experts and students residing in Shanghai Pudong New Area for over 1 year. The number of overseas tourists to Shanghai Pudong New Area includes those overseas tourists entering China through Shanghai Pudong New Area customs and through customs other than Shanghai.

第十二篇

CHAPTER 12

科学技术

SCIENCE AND TECHNOLOGY

表 12-1　历年科技成果
Achievements in Scientific & Technological Research
（1995～2015）

单位：项　　　　　　　　　　　　　　　　　　　　　　　　　　　　　　（item）

年　份 Year	获上海市高新技术成果转化百佳项目 Top 100 Projects Which Have Successfully Commercialized Achievements in Scientific & Technological Research	获上海市以上科技进步奖 Shanghai and Above Level Achievement Awards in Scienceand Technology	按奖项分 Award Grade								
			特等奖 Special Award	#国家级 National Grade	一等奖 First Prize	#国家级 National Grade	二等奖 Second Prize	#国家级 National Grade	三等奖 Third Prize	青年科技杰出贡献奖 Youth Science and Technology Outstanding Contribution Award	国际科技合作奖 International Technology Cooperate Award
1995		2					1		1		
1996											
1997		2					1		1		
1998		14					3		11		
1999		12			2		3		7		
2000		11					5		6		
2001		16					5		11		
2002		37			8		13		16		
2003	11	34			8		10		16		
2004	11	45			10		16		19		
2005	25	35			5	1	10	3	20		
2006	17	48			11	1	23	5	14		
2007		73			11	2	31	11	31		
2008		66			10		27	6	29		
2009		50			5		23	5	22		
2010		63			8		29	10	26		
2011		92			15		43	12	34		
2012		69			19	1	25	3	24	1	
2013		70			9		37	12	24		
2014		61	1	1	10		21	6	27	1	1
2015		83	1	1	7		27	8	48		

注：上海市高新技术成果转化百佳项目从 2001 年起评比。
Note：We started to appraise the above-mentioned Top 100 Projects since 2001.

表12-2 历年各类技术合同项目
All Kinds of Technical Contracts
(1994~2015)

单位:项 (item)

年 份 Year	各类合同项目 Item of Contracts	技术开发 Technical Development	技术转让 Technology Tranfer	技术咨询 Technical Consultation	技术服务 Technical Service
1994	595	25	43	98	429
1995	924	42	33	147	702
1996	1 525	12	16	215	1 282
1997	1 742	23	56	291	1 372
1998	1 659	57	49	282	1 271
1999	1 998	85	21	406	1 486
2000	1 940	79	24	458	1 379
2001	2 253	260	86	405	1 502
2002	2 281	372	116	465	1 328
2003	2 406	500	284	422	1 200
2004	2 362	580	148	406	1 228
2005	3 034	1 155	225	353	1 301
2006	2 636	1 448	100	204	884
2007	2 545	1 326	118	86	1 015
2008	2 294	1 448	94	262	490
2009	2 518	1 757	112	194	455
2010	2 550	1 774	139	100	537
2011	2 932	2 269	137	181	345
2012	2 722	2 133	124	116	349
2013	2 484	1 876	112	90	406
2014	2 753	1 938	132	8	675
2015	2 475	1 946	122	9	398

表 12-3　历年各类技术合同成交金额

Business Volume of All Kinds of Technical Contracts (1994 ~ 2015)

单位:万元　　(10 000 yuan)

年　份 Year	成交金额 Business Volume	技术开发 Technical Development	技术转让 Technology Tranfer	技术咨询 Technical Consultation	技术服务 Technical Service
1994	6 225	284	404	492	5 045
1995	12 514	3 863	2 105	936	5 610
1996	21 255	599	573	1 772	18 311
1997	15 644	749	1 286	2 386	11 223
1998	21 286	3 924	2 106	2 098	13 158
1999	24 788	7 194	1 509	2 929	13 156
2000	39 707	7 969	15 893	2 524	13 321
2001	62 892	30 778	8 709	3 317	20 088
2002	86 786	51 233	12 303	4 585	18 665
2003	112 355	79 274	12 978	5 217	14 886
2004	221 295	185 897	13 881	4 030	17 487
2005	386 406	335 848	33 096	3 087	14 375
2006	641 015	525 942	96 628	2 952	15 493
2007	839 052	694 197	125 175	2 586	17 094
2008	957 346	870 937	69 244	3 512	13 653
2009	1 299 693	1 145 384	137 907	2 111	14 291
2010	1 210 256	1 023 716	96 063	16 254	74 224
2011	1 269 191	1 125 001	66 825	2 508	74 857
2012	1 578 060	1 247 899	136 211	2 749	191 201
2013	1 747 328	870 741	164 063	22 137	690 387
2014	1 795 142	944 087	89 506	762	760 788
2015	1 770 611	1 100 769	231 052	13 985	424 805

表 12-4 历年专利申请情况
Statistics of Patent Claiming
(1999～2015)

单位:项 (item)

年 份 Year	专利申请 总 量 Total Patent Claimings	发 明 Inventions	实用新型 Utility Models	外观设计 Design in Appearance
1999	386	67	216	103
2000	718	209	241	268
2001	1 103	222	453	428
2002	2 397	467	591	1 339
2003	2 580	1 064	852	664
2004	2 871	1 676	719	476
2005	3 141	1 794	863	484
2006	6 767	2 557	1 224	2 986
2007	8 435	3 054	1 386	3 995
2008	8 980	3 065	1 893	4 022
2009	14 645	5 372	3 936	5 337
2010	17 587	6 576	4 902	6 109
2011	18 819	9 218	6 973	2 628
2012	21 972	12 902	7 158	1 912
2013	18 331	9 687	6 936	1 708
2014	19 002	10 279	7 127	1 596
2015	22 493	11 353	9 122	2 018

表 12-5 历年专利授权情况
Statistics of Patents Authorized
(2001～2015)

单位:项 (item)

年 份 Year	专利授权 总 量 Total Patents Authorized	发 明 Inventions	实用新型 Utility Models	外观设计 Design in Appearance
2001	519			
2002	668			
2003	1 542			
2004	1 066	95	528	443
2005	1 204	329	576	299
2006	1 432	375	655	402
2007	4 086	409	1 152	2 525
2008	3 677	841	1 442	1 394
2009	8 046	1 557	2 266	4 223
2010	12 764	1 503	3 950	7 311
2011	12 685	2 149	5 423	5 113
2012	11 226	2 789	6 653	1 784
2013	11 073	3 074	6 564	1 435
2014	10 896	3 139	6 454	1 303
2015	13 299	4 654	6 970	1 675

表12-6　区属企业、事业单位各类专业技术人员(2015年末)

Professional Personnel Working in Enterprises and Institutions in PNA (Total by the End of 2015)

单位:人　　(person)

指标	Indicators	合计 Total	#女性 Female	按学历分 By Education Level 研究生 Post Graduate	大学本科 University	高等专科 Junior University	中等专科 Specialized Secondary School	高中及以下 Senior High School and Below
总计	**Total**	**48 394**	**35 305**	**3 073**	**34 860**	**8 445**	**1 520**	**496**
工程技术人员	Engineering	2 228	563	269	1 248	378	140	193
农业技术人员	Agricultural	464	179	50	261	98	42	13
科学研究人员	Research	259	120	59	121	64	11	4
卫生技术人员	Healthcare	12 508	9 213	1 354	6 942	3 176	940	96
教学人员	Teaching	29 318	23 202	996	24 481	3 697	139	5
经济人员	Economic	1 239	469	206	545	333	64	91
会计人员	Financial/Accounting	1 266	914	55	657	419	108	27
统计人员	Statistical	168	115	7	89	51	15	6
翻译人员	Interpreter/Translator	16	11	5	9	2		
图书档案文博人员	Librarian/Archivist/Museum Staff	439	329	35	252	120	15	17
新闻、出版人员	News-Reporting/Publishing	72	30	6	58	7	1	
律师、公证人员	Lawyer/Notary	53	27	12	41			
工艺美术人员	Artisan	4			1	3		
体育人员	Sports	65	22		49	15		1
艺术人员	Actor/Actress	76	46	5	30	28	7	6
政工人员	Political	219	65	14	76	54	38	37

表12-7 区属企业、事业单位各年龄组专业技术职务及专业技术人员(2015年末)

Technical Professions and Technicians Grouped by Ages in PNA Enterprises and Institutions (Total by the End of 2015)

单位:人 (person)

指 标 Indicators		合 计 Total	按年龄分 By Age					
			35岁及以下 35 Year-old and Below	36至40岁 36~40 Year-old	41至45岁 41~45 Year-old	46至50岁 46~50 Year-old	51至54岁 51~54 Year-old	55岁以上 55 Year-old and Above
总 计	**Total**	**48 394**	**18 167**	**8 935**	**9 158**	**7 023**	**3 710**	**1 401**
按专业技术职务分	**By Professional Position**							
高级职务	Senior	4 445	26	426	1 194	1 511	945	343
中级职务	Intermediate	20 774	2 922	5 089	5 902	4 225	2 014	622
初级职务	Junior	21 189	13 487	3 317	2 002	1 238	715	430
未聘职务	Laid -off	1 986	1 732	103	60	49	36	6
按专业技术类别分	**By Profession**							
工程技术人员	Engineering	2 228	766	365	371	325	241	160
农业技术人员	Agricultural	464	159	43	53	92	61	56
科学研究人员	Scientific	259	64	67	40	46	22	20
卫生技术人员	Healthcare	12 508	4 910	2 706	2 195	1 448	846	403
教学人员	Teaching	29 318	11 289	5 006	5 845	4 560	2 098	520
经济人员	Economic	1 239	349	219	206	178	188	99
会计人员	Financial/Accounting	1 266	319	325	274	188	117	43
统计人员	Statistical	168	49	44	26	33	11	5
图书档案文博人员	Librarian/Archivist/Museum Staff	439	124	102	64	78	44	27
政工人员	Political	219	37	16	41	39	41	45
其他专业技术人员	Others	286	101	42	43	36	41	23

表 12-8 工业企业科技活动人员情况
Scientific and Technical Personnel of Industrial Enterprises
(2015)

指 标	Indicators	有科技活动企业数(个) Number of Enterprises with Scientific Technical Activities (unit)	从事科技活动人员(人) Total Number of Personnel Undertaking Scientific Technical Activities (person)	#本科及本科以上学历人员(人) Number of personnel with Bechelor Degree or Above (person)
总 计	**Total**	**485**	**67 997**	**57 057**
按注册登记大类分组	**Grouped by Type of Registration**			
国 有	State-owned	6	2 720	337
集 体	Collective-owned	2	33	31
股份制及其他有限公司	Share-holding	108	15 443	14 078
私 营	Private	146	7 363	5 763
外商及港澳台投资	Overseas Invested Enterprises	213	38 665	33 605
其 他	Others	10	3 773	3 243
按隶属关系分组	**Grouped by Subordination**			
中央工业	Central	25	14 405	9 426
地方工业	Local	460	53 592	47 631
按企业规模分组	**Grouped by Enterprise Scale**			
#大型企业	Large	54	41 203	34 882
中型企业	Medium	137	16 411	13 713
按工业行业大类分组	**Grouped by Sector**			
#农副食品加工业	Farm and Sideline Products Processing	7	326	253
食品制造业	Food Manufacturing	2	74	57
酒、饮料和精制茶制造业	Wine, Beverage and Refined Tea Manufacturing	2	83	83
烟草制品业	Tobacco Manufacturing	1	17	8
纺织业	Textile Industry	4	186	99
家具制造业	Furniture Manufacturing	2	1 314	1 303
造纸和纸制品业	Papermaking and Paper Products	7	250	215
印刷和记录媒介复制业	Printing and Record Medium Reproduction Industry	10	486	325
文教、工美、体育和娱乐用品制造业	Culture, Art, Sports and Recreation Supplies Manufacturing	2	92	49
石油加工、炼焦和核燃料加工业	Oil Processing, Coking and Nuclear Fuel Processing	2	143	72
化学原料和化学制品制造业	Raw Chemical Materials and Chemical Products	33	2 232	1 860
医药制造业	Medicine Manufacture	40	3 958	3 482
化学纤维制造业	Chemical Fiber Manufacturing	2	59	59
橡胶和塑料制品业	Rubber and Plastic Products Industry	18	952	728
非金属矿物制品业	Nonmetal Mineral Products	16	684	543
黑色金属冶炼和压延加工业	Smelting and Rolling of Nonferrous Metals	1	4	4
有色金属冶炼和压延加工业	Smelting and Rolling of Ferrous Metals	4	207	106
金属制品业	Metal Products	19	927	784
通用设备制造业	General Equipment Manufacture	59	4 777	4 288
专用设备制造业	Special Purpose Equipment Manufacturing	50	4 272	3 513
汽车制造业	Automobile Manufacturing	54	16 684	16 105
铁路、船舶、航空航天和其他运输设备制造业	Railroad, Ship, Aviation and Other Transportation Equipment Manufacturing	12	2 470	1 910
电气机械和器材制造业	Electric Equipment and Machinery Manufacturing	61	5 274	4 131
计算机、通信和其他电子设备制造业	Computer, Communications and Other Electronic Equipment Manufacturing	46	18 413	15 445
仪器仪表制造业	Instrument Manufacturing	19	1 400	1 325
废弃资源综合利用业	Comprehensive Utilization of Waste Resources	1	11	11
金属制品、机械和设备修理业	Metal Products, Machinery and Equipment Repair Industry	1	20	20
电力、热力生产和供应业	Production and Supply of Electricity and Thermal Power	7	2 625	251
燃气生产和供应业	Production and Supply of Fuel Gas	1	30	1
水的生产和供应业	Production and Supply of Water	1	6	6

注：本篇工业数据为年主营业务收入2000万及以上企业。
Note: In this chapter, industry data refer to enterprises with annual main business income of 20 million yuan and above.

表 12－9 工业企业技术开发项目和人员情况

Technical Development Projects and Personnel of Industrial Enterprises (2015)

指 标	Indicators	项目数（项）Number of Projects (item)	从事技术开发人数（人）Number of Technical Development Personnel (person)	科技项目经费内部支出（万元）Internal Expenditure for Projects of Science and Technology (10 000 yuan)
总 计	**Total**	**4 571**	**55 648**	**2 570 450**
按注册登记大类分组	**Grouped by Type of Registration**			
国 有	State-owned	244	1 611	31 723
集 体	Collective-owned	8	32	756
股份制及其他有限公司	Share-holding	909	11 502	628 646
私 营	Private	724	6 117	139 723
外商及港澳台投资	Overseas Invested Enterprises	2 518	33 151	1 612 966
其 他	Others	168	3 235	156 636
按隶属关系分组	**Grouped by Subordination**			
中央工业	Central	831	11 987	497 152
地方工业	Local	3 740	43 661	2 073 298
按企业规模分组	**Grouped by Enterprise Scale**			
#大型企业	Large	1 590	33 817	1 814 115
中型企业	Medium	1 487	13 199	515 753
按工业行业大类分组	**Grouped by Sector**			
#农副食品加工业	Farm and Sideline Products Processing	36	294	12 314
食品制造业	Food Manufacturing	18	73	3 088
酒、饮料和精制茶制造业	Wine, Beverage and Refined Tea Manufacturing	12	83	4 062
烟草制品业	Tobacco Manufacturing	3	15	286
纺织业	Textile Industry	14	144	6 068
家具制造业	Furniture Manufacturing	82	686	41 398
造纸和纸制品业	Papermaking and Paper Products	42	197	7 210
印刷和记录媒介复制业	Printing and Record Medium Reproduction Industry	57	421	10 412
文教、工美、体育和娱乐用品制造业	Culture, Art, Sports and Recreation Supplies Manufacturing	5	28	684
石油加工、炼焦和核燃料加工业	Oil Processing, Coking and Nuclear Fuel Processing	51	112	1 973
化学原料和化学制品制造业	Raw Chemical Materials and Chemical Products	234	1 819	87 510
医药制造业	Medicine Manufacture	456	3 438	126 447
化学纤维制造业	Chemical Fiber Manufacturing	8	55	1 249
橡胶和塑料制品业	Rubber and Plastic Products Industry	86	853	16 426
非金属矿物制品业	Nonmetal Mineral Products	111	625	25 037
黑色金属冶炼和压延加工业	Smelting and Rolling of Ferrous Metals	1	4	4
有色金属冶炼和压延加工业	Smelting and Rolling of Nonferrous Metals	24	148	7 037
金属制品业	Metal Products	105	899	18 957
通用设备制造业	General Equipment Manufacture	463	3 837	177 240
专用设备制造业	Special Purpose Equipment Manufacturing	288	3 517	111 133
汽车制造业	Automobile Manufacturing	975	14 045	903 208
铁路、船舶、航空航天和其他运输设备制造业	Railroad, Ship, Aviation and Other Transportation Equipment Manufacturing	167	2 062	101 465
电气机械和器材制造业	Electric Equipment and Machinery Manufacturing	357	3 849	118 191
计算机、通信和其他电子设备制造业	Computer, Communications and Other Electronic Equipment Manufacturing	650	15 920	725 813
仪器仪表制造业	Instrument Manufacturing	107	888	28 239
废弃资源综合利用业	Comprehensive Utilization of Waste Resources	1	11	392
金属制品、机械和设备修理业	Metal Products, Machinery and Equipment Repair Industry	2	7	144
电力、热力生产和供应业	Production and Supply of Electricity and Thermal Power	202	1 562	32 991
燃气生产和供应业	Production and Supply of Fuel Gas	3	29	37
水的生产和供应业	Production and Supply of Water	8	6	1 309

表 12-10 工业科技活动经费支出情况
（2015）

单位：万元

指 标	Indicators	企业内部科技活动支出合计 Total Expenditures of Scientific and Technological Activities Within Enterprises
总 计	**Total**	**2 924 047**
按注册登记大类分组	**Grouped by Type of Registration**	
国 有	State-owned	34 879
集 体	Collective-owned	756
股份制及其他有限公司	Share-holding	797 014
私 营	Private	155 046
外商及港澳台投资	Overseas Invested Enterprises	1 754 181
其 他	Others	182 171
按隶属关系分组	**Grouped by Subordination**	
中央工业	Central	554 744
地方工业	Local	2 369 303
按企业规模分组	**Grouped by Enterprise Scale**	
#大型企业	Large	2 020 820
中型企业	Medium	631 644
按工业行业大类分组	**Grouped by Sector**	
#农副食品加工业	Farm and Sideline Products Processing	14 764
食品制造业	Food Manufacturing	3 203
酒、饮料和精制茶制造业	Wine, Beverage and Refined Tea Manufacturing	4 348
烟草制品业	Tobacco Manufacturing	337
纺织业	Textile Industry	6 923
家具制造业	Furniture Manufacturing	57 609
造纸和纸制品业	Papermaking and Paper Products	7 650
印刷和记录媒介复制业	Printing and Record Medium Reproduction Industry	10 650
文教、工美、体育和娱乐用品制造业	Culture, Art, Sports and Recreation Supplies Manufacturing	895
石油加工、炼焦和核燃料加工业	Oil Processing, Coking and Nuclear Fuel Processing	2 792
化学原料和化学制品制造业	Raw Chemical Materials and Chemical Products	95 308
医药制造业	Medicine Manufacture	141 196
化学纤维制造业	Chemical Fiber Manufacturing	1 279
橡胶和塑料制品业	Rubber and Plastic Products Industry	17 529
非金属矿物制品业	Nonmetal Mineral Products	27 423
黑色金属冶炼和压延加工业	Smelting and Rolling of Ferrous Metals	4
有色金属冶炼和压延加工业	Smelting and Rolling of Nonferrous Metals	7 349
金属制品业	Metal Products	19 804
通用设备制造业	General Equipment Manufacture	193 847
专用设备制造业	Special Purpose Equipment Manufacturing	121 712
汽车制造业	Automobile Manufacturing	994 509
铁路、船舶、航空航天和其他运输设备制造业	Railroad, Ship, Aviation and Other Transportation Equipment Manufacturing	126 220
电气机械和器材制造业	Electric Equipment and Machinery Manufacturing	160 506
计算机、通信和其他电子设备制造业	Computer, Communications and Other Electronic Equipment Manufacturing	838 822
仪器仪表制造业	Instrument Manufacturing	29 372
废弃资源综合利用业	Comprehensive Utilization of Waste Resources	392
金属制品、机械和设备修理业	Metal Products, Machinery and Equipment Repair Industry	144
电力、热力生产和供应业	Production and Supply of Electricity and Thermal Power	37 977
燃气生产和供应业	Production and Supply of Fuel Gas	37
水的生产和供应业	Production and Supply of Water	1 309

Expenditures of Industrial Science and Technology Activities

(10 000 yuan)

委托外单位科技活动支出合计 Total Expenditures of Scientific and Technological Activities Organized by Other Enterprises	其他技术活动费用支出 Expenses of Other Technological Activities			
	技术改造经费支出 Expenditures on Technical Transformation	技术引进经费支出 Expenditures on Technical Introdnction	消化吸收经费支出 Expenditures on Technical Digestion and Absorption	购买国内技术经费支出 Expenditure in Buying Domestic Technology
262 711	**397 706**	**347 284**	**168 955**	**20 719**
5 655	13 812			
153 311	91 671	49 268	3 310	14 353
151	872			1 060
97 279	263 949	279 795	165 646	2 241
6 314	27 403	18 221		3 064
22 582	66 453	57 707	3 384	3 676
240 129	331 253	28 958	16 557	1 704
198 385	335 643	313 625	136 112	8 861
57 177	30 205	31 690	32 843	11 640
985	914			
156	154			
5 064				
6	378			
	19 503			
1 159	15 517	5 087		284
8 590	456			1 000
15				
				154
72	5 700	102	202	
5	232			
	1 359	28		
2 075	4 524	39 398	553	612
1 088		1 126	2 831	
184 165	298 046	264 066	132 786	1 721
5 231	22 045	18 218		3 064
15 526	672	15 689	11 796	
32 520	6 421	3 569	20 787	13 883
	264			
5 970	14 847			
47	5 199			
36	1 475			

表12-11 工业企业技术开发机构情况
Technical Development Institutions of Industrial Enterprises
(2015)

指标	Indicators	企业办技术开发机构数(个) Technical Development Institutions in Enterprises (unit)	技术开发机构科技活动人数(人) Technical Development Personnel (person)	技术开发机构科技经费内部支出(万元) Expenditure of Technical Development (10 000 yuan)
总 计	**Total**	**262**	**39 010**	**1 824 603**
按注册登记类型分	**Grouped by Type of Registration**			
国 有	State-owned	3	548	21 466
股份制及其他有限公司	Share-holding	55	8 315	420 393
私 营	Private	73	3 794	77 312
外商及港澳台投资	Overseas Invested Enterprises	125	23 603	1 179 925
其 他	Others	6	2 750	125 508
按隶属关系分	**Grouped by Subordination**			
中央工业	Central	19	9 464	435 112
地方工业	Local	243	29 546	138 949
按企业规模分	**Grouped by Enterprise Scale**			
#大型企业	Large	55	26 868	1 472 229
中型企业	Medium	77	8 127	259 955
按行业大类分	**Grouped by Sector**			
农副食品加工业	Farm and Sideline Products Processing	3	143	2 935
食品制造业	Food Manufacturing	1	40	2 552
酒、饮料和精制茶制造业	Wine, Beverage and Refined Tea Manufacturing			
烟草制品业	Tobacco Manufacturing			
纺织业	Textile Industry	2	54	3 643
家具制造业	Furniture Manufacturing	2	708	33 159
造纸和纸制品业	Papermaking and Paper Products	3	186	5 466
印刷和记录媒介复制业	Printing and Record Medium Reproduction Industry	6	218	8 026
文教、工美、体育和娱乐用品制造业	Culture, Art, Sports and Recreation Supplies Manufacturing			
石油加工、炼焦和核燃料加工业	Oil Processing, Coking and Nuclear Fuel Processing	1	65	920
化学原料和化学制品制造业	Raw Chemical Materials and Chemical Products	11	582	19 025
医药制造业	Medicine Manufacture	29	2 119	97 987
化学纤维制造业	Chemical Fiber Manufacturing	1	30	876
橡胶和塑料制品业	Rubber and Plastic Products Industry	9	359	6 990
非金属矿物制品业	Nonmetal Mineral Products	7	366	6 840
黑色金属冶炼和压延加工业	Smelting and Rolling of Ferrous Metals			
有色金属冶炼和压延加工业	Smelting and Rolling of Nonferrous Metals	4	189	859
金属制品业	Metal Products	10	522	9 652
通用设备制造业	General Equipment Manufacture	34	3 208	148 997
专用设备制造业	Special Purpose Equipment Manufacturing	22	1 858	53 992
汽车制造业	Automobile Manufacturing	23	11 927	729 412
铁路、船舶、航空航天和其他运输设备制造业	Railroad, Ship, Aviation and Other Transportation Equipment Manufacturing	7	1 908	62 390
电气机械和器材制造业	Electric Equipment and MachineryManufacturing	31	1 926	61 411
计算机、通信和其他电子设备制造业	Computer, Communications and Other Electronic Equipment Manufacturing	44	11 378	533 542
仪器仪表制造业	Instrument Manufacturing	9	740	18 447
废弃资源综合利用业	Comprehensive Utilization of Waste Resources			
金属制品、机械和设备修理业	Metal Products, Machinery and Equipment Repair Industry			
电力、热力生产和供应业	Production and Supply of Electricity and Thermal Power	2	478	17 440
燃气生产和供应业	Production and Supply of Fuel Gas			
水的生产和供应业	Production and Supply of Water	1	6	43

表 12－12 规模以上大中型工业企业专利情况
Patents Utilized by Large and Medium-sized Industrial Enterprises (2015)

单位:件 (item)

指 标	Indicators	专利申请数 Patent Applications	# 发明专利数 Patents of Creations and Inventions	有效发明专利数 Number of Effective Patents	# 境外授权 Authorized Overseas
总 计	**Total**	**7 507**	**4 614**	**10 073**	**840**
按注册登记大类分组	**Grouped by Type of Registration**				
国 有	State-owned	437	254	597	
集 体	Collective-owned	3		14	
股份制及其他有限公司	Share-holding	2 067	1 346	2 897	154
私 营	Private	655	204	694	7
外商及港澳台投资	Overseas Invested Enterprises	4 002	2 689	5 666	671
其 他	Others	343	121	205	8
按隶属关系分组	**Grouped by Subordination**				
中央工业	Central	1 429	990	2 199	80
地方工业	Local	6 078	3 624	7 874	760
按企业规模分组	Grouped by Enterprise Scale				
# 大型企业	Large	4 977	3 461	6 295	489
中型企业	Medium	1 273	659	2 090	159
按工业行业大类分组	**Grouped by Sector**				
# 农副食品加工业	Farm and Sideline Products Processing	11	1	11	
食品制造业	Food Manufacturing	4	4	18	11
酒、饮料和精制茶制造业	Wine, Beverage and Refined Tea Manufacturing	6			
烟草制品业	Tobacco Manufacturing	3			
纺织业	Textile Industry	86	1	8	
家具制造业	Furniture Manufacturing	39	26	44	
造纸和纸制品业	Papermaking and Paper Products	14	1	9	
印刷和记录媒介复制业	Printing and Record Medium Reproduction Industry	29	10	78	
文教、工美、体育和娱乐用品制造业	Culture, Art, Sports and Recreation Supplies Manufacturing	7	1	103	
石油加工、炼焦和核燃料加工业	Oil Processing, Coking and Nuclear Fuel Processing	8	7	12	
化学原料和化学制品制造业	Raw Chemical Materials and Chemical Products	165	104	353	24
医药制造业	Medicine Manufacture	127	79	355	23
化学纤维制造业	Chemical Fiber Manufacturing	10	3	5	
橡胶和塑料制品业	Rubber and Plastic Products Industry	49	29	119	
非金属矿物制品业	Nonmetal Mineral Products	50	31	103	9
黑色金属冶炼和压延加工业	Smelting and Rolling of Ferrous Metals	1			
有色金属冶炼和压延加工业	Smelting and Rolling of Nonferrous Metals	5	3	9	
金属制品业	Metal Products	95	16	64	
通用设备制造业	General Equipment Manufacture	527	173	516	25
专用设备制造业	Special Purpose Equipment Manufacturing	523	219	622	56
汽车制造业	Automobile Manufacturing	1 406	386	632	1
铁路、船舶、航空航天和其他运输设备制造业	Railroad, Ship, Aviation and Other Transportation Equipment Manufacturing	232	109	246	
电气机械和器材制造业	Electric Equipment and Machinery Manufacturing	410	107	292	5
计算机、通信和其他电子设备制造业	Computer, Communications and Other Electronic Equipment Manufacturing	3 252	3 014	5 784	686
仪器仪表制造业	Instrument Manufacturing	74	25	124	
废弃资源综合利用业	Comprehensive Utilization of Waste Resources				
金属制品、机械和设备修理业	Metal Products, Machinery and Equipment Repair Industry				
电力、热力生产和供应业	Production and Supply of Electricity and Thermal Power	365	257	561	
燃气生产和供应业	Production and Supply of Fuel Gas				
水的生产和供应业	Production and Supply of Water	1		2	

表12－13 规模以上工业企业新产品产出情况
Output of New Products of Large and Medium Industrial Enterprises (2015)

单位:万元 (10 000 yuan)

指 标	Indicators	新产品产值 Output of New Products	新产品销售收入 Sales Revenue	#出口 Export
总 计	**Total**	**23 094 212**	**24 285 408**	**4 750 678**
按注册登记大类分组	**Grouped by Type of Registration**			
国 有	State-owned	53 505	57 967	
集 体	Collective-owned			
股份制及其他有限公司	Share-holding	3 141 788	3 349 397	608 597
私 营	Private	1 051 147	1 110 092	81 547
外商及港澳台投资	Overseas Invested Enterprises	15 711 370	15 970 817	3 047 531
其 他	Others	3 136 403	3 797 134	1 013 004
按隶属关系分组	**Grouped by Subordination**			
中央工业	Central	4 570 373	4 680 093	2 027 512
地方工业	Local	1 852 384	1 960 532	272 317
按企业规模分组	**Grouped by Enterprise Scale**			
#大型企业	Large	17 166 746	18 007 629	3 757 293
中型企业	Medium	4 405 252	4 697 787	796 423
按工业行业大类分组	**Grouped by Sector**			
农副食品加工业	Farm and Sideline Products Processing	60 668	62 978	
食品制造业	Food Manufacturing	6 913	6 913	3 753
酒、饮料和精制茶制造业	Wine,Beverage and Refined Tea Manufacturing	6 498	5 697	
烟草制品业	Tobacco Manufacturing			
纺织业	Textile Industry	50 345	55 763	12 911
家具制造业	Furniture Manufacturing	239 744	239 744	
造纸和纸制品业	Papermaking and Paper Products	105 539	175 370	3 758
印刷和记录媒介复制业	Printing and Record Medium Reproduction Industry	150 187	179 255	20 663
文教、工美、体育和娱乐用品制造业	Culture, Art, Sports and Recreation Supplies Manufacturing	4 183	4 183	3 764
石油加工、炼焦和核燃料加工业	Oil Processing, Coking and Nuclear Fuel Processing	6 029	6 753	
化学原料和化学制品制造业	Raw Chemical Materials and Chemical Products	310 196	563 275	19 165
医药制造业	Medicine Manufacture	1 281 036	1 089 140	4 759
化学纤维制造业	Chemical Fiber Manufacturing	3 459	3 529	1 059
橡胶和塑料制品业	Rubber and Plastic Products Industry	113 670	119 924	8 190
非金属矿物制品业	Nonmetal Mineral Products	50 411	47 170	2 268
黑色金属冶炼和压延加工业	Smelting and Rolling of Ferrous Metals			
有色金属冶炼和压延加工业	Smelting and Rolling of Nonferrous Metals	108 558	108 532	7 732
金属制品业	Metal Products	90 675	99 963	14 667
通用设备制造业	General Equipment Manufacture	2 330 449	2 396 527	1 060 169
专用设备制造业	Special Purpose Equipment Manufacturing	802 434	836 122	363 603
汽车制造业	Automobile Manufacturing	10 167 408	11 001 071	55 946
铁路、船舶、航空航天和其他运输设备制造业	Railroad, Ship, Aviation and Other Transportation Equipment Manufacturing	2 510 883	2 582 573	1 013 004
电气机械和器材制造业	Electric Equipment and Machinery Manufacturing	1 782 123	1 712 305	577 421
计算机、通信和其他电子设备制造业	Computer, Communications and Other Electronic Equipment Manufacturing	2 459 899	2 533 883	1 554 524
仪器仪表制造业	Instrument Manufacturing	104 859	109 490	23 322
废弃资源综合利用业	Comprehensive Utilization of Waste Resources			
金属制品、机械和设备修理业	Metal Products,Machinery and Equipment Repair Industry			
电力、热力生产和供应业	Production and Supply of Electricity and Thermal Power	348 046	345 246	
燃气生产和供应业	Production and Supply of Fuel Gas			
水的生产和供应业	Production and Supply of Water			

表 12-14 主要年份科技企业主要经济指标
Major Economic Indicators of Technology Enterprises in Main Years

指 标	Indicators	单 位 Unit	2000	2005	2010	2013	2014	2015
企业单位数	Number of Enterprises	个 unit	828	700	2 525	1 773	2 035	3 189
企业专利总数	Number of Enterprise Patents	项 item			4 918	6 630	5 574	11 073
职工人数	Number of Employees	万人 10 000 persons	3.04	5.76	9.47	27.09	27.66	50.17
从事科技活动人员	Persons Employed in Science and Technology	万人 10 000 persons			1.59	11.6	12.81	20.30
资产总额	Total Assets	亿元 100 million yuan	122.40	575.47	766.56	5 655.14	6 208.57	12 027.05
技工贸销售总额	Total Sales	亿元 100 million yuan	82.01	521.45	858.06	8 346.95	4 318.22	7 505.49
产品销售收入	Income for Selling Products	亿元 100 million yuan			770.89	8 237.57	4 150.83	7 355.41
利润总额	Total Profits	亿元 100 million yuan	4.64	35.58	64.99	321.71	378.53	867.88
上交税收	Tax Payable	亿元 100 million yuan	2.70	18.22	44.66	182.43	509.96	369.53
创汇总额	Total Foreign Exchange	亿美元 USD 100 million	0.95	12.65	25.67	115.59	114.44	195.63
投入科研开发费	Investment in Research and Development	亿元 100 million yuan	4.18	34.72	26.56	300.44	393.41	674.70

注：2011 年起数据含2000 万以上科技企业。
Note: Data in 2011 include technology enterprises that have the output value of more than 20 million yuan.

主要统计指标解释

专　利

是专利权的简称，是对发明人的发明创造经审查合格后，由专利局依据专利法授予发明人和设计人对该项发明创造享有的专有权。包括发明、实用新型和外观设计。反映拥有自主知识产权的科技和设计成果情况。

发　明

指对产品、方法或者其改进所提出的新的技术方案。是国际通行的反映拥有自主知识产权技术的核心指标。

实用新型

指对产品的形状、构造或者其结合所提出的适于实用的新的技术方案。反映具有一定技术含量的技术成果情况。

外观设计

指对产品的形状、图案、色彩或者其结合所作出的富有美感并适于工业上应用的新设计。反映拥有自主知识产权的外观设计成果情况。

专业技术人员

专业技术人员指事业、企业单位中已被聘任专业技术职务的从事专业技术工作和专业技术管理的人员，以及虽未被聘任专业技术职务，但现在专业技术岗位上工作的人员。

国有企业

指企业全部资产归国家所有，并按《中华人民共和国企业法人登记管理条例》规定登记注册的非公司制的经济组织。不包括有限责任公司中的国有独资公司。

集体企业

集体企业指企业资产归集体所有，并按《中华人民共和国企业法人登记管理条例》规定登记注册的经济组织。

科技活动

指在自然科学、农业科学、医药科学、工程与技术科学、人文与社会科学领域（简称科学技术领域）中，与科技知识的产生、发展、传播和应用密切相关的有组织的活动。可分为研究与试验发展（R&D）、研究与试验发展成果应用及相关的科技服务三类活动。该定义是联合国教科文组织考虑成员国特别是发展中国家开展科技统计工作的需要，而对科技活动所作的统计界定。

科技活动人员

指直接从事科技活动、以及专门从事科技活动管理和为科技活动提供直接服务，累计从事科技活动的时间占全年制度工作时间10%及以上的人员。（1）直接从事科技活动的人员，包括：在独立核算的科学研究与技术开发机构、高等学校、各类企业及其他事业单位内设的研究室、实验室、技术开发中心及中试车间（基地）等机构中从事科技活动的研究人员、工程技术人员、技术工人及其它人员；虽不在上述机构工作，但编入科技活动项目（课题）组的人员；科技信息与文献机构中的专业技术人员；从事论文设计的研究生等。（2）专门从事科技活动管理和为科技活动提供直接服务的人员包括：独立核算的科学研究与技术开发机构、科技信息与文献机构、高等学校、各类企业及其他事业单位主管科技工作的负责人，专门从事科技活动的计划、行政、人事、财务、物资供应、设备维护、图书资料管理等工作的各类人员，但不包括保卫、医疗保健人员、司机、食堂人员、茶炉工、水暖工、清洁工等为科技活动提供间接服务的人员。该指标用来反映投入科技活动人力的规模。

科学家和工程师

科学家与工程师指科技活动人员中具有高、中级技术职称（职务）的人员和不具有高、中级技术职称（职务）的大学本科及以上学历人员。

科技活动经费筹集

指从各种渠道筹集到的计划用于科技活动的经费，包括政府资金、事业资金、企业资金、银行贷款和其他收入等。反映各社会经济主体对促进科技进步所作的努力。

政府资金

指从各级政府部门获得的计划用于科技活动的经费，包括科学事业费、科技三项费、科研基建费、科学基金、教育等部门事业费中计划用于科技活动的经费以及政府部门预算外资金中计划用于科技活动的经费等。

新产品

指采用新技术原理、新设计构思研制、生产的全新产品，或在结构、材质、工艺等某一方面比原有产品有明显改进，从而显著提高了产品性能或扩大了使用功能的产品。既包括政府有关部门认定并在有效期内的新产品，也包括企业自行研制开发、在统计规定的新产品跟踪期限内的产品。跟踪期限规定如下：装备类跟踪五年，消费品类跟踪二年，其他类跟踪三年。用来反映科技产出及对经济增长的直接贡献。

R&D

是“科学研究与试验发展”(Research and Development)的英文缩写。其含义是指在科学技术领域,为增加知识总量,以及运用这些知识去创造新的应用进行的系统的创造性的活动。R&D包括基础研究、应用研究、试验发展三类活动。

EXPLANATORY NOTES TO MAJOR STATISTICAL INDICATORS

Patent

Patent is an abbreviation for the patent right and refers to the exclusive right of ownership by the inventors or designers for the creation or inventions, given from the patent offices after due process of assessment and approval in accordance with the Patent Law. Patents are granted for inventions, utility models and designs. This indicator reflects the achievements of S&T and design with independent intellectual property.

Invention

Inventions refer to the new technical proposals to the products or methods or their modifications. This is universal core indicator reflecting the technologies with independent intellectual property.

Utility Models

Utility Models refer to the practical and new technical proposals on the shape and structure of the product or the combination of both. This indicator reflects the condition of technological results with certain technical content.

Exterior Design

Designs refer to the aesthetics and industrially applicable new designs for the shape, pattern and color of the product, or their combinations. This indicator reflects the appearance design achievements with independent intellectual property.

Professional and Technical Personnel

Professional and Technical Personnel refer to professional, technical and managerial staff members in institutions or enterprises who not only have professional and technical titles but also hold professional and technical posts. They also include those who work on professional and technical posts but do not have professional and technical titles.

State-owned Enterprises

State-owned Enterprises refer to non-corporation economic units where the entire assets are owned by the state and which have registered in accordance with the Regulation of the People's Republic of China on the Management of Registration of Corporate Enterprises. Excluded from this category are sole state-funded corporations in the limited liability corporations.

Collective-owned Enterprises

Collective-owned Enterprises refer to economic units where the assets are owned collectively and which have registered in accordance with the Regulation of the People's Republic of China on the Management of Registration of Corporate Enterprises.

Scientific and Technological Activities (S&T Activities)

Scientific and Technological Activities (S&T Activities) refer to organized activities which are closely related with the creation, development, dissemination and application of the scientific and technical knowledge in the fields of natural sciences, agricultural sciences, medical sciences, engineering and technological sciences, humanities and social sciences (referred to as scientific and technological fields). S&T activities can be classified into 3 categories: research and development (R&D) activities, application of R&D results, and related S&T services. This statistical definition is made by UNICHIEF for scientific and technological activities to meet the need of carrying out statistical work in this field for its member countries in particular those developing countries.

Personnel Engaged in S&T Activities

Personnel Engaged in S&T Activities refer to personnel directly engaged in S&T activities, in the management of S&T activities, and in providing direct service to S&T activities, who spend over 10% of the total working hours in a year in S&T activities. (1) Personnel directly engaged in S&T activities include researchers, engineers, technicians and other related personnel engaged in S&T activities in independent-accounting R&D institutions, institutions of higher learning, and in research institutes, laboratories, technology development centers and central experiment workshops under enterprises and institutions. Also included are people working in S&T information archiving institutes, and graduate students working on the design of their thesis. (2) Personnel engaged in the management of S&T activities and in providing direct service to S&T activities include senior management people responsible for S&T activities in independent-accounting R&D institutions, S&T information archiving institutes, institutions of higher learning, and in enterprises and institutions where S&T activities are undertaken. Also included are people responsible for the planning, administration, personnel management, financial management, logistics supply, equipment maintenance, information and library management that are related with S&T activities. People providing indirect services are excluded, such as security, medical service, drivers, plumbers, cleaners and those providing catering and related service. This indicator reflects the size of personnel engaged in S&T activities.

Scientists and Engineers

Scientists and Engineers refer to persons engaged in S&T activities who have obtained titles of senior and middle level professional positions, and those without such position but have completed university or higher education.

Funding for S&T Activities

Funding for S&T Activities refers to funds obtained from various sources for S&T activities, including government funds, self-raised funds by institutions, self-raised funds by enterprises, loans from banks and other funds. This indicator reflects the efforts made by various social economic entities in promoting the development of S&T.

Government Funds

Government Funds refer to funds obtained from government agencies at all levels to be used for S&T activities, including fund for scientific undertakings, 3 kinds of fund for S&T activities, fund for capital construction for scientific researches, science fund, funds from education expenditures by education departments for S&T activities, and extra-budget fund from government agencies for S&T activities.

New Products

New Products refer to new products produced with new technology and new design, or products that represent noticeable improvement in terms of structure, material, or production process so as to improve significantly the character or function of the older versions. They include new products certified by relevant government agencies within the period of certification, as well as new products designed and produced by enterprises within the new product track time limit prescribed by the statistical regulations. The new product track time limit is prescribed as following: equipment products 5 years, consumption products 2 years, other products 3 years. This indictor reflects the direct contribution of S&T output to economic growth.

R&D

R&D is an abbreviation which stands for 'Science Research and Experimental Development', which means systematic and creative endeavors aimed at expanding the overall volume of knowledge and applying the knowledge in systematic creation. R&D includes basic studies, application research and experimental development.

第十三篇

CHAPTER 13

人民生活

PEOPLE'S LIVELIHOOD

表13-1 从业人员工资总额
Wages of Employees
(2015)

单位:亿元 (100 million yuan)

指 标	Indicators	合 计 Total	国有单位 State-owned Enterprises	集体单位 Collective-owned Enterprises	港澳台及外商投资单位 Overseas Invested Enterprises	其他单位 Others
总 计	**Total**	**2 727.80**	**206.62**	**13.70**	**1 553.81**	**953.67**
按产业分	**By Industry**					
第一产业	Primary Industry	5.45	0.60			4.85
第二产业	Secondary Industry	621.64	13.67	3.93	396.77	207.28
第三产业	Tertiary Industry	2 100.71	192.35	9.77	1 157.04	741.54
按行业分	**By Sector**					
农、林、牧、渔业	Farming, Forestry, Animal Husbandry and Fishery	5.45	0.60			4.85
采矿业	Mining	0.55				0.55
制造业	Manufacturing	506.21	13.35	3.50	380.23	109.13
电力、热力、燃气及水生产和供应业	Production and Supply of Electricity, Heat, Gas and Water	12.29	0.22	0.06	2.67	9.35
建筑业	Construction	102.59	0.10	0.37	13.88	88.24
批发和零售业	Wholesale and Retail	483.87	1.37	1.00	433.51	48.00
交通运输、仓储和邮政业	Transportation, Warehousing and Post Service	227.39	19.62	0.10	34.91	172.76
住宿和餐饮业	Hotel and Catering	14.99	0.54	0.20	9.21	5.04
信息传输、软件和信息技术服务业业	Information Transmission, Software and Information Technology Services	286.40	0.57		170.90	114.92
金融业	Banking	430.60	38.14		159.45	233.00
房地产业	Real Estate	63.19	3.04	1.28	32.74	26.13
租赁和商务服务业	Leasing and Business Service	308.98	4.92	1.26	220.53	82.26
科学研究和技术服务业	Scientific Research and Technology Services	110.31	9.09	0.28	80.10	20.82
水利、环境和公共设施管理业	Water Conservancy, Environment and Public Facilities Administration	11.70	3.84	0.58	1.04	6.24
居民服务、修理和其他服务业	Residents Service, Repair and other Services	9.42	0.53	0.53	5.79	2.56
教 育	Education	56.45	41.42	0.82	2.94	11.27
卫生和社会工作	Healthcare and Social Work	39.14	29.34	2.78	0.44	6.58
文化、体育和娱乐业	Culture, Sports and Entertainment	10.22	2.77	0.25	5.47	1.72
公共管理、社会保障和社会组织	Public Management, Social Guarantee and Social Organizations	48.07	37.17	0.68	0.00	10.22

表13-2 从业人员平均工资
Average Wages of Employees
(2015)

单位:元 (yuan)

指　标 Indicators		合　计 Total	国有单位 State-owned Enterprises	集体单位 Collective-owned Enterprises	港澳台及外商投资单位 Overseas Invested Enterprises	其　他 单　位 Others
总　计	**Total**	**129 368**	**115 830**	**44 344**	**149 780**	**110 663**
按产业分	**By Industry**					
第一产业	Primary Industry	42 682	41 085	28 990	55 400	42 547
第二产业	Secondary Industry	90 049	92 090	36 792	92 194	88 372
第三产业	Tertiary Industry	149 214	117 841	48 484	190 326	120 341
按行业分	**By Sector**					
农、林、牧、渔业	Farming, Forestry, Animal Husbandry and Fishery	42 682	41 085	28 990	55 400	42 547
采矿业	Mining	129 788				129 788
制造业	Manufacturing	88 894	92 910	35 064	90 596	87 030
电力、热力、燃气及水生产和供应业	Production and Supply of Electricity, Heat, Gas and Water	140 955	56 199	62 716	131 322	150 583
建筑业	Construction	91 720	21 280	54 664	172 361	85 959
批发和零售业	Wholesale and Retail	155 844	56 789	38 001	176 944	79 407
交通运输、仓储和邮政业	Transportation, Warehousing and Post Service	118 826	100 429	26 404	99 267	126 757
住宿和餐饮业	Hotel and Catering	53 886	53 244	34 103	59 561	46 850
信息传输、软件和信息技术服务业	Information Transmission, Software and Information Technology Services	211 811	90 194	6 000	216 398	206 714
金融业	Banking	196 722	200 261		289 504	160 956
房地产业	Real Estate	90 269	96 430	40 147	118 070	72 725
租赁和商务服务业	Leasing and Business Service	156 290	109 208	33 742	234 163	86 349
科学研究和技术服务业	Scientific Research and Technology Services	173 623	123 661	75 182	207 993	120 460
水利、环境和公共设施管理业	Water Conservancy, Environment and Public Facilities Administration	67 815	69 841	45 991	118 175	64 929
居民服务、修理和其他服务业	Residents Service, Repair and other Services	53 183	73 969	39 704	67 328	36 371
教　育	Education	94 286	102 180	70 482	138 000	70 253
卫生和社会工作	Healthcare and Social Work	107 066	132 045	74 133	138 495	64 090
文化、体育和娱乐业	Culture, Sports and Entertainment	95 138	114 482	46 849	105 014	67 087
公共管理、社会保障和社会组织	Public Management, Social Guarantee and Social Organizations	99 690	110 976	65 682		74 656

表 13-3　居民家庭基本情况
Background of Urban Families

指　标　Indicators		单　位　Unit	2014	2015
调查户数	Households Surveyed	户 household	1 000	1 000
调查户总人口	Total Population of Households Surveyed	人 person	2 475	2 464
调查户就业人口	Employed Persons in Households Surveyed	人 person	1 316	1 303
平均每户常住人口	Average Number of Permanent Residents Per Household	人 person	2.48	2.46
平均每户就业人口	Average Number of Employed Persons Per Household	人 person	1.31	1.30
平均每户就业面	Average Employment Rate Per Household	%	53.2	52.9
平均每一就业者赡养人口	Number of Persons Supported by Each Employed Person	人 person	1.88	1.89
平均消费倾向	Average Propensity to Consumption	%	73.1	71.0
居民人均可支配收入	Annual Disposable Income Per Capita	元 yuan	46 709	50 726
居民人均消费支出	Annual Consumption Spending Per Capita	元 yuan	34 157	35 999

注：1. 表 13－5、表 13－6、表 13－7 非住户调查资料。
2. 根据国家住户调查城乡一体化改革，2015 年住户调查数据为城乡一体化新口径数据，同前期老口径数据没有可比性，为方便使用，本年鉴所公布的 2014 年住户调查数据为推算数据。

Note：1. The contents in from this table to Table 13－8 are the survey data of households in Pudong.
2. According to the Urban－Rural Integration Reform of the Nationsl Household Survey，survey data for 2015 are integrated data，which are not comparable with that for 2014. Thus，for convenience，data for 2014 in this book are forecasted.

表13-4 居民家庭人均收支情况

Income and Expenditure of Urban and Suburban Residents in Main Years

单位:元 (yuan)

指标	Indicators	2014	2015
居民人均可支配收入	**Per capita disposable income of vesidents**	**46 709**	**50 726**
工资性收入	Wage Income	31 563	33 425
经营净收入	Net Operational Income	989	1 152
财产净收入	Net Property Income	7 785	8 566
转移净收入	Net Transferable Income	6 372	7 583
居民人均消费支出	**Total Expenses Per Capita of Urban Residents**	**34 157**	**35 999**
食品烟酒	Food,Tobacco and Alcohol	7 833	8 178
衣　着	Clothing	1 635	1 678
居　住	Habitation	12 490	13 252
生活用品及服务	Household Appliances and Services	1 587	1 643
交通通信	Traffic and Communications	4 166	4 588
教育文化娱乐	Education, Culture and Amusement Services	3 558	3 895
医疗保健	Medical Care	2 038	1 938
其他用品和服务	Miscellaneous Commodities and Services	850	827
社会保障支出	Social Security Expenses	2 658	2 639

表 13-5　个人储蓄存款年末余额(2010～2015)
Household Balance of Saving Deposit at Year-end (2010～2015)

年　份 Year	个人储蓄存款余额（亿元） The Balance of Household Saving Deposts (100 million yuan)	人均储蓄存款余额（元） Per Capita Balance of Saving Deposit (yuan)
2010	2 943.49	63 746
2011	3 375.71	66 065
2012	3 886.60	74 463
2013	4 254.05	79 716
2014	4 381.03	80 680
2015	4 381.84	80 209

表 13-6　居民家庭生活基本情况(2010～2015)
Basic Information of Households' Living Conditions (2010～2015)

年　份 Year	调查户数(户) Households Surveyed (household)	平均每户 就业面(%) Average Employed Persons Per Household (%)	平均每一就业 者负担人数（人） Number of Dependents per Employee(person)	平均每人年可 支配收入（元） Annual Per Capita Disposable Income (yuan)
2010	600	53.9	1.86	32 330
2011	600	53.5	1.87	36 815
2012	600	53.2	1.88	40 901
2013	600	51.7	1.93	45 199
2014	800	50.9	1.96	49 629
2015	1 000	53.0	2.00	50 726

注：2015 年住户调查数据为城乡一体化新口径数据。
Note: Household Survey data is 2015 are iutegrated data of urban and household.

表 13-7　个人贷款年末余额(2010～2015)
Household Balance of Loans at Year - end (2010～2015)

年　份 Year	个人贷款余额（亿元） Household Balance of Loans (100 million yuan)	人均贷款余额（元） Per Capita Balance of Loans (yuan)
2010	1 007.62	21 821
2011	1 150.64	22 518
2012	1 233.31	23 629
2013	1 413.30	26 483
2014	1 519.35	27 980
2015	1 838.84	33 660

表 13-8 居民家庭人均收入与支出状况(按收入水平分)
Average Income and Expenses of Urban Families(by income level) (2015)

单位:元 (yuan)

指 标	Indicators	总平均 Overall Average	低收入户 Low-income Household	较低收入户 Lower-income Household	中等收入户 Medium-income Household	较高收入户 Medium Higher-income Household	高收入户 High-income Household
人均可支配收入	**Disposable Income Per Capita**	**50 726**	**18 782**	**32 724**	**45 683**	**61 103**	**107 168**
工资性收入	Wage Income	33 425	13 620	22 660	27 988	31 777	79 330
经营净收入	Net Operational Income	1 152	1 082	883	1 451	919	1 426
财产净收入	Net Property Income	8 566	1 816	4 054	7 920	11 792	20 092
转移净收入	Net Transferable Income	7 583	2 264	5 127	8 324	16 615	6 320
人均消费支出	**Consumption Expenses**	**35 999**	**15 786**	**24 581**	**32 966**	**43 608**	**70 251**
食品烟酒	Food, Tabacco and Alcohol	8 178	5 337	6 767	8 098	9 953	11 571
衣 着	Clothing	1 678	886	1 264	1 608	1 711	3 221
居 住	Habitation	13 252	4 573	7 845	12 147	17 733	26 971
生活用品及服务	Household Appliances and Services	1 643	643	1 192	1 389	1 978	3 370
交通通信	Traffic and Communications	4 588	2 105	3 815	3 615	4 527	9 853
教育文化娱乐	Education, Culture and Amusement Services	3 895	1 260	1 908	3 732	4 561	9 048
医疗保健	Medical Care	1 938	671	1 301	1 603	2 384	4 196
其他用品和服务	Miscellaneous Commodities and Services	827	311	489	774	761	2 021
财产性支出	Property Expenses	857	36	542	854	1 261	1 822
转移性支出	Transferable Expenses	4 315	1 474	2 423	3 299	4 625	11 009
社会保障支出	Social Security Expenses	2 639	1 103	1 873	2 568	2 778	5 422
购、建房支出	Expenses for Purchasing/ Building Houses	1 054		2 730	1 999		440

注：收入水平根据居民家庭人均可支配收入由低到高排序，分别按家庭数量的 20% 分为 5 组。
Note: Income levels are sorted from the low to the high according to the disposable income per capita of urban families. They are divided into five groups from 20% of the total number of families respectively.

表13-9　每百户居民家庭年末耐用消费品拥有量
Possession of Durable Consumer Goods Per 100 Urban Households at Year-end

指　标	Indicators	单　位　Unit	2014	2015
摩托车	Mototrcycle	辆 in number	7	8
助力车	Scooter	辆 in number	56	62
家用汽车	Household Car	辆 in number	23	26
洗衣机	Washing Machine	台 set	84	90
电冰箱	Household Refrigerator	台 set	92	95
彩色电视机	Color TV Set	台 set	167	167
家用电脑	Personal Computer	台 set	98	98
组合音响	Stereo System	套 set	12	11
摄像机	Video Camera	架 set	9	8
照相机	Camera	架 set	41	41
中高档乐器	Medium and High-grade Musical Instrument	架 set	6	4
微波炉	Microwave Oven	台 set	76	80
空调器	Air Conditioner	台 set	164	172
淋浴热水器	Water Heater	台 set	80	85
健身器材	Fitness Goods	套 set	3	4
普通电话	Fixed Telephone	部 set	75	69
移动电话	Mobile Phone	部 set	204	217

表13-10 居民家庭生活质量
Living Conditions of Urban Families

指　标	Indicators	单　位 Unit	2014	2015
生活用水	**Tap Water for Residential Use**			
独用自来水	Private Tap Water	%	98.0	98.2
公用自来水	Shared Tap Water	%	2.0	1.8
厕所使用	**Sanitary Equipment**			
本户独用	Without any Sanitary Equipment	%	88.0	89.7
几户合用	Shared Sanitary Equipment (with limited number of households)	%	5.8	4.9
公用厕所	Shared Sanitary Equipment	%	6.2	5.4
洗澡设施	**Bath Equipment**			
统一供热水	Unified Hot Water Supply	%	1.6	0.1
家庭自装热水器	Self-installed	%	78.3	83.9
其　他	Others	%	3.7	2.6
无洗澡设施	Without bath equipment	%	16.4	13.4
居室取暖设备	**Heating Equipment**			
无取暖设备	Without any Heating	%	20.2	16.5
冷暖空调	Air Conditioner	%	79.8	83.5
其　他	Others	%		
炊用燃气	**Gas for Cooking**			
天然气	Natural Gas	%	54.5	54.4
液化石油气	Liquefied Petroleum Gas	%	35.6	39.4
煤	Coal	%		
其　他	Others	%	9.9	6.2
通信设备	**Telecommunications Equipment**			
固定电话	Fixed Telephone	部/百户 set / hundred households	75	69
移动电话	Mobile Telephone	部/百户 set / hundred households	204	217

表 13－11　居民家庭人均年消费支出状况
Annual Nonproductive Expenditure Per Capita for Urban Families

指　标	Indicators	2014	2015
总　计	**Total**	**34 157**	**35 999**
食品烟酒	**Food, Tabacco and Alcohol**	**7 833**	**8 178**
#粮油类	Cereals & Oils	765	702
蔬菜类	Vegetables	699	687
肉禽蛋水产品	Meat, Poultry, Eggs and Aquatic Products	2 093	2 160
奶　类	Dairy Products	436	402
干鲜瓜果类	Dry and Fresh Pruits	635	656
糖果糕点类	Confection and Pastry	257	255
烟酒类	Tabacco and Alcohol	572	604
饮料类	Beverages	144	146
饮食服务及其他	Catering Services and Others	2 232	2 566
衣　着	**Clothing**	**1 635**	**1 678**
#服　装	Clothes	1 280	1 335
鞋　类	Shoes	355	343
居　住	**Housing**	**12 490**	**13 252**
租赁房房租	Rents	1 094	1 171
住房维修及管理	Maintaniance and Management	744	674
水电燃料及其他	Water, Electricity and Others	862	1 019
生活用品及服务	**Household Appliances and Services**	**1 587**	**1 643**
家具及室内装饰品	Furniture and Ornaments	325	209
家用器具	Household Appliances	306	344
家用纺织品	Household Textiles	126	118
家庭日用杂品	Daily Use Household Articles	306	327
个人用品	Personal Articles	300	392
家庭服务	Household Services	224	253
交通通信	**Transportation and Telecommunications**	**4 166**	**4 588**
交　通	Transportation	2 854	3 264
通　信	Telecommunications	1 312	1 324
教育文化娱乐	**Education, Culture nd Entertainment**	**3 558**	**3 895**
教　育	Education	1 292	1 490
文化娱乐	Culture and Entertainment	2 266	2 405
医疗保健	**Health Care**	**2 038**	**1 938**
医疗器具及药品	Medical Instrument and Medicines	349	417
医疗服务	Medical Services	1 689	1 521
其他用品和服务	**Other Articles and Services**	**850**	**827**

主要统计指标解释

从业人员工资总额

从业人员工资总额指各单位在一定时期内直接支付给本单位全部从业人员的劳动报酬总额。包括在岗职工工资总额和本单位其他从业人员劳动报酬两部分。

从业人员平均工资

平均工资指企业、事业、机关单位的职工在一定时期内平均每人所得的货币工资额。它表明一定时期从业人员工资收入的高低程度,是反映工资水平的主要指标。计算公式为:

平均工资 = 报告期实际支付的全部从业人员工资总额/报告期全部从业人员平均人数

城镇居民可支配收入

城镇居民可支配收入指居民可用于最终消费支出和其他非义务性支出以及储蓄的总和,即居民家庭可以用来自由支配的收入。它是家庭总收入扣除交纳的所得税、个人交纳的社会保障费以及调查户的记账补贴后的收入。不包括出售财物和借贷收入。

城镇居民家庭消费支出

指城镇居民家庭用于日常生活的全部支出,包括食品、衣着、家庭设备用品及服务、医疗保健、交通和通信、教育文化娱乐服务、居住、杂项商品和服务等八大类。

城镇居民家庭人均服务性消费支出

指调查户用于本家庭支付社会提供的各种文化和生活方面的非商品性服务费用。服务性消费的特点在于其劳动过程和消费过程在时间与空间上的统一。在居民家庭八大类消费中,服务消费支出包括:(1)食品类中加工服务费和部分在外饮食费用;(2)衣着类中衣着加工服务费;(3)家庭设备用品及服务类中家庭服务(如家政服务费用);(4)医疗保健类中医疗费(如诊疗费、上门出诊费、护工费用);(5)交通和通信类中交通工具服务费(如汽车使用、维修费用)、交通费中使用飞机、轮船、火车等交通工具费用、通信服务费(如电信费、邮费);(6)教育文化娱乐服务类中文化娱乐服务费(如参观、游览费用、健身活动费、团体旅游、其他文娱活动费)、文娱用品修理服务费、教育费(如义务、非义务教育支出)、成人教育支出、家教费、培训班费用、择校费;(7)居住类中租赁费用、部分房屋装潢费用(人工费用)、居住服务费(如物业管理、维修费用);(8)杂项商品和服务(如美容、洗澡、理发费用,旅馆住宿等费用)。

农村居民可支配收入

指一定时期内农村居民总收入中,扣除家庭经营费用支出、生产性固定资产折旧、交纳税金和上交承包金、公益性及转移支付后的(包括养老、失业、合作医疗、保险基金及罚款等支付),可用于生活消费、生产投资和储蓄的收入。它与纯收入的主要区别是扣除了转移性支付,加上实际得到的公益性及转移性收入后的余额。农村居民可支配收入包括:工资性收入、家庭经营净收入、财产性收入、转移性净收入。

农村居民家庭生活消费支出

指农村住户用于物质生活和精神生活方面的支出。包括食品、衣着、居住、家庭设备用品及服务、医疗保健、交通和通信、文化教育娱乐用品及服务、其他商品和服务等消费支出。

财产性收入

指金融资产或有形非生产性资产的所有者向其他机构单位提供资金或将有形非生产性资产供其支配,作为回报而从中获得的收入。

转移性收入

指农村住户和住户成员无须付出任何对应物而获得的货物、服务、资金或资产所有权等,不包括无偿提供的用于固定资本形成的资金。一般情况下,是指农村住户在二次分配中的所有收入。

基本养老保险

(1)参加保险人数:指报告期末按照国家法律、法规和有关政策规定参加基本养老保险的职工人数。包括不能正常缴费、已中断缴费但未终止保险关系的职工人数。

(2)社会统筹基金收入:指根据国家规定,由纳入基本养老保险范围的单位,按照国家规定的缴费基数和缴费比例缴纳的社会统筹基金,以及通过其他方式取得的形成基金来源的收入,包括:单位缴纳的社会统筹基金收入、财政补贴收入、利息收入、其他收入。

(3)社会统筹基金支出:指按照国家政策规定的开支范围和开支标准从社会统筹基金中支付给参加基本养老保险的离休、退休、退职人员个人的养老金、丧葬抚恤补助,以及由于保险关系转移、上下级之间调剂资金等原因而发生的支出。包括:基础性养老金、过渡性养老金、离休金、退休金、退职金、补贴、丧葬抚恤补助、其他支出。

(4)社会统筹基金结余:指截止报告期末基本养老保险

的社会统筹基金结余金额。包括银行存款、财政专户、债券投资和其他。

城镇登记失业人员

城镇登记失业人员指有非农业户口,在一定的劳动年龄内(16 岁以上及男 50 岁以下、女 45 岁以下),有劳动能力,无业而要求就业,并在当地就业服务机构进行求职登记的人员。

EXPLANATORY NOTES TO MAJOR STATISTICAL INDICATORS

Total Wages of Employees

Total Wages of Employees refers to total payment by various units to their employees during a certain period of time, including wages to permanent staff and workers and payment to other employees.

Average Wage

Average Wage refers to the average wage in money terms per person during a certain period of time for staff and workers in enterprises, institutions, and government agencies, which reflects the general level of wage income during a certain period of time and is calculated as follows: Average Wage = Total Wages of Staff and Workers at Reference Time / Average Number of Staff and Workers at Reference Time.

Disposable Income of Urban Households

Disposable Income of Urban Households refers to the actual income at the disposal of members of the households which can be used for final consumption, other non-compulsory expenditure and savings, which is part of the urban households´income that can be disposed by the urban households themselves. It is the income after deducting personal income tax, social insurance paid by individuals and investigation allowance from the total income of the households. The income from selling properties and borrowing are not included.

Consumption Expenditures of Urban Households

Consumption Expenditures of Urban Households refer to all the expenditures paid by urban households for consumption in daily life, including 8 categories as follows: food; clothing; household facilities, articles and services; medical care; traffic and telecommunication; education, culture and recreation services; housing; miscellaneous commodities and services.

Urbanities'per-capita Spending on Services

Urbanities'per-capita spending on services refers to urbanites pay for services rather than commodities. Services are offered and consumed at the same time and place. The service spending for an urban family falls into the following eight types: (1)Money paid for food processing and money spent while eating out; (2)Money paid for clothing processing; (3)Domestic services and services for home amenities; (4) Medical cost (including medical diagnosis and treatment, in-home medical services and nursing cost); (5)Transport tool service fees (such as for the use of a car and maintenance fee thereby arising), transport tools (plane, ship, train) fees, post and telecommunications fees; (6)Fees for culture and entertainment services (such as tour and fitness building), fees for repair of sports and entertainment items, education cost (spending on obligatory and non-obligatory education), adult education cost, tutor fees, training courses fees and extra money paid as sponsorship fee to a school a student outside his or her education community; (7)Housing rents, some interior decoration cost (for labor), residence service fees (such as for property management and repairs); (8)Fees for other services (such as at a beauty salon, bathhouse, hairdresser´s and hotels).

Disposable Income of Rural Households

Disposable Income of Rural Households refers to the part of the rural households´income in a certain period after deducting family business expenditure, depreciation of productive fixed assets, taxes, contract expenditure, welfare funds and transferred expenditure, (including pensions, unemployment relief, cooperative medical funds, premiums and fines), which can be used for personal consumption, production investment and deposit. It differs from the net income in that it is the balance of the actual welfare and transferred income after deducting transferred expenditure. The disposable income includes: wages and salaries, net income from household business, property income, net transferred income.

Living Expenditures for Consumption of Rural Households

Living Expenditures for Consumption of Rural Households refer to expenditures of material and culture life of rural household, including expenses on food, clothing, housing, household appliances and service, medical and health care, traffic and communication items, cultural, education and recreation items and service and other commodities and service.

Income from Properties

Income from Properties refers to the income received as returns by owners of financial assets or tangible non-productive assets by providing capitals or tangible non-productive assets to other institutional units.

Income from Transfers

Income from Transfers refers to the receipt by rural households and their members of goods, services, capitals or rights of assets without giving or repaying accordingly, excluding capitals provided to them for the formation of fixed assets. In general, it refers to all income received by rural households through redistribution.

Basic Endowment Insurance

(1) Number of people participating in the insurance program: by the end of reference period, number of staff and workers partici-

pating in the insurance program in line with national laws, regulations and related policies, including those who can not make regular payment or interrupt payment but not terminate the insurance program.

(2) Revenue of social comprehensive funds: according to national provision, payments made by units covered in basic endowment insurance program, and income from other resources, including: income of social comprehensive funds paid by unites, financial subsidies, interest income and others.

(3) Expenditure of social comprehensive funds: refer to payment made to those retired and resigned people covered in endowment insurance program in terms of pension or compensation within the expenditure scope and standards according to related national policies, and the expenditure occurred due to shift of the insurance relationship or adjustment funds among agencies, including: basic pension, transitional pension, pension for resigned people, pension for retired people, pension for people quitting jobs, subsidies, funeral subsidies and other expenditure.

(4) Balance of social comprehensive funds: refer to the balance of basic endowment insurance of social comprehensive funds at the end of the reference period, including: bank savings, special fiscal account, investment in bonds and others.

Registered Urban Unemployment

Registered Urban Unemployment refers to those non-agricultural population within working age (16 – 50 years for male and 16 – 45 years for females) who are able and willing to work but unemployed and have registered for job in local employment service agencies.

第十四篇

CHAPTER 14

就业与社会保障

EMPLOYMENT AND SOCIAL SECURITY

表 14-1　历年全社会从业人员数
Number of Whole Society Employees
(1993～2015)

单位:人　　(person)

年　份 Year	从业人员 Employed Persons	内资、外资、港澳台资单位从业人员 Employed Persons in Domestic-invested, Foreign-invested and HongKong/Macao/Taiwan-invested Institutions	其　他 Others
1993	1 043 985	788 821	255 164
1994	1 049 985	767 146	282 839
1995	1 079 744	798 884	280 860
1996	1 039 692	759 936	279 756
1997	981 826	703 890	277 936
1998	963 211	638 707	324 504
1999	983 401	645 583	337 818
2000	1 040 411	636 923	403 488
2001	1 114 514	650 633	463 881
2002	1 199 864	686 637	513 227
2003	1 268 717	674 381	594 336
2004	1 302 723	643 628	659 095
2005	1 440 763	746 714	694 049
2006	1 467 145	720 105	747 040
2007	1 490 809	708 308	782 501
2008	1 507 631	749 400	758 231
2009	2 009 539	920 081	1 089 458
2010	2 351 115	1 004 078	1 347 037
2011	2 806 796	1 488 778	1 318 018
2012	2 970 091	1 584 025	1 386 066
2013	2 905 942	1 547 059	1 358 883
2014	3 023 905	2 069 720	954 185
2015	2 946 963	2 052 760	894 203

注：2014 年从业人员数据根据第三次经济普查数据进行调整。
Note：The data of employed persons in 2014 has adapted according to the third economic census.

表14-2 全社会各行业从业人员数
Number of Whole Society Employees by Sectors

单位:人 (person)

指 标	Indicators	2013	2014	2015
总 计	**Total**	**2 905 942**	**3 023 905**	**2 946 963**
按三次产业分	**By Industry**			
第一产业	Primary Industry	133 905	136 340	131 872
第二产业	Secondary Industry	1 555 064	1 503 262	1 394 806
第三产业	Tertiary Industry	1 216 973	1 384 303	1 420 285
按行业分	**By Sector**			
农、林、牧、渔业	Farming, Forestry, Animal Husbandry and Fishery	134 226	136 340	131 872
采矿业	Mining	170	191	433
制造业	Manufacturing	1 269 976	1 258 765	1 204 211
电力、热力、燃气及水生产和供应业	Production and Supply of Electricity, Heat, Gas and Water	37 971	35 159	28 442
建筑业	Construction	271 891	209 147	161 720
批发和零售业	Wholesale and Retail	317 844	352 262	377 758
交通运输、仓储和邮政业	Transportation, Warehousing and Post Service	197 078	206 172	214 249
住宿和餐饮业	Hotel and Catering	39 722	40 105	42 706
信息传输、软件和信息技术服务业业	Information Transmission, Software and Information Technology Services	53 950	60 958	77 094
金融业	Banking	194 200	205 850	197 035
房地产业	Real Estate	57 388	58 109	60 718
租赁和商务服务业	Leasing and Business Service	45 450	48 860	64 731
科学研究和技术服务业	Scientific Research and Technology Services	34 341	35 046	88 096
水利、环境和公共设施管理业	Water Conservancy, Environment and Public Facilities Administration	12 825	134 163	22 364
居民服务、修理和其他服务业	Residents Service, Repair and other Services	129 047	130 197	137 719
教 育	Education	47 169	47 459	65 555
卫生和社会工作	Healthcare and Social Work	29 134	29 782	33 844
文化、体育和娱乐业	Culture, Sports and Entertainment	7 294	8 983	10 825
公共管理、社会保障和社会组织	Public Management, Social Guarantee and Social Organizations	26 266	26 357	27 591

表 14-3　历年职工人数
Staff and Workers
(1993~2015)

单位:人　　(person)

年　份 Year	职工人数 Staff and Workers	按登记注册类型分 Classified by Registration Categories			
		国有经济单位 State-owned Enterprises	集体经济单位 Collective-owned Enterprises	港澳台及外商投资单位 Overseas Investment Enterprises	其他单位 Others
1993	788 821	597 417	84 811		106 592
1994	767 146	582 477	76 023		108 646
1995	798 884	571 398	85 955		141 531
1996	719 634	469 966	85 030		164 638
1997	663 163	405 349	77 072	52 405	128 337
1998	661 406	354 408	60 633	111 015	135 350
1999	677 348	355 607	56 824	126 897	138 020
2000	677 544	340 605	44 654	137 332	154 953
2001	687 694	299 186	37 756	134 732	216 020
2002	701 949	276 876	33 390	160 884	230 799
2003	671 434	249 461	25 549	136 212	260 212
2004	614 014	238 073	23 217	119 658	233 066
2005	701 553	233 350	20 431	129 890	317 882
2006	665 680	173 204	16 196	145 534	330 746
2007	631 720	188 892	16 278	186 480	240 070
2008	667 882	175 428	11 823	225 566	255 065
2009	797 302	193 246	20 408	297 093	286 555
2010	850 176	201 002	17 155	336 022	295 997
2011	1 385 342	275 135	13 728	627 996	468 483
2012	1 451 359	282 539	24 766	695 262	448 792
2013	1 528 417	211 685	21 634	749 439	545 659
2014	1 978 127	177 932	29 731	999 677	770 787
2015	1 991 863	177 828	30 670	985 011	798 354

表14-4 各行业职工人数
Staff and Workers by Sectors
(2015)

单位:人 (person)

指 标	Indicators	职工人数 Staff and Workers	按登记注册类型分 Classified by Registration Categories			
			国有经济单位 State-owned Enterprises	集体经济单位 Collective-owned Enterprises	港澳台及外商投资单位 Overseas Investment Enterprises	其他单位 Others
总 计	**Total**	**1 991 863**	**177 828**	**30 670**	**985 011**	**798 354**
按三次产业分	**By Industry**					
第一产业	Primary Industry	11 229	148	344	763	9 974
第二产业	Secondary Industry	632 070	16 121	7 822	405 834	202 293
第三产业	Tertiary Industry	1 348 564	161 559	22 504	578 414	586 087
按行业分	**By Sector**					
农、林、牧、渔业	Farming, Forestry, Animal Husbandry and Fishery	11 229	148	344	763	9 974
采矿业	Mining	426				426
制造业	Manufacturing	532 675	15 375	6 922	396 923	113 455
电力、热力、燃气及水生产和供应业	Production and Supply of Electricity, Heat, Gas and Water	8 401	377	123	1 997	5 904
建筑业	Construction	90 568	369	777	6 914	82 508
批发和零售业	Wholesale and Retail	292 312	2 055	2 727	229 516	58 014
交通运输、仓储和邮政业	Transportation, Warehousing and Post Service	177 973	11 418	332	35 236	130 987
住宿和餐饮业	Hotel and Catering	22 087	1 158	438	11 785	8 706
信息传输、软件和信息技术服务业	Information Transmission, Software and Information Technology Services	134 154	528	9	77 631	55 986
#软件和信息技术服务业	Software and Information Technology Services	15 310	180	1	2 276	12 853
金融业	Banking	189 187	19 671		47 680	121 836
房地产业	Real Estate	66 001	3 527	3 443	28 239	30 792
租赁和商务服务业	Leasing and Business Service	202 158	10 457	5 430	91 999	94 272
科学研究和技术服务业	Scientific Research and Technology Services	59 672	6 660	268	36 779	15 965
水利、环境和公共设施管理业	Water Conservancy, Environment and Public Facilities Administration	15 518	5 346	1 190	825	8 157
#公共设施管理业	Public Facilities Administration	13 415	4 664	1 190	338	7 223
居民服务、修理和其他服务业	Residents Service, Repair and other Services	18 777	653	966	8 977	8 181
教 育	Education	53 583	38 478	1 047	1 719	12 339
卫生和社会工作	Healthcare and Social Work	35 407	23 378	3 578	215	8 236
文化、体育和娱乐业	Culture, Sports and Entertainment	10 212	2 268	376	5 199	2 369
公共管理、社会保障和社会组织	Public Management, Social Guarantee and Social Organizations	42 798	31 118	1 509		10 171

表14-5　享受居民最低生活保障人数
Number of Residents Benefiting from Guarantee of Minimum Standard of Living (2015)

单位:人　　(person)

指　标	Indicators	保障对象 Residents to be Guaranteed	城镇低保 Guarantee of Minimum Standard of Living in Urban Area	农村贫困户 Poverty Households in Rural Area
总　计	**Total**	**36 440**	**31 179**	**5 261**
潍坊新村街道	Weifangxincun Subdistrict	737	737	
陆家嘴街道	Lujiazui Subdistrict	1 361	1 361	
周家渡街道	Zhoujiadu Subdistrict	2 057	2 057	
塘桥街道	Tangqiao Subdistrict	831	831	
上钢新村街道	Shanggangxincun Subdistrict	1 424	1 424	
南码头路街道	Nanmatoulu Subdistrict	746	746	
沪东新村街道	Hudongxincun Subdistrict	1 069	1 069	
金杨新村街道	Jinyangxincun Subdistrict	1 114	1 114	
洋泾街道	Yangjing Subdistrict	900	900	
浦兴路街道	Puxinglu Subdistrict	1 536	1 536	
东明路街道	Dongminglu Subdistrict	845	845	
花木街道	Huamu Subdistrict	1 650	1 650	
川沙新镇	Chuansha New Town	2 521	1 960	561
高桥镇	Gaoqiao Town	638	612	26
北蔡镇	Beicai Town	1 711	1 693	18
合庆镇	Heqing Town	521	371	150
唐　镇	Tangzhen Town	210	179	31
曹路镇	Caolu Town	1 252	1 124	128

单位:人 表 14-5 续表 Continued (person)

指 标 Indicators		保障对象 Residents to be Guaranteed	城镇低保 Guarantee of Minimum Standard of Living in Urban Area	农村贫困户 Poverty Households in Rural Area
金桥镇	Jinqiao Town	196	194	2
高行镇	Gaohang Town	625	625	
高东镇	Gaodong Town	330	289	41
张江镇	Zhangjiang Town	911	911	
三林镇	Sanlin Town	1 713	1 663	50
惠南镇	Huinan Town	1 580	1 155	425
周浦镇	Zhoupu Town	624	560	64
新场镇	Xinchang Town	777	498	279
大团镇	Datuan Town	1 260	519	741
康桥镇	Kangqiao Town	420	417	3
航头镇	Hangtou Town	641	430	211
祝桥镇	Zhuqiao Town	2 893	2 011	882
泥城镇	Nicheng Town	791	492	299
宣桥镇	Xuanqiao Town	661	445	216
书院镇	Shuyuan Town	755	184	571
万祥镇	Wanxiang Town	378	198	180
老港镇	Laogang Town	577	194	383
南汇新城镇	Nanhui New Town	185	185	

表 14-6 劳动就业及社会保障
Employment and Social Security

指 标 Indicators		单 位 Unit	2010	2014	2015
劳动就业	**Employment**				
期末城镇登记失业人数	Actual Number of Those Registered as Unemployed at Year-end	人 person	43 453	41 759	39 874
招工录用总数	Total Recruitment	人 person	287 873	264 446	255 455
征地劳动力安置	Recruitment of Those Who Have Lost Jobs Because of Requisition of Land	人 person	29 310	3 401	2 635
新增就业岗位	Number of Newly Increased Employment	人 person	140 440	150 714	151 025
扶持创业人数	Number of Entrepreneurship Support	人 person		1 959	1 825
国家职业资格培训人数	Number of National Occupation Qualification Training	人 person		83 811	72 827
社会保险	**Social Security**				
失业保险金发放人次	Unemployment Insurance Payment Distribution	人次 person-time	294 180	230 566	229 448
失业保险金发放金额	Unemployment Insurance Payment	万元 10 000 yuan	17 156	26 572	31 808
期末城乡居民基本养老保险参保人数	Number of Persons Who Joined Endowment Insurance Program in Urban and Rural Areas at Year end	人 person	91 747	130 355	139 224
期末城乡居民基本养老保险享受人数	Number of Persons Who Benefited from Endowment Insurance Program in Urban and Rural Areas at Year end	人 person	58 432	73 713	83 315
社会救助	**Social Relief**				
城镇居民低保人数	Urban Residents Who Benefit from Subsistence Allowances from the State	人 person	72 424	33 843	31 179
城镇居民低保金额	Subsistence Allowances to Urban Residents	万元 10 000 yuan	24 902	23 457	24 668
农村居民低保人数	Number of Rural Population Benefiting from Subsistence Allowance	人 person	11 119	4 851	5 261
农村居民低保金额	Amount of Subsistence Allowance for Rural Population	万元 10 000 yuan	2 285	2 913	3 761

表 14-7 收养性单位基本情况
Background of Welfare Facilities
(2015)

指 标	Indicators	单 位 Unit	合 计 Total	社会福利院 Welfare Homes	敬老院 Homes for Senior Citizens
单位数	**Total Number**	**个 unit**	**137**	**2**	**135**
年末职工人数	**Number of Staff and Workers (Year End)**	**人 person**	**5 835**	**232**	**5 603**
#医护人员	Medical Personnel and Nurses	人 person	322	25	297
年末床位数	**Number of Beds**	**张 bed**	**25 010**	**858**	**24 152**
年末在院人数	**Persons Housed (Year End)**	**人 person**	**16 422**	**385**	**16 037**
#女 性	Female	人 person	10 857	237	10 620
#自费人员	Those at Their Own Expenses	人 person	15 744	385	15 359
在院人员按年龄分	Persons Housed by Age				
老 人	Old People	人 person	15 976	385	15 591
青壮年	Young and Middle-aged People	人 person	446		446
儿 童	Children	人 person			

表 14-8 残疾人事业及居家养老情况
Statistics of Disabled Persons & Home-based Care for the Aged

指 标	Indicators	单 位 Unit	2010	2014	2015
残疾人事业	**Disabled Persons**				
白内障复明手术	Operations for Recovery from Cataract	例 in number	2 281	628	600
低视力配用助视器人数	Number of Bad Eyesighted Persons Equipped with Typoscope	人 person	153	619	1 379
低听力配用助听器人数	Number of Bad Auditioned Persons Equipped with Haudiphone	人 person	336	939	851
精神病人数	Number of Mental Patients	人 person	15 735	23 856	24 516
监护精神病人数	Number of Mental Patients Supervised	人 person	15 230	23 450	24 415
城镇残疾人就业人数	Employed Disabled Persons in Towns and Subdistricts	人 person	125	452	414
居家养老	**Life of Disabled Persons Including the Aged**				
期末养老机构床位数	Number of Beds in Old-Aged Institutions at End of Term	张 bed	22 096	23 459	25 010
居家养老护理人员数	Number of Care Workers for the Old-Aged Living at Home	人 person	3 953	4 187	4 187
居家养老服务总数	Number of Services for the Old-Aged Living at Home	人 person	47 610	58 345	59 645
#补贴数	Number of the Old Disabled Persons	人 person	41 596	46 773	25 614

表14-9　红十字会基本情况
Statistics of Red Cross

指　标	Indicators	单　位 Unit	2010	2014	2015
救　灾	**Providing Disaster Relief**				
捐赠款物	Donation of Money and Clothes	万元 10 000 Yuan	2 790	102	14
救　助	**Salvage**				
救助款物	Salvation of Money and Clothes	万元 10 000 Yuan	1 186	4 259	4 788
受益人次	Number of Persons Benefited	人次 person-time	14 031	47 395	47 108
救　护	**Rescue**				
师资培训	Teachers Trained	人 person	29	132	9
救护员培训	Rescue Workers Trained	人 person	4 501	5 208	6 481
救护防病知识普及	Popularization of Rescue and Disease Protection	人次 person-time	59 265	127 756	83 522
预防艾滋病	Protection of AIDS	人次 person-time	31 520	524 492	400 065
遗体捐献登记	Registration of Body Donations	例 in number	202	273	265
基层组织	Grassroot Organizations	个 in number	281	296	296
社区公益服务站点	Community Public Service Stations	个 in number	523	1 197	1 291
志愿者	Volunteers	人 in number	6 491	19 547	15 017

表14-10　保障性住房
Indemnificatory Housing

指　标	Indicators	单位 Unit	2005	2010	2014	2015
廉租住房	**Low Rent Housing**					
人均居住面积认定标准	Approved Standard for Living Space Per Capita	平方米 sq·m	≦7	≦7	≦7	≦7
人均月收入认定标准	Approved Standard for Monthly Income Per Capita	元 yuan	300	≦1100	≦2500	≦2500
累计受益户数	Number of Households Registered	户 household	1 670	6 450	9 850	10 462
配租金额	Total Rent of Assisted Households	万元 10 000yuan	780	12 059	27 283	32 308
动迁房	**Resettlement Housing**					
动迁房套数	Number of Resettlement Housing	套 household			15 673	14 317
动迁房面积	Area of Resettlement Housing	万平方米 10 000 sq·m			137.74	118.40
共有产权房	**Limited-property-rights Housing**					
共有产权房套数	Number of Limited-property-rights Housing	套 household			262	8 110
共有产权房面积	Area of Limited-property-rights Housing	万平方米 10 000 sq·m			2.01	52.55

表 14-11 社会捐赠与帮困
Social Donations and Financial Aids

指 标 Indicators		单位 Unit	2010	2014	2015
社会捐赠	**Social Donations**				
捐赠款金额	Amount of Donations	万元 10 000 yuan	12 416	9 910	33 328
捐赠衣被	Clothes and Quilts for Donation	万件 10 000 unit	88	4	36
医疗救助	**Medical Assistance**				
医疗救助人次	Number of Medical Assistance	人次 person-time	13 096	68 494	88 489
医疗救助金额	Amount of Medical Assistance	万元 10 000 yuan	5 122	6 725	11 443
帮困助学	**Financial Aids for Students**				
帮困助学人次	Number of Financial Aids for Students	人次 person-time	18 136	21 070	12 602
帮困助学金额	Amount of Financial Aids for Students	万元 10 000 yuan	907	1 608	1 105

表 14-12 社会保障标准
Standard for Social Security

单位:元 (yuan)

指 标 Indicators		2010	2014	2015
职工月最低工资标准	Standard of Minimum Monthly Salary for Employees	1 120	1 820	2 020
城镇居民月最低生活保障标准	Standard of Minimum Monthly Living Expenses for Urban Residents	450	710	790
农村居民月最低生活保障标准	Standard of Minimum Monthly Living Expenses for Rural Residents	300	620	790
城乡居民基本养老保险金月最低标准	Minimum Monthly Pension Insurance for Urban and Rural Residents in PNA		725	835

主要统计指标解释

从业人员

从业人员指从事一定社会劳动并取得劳动报酬或经营收入的人员,包括在岗职工、再就业的离退休人员、私营业主、个体户主、私营和个体从业人员、乡镇企业从业人员、农村从业人员、其他从业人员(包括民办教师、宗教职业者、现役军人等)。这一指标反映了一定时期内全部劳动力资源的实际利用情况,是研究我国基本国情国力的重要指标。

各单位的从业人员指在各级国家机关、政党机关、社会团体及企业、事业单位中工作,取得工资或其他形式的劳动报酬的全部人员。包括在岗职工、再就业的离退休人员、民办教师以及在各单位中工作的外方人员和港澳台方人员、兼职人员、借用的外单位人员和第二职业者。不包括离开本单位仍保留劳动关系的职工。各单位的就业人员反映了各单位实际参加生产或工作的全部劳动力。

职　工

职工指在国有、城镇集体、联营、股份制、外商和港、澳、台投资、其他单位及其附属机构工作,并由其支付工资的各类人员。不包括下列人员:(1)乡镇企业就业人员;(2)私营企业就业人员;(3)城镇个体劳动者;(4)离休、退休、退职人员;(5)再就业的离、退休人员;(6)民办教师;(7)在城镇单位中工作的外方及港、澳、台人员;(8)其他按有关规定不列入职工统计范围的人员。(1998 年及以后的数据均为在岗职工数据,其他相关指标如职工工资总额,职工平均工资等指标也从 1998 年按此口径进行了相应调整)。

登记注册类型

登记注册类型是以工商行政管理机关登记注册的具有法人资格的各类企业为划分对象。产业活动单位和行政机关、事业单位、社会团体及其他经济组织参照执行。

国有企业指企业全部资产归国家所有,并按《中华人民共和国企业法人登记管理条例》规定登记注册的非公司制的经济组织。不包括有限责任公司中的国有独资公司。

集体企业指企业资产归集体所有,并按《中华人民共和国企业法人登记管理条例》规定登记注册的经济组织。

股份合作企业指以合作制为基础,由企业职工共同出资入股,吸收一定比例的社会资产投资组建,实行自主经营,自负盈亏,共同劳动,民主管理,按劳动分配与按股份分红相结合的一种集体经济组织。

联营企业指两个及两个以上相同或不同所有制性质的企业法人或事业单位法人,按自愿、平等、互利的原则,共同投资组成的经济组织。联营企业包括国有联营企业、集体联营企业、国有与集体联营企业和其他联营企业。

有限责任公司指根据《中华人民共和国公司登记管理条例》规定登记注册,由 2 个以上,50 个以下的股东共同出资,每个股东以其所认缴的出资额对公司承担有限责任,公司以其全部资产对其债务承担责任的经济组织。有限责任公司包括国有独资公司以及其他有限责任公司。

股份有限公司指根据《中华人民共和国公司登记管理条例》规定登记注册,其全部注册资本由等额股份构成并通过发行股票筹集资本,股东以其认购的股份对公司承担有限责任,公司以其全部资产对其债务承担责任的经济组织。

私营企业指由自然人投资设立或由自然人控股,以雇佣劳动为基础的营利性经济组织。包括按照《公司法》、《合伙企业法》、《私营企业暂行条例》规定登记注册的私营有限责任公司、私营股份有限公司、私营合伙企业和私营独资企业。

与港澳台商投资合资经营企业指港澳台地区投资者与内地企业依照《中华人民共和国中外合资经营企业法》及有关法律的规定,按合同的比例投资设立、分享利润和分担风险的企业。

港澳台商投资合作经营企业指港澳台地区投资者与内地企业依照《中华人民共和国中外合资经营企业法》及有关法律的规定,依照合同的约定进行投资或提供条件设立、分享利润和分担风险的企业。

港澳台商独资经营企业指依照《中华人民共和国外资企业法》及有关法律的规定,在内地由港澳台商地区投资者全额投资设立的企业。

港澳台商投资股份有限公司指根据国家有关规定,经外经贸部依法批准设立,其中港、澳、台商的股本占公司注册资本的比例达 25% 以上的股份有限公司。凡其中港、澳、台商的股本占公司注册资本的比例小于 25% 的,属于内资企业中股份有限公司。

中外合资经营企业指外国企业或外国人与中国内地企业依照《中华人民共和国中外合资经营企业法》及有关法律的规定,按合同规定的比例投资设立、分享利润和分担风险的企业。

中外合作经营企业指外国企业或外国人与中国内地企业依照《中华人民共和国中外合作经营企业法》及有关法律的规定,依照合作合同的约定进行投资或提供条件设立、分享利润和分担风险的企业。

外资企业指依照《中华人民共和国外资企业法》及有关法律的规定,在中国内地由外国投资者全额投资设立的企业。

外商投资股份有限公司指根据国家有关规定,经外经贸部依法批准设立,其中外资的股本占公司注册资本的比例达 25% 以上的股份有限公司。凡其中外资股本占公司注册资本的比例小于 25% 的,属于内资企业中的股份有限公司。

国民经济行业分类

《国民经济行业分类》国家标准于1984年首次发布，1994年对其进行了第一次修订,2011年新修订。

本年鉴的行业分类使用2011年修订的行业分类标准。

2011年新行业分类标准按照国际通行的经济活动同质性原则划分行业,进一步打破了部门管理界限,对原标准中不符合这一原则的分类进行了调整;根据我国社会经济活动的发展状况,重点加强了第三产业的分类,新增了大量服务业方面的活动类别;对新标准的每一个行业小类,全部与国际标准产业分类的最细一层分类建立了对应关系。新修订的《国民经济行业分类》主要目的之一是与联合国的《全部经济活动的国际标准产业分类》接轨,准确反映一定时期内国民经济行业的构成状况。

失业保险

①参加保险人数:指报告期末按照国家法律、法规和有关政策规定参加了失业保险的城镇企业事业单位的职工及地方政府规定参加失业保险的其他人员的人数。

②失业保险金:指为保障失业人员的基本生活而按规定支付的失业保险金金额。

社会福利事业单位

社会福利事业单位指集中收养社会孤老、残、幼的机构。包括由民政部门管理的社会福利院、儿童福利院、精神病人福利院和城镇集体办的福利院,以及农村集体办的敬老院。

优抚对象

优抚指政府对革命烈士家庭、病故残疾工作人员以及参战负伤致残的民兵、民工的抚恤和人民群众对其的优待。优抚对象包括革命烈士家属、因公牺牲和病故军人家属、革命伤残人员、现役军属、退伍红军老战士、红军失散人员、复员军人、退伍军人、在职退役军人、在乡退役军人、带病回乡退伍军人、复退军人精神病员、孤老优抚对象等。

EXPLANATORY NOTES TO MAJOR STATISTICAL INDICATORS

Employees

Employees refer to the persons who are engaged in social working and receive remuneration payment or earn business income, including total staff and workers, re-employed retirees, employers of private enterprises, self-employ ed workers, employees in private enterprises and individual economy, employees in township enterprises, employed persons in the rural areas , and other employed persons (including teachers in the schools run by the local people, people engaged in religious profession and the servicemen, etc.). This indicator reflects the actual utilization of total labor force during a certain period of time and is often used for the research on China′s economic situation and national power.

Employees in Various Units refer to all the persons working in government agencies of various levels, political and party organizations, social organizations, enterprises and institutions, and receiving wages or other forms of payment. They include fully-employed staff and workers, re-employed retirees, teachers in schools run by the local people, foreigners and Chinese compatriots from Hong Kong, Macao, and Taiwan working in various units, part-time employees, employees of other units working temporarily at current posts, and employees holding the second job, but exclude staff and workers who have left their working units while keeping their labor contract (employment relation) unchanged. This indicator reflects the total number of laborers actually engaged in production or other operations in various units.

Staff and Workers

Staff and Workers refer to persons working in, and receive payment from units of state ownership, collective ownership, joint ownership, share holding ownership, foreign ownership, and ownership by entrepreneurs from Hong Kong, Macao, and Taiwan, and other types of ownership and their affiliated units. They do not include 1) persons employed in township enterprises, 2) persons employed in private enterprises, 3) urban self-employed persons, 4) retirees, 5) re-employed retirees, 6) teachers in the schools run by the local people, 7) foreigners and persons from Hong Kong, Macao and Taiwan who work in urban units, and 8) other persons not to be included by relevant regulations. (Data of 1998 and afterward refer to fully employed staff and workers. Other related statistics such as total wages and average wage are adjusted since 1998 accordingly).

Registration Categories

Registration Categories are used to classify all kinds of enterprises that have the legal person status and have registered with the industrial and commercial administrations. The classification of business units, administrative and public institutions, social organizations and other economical bodies may refer to it.

The state-owned enterprises are economic organizations whose assets are solely owned by the state and whose registrations are made according to "Regulations of the People′s Republic of China for Controlling the Registration of Enterprises as Legal Persons" excluding the state-owned liability limited companies.

The collective-owned enterprises are economic organizations whose assets are owned by collecting and whose registration are made according to "Regulations of the People′s Republic of China for Controlling the Registration of Enterprises as Legal Persons."

Share-holding cooperative enterprises are a kind of collective economic organizations based on a cooperative system. In addition to the shares bought by their workers and staff, the enterprises also absorb a certain percentage of social capital. They enjoy the autonomy in operation and are responsible for their own losses and profits. The share-holders work together, conduct democratic management, and combine labor-based distribution with share-based dividends.

Joint-owned enterprises refer to economic organizations set up with joint investment from legal persons of two or more enterprises of different ownerships or institutions according to principle of voluntary participation, equality and mutual benefit. They include state-owned joint operation enterprises, collective joint operation enterprises, state-collective joint operation enterprises and other types of joint operation enterprises.

A company with limited liability is a company registered in accordance with the "Regulations of the People's Republic of China on Administration of Company Registration." Its investment comes from more than 2 and less than 50 shareholders. Each shareholder assumes limited liability for the company according to his subscription to capital stock. The company assumes liabilities for its debts according to all its assets. Such economic organizations include solely state – invested companies and other types of companies with limited liability.

A share-holding company with limited liability refers to economic organizations registered in accordance with the "Regulations of the People's Republic of China on Administration of Company Registration". All its registered capital is composed of shares of equal value and its capital is collected through share issuing. The shareholders bear limited liability for the company according to the amount of shares they have bought from the company and the company assumes liabilities for its debts according all its assets.

A private enterprise refers to profit-making economic organizations set up with investment from natural persons or with controlling interest in the hands of natural persons who employ laborers for operation. Such enterprises include private companies with limited liability private joint stock companies limited private partnership enterprises and solely individual-invested enterprises, which are registered according to the "Company Law," "Partnership Enterprises Law" and "Interim Regulations of Private Enterprises."

The joint ventures with investment from Hong Kong, Macao and Taiwan refer to those established according to the "Law of the People's Republic of China on Chinese-foreign Joint Ventures" and regulations stipulated in relevant laws, by investors from those regions and the Chinese mainland enterprises with contracted share of investment and sharing profits and ventures between the parties.

Cooperative businesses with investment from Hong Kong, Macao and Taiwan refer to enterprises jointly set up by investors from Hong Kong, Macao and Taiwan and mainland enterprises according to the "Law of the People's Republic of China on Chinese-foreign Contractural Joint Ventures" and other relevant regulations. They invest or provide conditions for establishment, decide profit distribution, and share risks according to provisions prescribed in the cooperative venture contracts.

Solely Hong Kong, Macao and Taiwan Funded enterprises refer to enterprises set up on the mainland according to the "Law of the People's Republic of China on Foreign Capital Enterprises and solely invested by investors from Hong Kong, Macao and Taiwan."

A share-holding company with limited liability with investment from Hong Kong, Macao and Taiwan refers to any joint stock company limited that is set up according relevant state regulations and is approved by the Ministry of Foreign Economic Relations and Trade. The investment from Hong Kong, Macao and Taiwan investors must account more than 25 per-cent of the company's total capital. If such investment is less than 25 percent, it shall be classified as a joint stock company limited invested by domestic investors.

A Sino-foreign joint venture refers to any enterprise that is jointly set up by foreign enterprises or foreigners with Chinese enterprises in accordance with the "Law of the People's Republic of China on Joint Ventures with Chinese and Foreign Investment." The investors shall put in investment, share profits and risks according to the contract on the joint venture.

Sino-foreign cooperative Businesses refer to the enterprises set up by foreign enterprises or foreigners with Chinese enterprises as their partners, in line with "The Sino-foreign Cooperative Ventures Law of the People's Republic of China" and other relevant laws and regulations. The partners of the cooperative ventures will invest, take profits and share risks according to the requirements of stipulated in the contract.

A Solely Foreign-Funded enterprises refers to any enterprise that is set up on the Chinese mainland according to the "Law of the People's Republic of China on Foreign-Capital Enterprises" and with all its investment coming from foreign investors.

The foreign-invested joint stock company limited refers to any joint stock company limited that is set up according to relevant state regulations and is approved by the Ministry of Foreign Economic Relations and Trade. The foreign investment must account more than 25 per-cent of the company's total capital. If such investment is less than 25 percent, it shall be classified as a joint stock company limited invested by Chinese investors.

Classification of the Sectors of the National Economy

Classification of the Sectors of the National Economy was first published in 1984 and revisions were made into it in 2011.

This Yearbook follows standards in the 2011 version of the Classification of the Sectors of the National Economy.

In the 2011 version, economic sectors are classified in accordance with the international categories of the economic activities, abolishing in definition between different administrative departments. Given the development of China's social and economic activities, more detailed classification is made of the service sector. The further breakdown of each economic sector in the latest version is geared to the most specific categorization in international practice. The latest version aims at, among others, an objective and precise presentation of the composition of the national economy in a certain period.

Unemployment Insurance

1. Number of people participated in unemployment insurance program: the number of staff and workers in urban enterprises or institutions and other people according to local government regulations participated in unemployment insurance program in line with national law, regulations and related policies by the end of the reference period.

2. Sum of Unemployment Insurance: refers to total amount of insurance paid to un-employees to guarantee their basic lives according to related regulations.

Social Welfare Institutions

Social Welfare Institutions refer to institutions taking care of old people without children, handicapped people and orphans. They include social welfare institutions run by civil affairs departments, children's welfare institutions, welfare institutions for mental patients, and collectively-run old people's homes in rural areas.

Special Care

Special Care is offered by the government to the family member of the martyrs, disabled or demobilized servicemen or laborers who were injured on duty. Entitled to the special care are family members of the revolutionary martyrs, family members of servicemen who dies on duty or died of an illness, disabled servicemen, family members of servicemen on active service, retired veteran Red Army soldiers, scattered Red Army soldiers, demobilized servicemen, ex-servicemen, servicemen who were demobilized while on duty, ex-servicemen back to their rural homes, ex-servicemen who were demobilized because of an illness and have gone back to their rural homes, ex-servicemen who suffer from mental illness and elderly persons with no family.

第十五篇

CHAPTER 15

教 育

EDUCATION

表 15-1　各级各类学校基本情况
Schools by Education Level and Type
(2015)

单位:人　　(person)

指　标 Indicators		学校(所) Schools (unit)	毕业生数 Graduates	招生数 Student Enrollment	在校学生数 Students Enrolled	教职员工数 Faculty and Staff	#专任教师 Full-time Faculty
总　计	**Total**	**346**	**76 219**	**87 239**	**362 449**	**30 121**	**25 891**
中等技术学校	Secondary Technical Schools	9	3 876	3 043	10 442	1 195	570
普通中学	High Schools	160	33 704	41 541	136 080	14 449	12 078
职业中学	Vocational Schools	7	5 243	4 094	13 713	1 081	934
小　学	Primary Schools	167	33 303	38 506	201 482	13 185	12 118
特殊教育学校	Special Education Schools	3	93	55	732	211	191

表 15-2　各级各类学校占地面积和校舍建筑面积
Ground Space of Schools and Floor Space of School Buildings by Education Level and Type
(2015)

单位:万平方米　　(10 000 sq·m)

指　标 Indicators		学校(所) Schools (unit)	占地面积 Ground Space	校舍建筑面积 Floor Space of School Buildings
总　计	**Total**	**346**	**889.02**	**522.36**
中等技术学校	Secondary Technical Schools	9	24.56	24.38
普通中学	High Schools	160	566.62	324.95
职业中学	Vocational Schools	7	34.82	25.82
小　学	Primary Schools	167	258.98	144.21
特殊教育学校	Special Education Schools	3	4.04	3.00

表 15-3 各级各类学校女学生和女教师
Female Students and Teachers by Education Level and Type
(2015)

单位:人 (person)

指标 Indicators		女学生 Female Students		女教师 Female Faculty	
		人数 Students	占学生总数(%) of Students(%)	人数 Teachers	占教师总数(%) of Teachers(%)
总计	**Total**	**170 203**	**47.0**	**19 298**	**74.5**
中等专业学校	Secondary Specialized Schools	4 636	44.4	325	57.0
普通中学	High Schools	65 712	48.3	8 384	69.4
职业中学	Vocational Schools	6 122	44.6	641	68.6
小学	Primary Schools	93 476	46.4	9 790	80.8
特殊教育学校	Special Education Schools	257	35.1	158	82.7

表 15-4 幼儿园基本情况
Statistics of Kindergartens
(2015)

指标 Indicators		幼儿园(所) Kindergartens (unit)	班级数(个) Classes (unit)	幼儿数(人) Children Enrolled (person)	教职员(人) Faculty and Staff (person)	#专任教师 Full-time Faculty
总计	**Total**	**290**	**4 035**	**119 113**	**10 632**	**7 892**
教育部门办	Run by Government Education Department	184	3 060	92 145	6 683	5 941
民办	Run by Entrepreneurs	105	971	26 861	3 929	1 940
其他部门办	Run by Other Organizations	1	4	107	20	11

表15-5　市、区实验性示范性中学基本情况一览
（2015）

指　标	Indicators	班级数（个）Classes (in Number)	初　中 Junior Schools	高　中 High Schools
总　计	Total	905	145	760
市实验性示范性中学	Experimental and Demonstrative High Schools in Shanghai	387	77	310
华东师范大学第二附属中学	Second High School Affiliated to Huadong Normal University	29		29
上海市浦东复旦附中分校	Shanghai Pudong High School Affiliated to Fudan University	11		11
上海市建平中学	Shanghai Jianping High School	39		39
上海市进才中学	Shanghai Jincai High School	38		38
上海师范大学附属中学	High School Affiliated to Shanghai Normal University	24		24
上海市洋泾中学	Shanghai Yangjing High School	36		36
上海南汇中学	Shanghai Nanhui High School	57	4	53
上海市川沙中学	Shanghai Chuansha High School	38	2	36
上海市实验学校	Shanghai Experimetnal High School	33	15	18
上海外国语大学附属浦东外国语学校	Pudong Foreign Languages High School Affiliated to Shanghai Foreign Languages University	46	32	14
上海中学东校	Shanghai High School East Campus	36	24	12
区实验性示范性中学	Experimental and Demonstrative High Schools in Pudong	518	68	450
华东师范大学附属东昌中学	Dongchang High School Affiliated to Huadong Normal University	37		37
上海市上南中学	Shanghai Shangnan High School	34		34
上海市高桥中学	Shanghai Gaoqiao High School	36		36
上海市三林中学	Shanghai Sanlin High School	33		33
上海市杨思高级中学	Shanghai Yangsi High School	24		24
上海海事大学附属北蔡高级中学	Beicai High School Affiliated to Shanghai Maritime University	18		18
上海市浦东中学	Shanghai Pudong High School	18		18
上海市陆行中学	Shanghai Luhang High School	24		24
上海市高行中学	Shanghai Gaohang High School	34	22	12
上海市香山中学	Shanghai Xiangshan High School	27	14	13
上海市建平世纪中学	Shanghai Jianping Century High School	18		18
上海市新川中学	Shanghai Xinchuan High School	24		24
上海交通大学附属中学浦东实验高中	Pudong Experimental High School Affiliated to Shanghai Jiaotong University	27		27
上海市文建中学	Shanghai Wenjian High School	18		18
上海海洋大学附属大团高级中学	Datuan High School Affiliated to Shanghai Maritime University	30		30
上海市新场中学	Shanghai Xinchang High School	30		30
华东师范大学附属周浦中学	Zhoupu High School Affiliated to Huadong Normal University	36		36
上海市南汇第一中学	Shanghai Nanhui First HIgh School	50	32	18

Statistics of Municipal and PNA Experimental and Demonstrative High Schools

在校学生(人) Students Enrolled (Persons)	初中 Junior Schools	高中 High Schools	教职员工(人) Faculty (Persons)	专任教师(人) Full-time Teachers	高中 High Schools	初中 Junior Schools	占地面积(平方米) Ground Space (sq. m)	校舍建筑面积(平方米) Floor Space of School Buildings (sq. m)	运动场地面积(平方米) Floor Space of Sports Grounds (Stadiums) (sq. m)
34 000	**5 491**	**28 509**	**3 787**	**3 210**	**2 800**	**410**	**1 683 905**	**972 101**	**436 260**
4 684	**2 876**	**11 808**	**1 733**	**1 434**	**1 221**	**213**	**1 001 561**	**599 164**	**229 695**
1 185		1 185	180	137	137		100 000	59 133	23 900
317		317	31	30	30		50 640	39 990	11 152
1 519		1 519	156	144	144		41 358	35 836	7 075
1 423		1 423	185	159	159		114 146	73 411	35 504
812		812	157	125	125		97 281	49 815	26 957
1 414		1 414	160	135	135		51 811	43 482	8 300
2 191	171	2 020	241	196	196		259 064	102 992	36 092
1 526	82	1 444	170	125	125		32 503	27 137	11 400
1 251	538	713	176	124	75	49	73 724	29 081	17 600
1 804	1 260	544	158	147	55	92	81 004	72 178	21 000
1 242	825	417	119	112	40	72	100 030	66 109	30 715
19 316	**2 615**	**16 701**	**2 054**	**1 776**	**1 579**	**197**	**682 344**	**372 937**	**206 565**
1 357		1 357	137	112	112		30 690	17 845	10 384
1 284		1 284	144	126	126		46 347	27 187	15 400
1 346		1 346	137	115	115		41 675	24 206	11 582
1 143		1 143	134	120	120		34 185	20 593	13 737
889		889	101	88	88		37 715	18 757	10 259
680		680	66	60	60		25 338	15 561	11 013
682		682	72	64	64		29 093	19 295	9 847
907		907	96	68	68		40 766	21 033	11 410
1 290	836	454	124	112	47	65	37 077	17 694	12 695
928	424	504	96	87	49	38	21 242	16 987	7 800
681		681	70	66	66		27 328	15 653	9 699
921		921	84	82	82		21 940	13 457	10 200
828		828	124	95	95		21 871	21 104	9 573
669		669	72	66	66		17 267	18 031	5 700
1 139		1 139	113	99	99		64 414	24 954	19 980
1 141		1 141	121	114	114		46 220	19 930	14 572
1 365		1 365	183	147	147		79 695	39 220	8 000
2 066	1 355	711	180	155	61	94	59 481	21 430	14 714

表 15-6 普通中学和小学专任教师学历情况
Education Level of Full-time Teachers at Junior and High Schools and Primary Schools (2015)

单位:人 (person)

指 标	Indicators	教师数 Faculty Contracts	大学本科毕业及以上 Graduated from University or Above	大学专科毕业 Graduated from Junior University	高中阶段毕业 Graduated from Senior High School	高中毕业以下 Below Senior High School or below
教师学历分布	**Education Level of Teachers**	**24 196**	**21 012**	**3 038**	**145**	**1**
高 中	High Schools	3 657	3 644	12	1	
初 中	Junior Schools	8 421	8 301	119	1	
小 学	Primary Schools	12 118	9 067	2 907	143	1
教师学历构成(%)	**Education Level Composition of Teachers (%)**	**100.0**	**86.8**	**12.6**	**0.6**	…
高 中	High Schools	100.0	99.7	0.3	…	
初 中	Junior Schools	100.0	98.6	1.4	…	
小 学	Primary Schools	100.0	74.8	24.0	1.2	…

表 15-7 民工子弟学校基本情况
Statistics of Schools for Children of Migrant Workers

指 标	Indicators	单 位 Unit	2005	2010	2014	2015
学校数	Total of Schools	所 in number	23	41	40	39
班级数	Total of Classes	个 in number	394	553	552	494
教职员工人数	Number of Teaching Staff	人 persons	851	1 526	1 504	1 370
在校学生人数	Total of Students	人 persons	20 520	25 768	24 019	19 480

主要统计指标解释

学 校

指按国家规定的设置标准和审批程序批准设立的，招收适龄人口实施各级各类教育活动的教育机构。

普通高等学校

指按照国家规定的设置标准和审批程序批准举办的，通过全国普通高等学校统一招生考试，招收高中毕业生为主要培养对象，实施高等教育的全日制大学、独立设置的学院和高等专科学校、高等职业学校和其他机构。

大学、独立设置的学院主要实施本科层次以上教育，高等专科学校、高等职业学校实施专科层次教育，其他机构是承担国家普通招生计划任务不计校数的机构。包括普通高等学校分校和批准筹建的普通高等学校等。

成人高等学校

指按国家规定的设置标准和审批程序举办的，通过全国成人高等教育统一招生考试，招收高中毕业或同等学历的人员为主要培养对象，利用函授、业余、脱产的多种形式对其实施高等学历教育的学校。包括：职工高等学校、农民高等学校、管理干部学院、教育学院、独立函授学院、广播电视大学、其他机构等。

民办的其他高等教育机构

指经省、自治区、直辖市教育行政部门审批并颁发办学许可证，但不具有颁发学历文凭资格的实施高等教育的单位。学历文凭考试机构是指民办的经教育行政部门专门批准，进行全日制高等教育的其他高等教育机构。

中等专业学校

指经县或县以上教育行政部门批准设立，招收初中毕业生实施中等专业课程教育的教学机构。

职业中学（职业高中、职业初中）

指经县或县以上教育行政部门批准设立，招收小学或初中毕业生实施中等职业技术教育的教学机构。按学校性质类别可分为：独立设置的职业中学（包括：职业初中、职业高中、职业初高中合设学校）；附设有普通中学班的职业中学。

普通中学（普通高中、普通初中）

普通中学分为普通高级中学和普通初级中学两个阶段。普通初级中学是指独立设置的招收小学毕业的适龄人口进行初级中等基础教育的机构；普通高级中学是指独立设置的招收初中毕业的适龄人口进行高级中等基础教育的机构；完全中学是指普通初、高中合设的教育机构；一贯制学校是指在一所学校连续实施中小学教育的机构。其中包括实施九年义务教育的九年一贯制学校和实施高中教育的十二年一贯制学校。（说明：一贯制学校的办学条件如能划分为小学、初中、高中，则分开填报；如不能划分清楚，可按就高不就低的方法填入初中、高中报表中，不能重复填写。）

普通小学

指由区或区以上教育行政部门批准，招收学龄儿童实施初等教育的教学机构。

幼儿园

指招收三周岁以上（含三周岁）学龄前幼儿，对其进行保育和教育的单位。

特殊教育学校

指本市独立设置的招收盲聋哑和智残儿童，以及其他特殊需要的儿童、青少年进行普通或职业初、中等教育的教学机构。

EXPLANATORY NOTES TO MAJOR STATISTICAL INDICATORS

School Institutions

School Institutions refer to education establishment set up according to the government evaluation and approval procedures, enrolling population of the right age, providing various phase education activity.

Regular Institutions of Higher Education

Regular Institutions of Higher Learning refer to educational establishments set up according to the government evaluation and approval procedures, enrolling graduates from senior secondary schools and providing higher education courses and training for senior professionals. They include full-time universities, colleges, high professional schools, high professional vocational schools and others.

Universities and colleges are mainly providing undergraduate courses; those high professional schools and high professional vocational schools are mainly providing professional trainings; and others refer to educational establishments, which are responsible for enrolling students but not covered in the total number of schools, including: branch schools of universities and colleges, and universities and colleges that have been proved and prepared to construct.

Institutions of Higher Education for Adults

Institution of Higher Learning for Adults refer to educational establishments, set up in line with relevant rules approved by the government, enrolling personnel with senior secondary schools or equivalent education, and providing higher education courses in many forms of correspondence, spare time, or full time for adults. Institutions of higher schools for adults include schools of higher educations for staff and workers, schools of higher education for peasants, colleges for management cadres, pedagogical colleges, independent correspondence colleges, Radio and TV universities and other educational establishment, etc.

Civil Other Institution of Higher Education

Civil Other Institution of Higher Education refer to educational establishment set up according to rules approved and permitted by educational administration department of municipal government and not be provided with qualification to awarding diploma.

Specialized Secondary schools

Specialized Secondary Schools refer to educational establishment set up according to approval and permission by educational administration department of district and above government, enrolling graduates from junior secondary schools and providing secondary professional education courses.

Vocational Secondary Schools (Senior Secondary Schools and Junior Secondary Schools)

Vocational Secondary Schools refer to educational establishment set up according to approval and permission by educational administration department of district and above government, enrolling graduates from primary schools and junior secondary schools and providing secondary vocational education courses.

Regular Secondary Schools (Senior Secondary Schools and Junior Secondary Schools)

Regular Secondary Schools are classified as senior secondary schools and junior secondary schools. Junior Secondary Schools refer to educational establishment enrolling graduates from primary schools and providing junior secondary educational courses. Senior Secondary Schools refer to educational establishment enrolling graduates from junior secondary schools and providing higher secondary educational courses.

Regular Primary Schools

Regular Primary Schools refer to educational establishment set up according to approval and permission by educational administration department of district and above government, enrolling graduates from children of school age and providing primary educational courses.

Kindergartens

Kindergartens refer to nursery and education establishment, enrolling children in 3 years old and above.

Special Education Schools

Special Education Schools refer to educational establishments set up independently, enrolling blind, deaf, dumb, amentia or other special children, and educational establishment, providing regular or vocational junior and senior secondary education for hobbledehoy.

第十六篇

CHAPTER 16

文化和体育

CULTURE AND SPORTS

表16－1　文化事业
Cultural Establishments

指　标　Indicators		单　位　Unit	2010	2014	2015
街道、镇社区文化活动中心	Culture and Activity Center for Sub-district and Town	个 unit	38	37	37
行政村(居委)综合文化活动室	Comprehensive Culture and Activity Room for Administrative Village (Neighborhood Committee)	个 unit	1 117	1 135	1 181
街镇图书馆藏书量	Number of Books Collected in Sub-district and Town Libraries	万册 10 000 Books	104.57	130.00	152.50
文化资源	**Cultural Resources**				
区属文化基层单位	PNA Grassroot Cultural Institutions	个 unit	16	15	15
公共文化设施数	Number of Public Cultural Facilities	个 unit	1 280	1 302	1 254
公益电影放映次数	Number of Welfare Films Screened	场次 in number	21 553	15 509	14 353
业余文艺团队个数	Number of Amateur Literary and Artistic Teams	个 unit	3 261	4 057	6 053
文化交流	**Cultural Exchanges**				
赴境外演出、展览次数	Number of Performances and Exhibitions in Foreign Countries and Regions	次 time	1		2
境外艺术团来访个数	Number of Overseas Artist Teams Visited	个 unit	18	7	4
境外艺术团演出场次	Number of Overseas Artist Teams Performed	场次 in number	54	4	1
文艺创作演出情况	**Literary and Artistic Creations and Performances**				
群众文艺创作数	Number of Literary and Artistic Creations	个 unit	1 169	1 297	1 198
获奖个数	Number of Prizes	个 unit	198	293	3501
获奖人次	Number of Person-times Who Get the Prizes	人次 person-time	2 500	2 521	2 890
获奖单位	Number of Units Who Get the Prizes	个 unit	198	90	198

表16-2 公共图书馆基本情况
Statistics of Public Libraries

指 标	Indicators	单 位 Unit	2005	2010	2014	2015
机构数	Number of Institutions	个 unit	1	3	3	3
职工人数	Staff and Workers	人 person	110	188	217	212
公用房屋建筑面积	Floor Space of Buildings for Public Use	平方米 sq·m	18 343	74 221	74 160	77 385
#书 库	Stack Rooms	平方米 sq·m	6 040	16 515	5 695	5 695
阅览室面积	Floor Space of Reading Rooms	平方米 sq·m	7 550	38 882	27 877	28 278
阅览室座席	Seats in Reading Rooms	个 unit	1 366	3 764	4 329	4 297
总藏书量	Total Book Volume	万册 10 000 volumes	126	290	371	470
#本年新购藏书	New Books Purchased in Current Year	万册 10 000 volumes	12	24	42	202
累计有效借书证数	Library Cards Distributed	张 in number			266 142	309 500
#当年发证数	Library Card distributed in Current Year	张 in number	10 524	56 598	72 064	53 190
图书流通人次	Books Circulation Persons-Time	万人次 10 000 person-times	150	242	484	429
图书外借册次	Borrowed Books-time	万册次 10 000 volume-times	99	177	469	565

表16-3　广播电视事业基本情况
Statistics of Broadcasting and Television

指　标 Indicators		单位 Unit	2005	2010	2014	2015
区广播电视台	PNA Radio and TV Station	座 unit	1	1	1	1
区有线网络中心	PNA Cabled Networking Center	座 unit	1	1	1	1
市属有线电视管理站	Municipal CATV Management Station	个 unit	10	10	10	10
区属有线电视管理站	PNA CATV Management Station	个 unit	3	7	2	2
广电工作从业人员	Persons Employed in Sectors of Broadcasting and Television	人 person	342	544	620	574
区台无线广播发射塔	Radio Broadcasting and TV Tower of PNA	座 unit	1	1	1	1
区台使用频率	Frequency Occupied by PNA	兆赫 MHz	106.5	106.5/100.1	106.5/100.1	106.5/100.1
区台无线广播覆盖率	Radio Broadcasting Coverage of PNA	%	100.0	100.0	100.0	100.0
有线广播电视专线	Cabled Broadcasting and Television Line	杆公里 pole. km	1 858	6 097	7 186	7 220
有线电视管道干线	CATV Trunk Line	公里 km	223	1 211	1 835	1 869
广播电视台播出节目时间	Broadcasting Duration of Radio and Television Stations	小时/日 hour/day		18	18	18
有线电视用户	CATV Subscribers	万户 10 000 households	73	131	150	155
村通播率	Rate of Villages Access to Broadcasting	%	100.0	100.0	100.0	100.0
区台平均日播音时间	Average Broadcasting Hours of PNA Radio Stations	小时 hour	1/14.5	1/21.0	2/36.0	2/36.0

表 16-4　文化馆基本情况
Statistics of Cultural Centers
(2015)

指　标	Indicators	单　位 Unit	合　计 Total	浦东文化馆 Pudong Cultural Center	浦南文化馆 Punan Cultural Center	川沙文化馆 Chuansha Cultural Center	文化艺术指导中心 Art Consulting Center
机构数	Number of Centers	个 unit	4	1	1	1	1
职工人数	Staff and Workers	人 person	162	22	18	21	101
公用房屋建筑面积	Floor Space of Buildings for Public Use	平方米 sq. m	34 239	7 392	2 510	3 333	21 004
组织文艺活动次数	Performances Organized	次 time	4 076	305	360	132	3 279
举办业余文艺训练班班次	Training Courses for Amateurs	班次 class-time	3 421	35	60	102	3 224
结业人数	Persons Graduated	人次 person-time	501 874	1 400	200	274	500 000

表 16-5　参加市级以上体育竞赛成绩情况
Sport Prize in State-level and International-level Competitions
(2015)

单位:次　　(time)

指　标	Indicators	第 1 名 First Place Winners	第 2 名 Second Place Winners	第 3 名 Third Place Winners	第 4 名 Fourth Place Winners	第 5 名 Fifth Place Winners	第 6 名 Sixth Place Winners	第 7 名 Seventh Place Winners
合　计	**Total**	**328**	**275**	**281**	**125**	**108**	**76**	**80**
市　级	Municipal Level	271	214	240	102	88	65	64
全　国	State Level	57	61	41	23	20	11	16
团　体	**Team**	**17**	**22**	**12**	**5**	**5**	**4**	**2**
市　级	Municipal Level	12	17	11	4	4	4	2
全　国	State Level	5	5	1	1	1	0	0
个　人	**Individual**	**311**	**253**	**269**	**120**	**103**	**72**	**78**
市　级	Municipal Level	259	197	229	98	84	61	62
全　国	State Level	52	56	40	22	19	11	16

表 16-6　举(承)办各级体育比赛情况
Sports Competitions of All Levels Held or Undertaken in PNA
(2015)

比赛级别	Levels	次数(次) Times (In Number)	参加人次数(人次) Athletes (person-time)
总　计	**Total**	**258**	**125 889**
区级比赛	PNA Competitions	173	77 291
市级比赛	Shanghai Competitions	61	36 300
全国比赛及以上	National or Above Competitions	24	12 298

表 16-7　等级运动员和裁判员情况
Graded Athletes and Referees
(2015)

单位:人　(person)

项　目	Item	二级运动员 Grade-Ⅱ Athletes	裁判员 Referees	
			二级 Grade-Ⅱ	三级 Grade-Ⅲ
合　计	**Total**	**102**	**90**	**309**
田　径	Track and Field	8		
排　球	Volleyball	6		
武　术	Martial Art	4		
篮　球	Basketball	12	18	96
射　击	Shooting	1		
足　球	Soccer		6	43
游　泳	Swimming	34	21	62
棒　球	Baseball		11	
散　打	Free Boxing			
击　剑	Fence-play	6		
围　棋	Go	4	8	25
象　棋	Chinese Chess		5	3
国际象棋	Chess			
乒乓球	Table Tennis	4		
举　重	Weight Lifting			
垒　球	Softball	1		
羽毛球	Badminton		9	80
台　球	Billiards			
门　球	Croquet			
健美操	Aerobics			
皮划艇	Canoeing/Kayaking	4		
赛　艇	Racing Boat	14		
摔　跤	Wrestling			
中国式摔跤	Chinese-style Wrestling			
花样游泳	Synchronized Swimming			
网　球	Tennis			
风　筝	Kite Flying			
航空模型	Model Plane			
车辆模型	Model Vehicle			
体育舞蹈	Ballroom Dancing			
拳　击	Boxing	2		
柔　道	Judo			
射　箭	Archery	1		
航海模型	Model Ship			
信　鸽	Carrier Pigeon			
桥　牌	Bridge		1	
健身秧歌	Fitness Yangko Dance			
马　术	Equestrianism			
跆拳道	Taekwondo			
毽　球	Shuttlecock			
台　球	Billiards		11	
短道速滑	Short-track Speed Skating	1		

表16-8 全民健身活动设施情况
Facilities for Fitness Activities

指 标	Indicators	单 位 Unit	2010	2014	2015
农民健身家园	**Fitness Garden for Farmers**				
篮球场	Basketball Court	片 in number	206	254	259
羽毛球场	Badminton Court	片 in number	5	5	7
网球场	Tennis Court	片 in number	2	3	3
门球场	Croquet Court	片 in number	68	89	99
社区公共运动场	**Community Public Sports Ground**				
篮球场	Basketball Court	片 in number	69	91	93
门球场	Croquet Court	片 in number	26	37	38
网球场	Tennis Court	片 in number	16	21	21
足球场	Soccer Field	片 in number	1	1	4
羽毛球场	Badminton Court	片 in number	3	5	5
健身苑(点)数量	**Number of Fitness Court (Center)**	**个 in number**	**1 689**	**3 079**	**3 099**
健身苑	Fitness Court	个 in number	67	67	67
街道、镇	Subdistrict or Town	个 in number	63	63	63
体育系统	Sports System	个 in number	2	2	2
学 校	School	个 in number	2	2	2
健身点	Fitness Center	个 in number	1 622	3 012	3 032
街道、镇	Subdistrict or Town	个 in number	1 622	3 012	3 032
健身苑(点)面积	**Floor Space for Fitness Court (Center)**	**万平方米 10 000sq·m**	**91.95**	**122.91**	**123.21**
健身苑	Fitness Court	万平方米 10 000sq·m	15.15	15.15	15.15
街道、镇	Subdistrict or Town	万平方米 10 000sq·m	14.00	14.00	14.00
体育系统	Sports System	万平方米 10 000sq·m	0.60	0.60	0.60
学 校	School	万平方米 10 000sq·m	0.55	0.55	0.55
健身点	Fitness Center	万平方米 10 000sq·m	76.80	107.76	108.06
街道、镇	Subdistrict or Town	万平方米 10 000sq·m	76.80	107.76	108.06
健身器材配置数	**Number of Body Fitness Apparatus**	**件 set**	**20 803**	**31 296**	**31 536**
街 道	Subdistrict	件 set	6 125	8 786	8 800
镇	Town	件 set	14 582	22 414	22 640
专业体育场馆	Professional Stadium and Gymnasium	件 set	60	60	60
学 校	School	件 set	36	36	36

主要统计指标解释

文化机构

是指专门从事文化工作具有法人资格，独立核算的事业，企业单位，以及单独核算，附属于事业单位的经营性专业文化活动单位。包括从事艺术、图书馆、档案馆、群众文化、文物保护、艺术教育、艺术研究、文化娱乐、新闻出版等机构，以及其他文化机构。

等级运动员人数

指经考核正式批准授予等级运动员称号的人数。运动员等级分为国际级运动健将、运动健将、一级运动员、二级运动员、三级运动员、少年级运动员。该指标主要反映运动员队伍的技术质量水平。

等级裁判员人数

指经考核正式批准授予等级裁判员称号的人数。裁判员等级分为国际裁判、国家级裁判、一级裁判、二级裁判、三级裁判。该指标主要反映裁判员队伍的技术质量水平。

EXPLANATORY NOTES TO MAJOR STATISTICAL INDICATORS

Cultural Institutions

Cultural Institution refers to undertaking and business institutions which specialize in cultural work and have legal personality and independent accounting system, and those professional cultural institutions attached to undertaking institutions and have independent accounting system. It includes institutions specialize in art, library, archives, mass culture, historical relic protection, art education, art research, entertainment, news and publication and other cultural institutions.

Number of Athletes in Grades

Number of Athletes in Grades refers to the number of athletes who have been given titles through examination. The titles of athletes include international masters of sports, masters of sports, first-grade, second-grade and third-grade sportsmen and young athletes. This indicator reflects skill of the athletes.

Number of Referees in Grades

Number of Referees in Grades refers to the number of referees who have been given titles after examination. They are classified as international referees, national referees and referees of the first, second and third grades. This indicator reflects the skill of referees.

第十七篇

CHAPTER 17

卫 生

PUBLIC HEALTH

表 17－1 各类卫生机构、床位及人员数
Healthcare Institutions, Hospital Beds and Professionals by Institution Type (2015)

指 标	Indicators	机构数(个) Institution (unit)	床位数(张) Beds (bed)	人员数(人) Staff (person)	#卫生技术人员 Healthcare Professional	管理人员 Administrator
总 计	**Total**	**1 057**	**21 098**	**35 560**	**29 237**	**1 958**
卫生部门合计	**Total by Healthcare Departments**	**176**	**16 323**	**28 313**	**23 568**	**1 385**
医院合计	Total of Hostpitals	25	13 116	20 275	17 224	995
综合性医院	Comprehensive Hospital	10	7 535	12 848	10 889	622
中医医院	Hospital of Traditional Chinese Medicine	4	1 434	2 477	2 101	135
中西医结合医院	Integrated Hospital of Traditonal Chinese and Western Medicine	1	694	1 248	1 105	65
专科医院	Special Hospital	8	2 643	2 349	1 950	108
妇幼保健院	Maternity and Pediatric Hospital	2	810	1 353	1 179	65
社区卫生服务中心(站)	Community Healthcare Service Center (Station)	138	3 207	6 707	5 570	287
妇幼保健所	Maternity and Pediatric Clinic	1		86	76	2
眼病牙病防治所	Visual and Dental Clinic	1		68	60	
疾病预防控制中心	Disease Prevention and Control Center	1		288	254	5
卫监监督所	Health Supervision Institution	1		152	125	2
急救中心	First-Aid Center	1		466	131	15
采供血机构	Blood Sampling and Supply Institution	1		72	46	13
其 他	Others	7		199	82	66
工业及其他部门合 计	**Total by Industry and other Departments**	**881**	**4 775**	**7 247**	**5 669**	**573**
医院合计	Total of Hospitals	40	4 775	4 783	3 468	497
工业医院	Industrial Hospital	5	2 553	1 670	1 204	297
综合性医院	Comprehensive Hospital	3	764	989	663	233
专科医院	Special Hospital	1	420	131	84	12
护理院	Nursing Home	1	1 369	550	457	52
民办医院	Private Hospital	35	2 222	3 113	2 264	200
诊所(含内设医疗机构)	Clinic (Medical Establishments Included)	537		2 464	2 201	76
村卫生室	Village Clinic	304				

表 17-2 各类卫生技术人员数
Number of Healthcare Professionals
(2015)

单位:人 (person)

指 标	Indicators	合 计 Total	执业医师 Medical Practitioners	执业助理医师 Assistant Medical Practitioners	注册护士 Registered Nurses	药师(士) Pharmacist	检验技师(士) Inspect technician	摄像技师(士) Video technician	其他卫生技术人员 Other Healthcare Professionals
总 计	**Total**	**29 237**	**10 466**	**333**	**12 741**	**1 645**	**1 190**	**503**	**2 359**
卫生部门合计	**Total by Healthcare Departments**	**23 568**	**8 186**	**228**	**10 548**	**1 400**	**999**	**411**	**1 796**
医院合计	Hostpitals	17 224	5 617	18	8 558	833	656	361	1 181
综合性医院	Comprehensive Hospital	10 889	3 595	2	5 412	426	394	262	798
中医医院	Hospital of Traditional Chinese Medicine	2 101	786	7	959	194	90	48	17
中西医结合医院	Integrated Hospital of Traditonal Chinese and Western Medicine	1 105	395	1	564	49	37	17	42
专科医院	Special Hospital	1 950	490	8	1 054	131	81	29	157
妇幼保健院	Maternity and Pediatric Hospital	1 179	351	0	569	33	54	5	167
社区卫生服务中心(站)	Community Healthcare Service Center (Station)	5 570	2 268	206	1 906	559	246	48	337
妇幼保健所	Maternity and Pediatric Clinic	76	48	0	12	4	5	2	5
眼病牙病防治所	Visual and Dental Clinic	60	33	0	17	2	1	0	7
疾病预防控制中心	Disease Prevention and Control Center	254	152	0	3	1	38	0	60
卫监监督所	Health Supervision Institution	125							125
急救中心	First-Aid Center	131	45	3	21	0	0	0	62
采供血机构	Blood Sampling and Supply Institution	46	4	1	26	0	14	0	1
其 他	Others	82	19	0	5	1	39	0	18
工业及其他部门合计	**Total by Industry and other Departments**	**5 669**	**2 280**	**105**	**2 193**	**245**	**191**	**92**	**563**
医院合计	Hospitals	3 468	1 086	39	1 486	172	131	60	494
工业医院	Industrial Hospital	1 204	246	13	516	53	46	14	316
综合性医院	Comprehensive Hospital	663	191	12	284	33	34	5	104
专科医院	Special Hospital	84	14	1	57	5	2	1	4
护理院	Nursing Home	457	41	0	175	15	10	8	208
民办医院	Private Hospital	2 264	840	26	970	119	85	46	178
诊所(含内设医疗机构)	Clinic (Medical Establishments Included)	2 201	1 194	66	707	73	60	32	69

注：以上含浦东区域内市属三级医院及分院数据。
Note: The above-mentioned data include those of municipal Grade III hospitals and their affiliated hospitals located in Pudong.

表17-3 区级医院基本情况
Statistics of PNA-level Hospitals
(2015)

指 标	Indicators	人员数（人）Staff (person)	#卫生技术人员 Healthcare Professionals	建筑面积（平方米）Floor Space (sq·m)	#业务用房 Floor Space for Treatment	床位数（张）Beds (bed)	全年诊疗人次（万人次）Annual Patients Treated (10 000 person-times)
总 计	**Total**	**12 819**	**10 919**	**796 611**	**688 228**	**8 962**	**1 454.14**
综合医院	**Comprehensive Hospitals**	**10 612**	**9 029**	**670 269**	**585 429**	**6 136**	**1 201.16**
东方医院	Oriental Hospital	2 854	2 385	157 584	148 911	1 473	275.03
第七人民医院	No. 7 People's Hospital	1 248	1 105	79 603	78 104	694	145.23
华山医院南汇分院	Nanhui Branch of Huashan Hospital	1 464	1 286	91 015	91 015	1 000	167.89
浦东新区人民医院	PNA People's Hospital	1 425	1 246	91 305	54 281	967	195.53
浦东新区公利医院	PNA Gongli Hospital	1 396	1 194	68 871	56 269	800	176.91
第九人民医院周浦分院	Zhoupu Branch of Shanghai No.9 People's Hospital	1 178	962	102 891	77 849	652	156.74
浦南医院	Punan Hospital	1 047	851	79 000	79 000	550	83.84
专科医院	**Specialized Hospitals**	**2 207**	**1 890**	**126 342**	**102 799**	**2 826**	**252.98**
传染病院	Infectious Disease Control Hospital	88	71	7 380	4 500	100	5.52
浦东新区中医医院	Hospital of Traditional Chinese Medicine, PNA	502	428	24 331	22 531	288	94.99
妇幼保健院	Maternity and Pediatric Hospital	380	333	20 031	15 770	200	32.33
光明中医医院	Guangming Chinese Medicine Hospital	534	468	16 000	13 800	325	93.41
南汇精神卫生中心	Nanhui Mental Health Center	117	92	12 500	10 725	340	5.01
浦东新区精神卫生中心	Mental Health Centre, PNA	201	175	21 771	18 219	800	9.36
南华医院	Nanhua Hospital	140	120	7 398	6 101	153	8.41
老年医院	Laonian Hospital	162	136	10 678	6 960	420	2.15
肺科医院	Pulmonary Disease Hospital	83	67	6 253	4 193	200	1.82

表 17 – 4 综合医院工作质量情况
Workload in Comprehensive Hospitals

指 标	Indicators	手术人数(人次) Operations (person-time)		入院病人数(人次) Inpatients(person-time)		出院病人数(人次) Inpatients Leaving for Home(person-time)	
		2014	2015	2014	2015	2014	2015
总 计	**Total**	**117 718**	**122 684**	**216 210**	**225 180**	**216 464**	**224 947**
东方医院	Oriental Hospital	34 018	35 510	58 217	60 585	58 238	60 640
第七人民医院	No. 7 People's Hospital	12 603	13 026	26 358	27 344	26 456	27 340
上海市浦东医院	Shanghai Pudong Hospital	16 813	15 231	36 813	35 127	36 833	35 174
浦东新区人民医院	PNA People's Hospital	15 140	15 326	31 553	31 970	31 553	31 856
浦东新区公利医院	PNA Gongli Hospital	14 698	16 381	25 231	29 098	25 291	29 000
浦东新区周浦医院	Zhoupu Hospital in Pudong New District	16 210	19 624	21 462	24 185	21 491	24 156
浦南医院	Punan Hospital	8 236	7 586	16 576	16 871	16 602	16 781

表 17 – 4 续表 Continued

指 标	Indicators	出院者平均住院日数(日) Average Days of Inpatients at Hospital(day)		平均病床工作日(日) Average Beds Exploitation(day)		病床使用率(%) Rate of Beds Exploitation(%)	
		2014	2015	2014	2015	2014	2015
总 计	**Total**	**9.17**	**8.97**	**343.76**	**337.66**	**94.18**	**92.51**
东方医院	Oriental Hospital	8.18	8.06	339.59	328.07	93.04	89.88
第七人民医院	No. 7 People's Hospital	9.30	8.68	354.39	342.58	97.09	93.00
上海市浦东医院	Shanghai Pudong Hospital	9.62	9.53	353.28	334.18	96.79	93.86
浦东新区人民医院	PNA People's Hospital	9.51	9.61	358.80	353.81	98.30	96.93
浦东新区公利医院	PNA Gongli Hospital	8.71	8.47	319.05	324.09	87.41	88.79
浦东新区周浦医院	Zhoupu Hospital in Pudong New District	8.77	8.27	360.25	317.78	98.70	87.06
浦南医院	Punan Hospital	12.05	12.18	318.76	379.65	87.33	104.01

注：1. 原华山医院南汇分院更名为上海市浦东医院。
2. 原第九人民医院周浦分院更名为浦东新区周浦医院。

Note: 1. Nanhui Branch of Huashan Hospital has changed its name into Shanghai Pudong Hospital.
2. Zhoupu Branch of Shanghai No. 9 People's Hospital Has changed its name into Zhoupu Hospital of Pudong New Area.

表 17-5　医院诊疗人次和入院人数

Outpatients and Inpatients Treated

(2015)

指　标	Indicators	诊疗人次（万人次） Total Patients Treated (10 000 person-times)	#门、急诊 Outpatients or Emergency Treatment	入院人数（人次） Inpatients (person-times)	每百诊次的入院人数(人) Inpatients Per 100 Total Patient/time (person)	出院人数（人次） Inpatients Leaving for Home (person-times)
总　计	**Total**	**4 826.84**	**4 748.66**	**385 752**	**0.80**	**559 675**
卫生部门合计	**Total by Healthcare Departments**	**4 162.71**	**4 099.02**	**328 912**	**0.79**	**502 963**
医院合计	Hostpitals	2 246.09	2 217.44	303 249	1.35	477 152
综合性医院	Comprehensive Hospital	1 397.31	1 369.25	211 306	1.51	303 344
中医医院	Hospital of Traditional Chinese Medicine	404.37	404.37	18 357	0.45	61 864
中西医结合医院	Integrated Hospital of Traditonal Chinese and Western Medicine	145.23	144.95	27 344	1.88	27 340
专科医院	Special Hospital	189.94	189.62	35 198	1.85	39 960
妇幼保健院	Maternity and Pediatric Hospital	109.25	109.25	11 044	1.01	44 644
社区卫生服务中心(站)	Community Healthcare Service Center (Station)	1 906.79	1 871.75	25 663	0.13	25 811
专业公共卫生机构	Special Public Health Institution	9.83	9.83			
工业及其他部门合计	**Total by Industry and other Departments**	**664.13**	**649.64**	**56 840**	**0.86**	**56 712**
医院合计	Hospitals	433.33	418.84	56 840	1.31	56 712
工业医院	Industrial Hospital	44.90	44.90	20 311	4.52	20 154
综合性医院	Comprehensive Hospital	43.52	43.52	9 618	2.21	9 565
专科医院	Special Hospital			19		26
护理院	Nursing Home	1.38	1.38	10 674	77.19	10 563
民办医院	Private Hospital	388.43	373.94	36 529	0.94	36 558
诊　所（含门诊部）	Clinic (including health rooms)	230.79	230.79			

注：1. 业务指标不包括村卫生室。
2. 以上数据除入院人数指标外均包含浦东地域市属三级医院分院数据。

Note: 1. Business indicators exclude those of village health rooms.
2. Except the number of inpatients, the above mentioned data include those of municipal Grade III hospitals and their affiliated hospitals located in Pudong.

表 17-6 医疗业务效益指标
Indicators of Medical Results

指 标	Indicators	单 位 Unit	2005	2010	2014	2015
医院(卫生部门)	**Hospitals (Healthcare Departments)**					
手术人次数	Operation Person-times	人次 person-time	32 404	69 354	144 884	150 577
病床周转率	Turnover of Beds	次/床 time/bed	26.77	24.95	30.73	30.75
病床平均工作日	Average Bed in Service	日/床 day/bed	374.72	344.26	355.23	347.82
病床使用率	Rate of Bed Exploitation	%	102.66	94.32	97.32	95.29
出院者平均住院日	Average Days of Inpatient at Hospital	日 day	13.37	13.06	10.83	10.45
综合医院出院病人平均医疗费	**Average Medical Fee of Inpatients at Comprehensive Hospitals**	**元/人 yuan/person**	**7 499.06**	**10 362.34**	**13 857.31**	**14 652.68**

注：1. 2009 年始，平均每张处方费用不作统计。
2. 本表不含浦东区域内市属三级医院分院数据

Note: 1. The average expense of every medical prescription has not been put into statistics since 2009.
2. Data in this table exclude those of municipal Grade III hospitals and their affiliated hospitals located in Pudong.

表 17-7 公民义务献血、用血情况
Voluntary Blood Donation and Blood Transfusion

指 标	Indicators	单 位 Unit	2010	2014	2015
献血人次	Number of Person-times Who Voluntarily Donate Their Blood	人份 in number	49 902	53 073	52 882
无偿献血占献血人次比重	Ratio of Person-times Who Voluntarily Donate Their Blood in Total Number of Blood Donations	%	93.0	97.0	98.0
用血量	Amount of Blood Transfusion				
#全 血	Whole Blood	人次 person-time	96	60	34
红细胞	Red Blood Cell	人次 person-time	41 729	47 254	44 068
血 浆	Blood Plasma	人次 person-time	37 740	51 093	50 085

表17-8 主要年份前十位疾病死亡原因及构成
Death Causes of 10 Major Diseases and Their Composition in Main Years

单位:% (%)

疾病死亡原因	Cause of Death	构成比 Composition Rate 1997	2000	2005	2010	2014	2015
循环系统病	Circulatory System Disease	35.85	32.40	34.55	34.24	36.98	37.99
肿　瘤	Tumor	26.87	30.40	31.04	32.52	32.15	31.21
呼吸系病	Respiratory Disease	16.11	13.80	11.00	9.66	9.68	9.61
损伤和中毒	Trauma & Toxicosis	5.86	6.30	5.48	5.73	4.61	4.90
消化系病	Digestive Disease	2.57	2.90	2.70	2.78	2.49	2.21
内分泌代谢免疫病	Internal Secretion, Metabolic and Immunity Diseases	2.64	2.70	4.10	4.03	4.66	5.03
传染病寄生虫病	Infectious Disease and Pardsitic Disease	1.94	2.10	1.52	1.19	0.98	1.08
精神病	Mental Disease	1.66	1.90	0.97	0.65	0.45	0.88
泌尿生殖系病	Genitourinary Disease	1.10	1.11	0.93	0.85	0.67	0.64
神经系病	Neuro Disease	0.66	0.62	0.78	1.05	1.22	1.30

表17-9 主要年份婴儿疾病死亡原因及构成
Disease Cause of Infant Death in Main Years

单位:% (%)

主要疾病死亡原因	Main Cause of Death	构成比 Composition Rate 2005	2010	2012	2013	2014	2015
新生儿病	Disease of the New-borns	34.20	40.98	45.61	49.26	49.43	42.31
先天异常	Congenital Anomaly	43.90	40.98	36.84	47.76	37.93	40.38
呼吸系病	Respiratory Disease	4.90	4.92	5.26	1.49		
传染病寄生虫病	Infectious Disease and Pardsitic Disease		3.28	5.26			
神经系统疾病	Nervous System Disease				1.49	3.45	3.85
损伤中毒	Trauma & Toxicosis	7.30	3.28	3.51		3.45	3.85
肿　瘤	Tumor	2.40	1.64			1.15	
血液系病	Blood System Disease		1.82				
内分泌、营养和代谢疾病	Endocrine, Nutritional and Metabolic Disease						3.85

表 17－10　家庭病床情况
Statistics of Family Ward Beds

指　标　Indicators		单　位　Unit	2005	2010	2014	2015
中西医师(士)赴家庭病床诊疗总人次	Total Number of Doctors of Traditional Chinese Medicine and of Western Medicine Treating Patients in Family Ward Beds	人次 person-times	109 579	162 608	112 616	118 108
期初原有家庭病床数	Number of Family Ward Beds at Beginning of Term	张 bed	2 097	2 555	2 857	2 634
期内新建家庭病床数	Number of New Established Family Ward Beds During the Term	张 bed	4 340	5 005	6 461	8 316
期内撤床病人数	Number of Patients Leaving Family Ward Beds During the Term	人 person	4 260	4 928	6 194	8 039
治　愈	Patients Cured	人 person	1	2	16	30
好　转	Patients Getting Better	人 person	149	264	574	1 463
稳　定	Patients Turning Stablized	人 person	3 452	3 711	4 362	4 873
转　院	Patients Turning to Another Hospital	人 person	419	618	690	680
要求撤床	Patients Asking to Cancel the Ward Beds	人 person	204	279	468	884
死　亡	Dead Patients	人 person	35	54	84	109
期末实有家庭病床数	Acutual Number of Family Ward Beds at End of Term	张 bed	2 177	2 632	3 124	2 911
期内家庭病床病人住床总床日数	Total Bed-days of Patients Staying in Familiy Ward Beds During the Term	天 day	777 590	1 042 073	979 701	1 135 093
期内撤床病人住床总床日数	Total Bed-days of Patients Who Have Stayed in Ward Beds Asking to Cancel Ward Beds During the Term	天 day	610 522	589 302	599 794	691 137
期内撤床病人诊疗总人次数	Total person-times of Patients Who Have Taken Medical Care Asking to Cancel Ward Beds During the Term	人次 person-times	90 942	100 068	70 157	92 459

主要统计指标解释

卫生机构

卫生机构是指从卫生行政部门取得《医疗机构执业许可证》,或从民政、工商行政、机构编制管理部门取得法人单位登记证书,为社会提供医疗保健、疾病控制、卫生监督服务或从事医学研究、医学教育等卫生单位和卫生社会团体。

医疗机构

医疗机构是指根据《医疗机构管理条例》的规定,经登记取得《医疗机构执业许可证》的机构。包括医院、社区卫生服务中心(站)、卫生院、门诊部、诊疗所、医务室、村卫生室、妇幼保健院(所、站)、专科疾病防治院(所、站)、急救中心、临床检验中心。

医 院

医院指设有固定床位,能收容病人住院并能为病人提供医疗、护理服务的医疗机构,包括县及县以上医院、农村乡卫生院和其他医院三部分。县及县以上医院按业务性质不同分为综合医院和专科医院。

卫生技术人员

卫生技术人员指从事卫生技术工作并在卫生事业机构领取劳动报酬的专业人员。包括中医师、西医师、中西医结合高级医师、护师、中药师、西药师、检验师、其他技师、中医士、西医士、护士、助产士、中药剂士、西药剂士、检验士、其他技士、其他中医、护理员、中药剂员、西药剂员、检验员、其他初级卫生技术人员。

医 生

医生指在医疗、预防保健机构工作且取得《执业医师证书》的执业医师和执业助理医师。

EXPLANATORY NOTES TO MAJOR STATISTICAL INDICATORS

Health Care Institutions

Health Care Institution refers to medical institutions and corporations providing health care, disease control and medical supervision service or engaged in medical research and medical education, which obtain Medical Institution Practice License from Medical Administration or Corporative Registration Certificate from Civil Administration, Commercial Administration or Organizational Management Administration.

Medical Organizations

Medical Institution refers to institutions which register Medical Institution Practice License according to Medical Institution Management Regulation, including hospitals, community medical service centers, medical house, clinics, dispensaries, medicine rooms, village medicine rooms, hospitals for maternity and kids care, special disease cure hospitals, first-aid center, clinical inspection centers.

Hospitals

Hospitals refer to medical institutions with permanent hospital beds, which are able to take in patients and provide them with medical and nursing services. Hospitals are classified into three categories: hospitals at or above the county level, hospitals of rural townships, and other hospitals. Hospitals at or above county level are divided into comprehensive and specialized hospitals.

Medical Professionals

Medical Professionals refers to those professionals engaged in medical work and receive salaries from medical institutions, including doctors of Chinese and Western medicine, senior doctors of integrated Chinese-Western medicine, head nurses, pharmacists of Chinese and Western medicine, laboratory specialists , other specialists, junior doctors of Chinese and Western medicine, nurses, midwives, druggists of Chinese and Western medicine, laboratory technicians, other technicians, other practitioners of Chinese medicine, nursing attendants, pharmacological workers of Chinese and Western medicine, laboratory workers and other primary medical personnel.

Doctors

Doctors refer to certified physicians and certified assistant physicians with certifications working in medical and health care and prevention agencies.

第十八篇

CHAPTER 18

法律、社会治安及其他

LAWS, PUBLIC ORDER AND OTHERS

表18-1 主要年份律师、公证及调解工作基本情况
Lawyers, Notaries and Mediations in Main Years

指 标 Indicators		单位 Unit	2010	2014	2015
律师事务所	**Law and Lawyers' Offices**	**个 unit**	**214**	**229**	**233**
合伙所	Partner Offices	个 unit	172	181	185
个人所	Individual Offices	个 unit	42	48	48
律师工作人员	**Lawyer Staff**	**人 person**	**2 958**	**4 136**	**4 456**
#专职律师	Full-time Lawyers	人 person	2 842	3 989	4 306
兼职律师	Part-time Lawyers	人 person	116	147	150
律师办理各类法律事务	**All Kinds of Legal Affairs Handled by Lawyers**				
担任法律顾问	Legal Advisers	家 unit	9 170	9 258	9 300
刑事诉讼辩护及代理	Litigation Defense and Legal Representation in Criminal Cases	件 unit	2 392	5 940	5 556
民事案件诉讼代理	Legal Representation in Civil Cases	件 unit	6 152	23 977	24 058
行政案件诉讼代理	Legal Representation in Administrative Cases	件 unit	98	389	393
非诉讼法律事务	Non-Litigation Legal Affairs	件 unit	5 741	15 621	19 424
法律援助工作	**Legal Aid Work**				
办理法律援助案件数	Number of Legal Aid Work Transaction	件 unit		4 314	5 327
刑事案件法律援助	Number of Criminal Case Legal Aid Work	件 unit		1 686	1 291
民事案件法律援助	Number of Civil Case Legal Aid Work	件 unit		2 628	4 036
公证工作	**Notarization**				
公证处	Notary Offices	个 unit	1	1	1
公证人员	Notarization	人 person	40	52	63
#公证员	Notaries	人 person	26	37	37
办理各类公证文件	All Kinds of Notarial Documents Conducted	件 unit	27 535	45 240	51 084
国内公证	Notarization for Domestic Affairs	件 unit	13 205	19 835	22 464
涉外公证	Notarization Concerning Foreign Affairs	件 unit	13 447	24 389	27 774
涉港澳台公证	Notarization Concerning Affairs in Macao, Hong Kong and TaiWan	件 unit	883	1 016	846
人民调解工作	**Mediation Work**				
专职司法助理员	Full-time Judicial Assistants	人 person	124	152	152
人民调解委员会	People's Mediation Commission	个 person	1 142	1 201	1 313
调解员	Mediators	人 person	5 386	5 417	5 417
调解民间纠纷	Mediation for Disputes among the People	件 unit	41 622	59 574	82 831

表 18-2 道路交通事故
Road Traffic Accidents

指　标	Indicators	单 位 Unit	2013	2014	2015
次　数	Number of Traffic Accidents	起 in number	17 952	15 406	13 970
死亡人数	Death Toll	人 person	252	286	344
伤残人数	Number of Wounded and Disabled	人 person	18 559	15 647	14 175

表 18-3 火灾事故
Fire Accidents

指　标	Indicators	单 位 Unit	2010	2014	2015
次　数	Number	起 in number	1 274	1 051	857
#纵　火	Arson	起 in number	19	19	18
电　气	Electric	起 in number	500	406	356
违章操作	False Operations	起 in number	59	34	14
吸　烟	Cigarette Smoking	起 in number	38	43	25
生活用火不慎	Careless Use of Fire in Daily Life	起 in number	218	164	97
玩　火	Playing with Fire	起 in number	33	19	18
自　燃	Spontaneous Ignition	起 in number	8	18	11
死亡人数	Death Toll	人 person	8	7	9
伤残人数	Number of Wounded and Disabled	人 person	6	15	5
损失折款	Amount Converted from the Losses	万元 10 000 yuan	1 083	2 058	6 441

表 18-4 社会治安
Public Order

指　标	Indicators	单 位 Unit	2010	2014	2015
刑事案件立案数	Number of Registered Criminal Cases	件 piece	23 517	23 968	29 600
行政(治安)案件查处	Investigation and Prosecution of Administrative (Public Order) Cases	件 piece	622 580	1 810 596	1 878 647
治安案件查处数	Number of Investigation and Prosecution of Public Order Cases	件 piece	95 669	140 994	157 772

表 18-5 档案管理
Archives Management

指 标	Indicators	单 位 Unit	2010	2014	2015
机构数	**Number of Institutions**	**个 Unit**	**1**	**1**	**1**
档案局(馆)	Archives Bureaus (Chanceries)	个 unit	1	1	1
从业人员	**Employees**	**人 person**	**93**	**83**	**84**
专 职	Full-time Employees	人 person	93	83	84
馆藏档案	**Collected Files**				
全 宗	Whole File	个 unit	359	362	362
案 卷	Rolls	万卷 10 000 rolls	235	272	275
录音、录像、影片档案	Archives of Records, Videos and Films	万盘 10 000 discs	0.16	0.17	0.17
照片档案	Photo Archives	万张 10 000 pieces	12.91	19.00	20.00
底 图	Base Maps	万张 10 000 pieces	0.21	0.21	0.21
电子档案	**Electric Archives**				
磁 盘	Discs	万盘 10 000 discs	0.03	0.03	0.03
光 盘	Compact Discs	万盘 10 000 discs	0.43	0.76	0.77
微缩胶片	**Microfiches**				
平 片	Plain Films	万张 10 000 Pieces	0.20	0.20	0.20
卷 片	Coiled Films	万米 10 000 meters	12.93	13.08	13.08
档案利用情况	**Utilization of Archives**				
利用卷次	Number of Roll-times Utilized	万卷次 10 000 roll-times	6.89	4.71	6.18
利用人次	Number of Person-times Utilized	万人次 10 000 Person-times	5.71	6.71	7.27
综合档案开放利用情况	**Open and Utilization of Comprehensive Archives**				
建国前案卷	Rolls Archived Before Liberation	卷 roll	425	2 951	2 951
建国后案卷	Rolls Archived After Liberation	万卷 10 000 rolls	5.88	6.19	6.18
建筑面积	**Floor Space**	**平方米 sq · m**	**17 524**	**17 524**	**17 524**
#库 房	Storeroom	平方米 sq · m	8 200	8 200	8 200

表 18-6　信访情况
Complaint Letters and Visits

指　标	Indicators	单位 Unit	2010	2014	2015
信访办受理人民来信、来访	**People's Letters and Visits Handled by Offices of Complaint Letters and Visits**	**件(批) piece (batch)**	**27 741**	**25 180**	**20 323**
来信数	Number of People's Letters	件(批) piece (batch)	12 453	8 810	6 390
电子邮件	E-mails	件(批) piece (batch)	9 452	9 139	7 604
来访数	Number of Visits	件(批) piece (batch)	1 893	6 306	5 445
来电数	Number of Calls	件(批) piece (batch)	3 943	925	884
进京非正常上访人次数	Number of Person-times Visiting Beijing in Secret	人次 person-times		604	240
到市政府集体上访批次	Number of Patch-times Visiting Municipal Government	批次 batch-times	145	174	201
到市政府集体上访人次数	Number of Person-times with Three and More Persons Visiting Municipal Government	人次 person-times	2 947	4 752	2 792

表18-7　法院收、结案情况
Cases Accepted and Ended by Courts

指　标	Indicators	单位 Unit	2010	2014	2015
法院收案数	Number of Cases Accepted by Courts	件 piece	76 028	103 436	110 335
#刑　事	Criminal	件 piece	3 406	6 059	5 651
民　事	Civil	件 piece	52 356	69 185	77 524
#经　济	Economic	件 piece	11 091	21 342	26 368
婚姻家庭类	Marriage and Family	件 piece	6 746	5 753	6 368
行　政	Administrative	件 piece	381	521	830
法院结案数	Number of Cases Ended by Courts	件 piece	75 899	102 917	108 436
法院未结案数	Number of Cases Not Ended by Courts	件 piece	8 556	8 801	10 700
同期结案率	Corresponding Claim Settlement Rate	%		92.1	97.7
均衡结案度	Balanced Claim Settlement Rate	%		4.9	4.5
法院上诉率	Rate of Appeals by Courts	%	23.4	16.9	18.6
法院实际执行率	Rate of Actual Executions by Courts	%	82.5	73.7	54.6
法院审限内结案率	Rate of Cases Ended by Courts Within Time Limit	%	98.3	99.5	99.6

表 18-8 外事活动情况
Activities in Foreign Affairs

指　标	Indicators	2014		2015	
		批　数（批）Delegations (in number)	人　数（人）Visitors (person)	批　数（批）Delegations (in number)	人　数（人）Visitors (person)
接待外国人来访总计	**Foreigners Received**	**218**	**1 421**	**294**	**2 709**
# 副总理以上国宾团	Deputy Prime Ministers and Above	3	20	2	30
部长级（含副部长）团	Ministers (Including Deputy Ministers)	7	88	9	92
其他政界人士团	Persons of Other Political/Government Circles	46	435	63	582
经贸界团	Businessmen	101	486	106	546
新闻界团	Newsreporters	6	33	5	38
其他团	Others	55	359	81	1 256
邀请外国人来访总计	**Foreigners Invited**	**10 765**	**12 205**	**10 052**	**11 614**
按签证性质分	By Type of Visa				
多次签证	Multi-Entry	2 156	2 192	1 736	1 747
一次性签证	Single-Entry	2 977	3 295	2 495	2 817
按国别（地区）分	By Country/Region				
# 美　国	United States of America	1 166	1 417	1 138	1 368
德　国	Germany	947	1 073	703	795
日　本	Japan	1 428	1 529	1 412	1 516
审批因公出国访问总计	**Approved Overseas Visits on State Missions**	**943**	**2 442**	**1 057**	**3 103**
按出国性质分	By Purpose				
经　贸	Business	832	2 048	894	2 543
非经贸	Non-Business	111	394	163	560
按出访国家（地区）分	By Country/Region				
# 美　国	United States of America	234	509	229	487
日　本	Japan	30	74	50	186
中国香港	Hong Kong, China	80	189	100	251

表18-9 主要年份人大情况
Statistics of Deputies to the People's Congress in Main Years

指标	Indicators	单位 Unit	2005	2010	2014	2015
全国人大代表人数	Number of Deputies to the National People's Congress	人 person	1			
全国人大代表提出议案	Proposals Suggested by Deputies to NPC	人 piece	5			
市人大代表人数	Number of Deputies to the Municipal People's Congress	人 person	80	118	117	117
#女 性	Female	人 person	19	37	47	48
市人大常委人数	Number of Standing Committee Members in MPC	人 person	4	6	5	4
市人大代表提出议案	Proposals Suggested by Deputies to MPC	件 piece	4	8	5	5
新区人大代表人数	Number of Deputies to PNA People's Congress	人 person	436	443	440	439
#女 性	Female	人 person	158	136	139	139
新区人大常委人数	Number of Standing Committee Members in PPC	人 person	28	34	30	33
#女 性	Female	人 person	4	11	8	8
新区人大代表提出议案	Proposals Suggested by Deputies to PPC	件 piece	9	4	2	3

表18-10 主要年份政协情况
Statistics of Political Consultative Conference Affairs in Main Years

指标	Indicators	单位 Unit	2005	2010	2014	2015
全国政协委员人数	National Political Consultative Conference Commissioners	人 person	7	10	17	17
市政协委员人数	Municipal Political Consultative Conference Commissioners	人 person	58	66	105	105
#女 性	Female	人 person	6	8	25	25
新区政协委员人数	PNA Political Consultative Conference Commissioners	人 person	379	645	536	537
#女 性	Female	人 person	84	161	148	149
新区政协常委人数	Standing Commissioners of PNA Political Consultative Conference	人 person	55	93	83	80
#女 性	Female	人 person	8	13	16	15
新区政协委员提案	Proposals Submitted by PNA Political Consultative Conference Commissioners	件 piece	205	528	265	287
#被采纳提案	Proposals Accepted	件 piece	165	467	152	185

注："全国政协委员人数"和"市政协委员人数"均指在浦东工作的政协委员人数。
Note: Both the item of "National Political Consultative Conference Commissioners" and that of "Municipal Political Consultative Conference Commissioners" refer to those who work in Pudong New Area.

表 18-11 主要年份精神文明建设情况
Construction of Role Models in Main Years

单位:个 (unit)

指 标	Indicators	2005	2010	2014	2015
市级文明社区	Model Communities at Municipal Level	6	12	12	14
市级文明镇	Model Towns at Municipal Level	6	16	16	19
文明小区	Model Quarters	393	908	874	874
#市 级	Municipal-level	208	414	340	340
文明村	Model Villages	101	254	206	206
#市 级	Municipal-level	53	112	93	93
文明开发园区	Model Development Parks	6	11	14	14
文明大厦	Model Mansions	22	45	48	48
文明单位	PNA Model Institutions	484	1 081	1 025	1 025
#市 级	Municipal-level	113	245	305	305
军民共建先进集体(对)	Model Collectives of Army-civilian (pair)	76	97		
#市 级	Municipal-level	24	22		
五好文明家庭(户)	Model Families (household)	203	241	580	
"三八"红旗手(人)	Female Models (person)	306	192	40	1
#国 家	State Level		1		1
市 级	Municipal-level	32	41	40	
"三八"红旗集体	Female Model Groups	99	88	11	1
#国 家	State Level		3		1
市 级	Municipal-level	11	10	11	
文明班组	Model Crews	338	479	483	
#市 级	Municipal-level	12			
区文明岗位	PNA-level Model Posts	202	227	229	
市级文明岗	Municipal Model Posts				

注：表列各项均为每两年评选一次。
Note: All the items in the listed table are choosen through public appraisal every two years.

主要统计指标解释

律　师

指依法取得律师执业证书，担任法律顾问，民事（刑事、行政）案件代理人、刑事案件辩护人、办理非诉讼业务，解答法律询问，代写法律事务文书等，为社会提供法律服务的人员。

公证人员

指在国家机关依法办理公证事务的司法人员。包括公证员、助理公证员和在公证处工作的其他人员。

公证文书

指公证处根据当事人申请，依照事实和法律，按照法定程序制作的，具有法律效力的司法证明文书。根据公证书用途和使用地，公证书分为国内公证书、国内经济公证书、涉外民事公证书、涉外经济公证书四类。

调解民间纠纷

指调解委员会按照法律规定，根据自愿原则，用说服教育的方法调解民间发生的有关民事权利和义务争执的件数，包括调解成功数和调解未成功数。该指标主要反映人民调解委员会的工作量。

立　案

指人民检察院对受理的报案、控告、举报或自首及自行发现的犯罪线索、犯罪嫌疑人进行初步调查后，认为存在职务犯罪事实和应追究刑事责任，并决定作为刑事案件进行侦查的诉讼活动，是追究犯罪的开始。该指标主要反映人民检察院依法将职务犯罪线索作为刑事案件进行侦查的诉讼活动。

EXPLANATORY NOTES TO MAJOR STATISTICAL INDICATORS

Lawyers

Lawyers are certified legal workers according to law, and who are employed by legal counseling firms to act as legal advisers, agents in criminal or civil lawsuits, or defenders in criminal lawsuits, or to handle non-litigious legal affairs, to advise on matters of law or to write legal papers for others, and provide service to the public.

Notary Personnel

Notary Personnel are judicial workers of the state notary organs handling notarization work according to law. They include notaries, assistant notaries, and other people working in notary firms.

Notary Documents

Notary Documents refer to the judicatory notary documents drawn up by the request of the party and are in accordance with facts and laws and following certain legal proceedings. According to usage and locality, the notary documents are divided into following 4 types: domestic notary documents, domestic economic notary documents, foreign-related civil notary documents and foreign-related economic notary documents.

Mediation of Civil Disputes

Mediation of Civil Disputes refers to number of cases made by mediation committees in mediating in civil disputes concerning civil rights and duties through persuasion and education in accordance with the provisions of law on a voluntary basis, so as to solve disputes by helping the parties involved come to an agreement and understanding, including those unsuccessful ones. This indicator reflects the workload of the mediation committees.

Acceptance of Case

Acceptance of Case refers to the decision made by the people's procuratorate office on reported cases, prosecution, impeachment, surrender, self-found criminal clues or suspects after initial investigation to confirm the act of crime and to start legal proceedings of the case as criminal case.

第十九篇

CHAPTER 19

城市建设和环境保护

URBAN CONSTRUCTIONS AND ENVIRONMENTAL PROTECTION

表 19-1　八层以上房屋分布(至 2015 年累计)
Distribution of 8-storey and Above Buildings (Total by the End of 2015)

单位:万平方米　　　　(10 000 sq · m)

指　标 Indicators		总　计 Total	8～10 层 8～10 Storeys	11～15 层 11～15 Storeys	16～19 层 16～19 Storeys	20～29 层 20～29 Storeys	30 层及以上 30 Storeys and Above
幢	In number	9 448	1 124	4 900	2 185	949	290
面　积	Area	9 233	869	3 434	2 072	1 678	1 180

表 19-2　市政工程设施
Public Utilities

指　标　Indicators		单　位　Unit	2005	2010	2014	2015
城市道路长度	Length of Urban Roads	公里 km	960	1 224	1 274	1 602
城市道路面积	Area of Urban Roads	万平方米 10 000 sq · m	1 704	2 463	2 773	2 962
城市桥梁	Urban Bridges	座 unit	169	370	649	785
雨水、污水泵站	Pump Stations for Rain/Sewage	座 unit	148	176	171	277
雨水、污水管长度	Length of Rain/Sewage Pipe	公里 km	1 858	2 805	3 150	5 825
公路里程	Length of Rural Highways	公里 km	905	1 937	2 278	2 342
公路面积	Area of Rural Highways	万平方米 10 000 sq · m	1 360	3 173	3 316	3 899
公路桥梁	Highway Bridges	座 unit	635	1 533	1 979	2 075

注：2007 年起道路长度和道路面积统计口径改变。
Note：The statistical approach has changed for the length and coverage of roads since 2007.

表19-3 环境保护
Environmental Protection

指 标	Indicators	单 位 Unit	2005	2010	2014	2015
工业固体废物产生量	Amount of Industrial Solid Waste	万吨/年 10 000 tons/year	250	268	239	244
工业固体废物综合利用量	Comprehensive Utilization of Industrial Solid Waste	万吨 /年 10 000 tons/year	242	243	227	220
工业废水排放量	Discharge of Industrial Waste Water	万吨/年 10 000 tons/year	7 103	6 679	5 939	5 909
工业废气排放总量	Total Emission of Industrial Waste Gases	亿标立方米/年 100 million cu · m/year	1 112	1 696	1 987	2 104
二氧化硫日平均值	Daily Average Amount of Sulphur Dioxide	毫克/立方米 milligram / cu · m	0.056	0.035	0.019	0.018
二氧化氮日平均值	Daily Average Amount of Nitrogen Dioxide	毫克/立方米 milligram / cu · m	0.046	0.041	0.037	0.039
可吸入颗粒物日平均值	Daily Average Amount of Inhalable Particles	毫克/立方米 milligram / cu · m	0.081	0.071	0.064	0.061
PM2.5 日平均值	Daily Average Amount of PM2.5	毫克/立方米 milligram / cu · m			0.048	0.050
区域环境噪声平均值	Average Value of Regional Ambient Noise	分贝 decibel	57.4	54.8	56.3	55.3
空气质量优良率	Rate of Fine Air Quality	%	89.3	92.6	76.7	73.6
污水纳管率	Rate of Sewage Piping	%	70.4	81.9	89.0	87.2

表19-4　城市环境卫生
Urban Environmental Sanitation

指　标 Indicators		单　位 Unit	2005	2010	2014	2015
清运垃圾	**Garbage Disposal**	**万吨 10 000 tons**	**104.22**	**169.86**	**215.56**	**245.51**
生活垃圾	Domestic Waste	万吨 10 000 tons	103.10	168.98	145.56	210.62
建筑垃圾	Construction Refuse	万吨 10 000 tons	1.12	0.88	70.00	34.89
清运粪便	**Night Soil Disposal**	**万吨 10 000 tons**	**31.45**	**35.31**	**24.06**	**23.86**
环境卫生设施	**Facilities of Environmental Sanitation**					
公共厕所	Public Restrooms	所 unit	219	900	1 016	896
垃圾箱	Garbage Bins/Cans	只 unit	9 216	4 013	3 837	3 797
废物箱	Litterbins	只 unit	8 317	19 384	28 837	22 083
倒粪站	Manure-Dumping Stations	个 unit	89	102	98	101
化粪池	Septic Tanks	个 unit	4 711	5 855	5 834	5 653
垃圾处理	**Trash Disposal**					
垃圾焚烧	Trash Burning	万吨 10 000 tons	44.49	44.40	88.65	125.27
焚烧垃圾发电量	Power Output by Trash Burning	万千瓦·时 10 000 kw·h	10 841	12 619	27 662	42 777
环卫机械总数	**Machineries Used in Environmental Sanitation**	**辆 set**	**598**	**1 191**	**1 203**	**1 222**

注：1. 2009 年起，垃圾箱统计口径作调整。
2. 2013 年起，清运垃圾的分类方法有调整，含装修垃圾、集贸垃圾、地沟油等。

Note：1. The statistical approach for garbage bins has been readjusted since 2009.
2. Since 2013, the diversification of garbage disposal has changed, including decoration garbage, trading garbage, and illegal cooking oil.

表 19-5 园林绿化
Parks,Gardens and Green Space

指标	Indicators	单位 Unit	2005	2010	2014	2015
园林绿地面积	Total Area of Parks, Gardens and Green Space	万平方米 10 000 sq·m	8 439.52	12 019.49	13 456.00	13 831.00
#公共绿地	Public Green Space	万平方米 10 000 sq·m	4 154.71	5 565.51	6 242.00	6 412.00
单位附属绿地	Green Space of Organizations	万平方米 10 000 sq·m	1 508.15	2 479.00	2 828.00	2 928.00
居住区绿地	Residential Green Space	万平方米 10 000 sq·m	1 139.81	2 834.12	3 231.00	3 336.00
建成区绿化覆盖面积	Green Coverage of Built Area	万平方米 10 000 sq·m	6 426.88	12 283.46	14 118.00	14 580.00
建成区绿化覆盖率	Coverage Rate of Urban Green Areas (%) in PNA	%	37.8	36.1	36.2	36.0
新辟、扩大各类绿地	New and Extended Green Space	万平方米 10 000 sq·m	199.50	516.76	290.00	375.00
#公共绿地	Public Green Space	万平方米 10 000 sq·m	78.97	294.71	90.00	170.00
公园个数	Parks	个 unit	17	20	26	31
#免费公园	Ticket-free Parks	个 unit	15	17	22	28
公园面积	Area of Parks	万平方米 10 000 sq·m	214.25	486.27	563.91	588.90
#免费公园	Ticket-free Parks	万平方米 10 000 sq·m	68.88	78.31	155.95	180.94
人均公共绿地	Public Green Space Per Capita	平方米/人 sq·m/person	24.42	22.71	24.00	24.10
行道树年末累计数	Accumulated Trees on Streets at Year-end	万株 10 000 pcs	36.79	23.20	36.25	41.30

表19-6 水、电、煤气供应
Supply of Tap Water, Electricity and Gas

指 标 Indicators		单 位 Unit	2005	2010	2014	2015
自来水	**Tap Water**					
水厂生产能力	Capacity of Tap Water Plants	万立方米/日 10 000 cu. m/day	171.20	241.00	228.00	228.00
供水管道总长度	Length of Water Supply Pipes	公里 km	3 100	8 471	13 250	11 059
全年售水总量	Total Annual Volume of Water Sold	万立方米 10 000 cu·m	41 926	60 088	60 860	60 908
#工业用水	Industrial Water	万立方米 10 000 cu·m	10 526	14 541	11 473	11 130
生活用水	Domestic Water	万立方米 10 000 cu·m	21 749	21 876	22 587	23 225
每日平均售水量	Average Daily Tap Water Consumption	万立方米 10 000 cu·m	115	165	167	167
电 力	**Electricity**					
用电最高日负荷	Maximum Daily Load of Electricity	万千瓦 10 000 kw	285.70	553.00	657.70	709.00
全年售电量	Annual Electricity Sold	亿千瓦·时 100 million kwh	128.19	229.71	261.01	276.42
各类用电户数	Various Electricity Users	万户 10 000 households	117.91	190.03	215.73	221.99
天然气	**Natural Gas**					
管线长度	Length of Gas Pipes	公里 km	3 574	6 463	6 701	6 862
全年销售量	Annual Volume of Gas Sold	万立方米 10 000 cu·m	44 300	64 200	74 872	79 848
#生活用气	Domestic Use	万立方米 10 000 cu·m	18 700	23 926	32 058	34 635
家庭用天然气户数	Natural Gas-using Households	万户 10 000 households	75.50	121.25	148.78	155.85
液化石油气	**Liquified Petroleum Gas (LPG)**					
全年销售量	Annual Volume of Gas Sold	吨 ton	52 000	66 700	11 830	76 942
#生活用气	Domestic Use	吨 ton	50 000	54 000	57 300	53 846
家庭用液化气户数	LPG-using Households	万户 10 000 households	45.90	69.11	80.89	71.12

表 19-7 交通运输
Transportation

指 标	Indicators	单 位 Unit	2005	2010	2014	2015
公共交通	**Public Transport**					
年末实有公交线路条数	Routes of Public Transport at year-end	条 route	108	232	331	346
年末运营线路长度	Length of Public Transport Routes at year-end	公里 km	2 125	4 770	5 242	5 187
年末运营公共车辆	Buses in Operation at year-end	辆 vehicle	2 041	3 450	3 877	3 926
全年运客量	Annual Passengers Carried	万人次 10 000 person-times	34 894	60 317	59 736	55 158
郊区行政村通达率	Rate of Village Access in Rural Area	%			100	100
公交线网密度	Density of Bus Net	公里/平方公里			1.5	1.3
隧道大桥	**Tunnels and Bridges**					
越江隧道条数	Tunnels across the Huangpu River	条 route	6	12	12	12
越江大桥座数	Bridges across the Huangpu River	座 in number	4	4	4	4
越江桥隧道车道数	Number of Lanes on Tunnels and Bridges across the Huangpu River	条 lane	54	84	84	84
轨 道	**City Railways**					
运营条数	Number of Railways in Operation	条 route		7	13	13
运营线路里程	Length of Routes in Operation	公里 km		109	186	186
站点数	Number of City Railway Stations	个 Unit		73	97	97
港 口	**Ports**					
港口货物吞吐量	Volume of Cargo Handled at Ports	万吨 10 000 tons		22 470	29 918	30 162
外高桥港区货物吞吐量	Volume of Cargo Handled at Waigaoqiao Port	万吨 10 000 tons		13 570	15 762	16 387
洋山港货物吞吐量	Volume of Cargo Handled at Yangshan Port	万吨 10 000 tons		8 900	14 156	13 775
集装箱吞吐量	Volume of Containers Handled	万标箱 10 000 TEUs		2 510	3 237	3 357
外高桥港区集装箱吞吐量	Volume of Containers Handled at Waigaoqiao Port	万标箱 10 000 TEUs		1 499	1 716	1 816
洋山港集装箱吞吐量	Volume of Containers Handled at Yangshan Port	万标箱 10 000 TEUs		1 011	1 520	1 541
民用航空	**Civil Aviation**					
浦东机场旅客吞吐量	Passenger Capacity at Pudong International Airport	万人次 10 000 person-times	2 358	4 041	5 169	6 009
浦东机场货邮吞吐量	Volume of Cargo and Post Handled at Pudong International Airport	万吨 10 000 tons	185	322	318	327

表19-8 邮电通信设施和邮电业务量

Post and Telecommunications Facilities and the Volume of Business

指 标	Indicators	单 位 Unit	2005	2010	2014	2015
邮政设施	**Postal Facilities**					
邮电局、所	Post Offices	个 unit	93	136	102	102
信筒、信箱	Mailboxes	处 unit	624	641	632	639
报刊发行站	Newpaper and Magazine Distributors	个 unit	728	392	1 309	1 329
邮路单程长度	Length of Single-Way Post	公里 km	3 282	822	684	1 268
农村投递路线总长度	Total Length of Postal Routes	公里 km	3 691	6 688	5 464	6 729
邮运汽车	Postal Vehicle	辆 vehicle	108	144	267	267
邮政业务总量	**Business Value of Postal Service**					
邮政业务收入	Postal Service Income	万元 10 000 yuan	35 300	43 990	64 230	74 391
函 件	Mails	万件 10 000 pieces	5 409	15 112	26 480	24 036
包 件	Parcels	万件 10 000 pieces	94	93	476	331
汇 票	Drafts	万张 10 000 pieces	98	162	103	84
订销报刊累计数	Accumulated Circulation of Newspapers and Magazines	万份 10 000 pieces	11 750	7 326	17 970	17 527
特快专递	Special Express	万份 10 000 pieces	281	618	47	15
集邮业务	Stamp-collecting Business	万枚 10 000 pieces	354	663	938	1 027
邮政储蓄年末收储余额	Postal Savings Balance at Year-end	万元 10 000 yuan	235 230	1 008 020	1 554 994	1 524 321
电讯设施、用户及业务收入	**Telecommunication Facilities, Subscribers and Operating Income**					
本地电话局用交换机容量	Urban Switchboard Capacity	万门 10 000 units	146	218	205	204
本地电话用户数	Local Telephone Users	万户 10 000 households	118	161	136	112
电信宽带用户数	Subscribers of Telecommunication Broad-Band	门 unit	281 408	806 341	1 071 202	1 062 342
电信业务收入	Telecommunication Income	万元 10 000 yuan	119 250	353 092	409 745	381 325
网络互动电视(IPTV)	Internet Interactive TV Network	线 Line		263 280	332 516	386 213
“我的 e 家”用户	“My e-Home” Subscribers	户 Household		625 799	329 454	198 345
光纤入户(FTTH)	Fiber To The Home(FTTH)	户 Household		53 731	768 383	876 573

注：电信业务收入，不包括移动通信和中国联通以及与其结算的业务量。报刊发行站、邮路单程长度、订销报刊不包括邮政投递的业务量。

Note: The business value of China Mobile and China Unicom as well as the related business is not included in the Telecommunication Income. Fields of newspaper distribution stations, one-way length of postal routes, subscrions and unsubscriptions and unsubscriptions of newspapers and magazines do not include the postal delivery volume.

表 19-9 房屋拆迁情况
Housing Demolition and Resettlement

指 标	Indicators	单 位 Unit	2005	2010	2014	2015
房屋完成拆迁总户数	**Total Households Domolished and Resettled**	**户 household**	**23 294**	**3 725**	**2 240**	**3 457**
重大项目拆迁	Demolished Because of Key Investment Projects	户 household	18 288	1 175	126	95
企事业单位	Enterprises and Institutions	户 household	351	77	8	
公 房	Public Housing	户 household	4 487			
私 房	Private Housing	户 household	13 361	1 085	118	95
个体工商	Individuals Engaged in Industry and Commerce	户 household	89	13		
旧城改造拆迁	Demolished Because of Renovation of Old Towns	户 household	211		50	38
其 他	Others	户 household	4 795	2 550	2 064	3 324
完成拆迁总面积	**Tota Area of Demolition Finished**	**万平方米 10 000 sq · m**	**474.63**	**139.78**	**36.46**	**50.68**
重大项目拆迁	Demolished Because of Key Investment Projects	万平方米 10 000 sq · m	363.14	26.79	2.61	1.77
企事业单位	Enterprises and Institutions	万平方米 10 000 sq · m	59.67	5.06	0.94	
公 房	Public Housing	万平方米 10 000 sq · m	22.34			
私 房	Private Housing	万平方米 10 000 sq · m	277.46	18.83	1.67	1.77
个体工商	Individuals Engaged in Industry and Commerce	万平方米 10 000 sq · m	3.67	2.90		
旧城改造拆迁	Demolition Because of Renovation of Old Towns	万平方米 10 000 sq · m	5.83		0.45	0.52
# 企事业单位	Enterprises and Institutions	万平方米 10 000 sq · m	3.81			
其 他	Others	万平方米 10 000 sq · m	105.66	112.99	33.40	48.39

主要统计指标解释

城市基础设施

城市基础设施包括电力建设、交通运输、邮电通信、市内公共交通、自来水、煤气、市政建设、园林绿化、环境卫生等。

道路长度

道路长度指除土路外，路面经过铺装宽度在3.5米以上的道路，包括高级、次高级道路和普通道路。

城市园林绿地面积

指报告期末用作园林和绿化的各种绿地面积。包括公共绿地、居住区绿地、单位附属绿地、防护绿地、生产绿地、道路绿地和风景林地面积。

不包括：

(1)屋顶绿化、垂直绿化、阳台绿化和室内绿化。

(2)以物质生产为主的林地、耕地、牧草地、果园和竹园等。

(3) 城市总体规划中不列入绿地的水域。

公共绿地

公共绿地指向公众开放的市级、区级、居住区级各类公园、街旁游园，包括其范围内的水域。其中居住区级公园应不小于1万平方米，街旁游园的宽度不小于8米，面积不小于400平方米。

供水管道长度

指从送水泵至用户水表之间所有管道的长度。不包括新安装尚未使用的管道。

生活用水

生活用水包括公共服务用水和居民家庭用水。公共服务用水指为城市社会公共生活服务的用水。包括行政事业单位、部队营区和公共设施服务、社会服务业、批发零售贸易业、旅馆饮食业以及其他公共服务业等单位的用水。居民家庭用水指城市范围内所有居民家庭的日常生活用水。包括城市居民、农民家庭、公共供水站用水。

工业固体废弃物产生量

指报告期内企业在生产过程中产生的固体状、半固体状和高浓度液体状废弃物的总量，包括危险废物、冶炼废渣、粉煤灰、炉渣、煤矸石、尾矿、放射性废物和其他废物等；不包括矿山开采的剥离废石和掘进废石（煤矸石和呈酸性或碱性的废石除外）。酸性或碱性废石指采掘的废石其流经水、雨淋水的pH值小于4或pH值大于10.5者。

工业固体废物综合利用量

指通过回收、加工、循环、交换等方式，从固体废物中提取或者使其转化为可以利用的资源、能源和其他原材料的固体废物量（包括当年利用往年的工业固体废物累计贮存量），如用作农业肥料、生产建筑材料、筑路等。综合利用量由原产生固体废物的单位统计。

工业废水排放量

工业废水排放量指经过企业厂区所有排放口排到企业外部的工业废水量。包括生产废水、外排的直接冷却水、超标排放的矿井地下水和与工业废水混排的厂区生活污水，不包括外排的间接冷却水（清污不分流的间接冷却水应计算在内）。

工业废水排放达标量

指报告期内废水中各项污染物指标都达到国家或地方排放标准的外排工业废水量，包括未经处理外排达标的，经废水处理设施处理后达标排放的，以及经污水处理厂处理后达标排放的。

工业废气排放量

工业废气排放量指企业厂区内燃料燃烧和生产工艺过程中产生的各种排入空气的含有污染物的气体总量，按标准状态〔273K，101 325Pa〕计算。测算公式为：

工业废气排放量 = 燃料燃烧过程中废气排放量 + 生产工艺过程中废气排放量

生活垃圾清运量

指报告期内收集和运送到垃圾处理厂（场）的生活垃圾数量。生活垃圾指城市日常生活或为城市日常生活提供服务的活动中产生的固体废物以及法律行政规定的视为城市生活垃圾的固体废物。包括：居民生活垃圾、商业垃圾、集市贸易市场垃圾、街道清扫垃圾、公共场所垃圾和机关、学校、厂矿等单位的生活垃圾。

运营公交车辆数

指年末公交企业（单位）用于运营业务的全部车辆数。以企业（单位）固定资产台帐中已投入运营的车辆数为准。

邮政业务总量

指以货币表现的邮政部门用于邮政服务的总数量。它综合反映了一定时期邮政工作的总成果,是研究邮政业务量构成和发展趋势的重要指标。它用各种邮政分类业务量,如函件件数、电报份数、订销报刊累计份数等,分别乘以相应的平均单位(不变价),加总后再加上其他业务收入求得。

局用交换机容量

指安装在电信企业用于接续本地固定电话的电话交换机容量。

住宅电话用户

指安装在居民住宅或农民家里并按照住宅电话用户登记注册和收费的电话用户。包括私人付费、单位付费和按规定免费安装的住宅电话用户。

EXPLANATORY NOTES TO MAJOR STATISTICAL INDICATORS

Urban Infrastructure Facilities

Urban Infrastructure Facilities include facilities for power generating, transportation, post and telecommunication, urban public transportation, supply of tap water and gas, development of municipal engineering, city landscaping and sanitation.

Length of Roads

Length of Roads refers to the roads with a paved surface, and with a width of more than 3 – 5 meters, including high quality, medium quality and ordinary roads.

Area of Urban Gardens and Green Areas

Area of Urban Gardens and Green Areas refers to the total area occupied for green projects at the end of the reference period, including public green land, green land in residential quarters, green land attached to institutions, protection green land, production green land, roadside green land and forest in scenic spots. It does not include the following:

(1) Greenery and plants on roofs, balconies, indoors and vertical green areas;

(2) Forest, cultivated land grassland, orchards and bamboo grooves that are for production purpose and etc.;

(3) Water areas that are not included in urban master plan as green land.

Public Green Area

Public Green Area refers to green areas open to the public such as municipal, community and neighborhood parks and roadside parks, including waters within parks. Neighborhood parks should occupy an area larger than 10,000 square meters, and the width of roadside parks should occupy an area larger than 400 square meters, with a width of more that 8 meters.

Length of Water Supply Pipelines

Length of Water Supply Pipelines refers to the total length of all the pipelines between the water pumps and the user's water meters, excluding pipelines newly installed but not used yet.

Consumption of Water for Residential Use

Consumption of Water for Residential Use refers to the water consumption of households for daily life and the water consumption of public service facilities. The latter refers to water consumption for urban public services, including the consumption of government agencies and public institutions, military barracks, public facilities, wholesale and retail outlets, restaurants, hotels, and other units providing public services. Household water consumption refers to consumption of water for daily life of all households in the boundary of cities, including households of urban residents and farmers, and public water supply stations.

Industrial Solid Wastes Produced

Industrial Solid Wastes Produced refers to total volume of solid, semi-solid and high concentration liquid residues produced by industrial enterprises from production process in a given period of time, including hazardous wastes, slag, coal ash, gangue, tailings, radioactive residues and other wastes, but excluding stones stripped or dug out in mining (gangue and acid or alkaline stones not included). A stone is acid or alkaline depending on the pH value of the water below 4 or above 10.5 when the stone is in, or soaked by, the water.

Volume of Industrial Solid Wastes Utilized in a Comprehensive Way

Volume of Industrial Solid Wastes Utilized in a Comprehensive Way refers to the volume of solid wastes from which useful materials can be extracted or which can be changed into utilizable resources, energy or other materials, including the volume of industrial solid wastes stored up in previous years and utilized in the current year, such as the solid wastes utilized as fertilizers, building materials, for making roads or for other purposes. Statistical data on utilization of industrial solid wastes are collected by solid wastes producing units.

Volume of Industrial Waste Water Discharged

Volume of Industrial Waste Water Discharged refers to the volume of industrial waste water discharged, through all outlets, to the outside of industrial enterprises, including waste water produced, direct-cooling water, underground water from mines that does not meet the standard of discharge, and the domestic sewage mixed up with industrial waste water when discharged, but excluding discharged indirect-cooling water.

Industrial Waste Water Meeting Discharge Standards

Industrial Waste Water Meeting Discharge Standards refers to volume of industrial waste water discharge which, with or without treatment, reaches national or local standards with regard to all pollutants.

Volume of Waste Industrial Gas Emission

Industrial Waste Air Emission refers to discharge into atmosphere of waste air containing pollutants generated from fuel burning and production process in enterprises within a given period of time. It is calculated at standard status (273K, 101325Pa) as:

Industrial waste air emission = emission through fuel burning + emission through production process

Consumption Wastes Transported

Consumption Wastes Transported refers to volume of consumption wastes collected and transported to disposal factories or sites. Consumption Wastes are solid wastes produced from urban households or from seryice activities for urban households , and solid wastes regarded by laws and regulations as urban consumption wastes, including those from households, commercial activities, markets cleaning of streets, public sites, offices, schools, factories, mining units and other sources.

Number of Vehicles under Operation

Number of Vehicles under Operation refers to the total number of vehicles under operation by public transport enterprises (units) at the end of the year, based on the records of operational vehicles by the enterprises (units).

Volume of Post Business

Volume of Post Business refers to the total amount of post services provided by the post department, which reflects the total achievements by the post departments during a given period of time in a comprehensive way, and is an important indicator to study the composition and development of the post business. It is arrived by first multiplying the business volume of different types, such as number of letters, telegrams and accumulated number of newspaper and journals subscribed and sold, etc. by their respective average unit price (fixed price) and then adding these products together, plus the income from other business revenues.

Capacity of Office Telephone Exchanges

Capacity of Office Telephone Exchanges refers to the capacity of telephone exchanges installed in the office of telecommunication service providers for communication between fixed telephones.

Household Telephone Subscribers

Household Telephone Subscribers refer to telephone sets installed in the dwelling units of urban or rural residents, and registered as residence subscribers for payment, including 3 types of payment for the service: private payment, public payment and free service.

第二十篇

CHAPTER 20

重点开发区和街镇

KEY DEVELOPMENT ZONES
AND SUB-DISTRICTS AND TOWNS

表 20－1 陆家嘴金融贸易区主要经济指标
Major Economic Indicators in Lujiazui Finance and Trade Zone

指 标	Indicators	单 位 Unit	2014	2015
税收总额(税务部门口径)	Total Amount of Tax Revenues (from the Tax Departments)	亿元 100 million yuan	570.77	671.92
一般公共预算收入	Local Fiscal Revenue	亿元 100 million yuan	165.23	204.60
固定资产投资额	Investment in Fixed Assets	亿元 100 million yuan	231.07	195.64
#房地产开发投资额	Investment in Real Estate	亿元 100 million yuan	200.96	179.95
#办公楼及商业营业用房	Office and Commercial Buildings	亿元 100 million yuan	84.32	103.72
房地产新开工面积	Floor Space of New Construction of Buildings	万平方米 10 000 sq·m	49.26	101.91
房地产竣工面积	Floor Space of Completed Buildings	万平方米 10 000 sq·m	20.16	27.59
外商直接投资项目	Projects of Foreign Direct Investment	个 unit	175	373
外商直接投资合同金额	Contracted Amount of Foreign Direct Investment	亿美元 USD 100 million	21.10	58.10
外商直接投资实际到位金额	Actual Paid Amount of Foreign Direct Investment	亿美元 USD 100 million	12.65	13.53
新增内资企业注册户数	Number of New Domestic Enterprises Registered	个 unit	1 983	4 396
新增内资企业注册资本	Capital of New Domestic Enterprises Registered	亿元 100 million yuan	543.34	3 356.93
金融业增加值	Added Value of Finance Industry	亿元 100 million yuan	1 288.05	1 605.98
期末金融机构数	Number of Financial Institutions at End of Term	个 unit	728	754
#外资银行法人行	Foreign Banks and Corporate Banks	个 unit	18	18
基金总公司	Head Office of Funds	个 unit	46	47
期末认定跨国公司地区总部个数	Number of Approved Regional Headquarters of Transnational Companies at End of Term	个 unit	87	90
举办展览(博览)次数	Number of Exhibitions (Fairs) Hosted	次 time	135	168
商品销售总额(限额以上)	Gross Sales of Commodities (Above Quota)	亿元 100 million yuan	12 974.02	14 288.03
社会消费品零售总额(限额以上)	Total Volume of Retail Sales for Social Consumer Goods (Above Quota)	亿元 100 million yuan	521.36	473.87
期末星级宾馆个数	Number of Star Hotels at End of Term	个 unit	34	34
主要景点接待人次	Person-times Received by Main Sight Spots	万人次 10 000 persom-times	2 046.80	2 026.10
商办楼宇数	Number of Office Buildings	幢 in number	235	235
商办楼宇建筑面积	Floor Space of Office Buildings	万平方米 10 000 sq·m	1 432.40	1 432.28
商办楼宇平均入驻率	Average Occupancy Rate of Office Buildings	%	96.8	95.5

注：地方财政收入即为原“地方税收”口径,后续相关指标口径相同。
Note: The local fiscal revenue is the former local tax approach. The relevant indicators hereinafter have the same statistical approach.

表20-2 金桥经济技术开发区主要经济指标
Major Economic Indicators in Jinqiao Economy and Technology Zone

指 标 Indicators		单 位 Unit	2014	2015
税收总额(税务部门口径)	Total Amount of Tax Revenues (from the Tax Departments)	亿元 100 million yuan	335.95	337.05
一般公共预算收入	Local Fiscal Revenue	亿元 100 million yuan	37.27	40.93
固定资产投资额	Investment in Fixed Assets	亿元 100 million yuan	60.51	64.41
#房地产开发投资额	Investment in Real Estate	亿元 100 million yuan	11.99	16.20
工业投资额	Investment in Industries	亿元 100 million yuan	42.10	41.72
房地产新开工面积	Floor Space of New Construction of Buildings	万平方米 10 000 sq·m	9.24	20.55
房地产竣工面积	Floor Space of Completed Buildings	万平方米 10 000 sq·m	13.32	43.81
外商直接投资项目	Projects of Foreign Direct Investment	个 unit	35	88
外商直接投资合同金额	Contracted Amount of Foreign Direct Investment	亿美元 USD 100 million	4.92	8.2
外商直接投资实际到位金额	Actual Paid Amount of Foreign Direct Investment	亿美元 USD 100 million	1.95	1.34
新增内资企业注册户数	Number of New Domestic Enterprises Registered	个 unit	349	446
新增内资企业注册资本	Capital of New Domestic Enterprises Registered	亿元 100 million yuan	25.84	67.89
工业总产值	Gross Value of Industrial Output	亿元 100 million yuan	2 047.94	1 825.63
#高技术产业产值	Output Value of High-tech Industries	亿元 100 million yuan	540.73	485.04
工业重点发展行业产值	Output Value of Key Industrial Sectors for Development	亿元 100 million yuan	1 730.70	1 578.83
#电子信息产品制造业	Manufacturing of Electronic and Information Products	亿元 100 million yuan	463.68	411.87
汽车制造业	Automobile Industry	亿元 100 million yuan	1 138.03	999.69
成套设备制造业	Manufacturing of Complete Equipment	亿元 100 million yuan	100.25	75.67
生物医药制造业	Manufacturing of Biological Medicine	亿元 100 million yuan	97.97	91.60
工业出口交货值	Delivery Value of Industrial Exports	亿元 100 million yuan	353.92	339.11
生产性服务业经营收入	Operating Income of Productive Services	亿元 100 million yuan	3 154.43	3 077.28
期末从业人员数	Number of Employed Persons at End of Term	万人 10 000 persoms	13.94	14.56

注：工业总产值为规模以上口径。后续相关指标口径相同。

Note: The gross value of industrial output has the approach for enterprises above certain scales. The relevant indicators hereinafter have the same statistical approach.

表20-3 南汇工业园区主要经济指标
Major Economic Indicators in Nanhui Industrial Park

指标 Indicators		单位 Unit	2014	2015
税收总额(税务部门口径)	Total Amount of Tax Revenues (from the Tax Departments)	亿元 100 million yuan	7.39	9.11
一般公共预算收入	Local Fiscal Revenue	亿元 100 million yuan	2.04	2.04
固定资产投资额	Investment in Fixed Assets	亿元 100 million yuan	17.85	13.32
#工业投资额	Investment in Industries	亿元 100 million yuan	4.97	6.54
外商直接投资项目	Projects of Foreign Direct Investment	个 unit	6	7
外商直接投资合同金额	Contracted Amount of Foreign Direct Investment	亿美元 USD 100 million	0.69	4.14
外商直接投资实际到位金额	Actual Paid Amount of Foreign Direct Investment	亿美元 USD 100 million	0.22	3.63
工业总产值	Gross Value of Industrial Output	亿元 100 million yuan	142.24	149.2
#高技术产业产值	Output Value of High-tech Industries	亿元 100 million yuan	13.72	17.59
工业重点发展行业产值	Output Value of Key Industrial Sectors for Development	亿元 100 million yuan	86.19	94.93
#电子信息产品制造	Manufacturing of Electronic and Information Products	亿元 100 million yuan	34.69	36.13
汽车制造业	Automobile Industry	亿元 100 million yuan	16.46	18.49
成套设备制造业	Manufacturing of Complete Equipment	亿元 100 million yuan	30.42	35.67
生物医药制造业	Manufacturing of Biological Medicine	亿元 100 million yuan	2.48	2.86
工业出口交货值	Delivery Value of Industrial Exports	亿元 100 million yuan	33.99	33.27
工业利润总额	Total Amount of Industrial Profits	亿元 100 million yuan	4.54	3.01

表20-4 张江高科技园区主要经济指标
Major Economic Indicators in Zhangjiang High-tech Park

指 标	Indicators	单 位 Unit	2014	2015
税收总额(税务部门口径)	Total Amount of Tax Revenues (from the Tax Departments)	亿元 100 million yuan	169.79	195.96
一般公共预算收入	Local Fiscal Revenue	亿元 100 million yuan	47.09	54.4
固定资产投资额	Investment in Fixed Assets	亿元 100 million yuan	131.37	160.19
#房地产开发投资额	Investment in Real Estate	亿元 100 million yuan	40.93	67.6
工业投资额	Investment in Industries	亿元 100 million yuan	50.32	56.45
外商直接投资项目	Projects of Foreign Direct Investment	个 unit	85	132
外商直接投资合同金额	Contracted Amount of Foreign Direct Investment	亿美元 USD 100 million	10.31	32.3
外商直接投资实际到位金额	Actual Paid Amount of Foreign Direct Investment	亿美元 USD 100 million	6.80	10.97
新增内资企业注册户数	Number of New Domestic Enterprises Registered	个 unit	991	1 845
新增内资企业注册资本	Capital of New Domestic Enterprises Registered	亿元 100 million yuan	56.26	223.63
工业总产值	Gross Value of Industrial Output	亿元 100 million yuan	758.37	848.82
#高技术产业产值	Output Value of High-tech Industries	亿元 100 million yuan	603.31	648.33
工业重点发展行业产值	Output Value of Key Industrial Sectors for Development	亿元 100 million yuan	714.52	799.39
#电子信息产品制造业	Manufacturing of Electronic and Information Products	亿元 100 million yuan	392.12	419.54
汽车制造业	Automobile Industry	亿元 100 million yuan	72.22	116.56
生物医药制造业	Manufacturing of Biological Medicine	亿元 100 million yuan	207.76	216.21
工业出口交货值	Delivery Value of Industrial Exports	亿元 100 million yuan	266.04	275.33
信息传输、计算机服务和软件业营业收入	Operating Income of Information Transmission, Computer Services and Software Industry	亿元 100 million yuan	762.21	842.53
文化产业营业收入	Operating Income of Cultural Industry	亿元 100 million yuan	988.79	1 090.51
知识产权授权数	Number of Authorizations for Intellectual Property	件 item	5 247	5 640
#专利授权数	Number of Patent Authorizations	件 item	4 015	4 206
技术交易数量	Number of Technology Transfers	件 item	1 051	977
技术合同金额	Contracted Value of Technologies	亿元 100 million yuan	57.48	65.15
经认定高新技术企业数	Number of Approved High-tech Enterprises	个 unit	596	679
期末从业人员数	Number of Employed Persons at End of Term	万人 10 000 persons	23.99	26.65

表20－5　康桥工业开发区主要经济指标
Major Economic Indicators in Kangqiao Industrial Development Zone

指　标　Indicators		单　位　Unit	2014	2015
税收总额(税务部门口径)	Total Amount of Tax Revenues (from the Tax Departments)	亿元 100 million yuan	34.72	35.92
一般公共预算收入	Local Fiscal Revenue	亿元 100 million yuan	7.59	9.50
固定资产投资额	Investment in Fixed Assets	亿元 100 million yuan	52.68	51.36
#工业投资额	Investment in Industries	亿元 100 million yuan	40.42	39.73
外商直接投资项目	Projects of Foreign Direct Investment	个 unit	5	4
外商直接投资合同金额	Contracted Amount of Foreign Direct Investment	亿美元 USD 100 million	1.02	1.48
外商直接投资实际到位金额	Actual Paid Amount of Foreign Direct Investment	亿美元 USD 100 million	0.36	1.15
工业总产值	Gross Value of Industrial Output	亿元 100 million yuan	1 496.47	1 827.26
#高技术产业产值	Output Value of High-tech Industries	亿元 100 million yuan	986.64	1 278.90
工业重点发展行业产值	Output Value of Key Industrial Sectors for Development	亿元 100 million yuan	1 281.19	1 592.07
#电子信息产品制造	Manufacturing of Electronic and Information Products	亿元 100 million yuan	986.13	1 278.74
汽车制造业	Automobile Industry	亿元 100 million yuan	142.25	160.29
成套设备制造业	Manufacturing of Complete Equipment	亿元 100 million yuan	124.15	122.29
工业出口交货值	Delivery Value of Industrial Exports	亿元 100 million yuan	1 013.03	1 385.95
工业利润总额	Total Amount of Industrial Profits	亿元 100 million yuan	80.08	95.27

表20-6 国际医学园区主要经济指标
Major Economic Indicators in International Medical Park

指 标	Indicators	单 位 Unit	2014	2015
税收总额(税务部门口径)	Total Amount of Tax Revenues (from the Tax Departments)	亿元 100 million yuan	4.17	4.8
一般公共预算收入	Local Fiscal Revenue	亿元 100 million yuan	1.17	1.5
固定资产投资额	Investment in Fixed Assets	亿元 100 million yuan	30.21	30.65
#工业投资额	Investment in Industries	亿元 100 million yuan	5.72	6.4
#医疗仪器设备及器械投资额	Investment in Medical Equipment, Apparatus and Appliances	亿元 100 million yuan	5.72	6.4
外商直接投资项目	Projects of Foreign Direct Investment	个 unit	7	7
外商直接投资合同金额	Contracted Amount of Foreign Direct Investment	亿美元 USD 100 million	0.39	0.53
外商直接投资实际到位金额	Actual Paid Amount of Foreign Direct Investment	亿美元 USD 100 million	0.10	0.16
工业总产值	Gross Value of Industrial Output	亿元 100 million yuan	41.75	42.20
#高技术产业产值	Output Value of High-tech Industries	亿元 100 million yuan	39.54	39.97
工业重点发展行业产值	Output Value of Key Industrial Sectors for Development	亿元 100 million yuan	41.20	41.62
#生物医药制造业	Manufacturing of Biological Medicine	亿元 100 million yuan	37.08	37.94
工业出口交货值	Delivery Value of Industrial Exports	亿元 100 million yuan	18.80	20.30
生物医药产业营业收入	Operating Income of Bio-medicine Industry	亿元 100 million yuan	96.23	106.00
期末生物医药企业签约个数	Number of Contracted Bio-medicine Enterprises at End of Term	个 unit	133	190
期末医院签约个数	Number of Contracted Hospitals at End of Term	个 unit	11	11

表20-7 外高桥保税区主要经济指标
Major Economic Indicators in Waigaoqiao Free Trade Zone

指 标 Indicators		单 位 Unit	2014	2015
税收总额(税务部门口径)	Total Amount of Tax Revenues (from the Tax Departments)	亿元 100 million yuan	519.10	499.91
一般公共预算收入	Local Fiscal Revenue	亿元 100 million yuan	117.54	105.90
海关部门税收	Tax Revenues by Customs Departments	亿元 100 million yuan	588.39	649.67
固定资产投资额	Investment in Fixed Assets	亿元 100 million yuan	25.58	21.73
外商直接投资项目	Projects of Foreign Direct Investment	个 unit	1 893	2 693
外商直接投资合同金额	Contracted Amount of Foreign Direct Investment	亿美元 USD 100 million	81.82	518.90
外商直接投资实际到位金额	Actual Paid Amount of Foreign Direct Investment	亿美元 USD 100 million	5.09	3.65
新增内资企业注册户数	Number of New Domestic Enterprises Registered	个 unit	8 622	6 512
新增内资企业注册资本	Capital of New Domestic Enterprises Registered	亿元 100 million yuan	3 067.07	4 304.73
港口货物吞吐量	Cargo Handling Capacity	万吨 10 000 tons	15 761.9	16 386.8
集装箱吞吐量	Container Handling Capacity	万标箱 10 000 TEUs	1 716.4	1 816.4
商品销售总额(限额以上)	Gross Sales of Commodities (Above Quota)	亿元 100 million yuan	2 499.57	2 807.26
商品销售总额(注册地口径)	Gross Sales of Commodities (Approach of Registered Place)	亿元 100 million yuan	12 786.96	12 804.80
保税市场交易额	Volume of Transactions in Free Trade Markets	亿元 100 million yuan	1 454.15	11 750.21
仓储业营业收入(注册地口径)	Operating Income of Storage Industry (Approach of Registered Place)	亿元 100 million yuan	72.00	84.04
工业总产值	Gross Value of Industrial Output	亿元 100 million yuan	572.70	509.83
#高技术产业产值	Output Value of High-tech Industries	亿元 100 million yuan	351.80	269.70
工业重点发展行业产值	Output Value of Key Industrial Sectors for Development	亿元 100 million yuan	485.86	412.35
#电子信息产品制造业	Manufacturing of Electronic and Information Products	亿元 100 million yuan	352.95	272.30
汽车制造业	Automobile Industry	亿元 100 million yuan	59.42	72.51
石化及精细化工制造业	Manufacturing of Petrochemical Industry and Refined Industry	亿元 100 million yuan	43.25	41.79
工业出口交货值	Delivery Value of Industrial Exports	亿元 100 million yuan	210.79	196.78
外贸进出口总额	Total Volume of Foreign Trade	亿美元 USD 100 million	1 042.71	1 012.10
出口额	Amount of Exports	亿美元 USD 100 million	262.57	257.40
进口额	Amount of Imports	亿美元 USD 100 million	780.14	754.71
期末从业人员数(注册地口径)	Number of Employed Persons at End of Term (Approach of Registered Place)	万人 10 000 persoms	26.44	26.50
期末历年累计竣工房屋面积	Floor Space of Accumulated Completed Buildings in Main Years at End of Term	万平方米 10 000 sq·m	904.61	921.59

表20-8 洋山保税港区主要经济指标
Major Economic Indicators in Yangshan Bonded Area Port

指标 Indicators		单位 Unit	2014	2015
税收总额(税务部门口径)	Total Amount of Tax Revenues (from the Tax Departments)	亿元 100 million yuan	53.68	82.38
海关部门税收	Tax Revenues by Customs Departments	亿元 100 million yuan	382.91	326.20
固定资产投资额	Investment in Fixed Assets	亿元 100 million yuan	2.74	2.27
外商直接投资项目	Projects of Foreign Direct Investment	个 unit	88	66
外商直接投资合同金额	Contracted Amount of Foreign Direct Investment	亿美元 USD 100 million	16.30	17.68
外商直接投资实际到位金额	Actual Paid Amount of Foreign Direct Investment	亿美元 USD 100 million	0.03	7.49
新增内资企业注册户数	Number of Actual Registered Domestic Enterprises at End of Term	个 unit	542	183
新增内资企业注册资本	Registered Capital of Actual Domestic Enterprises at End of Term	亿元 100 million yuan	231.72	82.28
港口货物吞吐量	Cargo Handling Capacity at Port	万吨 10 000 tons	14 156	13 775
集装箱吞吐量	Container Handling Capacity	万标箱 10 000 TEUs	1 520.2	1 540.7
#洋山港国际中转量	International Transferring Amount at Yangshan Port	万标箱 10 000 TEUs	167.0	148.7
#洋山港水水中转	Ship-to-ship Transferring Amount at Yangshan Port	万标箱 10 000 TEUs	755.5	763.7
进出口总额	Total Volume of Foreign Trade	亿美元 USD 100 million	121.82	117.28
出口额	Amount of Exports	亿美元 USD 100 million	44.17	41.35
进口额	Amount of Imports	亿美元 USD 100 million	77.65	75.92

表20－9　临港产业区主要经济指标
Major Economic Indicators in Lingang Industrial Park

指　标	Indicators	单　位　Unit	2014	2015
税收总额(税务部门口径)	Total Amount of Tax Revenues (from the Tax Departments)	亿元 100 million yuan	57.86	56.29
一般公共预算收入	Local Fiscal Revenue	亿元 100 million yuan		22.95
固定资产投资额	Investment in Fixed Assets	亿元 100 million yuan	183.11	214.89
#工业投资额	Investment in Industries	亿元 100 million yuan	66.71	43.05
外商直接投资项目	Projects of Foreign Direct Investment	个 unit	86	100
外商直接投资合同金额	Contracted Amount of Foreign Direct Investment	亿美元 USD 100 million	1.55	3.82
外商直接投资实际到位金额	Actual Paid Amount of Foreign Direct Investment	亿美元 USD 100 million	0.06	0.32
工业总产值	Gross Value of Industrial Output	亿元 100 million yuan	249.17	262.96
#高技术产业产值	Output Value of High-tech Industries	亿元 100 million yuan	3.94	4.99
工业重点发展行业产值	Output Value of Key Industrial Sectors for Development	亿元 100 million yuan	146.24	146.34
#汽车制造业	Automobile Industry	亿元 100 million yuan	12.18	11.22
成套设备制造业	Manufacturing of Complete Equipment	亿元 100 million yuan	105.08	125.43
工业出口交货值	Delivery Value of Industrial Exports	亿元 100 million yuan	36.28	35.45
工业利润总额	Total Amount of Industrial Profits	亿元 100 million yuan	11.42	9.78

表20－10 各镇财政收入及工业总产值
Financial Revenue and Gross Output Value of Industry in Towns

单位:亿元 100 million yuan

镇 Town		财政收入 Financial Revenue			工业总产值 Gross Output Value of Industry		
		2013	2014	2015	2013	2014	2015
总　计	**Total**	**412.20**	**474.81**	**514.91**	**2 313.69**	**2 261.42**	**2 138.13**
川沙新镇	Chuansha New Town	21.92	19.06	20.96	132.36	134.05	120.21
高 桥 镇	Gaoqiao Town	20.86	22.71	26.44	129.41	133.26	112.53
北 蔡 镇	Beicai Town	23.11	27.01	27.87	65.75	73.14	68.21
合 庆 镇	Heqing Town	12.64	14.74	15.75	180.40	184.37	147.53
唐　　镇	Tangzhen Town	24.60	27.01	33.09	47.80	49.62	44.46
曹 路 镇	Caolu Town	20.81	22.94	26.15	203.14	194.54	188.94
金 桥 镇	Jinqiao Town	24.04	23.13	26.89	22.66	24.85	23.35
高 行 镇	Gaohang Town	23.97	29.32	27.08	148.16	139.46	121.93
高 东 镇	Gaodong Town	29.69	32.26	31.18	315.60	197.36	181.05
张 江 镇	Zhangjiang Town	15.70	18.84	19.78	38.38	36.35	36.65
三 林 镇	Sanlin Town	40.52	55.57	52.2	42.05	39.09	39.32
惠 南 镇	Huinan Town	9.29	13.23	10.73	13.48	13.09	12.72
周 浦 镇	Zhoupu Town	17.68	20.69	21.01	94.45	99.58	100.47
新 场 镇	Xinchang Town	8.38	9.33	8.82	88.00	89.03	84.86
大 团 镇	Datuan Town	3.05	3.65	3.59	14.26	14.77	14.13
南汇新城	Nanhui New Town	18.18	31.65	39.59	174.57	202.40	209.92
康 桥 镇	Kangqiao Town	21.14	21.90	29.79	200.35	210.17	215.96
航 头 镇	Hangtou Town	12.63	12.84	11.90	96.75	107.28	107.35
祝 桥 镇	Zhuqiao Town	33.90	33.64	40.23	150.95	145.17	140.37
泥 城 镇	Nicheng Town	11.28	12.54	13.99	11.41	12.21	10.67
宣 桥 镇	Xuanqiao Town	3.82	4.44	5.09	56.08	52.74	49.74
书 院 镇	Shuyuan Town	6.19	7.16	9.08	22.49	22.98	23.11
万 祥 镇	Wanxiang Town	5.24	6.37	7.48	22.95	21.06	19.26
老 港 镇	Laogang Town	3.57	4.78	6.21	42.14	64.85	65.40

主要统计指标解释

货物流量包括货物运输总量和货物进出仓量

货物运输总量

指在报告期内,以重量单位吨位计算的各种运输工具实际完成运输过程的货物数量,公路和水路的货运量按报告期到达货物数量统计,即报告期内已送达目的地并投卸完的货物数量为该报告期的货物运输总量。

货物进仓量

指在报告期内进入本企业仓库和堆放场地的各种货物的重量。按来源分为来自国外、来自国内一般地区和来自国内特殊监管区域(即保税区、出口加工区、保税物流园区等海关特殊监管区域)。

货物出仓量

指在报告期内运出本企业仓库和堆放场地的各种货物的重量。按流向分为流向国外、流向国内一般地区和流向国内特殊监管区域(即保税区,出口加工区、保税物流园区等海关特殊监管区域)。

上海市高新技术企业认定条件

(一)在本市注册的企业,近三年内通过自主研发、受让、受赠、并购等方式,或通过在全球范围内5年以上的独占许可方式,对其主要产品(服务)的核心技术拥有在中国内地得到中国法律保护的自主知识产权;

(二)产品(服务)属于高新技术企业认定管理办法的附件《国家重点支持的高新技术领域》规定的范围;

(三)具有大学专科以上学历的科技人员占企业当年职工总数的30%以上,其中研发人员占企业当年职工总数的10%以上;

(四)企业为获得科学技术(不包括人文、社会科学)新知识,创造性运用科学技术新知识,或实质性改进技术、产品(服务)而持续进行了研究开发活动,且近三个会计年度的研究开发费用总额占销售收入总额的比例符合如下要求:

1、最近一年销售收入小于5000万元的企业,比例不低于8%;

2、最近一年销售收入在5000万元至20000万元的企业,比例不低于4%;

3、最近一年销售收入在20000万元以上的企业,比例不低于3%。

其中,企业在中国内地发生的研究开发费用总额占全部研究开发费用总额的比例不低于60%。企业注册成立时间满一年但不足三年的,按实际经营年限计算;

(五)高新技术产品(服务)收入占企业当年总收入的60%以上;

(六)企业研究开发组织管理水平、科技成果转化能力、自主知识产权数量、销售与总资产成长性等指标符合《高新技术企业认定管理工作指引》的要求。

EXPLANATORY NOTES TO MAJOR STATISTICAL INDICATORS

The Flow of Goods Includes the Total of Goods and the Amount of Goods Entered and Left the Warehouse

Total of Cargo Transport

Refers to the number of cargoes that have been completely finished by all kinds of transportation means that are calculated by weight with the unit of ton during the reference period. The transport volume by road and that by water are calculated by the number of cargoes that have actually arrived during the reference period, namely the volume of goods that has been transported to its destination and discharged during the reference period is the total of cargo transport during the reference period.

Amount of Goods Entered the Warehouse

Refers to the weight of all kinds of goods that have entered the warehouse and storage space of this enterprise during the reference period. Grouped by its sources, they are from the overseas, ordinary domestic regions and specially-supervised domestic regions (namely special regions supervised by the Customs House such as bonded zones, export processing zones, bonded logistics parks).

Amount of Goods Left the Warehouse

Refers to the weight of all kinds of goods that have left the warehouse and storage space of this enterprise during the reference period. Grouped by its flows, they are to the overseas, ordinary domestic regions and specially-supervised domestic regions (namely special regions supervised by the Customs House such as bonded zones, export processing zones, bonded logistics parks).

Conditions for Identification of High-tech Enterprises in Shanghai

(I) Enterprises, which have registered in Shanghai, possess independent intellectual property rights protected by Chinese laws in China for the core technology of their main products or services, by means of independent research and development, transferring, donation and purchasing, or in possession of exclusive licenses for over five years all over the world.

(II) Their products or services belong to the scope specified in the Appendix: High-tech Fields Key Supported by the State of Identification and Management Methods of High-tech Enterprises.

(III) High-tech employees with education levels of college degrees or above occupy over 30% of the total number of employees in that year, in which R&D persons are over 10%.

(IV) In order to obtain the new knowledge of science and technology (excluding human studies), take advantage of the new knowledge of science and technology in a creative way, or improve their products or services in a substantial way, enterprises have continued to conduct R&D activities and the ratios of the sum of expenses for research and development in the total sales revenue during the current three fiscal years should accord with the following requirements:

1. This ratio is not less than 8% for enterprises with its sales revenue of the previous year less than RMB 50 million.

2. This ratio is not less than 4% for enterprises with its sales revenue of the previous year between RMB 50 million and RMB 200 million.

3. This ratio is not less than 3% for enterprises with its sales revenue of the previous year over RMB 200 million.

Which the sum expenses for research and development in domestic regions of China of the enterprise should account for more than 60% of the total R&D expenses. If the enterprise has registered for more than one year and less than three years, we will calculate its actual operation period.

(V) The revenue of high-tech products or services accounts for over 60% of the total income of the enterprise at the year.

(VI) Indicators such as the level of R&D organization and management, the transferring capability of scientific and technical achievements, the number of independent intellectual property rights, and sales and total assets growth accord with the requirements of the Working Guidance of Identification and Management for High-tech Enterprises.

第二十一篇

CHAPTER 21

上海市统计资料

STATISTICS OF SHANGHAI MUNICIPALITY

表21-1 主要年份人口、从业人员、工资和婚姻情况
Population, Employment, Wages and Marriage in Main Years

指 标	Indicators	1990	2000	2010	2014	2015
年末总人口（万人）	**Year-end Population (10 000 persons)**	**1 283.35**	**1 321.63**	**1 412.32**	**1 438.69**	**1 442.97**
按性别分	Grouped by Sex					
男	Male	647.13	665.51	703.57	714.71	716.37
女	Female	636.22	656.12	708.75	723.99	726.60
按农业、非农业分	Grouped by Agriculture and Non-agriculture					
农业人口	Agriculture	418.89	335.47	157.37	139.19	
非农业人口	Non-agriculture	864.46	986.16	1 254.95	1 299.5	
常住人口(万人)	Year-end Resident Population (10 000 persons)	1 334.00	1 608.60	2 302.66	2 425.68	2 415.27
人口密度(人/平方公里)	Density of Population (persons/sq · km)	2 104	2 537	3 632	3 826	3 809
总户数(万户)	Total Households (10 000 household)	415.28	475.73	519.27	532.55	536.76
每户平均人口(人)	Average Persons Per Household (persons)	3.1	2.8	2.7	2.7	2.7
人口自然变动	**Natural Change**					
出生人口(万人)	Number of Birth (10 000 persons)	13.12	6.95	10.02	12.41	10.59
出生率(‰)	Birth Rate (‰)	10.20	5.30	7.13	8.64	7.35
死亡人口(万人)	Number of Death (10 000 persons)	8.63	9.45	10.87	11.95	12.42
死亡率(‰)	Death Rate (‰)	6.70	7.20	7.73	8.32	8.62
自然增长率(‰)	Natural Growth Rate (‰)	3.51	-2.50	-0.60	0.32	-1.27
人口迁徙变动	**Migration Change**					
迁入人口(万人)	Inflows (10 000 persons)	12.18	15.16	17.22	11.55	11.61
迁入率(‰)	Rate of Inflows (‰)	9.52	11.51	12.24	8.05	8.06
迁出人口(万人)	Outflows (10 000 persons)	10.72	5.32	4.97	5.78	5.32
迁出率(‰)	Rate of Outflows (‰)	8.38	4.04	3.53	4.02	3.69
从业人员(万人)	**Employment (10 000 persons)**	**787.72**	**828.35**	**1 090.76**	**1 365.63**	**1 361.51**
职工人数(万人)	Staff and Workers (10 000 persons)	508.10	390.14	648.49		
职工工资总额(亿元)	Wages of Staff and Workers (100 million yuan)	146.78	614.53	3018.55	7643.73	8318.57
职工年平均工资(元)	Average Annual Wages of Staff and Workers (yuan)	2 917	15 420	46 757	65 417	71 268
婚姻登记	**Registered Marriage**					
准予登记结婚(万对)	Marriage Registration Permitted (10 000 couples)	10.77	9.31	13.03	14.19	14.18
初 婚(万人)	First Marriage (10 000 persons)	19.49	15.08	20.10	20.14	19.89
再 婚(万人)	Remarriage (10 000 persons)	2.04	2.89	5.96	8.25	8.47
离婚件数(万件)	Divorce (10 000 persons)	1.64	3.18	4.67	6.15	6.66

表21-2 主要年份上海市生产总值和指数
Value Added and Index in Main Years

指 标	Indicators	1990	2000	2010	2014	2015
上海市生产总值(亿元)	**Gross Domestic Product (100 million yuan)**	**781.66**	**4 771.17**	**17 165.98**	**23 567.7**	**25 123.45**
#第一产业	Primary Industry	34.24	76.68	114.15	124.26	109.82
第二产业	Secondary Industry	505.60	2 207.63	7 218.32	8 167.71	7 991.00
第三产业	Tertiary Industry	241.82	2 486.86	9 833.51	15 275.73	17 022.63
#工　业	Industry	469.83	1 998.96	6 536.21	7 362.84	7 162.33
建筑业	Construction	35.77	208.67	682.11	831.86	855.22
构　成(%)	**Composition (%)**					
#第一产业	Primary Industry	4.3	1.8	0.7	0.5	0.4
第二产业	Secondary Industry	63.8	47.6	42.0	34.7	31.8
第三产业	Tertiary Industry	31.9	50.6	57.3	64.8	67.8
#工　业	Industry	59.1	43.0	38.0	31.2	28.5
建筑业	Construction	4.7	4.6	4.0	3.5	3.4
人均生产总值(元)	**Average GDP Per Capita (yuan)**	**5 911**	**30 047**	**76 074**	**97 370**	**103 796**
上海市生产总值指数(以1990年为100)	**Indices of GDP (1990 = 100)**	**100.0**	**319.1**	**953.0**	**1 278.9**	**1 367.1**
第一产业	Primary Industry	100.0	126.8	112.8	109	94.3
第二产业	Secondary Industry	100.0	305.0	915.8	1 107.8	1 121.2
第三产业	Tertiary Industry	100.0	375.9	1 143.6	1 644.2	1 818.5
上海市生产总值指数(以上年为100)	**Indices of GDP (preceding year = 100)**	**103.5**	**111.0**	**110.3**	**107**	**106.9**
第一产业	Primary Industry	104.3	103.4	93.4	100.1	86.4
第二产业	Secondary Industry	102.8	109.8	116.8	104.2	101.2
第三产业	Tertiary Industry	105.3	113.5	105.7	108.8	110.6

表21-3　主要年份全社会固定资产投资主要指标
Major Indicators of Total Investment in Fixed Assets in Main Years

指　标	Indicators	1990	2000	2010	2014	2015
投资总额(亿元)	**Total Investment (100 million yuan)**	**227.08**	**1 869.67**	**5 317.67**	**6 016.43**	**6 352.70**
#房地产	Real Estate	8.16	566.17	1 980.68	3 206.48	3 468.94
在投资总额中按构成分	In Total Investment Grouped by Use of Funds					
#建筑安装工程	Construction and Installation	127.63	882.91	2 820.17	3 713.25	3 787.88
设备、工具、器具购置	Purchase of Equipment, Tools and Instrument	79.51	482.47	991.10	624.83	761.20
按建设性质分	Grouped by Type of Construction					
#新　建	New Construction	78.01	730.76	2 052.69	1 913.30	1 837.92
改建和技改	Reconstruction and Technical Renovation	70.48	216.40	513.80	335.59	345.03
扩　建	Expansion	47.50	216.71	368.07	303.63	289.65
按三次产业分	Grouped by Type of Industry					
第一产业	Primary Industry	3.20	7.87	16.40	11.86	3.95
第二产业	Secondary Industry	133.00	615.94	1435.37	1 157.27	958.84
第三产业	Tertiary Industry	90.88	1 245.86	3 865.90	4 847.30	5 389.91
按经济类型分	Grouped by Economic Types					
#国有经济	State-owned	192.24	829.98	2234.12	1 796.22	1 974.08
集体经济	Collective-owned	18.29	156.34	183.07	55.07	53.62
联营经济	Joint Owned		41.20	11.52	6.11	5.55
股份制经济	Share-holding		421.53	1 200.26	1 812.77	2 124.52
外商投资经济	Foreign Funded		222.86	439.28	637.9	534.11
港澳台投资经济	Hong Kong, Macao and Taiwan Funded		96.19	247.67	465.14	630.61
房屋建筑面积(万平方米)	**Floor Space of Buildings (10 000 sq. m)**					
施工面积	Floor Space Under Construction	3801.46	8 636.31	15 020.76	18 010.06	17 885.94
#住　宅	Residential Housing	2 269.06	4 804.12	7 344.07	8 573.04	8 443.82
竣工面积	Floor Space Completed	2 138.44	3 266.52	2 776.21	2 682.42	2 923.42
#住　宅	Residential Housing	1 339.02	1 724.02	1 415.44	1 549.64	1 617.86
房屋建筑面积竣工率(%)	Rate of Floor Space of Buildings Completed (%)	56.3	37.8	18.5	14.9	16.3
资金来源合计(亿元)	**Total Capital Source (100 million yuan)**	**261.46**	**2 061.66**	**7 997.62**	**10 524.10**	**10 652.67**
上年末结余资金	A Balance at End of Previous Year	28.85	241.05	1 440.57	2 562.48	2 472.7
当年资金来源小计	Sub-total Capital Source of the Year	232.61	1 820.61	6 557.05	7 961.62	8 179.97
国家预算内资金	Capital Within the State Budget	14.39	48.30	116.71	417.89	501.61
国内贷款	Domestic Loans	62.52	379.21	1 568.79	2 068.08	2 050.79
债　券	State Treasury Bond		4.85	10.06		0.50
利用外资	Foreign Capital Absorbed	35.46	161.83	239.18	205.05	130.13
自筹资金	Self-raised Capital	94.13	905.46	3 273.11	3 243.55	3 010.99
其他资金	Other Capital	26.11	320.96	1 349.21	2 027.05	2 485.96

表21-4 主要年份城市基础设施投资额和公用事业
Investment in Urban Infrastructure and Public Utilities in Main Years

指 标	Indicators	1990	2000	2010	2014	2015
城市基础设施投资额（亿元）	**Investment in Urban Infrastructure (100 million yuan)**	**47.22**	**449.90**	**1497.46**	**1057.25**	**1425.08**
电力建设	Electric Construction	17.53	64.61	148.50	134.22	129.36
交通邮电	Traffic and Post	10.06	117.52	866.20	422.48	759.23
公用设施	Public Facilities	19.63	267.77	482.76	412.61	440.83
公用事业	Public Utilities	10.83	104.43	86.58	32.80	66.73
自来水	Tap Water	1.06	5.35	61.63	20.00	58.63
燃 气	Gas	1.81	6.88	24.95	12.80	8.10
市政建设	Municipal Construction	8.80	163.34	396.18	379.81	374.10
#园林建设	Parks, Gardens and Green Areas	0.11	38.76	35.87	56.46	34.84
环境卫生	Environment Sanitation	0.37	19.34	10.80	9.41	18.49
市政工程	Urban Municipal Engineering	8.31	102.36	349.27	313.94	320.77
自来水	**Tap Water**					
自来水管道长度(公里)	Length of Tap Water Pipelines (km)	3 483	15 943	31 182	35 068	36 383
自来水供应能力（万立方米/日）	Tap Water Supply (10 000 cu · m/day)	462	1 048	1131	1137	1137
售水量(亿立方米)	Sales of Tap Water (100 milion cu · m)	12.25	19.75	24.44	24.82	24.58
#生产用水	Industrial Use	5.90	5.49	5.80	5.16	4.94
生活用水	Residential Use	6.11	11.88	18.64	19.66	19.64
天燃气、液化气	**Natural Gas and Liquefied Gas**					
天燃气	Natural Gas					
管线长度(公里)	Length of Natural Gas Pipelines (km)		1 742	17 316	26 057	28 601
天然气销售量(亿立方米)	Sales of Natural Gas (100 million cu · m)		2.16	42.66	66.39	69.73
#家庭用	Family Use		0.45	7.79	12.44	13.50
家庭用液化气户数(万户)	Household of Family Use Petroleum Gas (10 000 households)	113.19	255.89	316.37	334.68	33.55
道 路	**Road**					
铺装道路长度(公里)	Length of Road Paved (km)	1 631	6 641	16 687	17 797	18 184
铺装道路面积(万平方米)	Area of Road Paved (10 000 sq. m)	1 787	8 147	25 607	27 918	28 567
交 通	**Traffic**					
年末实有公交线路条数(条)	Lines of Public Traffic (year-end) (route)	390	978	1 165	1 377	1 429
年末实有公交线路长度(公里)	Lines of Public Traffic Routes (year-end) (km)	18 593	23 260	23 131	23 897	24 027
年末运营公交车辆(辆)	Public Transportation Vehicles (year-end) (vehicle)	6 264	17 939	17 455	16 155	16 531
客运总量(亿人次)	Passengers Carried (100 million person-times)	54.37	26.49	28.08	26.65	25.49
出租汽车运营车辆数(辆)	Taxi in Operation (vehicle)	11 298	42 943	50 007	50 738	49 586
隧 道	**Tunnels**					
越江隧道条数(条)	Routes of Tunnels Across the Huangpu River (route)	2	2	12	13	13
越江大桥座数(座)	Number of Bridges Across the Huangpu River (unit)	1	5	10	11	11
城市绿化	**Urban Greenbelt**					
城市绿地面积(公顷)	Area of Parks, Gardens and Green Areas (hectare)	3 570	12 601	120 148	125 741	127 332
人均公共绿地面积（平方米/人）	Public Green Area Per Capita (sq · m/person)	1.02	4.60	13.00	7.3	7.6
绿化覆盖率(%)	Green Area Coverage (%)	12.4	22.2	38.2	38.4	38.5
公园数(个)	Number of Parks (unit)	83	122	148	161	165

注：2009年原园林绿地面积改为城市绿地面积，统计分类作了调整。
Note: As the field of green-land area was changed into that of urban green space in 2009, the classification has been readjusted thereafter.

表21-5　主要年份农业主要指标
Major Indicators of Agriculture in Main Years

指　标 Indicators		1990	2000	2010	2014	2015
农业总产值(亿元)	**Gross Output Value of Agriculture (100 million yuan)**	**68.16**	**216.50**	**287.03**	**322.22**	**302.62**
#种植业	Planting	29.09	89.82	155.27	169.51	162.04
林　业	Forestry	0.37	1.41	7.53	8.78	12.15
牧　业	Animal Husbandry	30.25	87.35	62.90	69.93	65.61
渔　业	Fishery	8.04	37.92	52.62	62.50	51.79
主要农副产品产量	**Output of Major Farm and Sideline Products**					
粮　食(万吨)	Grain (10 000 tons)	244.36	174.00	118.40	112.89	112.08
油菜籽(万吨)	Rapeseed (10 000 tons)	18.17	15.71	2.04	1.05	0.96
蔬　菜(万吨)	Vegetables (10 000 tons)	186.79	377.00	380.35	377.95	349.35
食用菌(万吨)	Edible Fungus(10 000 tons)			8.73	15.23	15.12
水　果(万吨)	Fruit (10 000 tons)	9.42	22.54	44.16	45.85	32.76
年末圈存量(万头)	Hogs at year-end (10 000 in number)	237.53	241.60	171.87	171.68	143.86
猪肉产量(万吨)	Pork (10 000 tons)	23.32	25.96	17.87	18.83	16.12
牛奶产量(万吨)	Cow Milk (10 000 tons)	22.68	25.95	24.71	27.05	27.69
鲜蛋上市量(万吨)	Poulty Eggs (10 000 tons)	15.07	16.64	6.28	5.23	4.89
水产品(万吨)	Aquatic Products (10 000 tons)	27.36	28.87	28.97	30.90	29.16
淡水产品	Freshwater Aquatic Products	10.32	16.64	16.82	13.03	12.21
海水产品	Seawater Aquatic Products	17.04	12.23	12.15	17.87	16.95
农业机械总动力(万千瓦)	**Total Power of Agricultural Machinery (10 000 kw)**	**276.50**	**142.50**	**28.97**	**117.76**	**119.01**

表21-6　规模以上工业企业主要指标
Major Indicators of the Above-certain-scale Industrial Enterprises
(2015)

指　标	Indicators	单位数（个）Number of Enterprises (unit)	从业人员（万人）Employees (10 000 persons)	工业总产值（亿元）Gross Output Value of Industry (100 million yuan)	年末资产总计（亿元）Total Assets (year-end) (100 million yuan)	利润总额（亿元）Total After-tax Profits (100 million yuan)	税金总额（亿元）Total Tax and Duties (100 million yuan)
总　计	**Total**	**8994**	**224.65**	**31 322.62**	**37 306.95**	**2 680.53**	**2 009.73**
按隶属关系分	**Grouped by Subordination**						
中央工业	Central Government	152	17.51	5 963.89	9 440.85	450.27	1 171.26
地方工业	Local Government	8 842	207.14	25 358.73	27 866.10	2 230.26	838.47
按登记注册类型分	**Grouped by Registration Categories**						
内　资	Domestic	5 177	97.46	12 295.92	2 0578.43	1 138.59	1 236.28
国　有	State-owned	59	3.00	947.64	2 106.37	43.71	34.75
集　体	Collective-owned	73	0.87	60.33	59.15	2.43	2.30
股份合作	Share-holding Coorperation	37	0.51	28.34	24.79	1.17	0.90
联　营	Joint Owned	13	0.13	15.17	12.59	-0.23	0.42
有限责任公司	Companies with Limited Liabilities	976	32.43	5 577.10	8 620.94	465.94	892.53
股份有限公司	Share-holding Companies with Limited Liabilities	170	10.10	1 926.82	5 469.73	403.87	189.24
私　营	Private	3 840	50.29	3 730.96	4 273.90	220.68	114.51
其　他	Others						
港澳台商投资	Hong Kong, Macao and Taiwan Funded	1 081	34.82	4 561.15	3 970.37	267.57	228.17
外商投资	Foreign Funded	2 736	92.37	14 465.55	12 758.15	1 274.37	545.28
按企业规模分	**Grouped by Size of Enterprises**						
大型企业	Large	272	80.49	16 735.42	19 997.96	1 709.19	1 562.58
中型企业	Medium	1 248	65.03	6 556.84	7 896.06	535.70	203.38
小型企业	Small	7 474	79.14	8 030.37	9 412.93	435.64	243.77

注：本表为国有企业及销售收入在2000万元以上的非国有企业。
Note: Data in this table is collected from state-owned enterprises and non-state-owned enterprises with revenue of sales more than 20 million yuan.

表21－7　主要年份国内外贸易主要指标
Major Indicators of Domestic and Foreign Trade in Main Years

指　标	Indicators	1990	2000	2010	2014	2015
社会消费品零售总额(亿元)	**Total Retail Sales Value of Consumer Goods (100 million yuan)**	**333.86**	**1 865.28**	**6 070.50**	**9 303.49**	**10 131.50**
按用途分	Grouped by Type of Goods					
吃的商品	Food	142.15	743.31	1 830.64	2 065.56	2 248.70
穿的商品	Clothing	52.33	248.94	686.15	1 313.05	1 531.97
用的商品	Articles	137.23	858.33	3 197.85	5 210.09	5 769.28
烧的商品	Fuels	2.15	14.70	355.86	714.79	581.55
按行业分	Grouped by Sector					
# 批发零售贸易业	Wholesale and Retail Trade	265.67	1 493.13	5 494.69	8 363.90	9 116.93
住宿餐饮业	Hotels and Catering Trade	17.08	134.12	691.89	939.59	1 014.57
外贸出口商品总额(亿美元)	Total Value of Exports (USD 100 million)	53.21	253.54	1 807.84	2 102.77	1 969.69
外贸进口商品总额(亿美元)	Total Value of Imports (USD 100 million)	21.10	293.56	1 880.85	2 563.45	2 547.64
外商直接投资签约项目数(个)	Projects of Foreign Direct Investment (unit)	203	1 814	3 906	4 697	6 007
# 中外合资	Joint Venture	161	441	445	887	1 391
中外合作	Cooperative Operation	12	226	14	7	6
外商独资	Foreign Enterprise	30	1 146	3 443	3 796	4 600
外商直接投资合同金额(亿美元)	Contracted Foreign Capital of Foreign Direct Investment (USD 100 million)	3.75	63.90	153.07	316.09	589.43
# 中外合资	Joint Venture	1.98	13.86	21.54	70.13	101.76
中外合作	Cooperative Operation	0.40	5.86	1.11	1.91	2.71
外商独资	Foreign Enterprise	1.36	44.14	128.17	230.19	457.41

表21-8 主要年份口岸进出口商品总额
Total Export and Import at Port in Main Years

单位:亿美元 (USD 100 million)

指 标	Indicators	1990	2000	2010	2014	2015
口岸进出口总额	**Total Value of Import and Export**	**172.89**	**1 093.11**	**6 846.45**	**8 634.55**	**8 187.86**
出口总额	Total Value of Export	86.62	615.72	4 233.40	5 232.12	5 005.80
#一般贸易	Original Trade	51.39	341.02	2 183.98	3 112.37	3 016.20
来料加工装配贸易	Processing and Assembly Trade	3.20	64.21	178.52	126.18	133.26
进料加工贸易	Processing Trade of Imported Material	30.67	205.13	1 639.70	1601.78	1 497.66
对外承包工程货物	Contracted Projects in Foreign Countries	0.41	1.25	60.55	85.04	67.43
进口总额	**Total Value of Import**	**86.27**	**477.39**	**2613.05**	**3 402.43**	**3 182.06**
#一般贸易	Original Trade	51.79	212.65	1 209.42	1 777.08	1 616.79
来料加工装配贸易	Processing and Assembly Trade of Import	2.40	44.87	169.36	164.31	155.92
进料加工贸易	Processing Trade of Imported Material	19.70	125.13	552.83	568.61	502.04
租赁贸易	International Leasing		2.47	18.56	40.52	23.12
外商投资进口设备	Imported Equipment of Foreign Funded Enterprise	6.11	40.26	43.81	26.63	13.89

表21-9　主要年份财政收支和保险

Major Indicators of Fiscal Revenue and Expenditure and Insurance in Main Years

单位:亿元　　(100 million yuan)

指　标	Indicators	1990	2000	2010	2014	2015
全市财政收入	**Fiscal Revenue**	**284.36**	**1 752.70**			
#中央财政收入	Central Fiscal Revenue	114.33	1 246.47			
一般公共预算收入	Local Fiscal Revenue	170.03	497.96	2 873.58	4 871.76	5 519.50
#增值税	Value-added Tax		93.55	388.62	969.14	1 012.80
营业税	Sales Tax		153.81	933.91	1 001.92	1 215.49
企业所得税	Enterprise Income Tax		103.03	606.05	942.46	1 104.08
个人所得税	Individual Income Tax		60.24	261.20	408.61	487.61
#市级财政收入	Financial Revenue at Prefectural Level		215.81	1 393.23	2 209.25	2 806.13
区县级财政收入	Financial Revenue at District (Country) Level		282.15	1 480.35	2 376.30	2 713.37
一般公共预算支出	**Local Fiscal Expenditure**	**75.56**	**622.84**	**3 302.89**	**5 182.65**	**6 191.56**
保险费收入	**Premium Income**	**8.99**	**127.23**	**883.86**	**986.75**	**1 125.16**
赔款及给付	Indemnity Expenditure and Payment	2.23	36.20	194.54	378.66	473.59
赔款率(%)	Indemnity and Premium Ratio(%)	24.7	28.5	22.0	38.4	42.1

表21-10 主要年份交通运输
Transportaion in Main Years

指 标	Indicators	1990	2000	2010	2014	2015
铁路运输	**By Railway**					
运营里程(公里)	Operations in Length (km)	259	257	414	456	456
正线延展里程(公里)	Extension of Main Tracks in Length (km)	356	397	697	825	825
旅客发送量(万人次)	Volume of Passengers Carried (10 000 person-times)	2 476	2 980	6 095	9 194	9 692
旅客周转量(亿人·公里)	Volume of Passengers Circulated (100 million persons · km)	26.85	35.40	60.16	84.46	88.95
货物运输量(万吨)	Volume of Goods Transported (10 000 tons)	1 257	1 055	959	549	471
货物周转量(亿吨·公里)	Volume of Goods Circulated (100 million tons · km)	111	122	26	12	11
公路运输	**By Road**					
通车里程(公里)	Available for Traffic in Length (km)	3 050	6 078	11 974	12 945	13 195
#高速公路	Expressway	36	98	775	825	825
旅客发送量(万人次)	Volume of Passengers Carried (10 000 person-times)	605	2 482	3 634	3 754	3 766
旅客周转量(亿人·公里)	Volume of Passengers Circulated (100 million persons · km)	8.42	16.44	115.44	124.34	125.45
货物运输量(万吨)	Volume of Goods Transported (10 000 tons)	605	2 482	40 890	42 848	40 627
货物周转量(亿吨·公里)	Volume of Goods Circulated (100 million tons · km)	11	56	266	301	290
水路运输	**By Water**					
旅客周转量(亿人·公里)	Volume of Passengers Circulated (100 million persons · km)	40.84	6.77	3.69	1.04	0.81
货物运输量(万吨)	Volume of Goods Transported (10 000 tons)	12 864	18 442	38 803	46 583	49 770
#远洋运输(万吨)	Ocean Transportation (10 000 tons)	2 246	7 022	15 172	16 541	18 145
货物周转量(亿吨·公里)	Volume of Goods Circulated (100 million tons · km)	3 236	6 430	15 818	18 320	19 196
#远洋运输(亿吨·公里)	Ocean Transportation (100 million tons · km)	1 957	5 285	14 535	14 487	15 150
港 口	**Ports**					
港口旅客发送量(万人次)	Volume of Passengers Carried at Ports (10 000 person-times)	555	539	85	90	113
民用航空	**Civil Aviation**					
旅客发送量(万人次)	Volume of Passengers Carried (10 000 person-times)	199	892	3 642	4 522	5 000
旅客周转量(亿人·公里)	Volume of Passengers Circulated (100 million persons · km)	37.84	176.11	1 034.96	1 217.26	1 445.81
货物运输量(万吨)	Volume of Goods Transported (10 000 tons)	13	88	371	361	371
货物周转量(亿吨·公里)	Volume of Goods Circulated (100 million tons · km)	1	12	63	57	57

注：港口旅客发送量从2006年起不包含海港到内河部分。
Note: The volume of Passenger Departures excludes those from seaports to freshwater since 2006.

表21-11　主要年份教育、卫生事业情况
Statistics of Education and Healthcare in Main Years

指　标	Indicators	1990	2000	2010	2014	2015
学　校(所)	**School (unit)**					
高等学校	Institutions of Higher Education	50	37	66	68	67
中等专业学校	Special Secondary Schools	110	84	65	54	51
职业中学	Vocational Middle Schools	80	60	26	28	27
普通中学	Regular Secondary Schools	712	861	755	768	790
小　学	Primary Schools	2630	1021	766	757	764
特殊教育学校	Special Schools	29	34	29	29	29
在校学生数(万人)	**Student Enrollment (10 000persons)**					
高等学校	Institutions of Higher Education	12.13	22.68	51.57	50.66	56.16
中等专业学校	Special Secondary Schools	6.17	11.89	10.91	7.74	7.24
职业中学	Vocational Middle Schools	3.66	8.48	3.77	2.72	2.32
普通中学	Regular Secondary Schools	48.31	79.54	59.44	58.42	57.05
小　学	Primary Schools	110.19	78.86	70.16	80.30	79.87
特殊教育学校	Special Schools	0.33	0.54	0.50	0.46	0.45
教职员工(万人)	**Staff and Workers (10 000persons)**					
高等学校	Institutions of Higher Education	7.06	6.08	7.42	7.34	7.36
中等专业学校	Special Secondary Schools	1.49	1.27	0.91	0.80	0.78
职业中学	Vocational Middle Schools	0.53	0.66	0.43	0.39	0.38
普通中学	Regular Secondary Schools	6.62	7.66	6.73	6.95	7.02
小　学	Primary Schools	7.48	6.13	5.58	5.96	6.03
特殊教育学校	Special Schools	0.11	0.16	0.16	0.16	0.16
卫生机构数(个)	**Health Care Institutions(unit)**	**7 690**	**4 400**	**3 270**	**4 987**	**5 016**
#医　院	Hospital	462	459	306	332	338
医院床位数(张)	**Hospital Beds (bed)**	**62 100**	**73 070**	**84 825**	**98 261**	**103 526**
卫生技术人员(万人)	**Medical Technical Personnel (10 000persons)**	**15.85**	**10.71**	**13.54**	**16.40**	**17.02**
#执业医生	Medical Parctitioners	5.82	4.99	5.13	6.13	6.31
护师、护士	Senior and Junior Nurses	3.27	3.68	5.59	7.19	7.54
医院治疗人次(万人次)	**Total Patients Treated (10 000person-times)**	**8 395.00**	**8 631.67**	**21 002.46**	**25 834.62**	**26 522.32**
#门、急诊	Out-patients and Emergency Patients		8 432.29	20 676.24	24 043.26	24 748.83
医院入院人数(万人次)	**In Patients (10 000person-times)**	**95.28**	**122.79**	**285.68**	**345.08**	**362.33**
医院每百诊次的入院人数(人)	**In Patients Per 100 Patient-times (person)**	**1.10**	**1.40**	**1.40**	**1.34**	**1.37**

表21-12 居民消费价格指数(以上年价格为100)
Consumer Price Index of Residents(Preceding Year = 100)

指 标	Indicators	2015
居民消费价格指数	**Overall Residents Consumer Price Index**	
食 品	**Food**	**102.9**
粮 食	Grain	103.0
淀粉及制品	Starch and Related Products	103.9
干豆类及豆制品	Dry Beans and Bean Prcducts	101.2
油 脂	Oil and Fat	98.5
肉禽及其制品	Meat Poultry and Their Products	105.3
蛋	Eggs	98.0
水产品	Aquatic Products	101.3
菜	Vegetables	107.5
#鲜 菜	Fresh Vegetables	
调味品	Flavoring	104.9
糖	Sugar	102.2
茶及饮料	Tea and Beverages	103.9
干鲜瓜果	Dried and Fresh Fruits	96.8
#鲜瓜果	Fresh Fruits	
糕点饼干面包	Cakes, Biscuits and Bread	101.8
液体乳及乳制品	Milk and Its Products	99.2
在外用膳食品	Out-of-home Food	104.1
其他食品	Other Food	104.2
烟 酒	**Tobacco, Alcohol and Related Products**	**104.2**
烟 草	Tobacco	104.9
酒	Liquor	102.5
衣 着	**Clothing**	**107.8**
服 装	Garments	107.3
男式服装	Men's Wear	
女式服装	Women's Wear	
儿童服装	Children's Wear	
衣着材料	Clothing Materials	106.3
鞋袜帽	Shoes, Socks and Hats	
#鞋	Shoes	109.8
衣着加工服务	Garment Processing Service	105.5
家庭设备用品及维修服务	**Home Appliances and Required Service**	**102.9**
耐用消费品	Durable Consumer Goods	101.8
室内装饰品	Interior Decorations	102.2
床上用品	Bed Articles	103.4
家庭日用杂志	Daily Use Household Articles	101.4
家庭服务及加工维修服务	Other Daily Use Articles	108.5
医疗保健和个人用品	**Medicine, Medical Services and Personal Articles**	**99.3**
医疗保健	Medicine and Medical Services	100.7
#中药材及中成药	Chinese Medicinal Crop and Patent Medicine	
西 药	Western Medicine	
保健器具及用品	Healthcare and Equipment	
医疗保健服务	Medical and Healthcare Services	
个人用品及服务	Personal Articles and Service	98.0
交通和通信	**Means of Transportation and Communication**	**97.6**
交 通	Transport	97.3
#交通工具	Transport Tools	
通 信	Communications	98.2
通信工具	Communications Tools	
通信服务	Communications Service	
娱乐教育文化用品及服务	**Recreation, Education and Culture Articles**	**100.3**
文娱用耐用消费品及服务	Durable Consumer Goods for Recreational Use	95.9
教 育	Education	102.5
文化娱乐用品	Recreation and Culture Articles	100.7
旅 游	Tourism	97.9
居 住	**Residence**	**104.6**
建房及装修材料	Housing Construction And Finishing Materials	101.4
住房租金	Rents	107.3
自有住房	Self-owned House	105.5
水电燃料	Tap Water, Electricity and Fuels	102.4
#水	Tap Water	
电	Electricity	
液化石油气	LPG	
管道燃气	Pipelined Gas	

表21-13　主要年份商品零售价格指数(以上年价格为100)
Classified Retail Price Index in Main Years (Preceding Year = 100)

指　标	Indicators	2001	2004	2005	2010	2014	2015
商品零售价格指数	**Overall Retail Price Index**	**98.6**	**100.9**	**99.4**	**101.7**	**100.9**	**101.1**
食品类	Food	98.4	108.6	104.7	107.6	103.2	102.8
粮　食	Grain	100.1	128.8	102.1	112.0	102.0	103.0
淀粉及制品	Starch and Related Products	100.4	107.2	105.2	95.5	102.5	103.9
干豆类及豆制品	Dry Beans and Bean Products	111.3	124.8	103.6	108.7	100.4	101.2
油　脂	Oil or Fat	81.4	114.4	91.2	105.6	95.0	98.0
肉禽及其制品	Meat Poultry and Their Products	100.4	117.6	105.5	104.2	101.4	105.3
蛋	Eggs	110.7	118.6	105.8	106.1	106.0	98.0
水产品	Aquatic Products	90.1	107.7	114.4	116.1	102.7	101.3
菜	Vegetables	107.1	95.5	103.4	111.0	101.5	107.5
调味品	Flavoring	99.5	103.0	102.1	106.5	103.1	104.8
糖	Sugar	104.4	103.1	103.8	103.8	102.0	102.2
干鲜瓜果	Dried and Fresh Fruits	107.3	118.3	99.4	112.1	111.6	96.8
糕点饼干面包	Cakes, Biscuits and Bread	99.8	100.9	98.4	100.5	102.6	101.8
液体乳及乳制品	Milk and Its Products	99.8	99.6	100.8	102.3	110.1	99.2
在外用膳食品	Out-of-home Food	100.7	103.1	104.4	105.6	101.9	104.1
其它食品	Other Food	99.5	96.9	101.1	105.0	103.4	104.2
饮料、烟酒	Beverages, Tobacco and Liquor	98.4	98.8	99.6	101.9	101.4	103.9
服装、鞋帽	Garments, Shoes and Hats	107.7	93.9	92.6	98.4	103.6	107.9
纺织品	Textiles	98.8	102.2	99.4	103.9	99.1	104.1
家用电器及音像器材	Household Appliances and Audio-video Appliances	95.0	93.4	93.1	92.4	96.5	99.3
文化办公用品	Cultural and Office Articies	98.7	91.9	91.6	97.7	98.2	99.2
日用品	Daily Use Articles	99.0	98.4	100.5	100.3	99.9	101.5
体育娱乐用品	Sports and Recreation Goods	99.1	96.8	94.7	95.9	98.6	99.4
交通、通信用品	Transportation and Communication Goods	97.4	90.2	88.5	94.0	98.8	97.8
家　具	Furniture	90.4	98.2	100.1	101.1	102.6	101.8
化妆品	Cosmetics	100.7	99.0	96.1	101.0	102.3	100.1
金银珠宝	Jewelry	87.2	107.9	107.3	111.7	93.7	95.2
中西药品及医疗保健用品	Traditional Chinese and Western Medicines	98.7	95.6	97.7	99.8	101.7	100.6
书报杂志及电子出版物	Books, Newspapers, Magazines and Electronic Publications	99.5	99.6	98.0	103.2	100.6	101.7
燃　料	Fuels	111.4	107.0	109.1	112.8	99.8	91.2
建筑材料及五金电料	Building Materials and Hardwares	101.8	104.7	104.0	103.3	99.3	99.6

主要统计指标解释

居民消费价格指数

居民消费价格指数是度量一组代表性消费商品及服务项目价格水平随着时间而变动的相对数，反映居民家庭购买的消费品及服务价格水平的变动情况。它是宏观经济分析和决策、价格总水平监测和调控以及国民经济核算的重要指标。其按年度计算的变动率通常被用来作为反映通货膨胀或紧缩程度的指标。

现行的居民消费价格指数按用途分为八个大类，包括食品、烟酒及用品、衣着、家庭设备用品及维修服务、医疗保健和个人用品、交通和通信、娱乐教育文化用品及服务、居住。

商品零售价格指数

商品零售价格指数是反映一定时期内城乡商品零售价格变动趋势和程度的相对数。商品零售价格的变动直接影响城乡居民的生活支出和国家的财政收入，影响居民购买力和市场供需的平衡，影响消费与积累的比例关系。因此，该指数可以从一个侧面对上述经济活动进行观察和分析。

EXPLANATORY NOTES TO MAJOR STATISTICAL INDICATORS

Consumer Price Index

The Consumer Price Index is an index that reflects the time-based change of prices of a group of representative consumption commodities and services. It is an important reference factor for macro-economic analysis and strategy, monitoring and adjustment of overall price level and the national economic budgeting. The year-on-year change of the index is often a norm reflecting the inflation or deflation.

The current CPI covers eight categories of goods and services: food; tobacco, liquor and related articles; garments; household facilities, articles and repair services; medical and health care and personal items; traffic and telecommunications; education, culture and recreation articles and services and residence.

Retail Price Index

Retail Price Index reflects the trend and degree of change in retail prices of commodities during a given period. The change in retail prices of commodities directly affect the living expenditure of urban and rural residents, government revenue, purchasing power of residents and the equilibrium of market supply and demand, and the ratio of consumption to accumulation. Therefore, the retail price indices are useful to analyze the changes of the above economic activities.

图书在版编目(CIP)数据

上海浦东新区统计年鉴. 2016 / 上海市浦东新区统计局，国家统计局浦东调查队编.
-- 北京 ：中国统计出版社，2016.9
ISBN 978-7-5037-7910-7

Ⅰ. ①上…
Ⅱ. ①上… ②国…
Ⅲ. ①统计资料－浦东新区－2016－年鉴
Ⅳ. ①C832.513-54

中国版本图书馆CIP数据核字(2016)第198471号

上海浦东新区统计年鉴—2016

作　　者/上海市浦东新区统计局　国家统计局浦东调查队
责任编辑/陈越月
执行编辑/施湘君　计勤敏
封面设计/蔡旭洲
出版发行/中国统计出版社
通信地址/北京市西城区月坛南街57号
邮　　编/100826
办公地址/北京市丰台区西三环南路甲6号
邮政编码/100073
电　　话/邮购（010）63376909　书店（010）68783171
网　　址/http://csp.stats.gov.cn
印　　刷/上海万卷印刷有限公司
经　　销/新华书店
开　　本/890×1240毫米1/16
字　　数/915.5千字
印　　张/22.75
印　　数/1～1500册
版　　别/2016年9月第1版
版　　次/2016年9月第1次印刷
书　　号/ISBN 978-7-5037-7910-7
定　　价/320.00元

如有印装错误，本社发行部负责调换。